6

Story and Art by
Rumiko Takahashi

Characters

TAISHO ERA

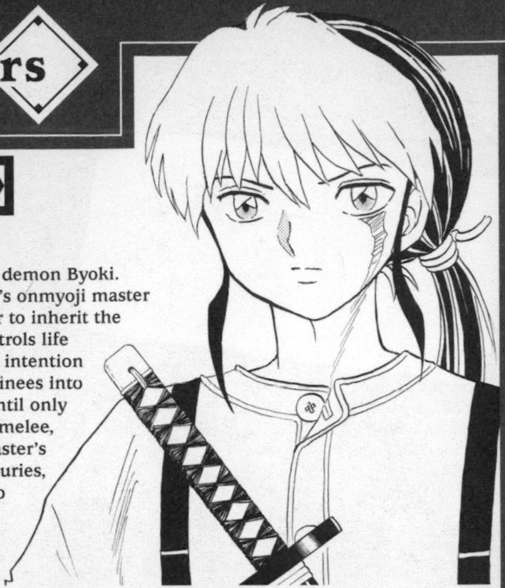

MAO

An exorcist cursed by the cat demon Byoki. Nine hundred years ago, Mao's onmyoji master proclaimed Mao his successor to inherit the Taizanfukun spell, which controls life spans. In reality, the master's intention was to goad the other five trainees into killing Mao and each other until only one survived. In the ensuing melee, Mao might have killed his master's daughter, Sana. For nine centuries, Mao has searched for Byoki to uncover the truth and purge his curse.

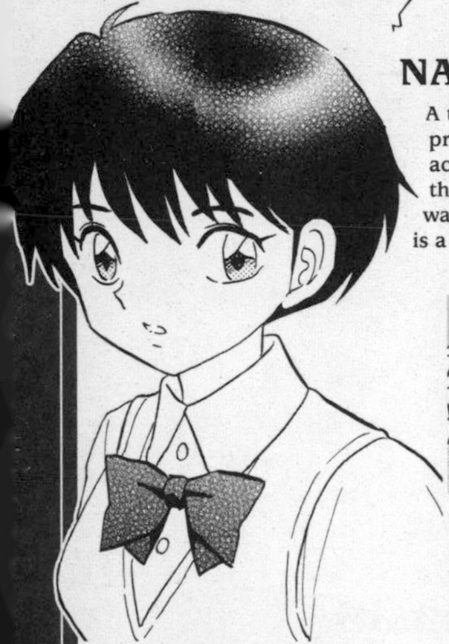

NANOKA KIBA

A third-year middle school student living in the present day. As a child, she was involved in a car accident that killed her parents and temporarily thrust her into the Taisho era. There, her body was cursed by Byoki. Nanoka's body, like Mao's, is a potential vessel that Byoki seeks to inhabit.

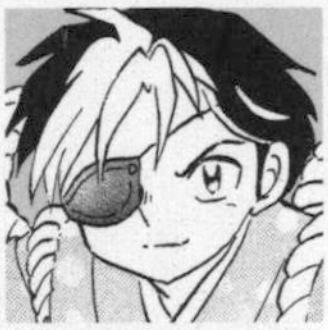

HATSUKA

Mao's senior student apprentice. Wields fire spells.

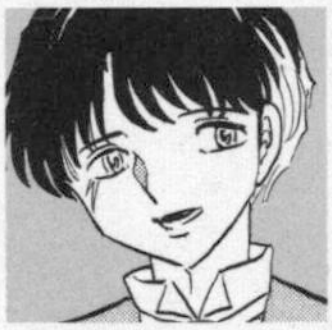

KAMON (KUCHINAWA)

Mao's senior student apprentice. Wields tree spells.

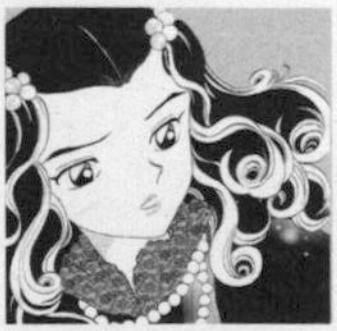

YURAKO

Her true identity is Sana. For some mysterious reason, she is secretly working for Shiranui.

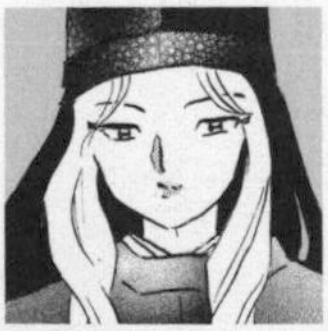

SHIRANUI

Mao's senior student apprentice. Wields water spells. Seeks vengeance from Mao.

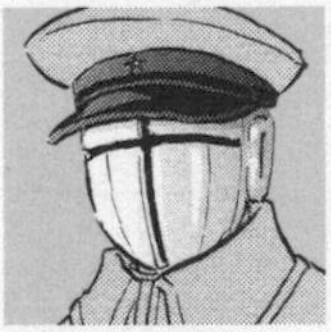

HAKUBI (Captain/lieutenant Shirasu)

A soldier working on Shiranui's side. Wields metal spells.

HEIAN PERIOD

HOUSE OF GOKO

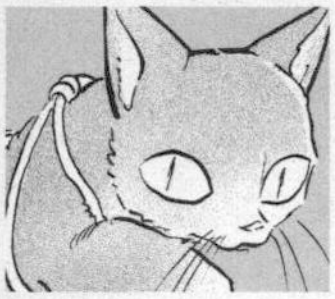

HAIMARU
Sana's beloved cat who only liked her and Mao.

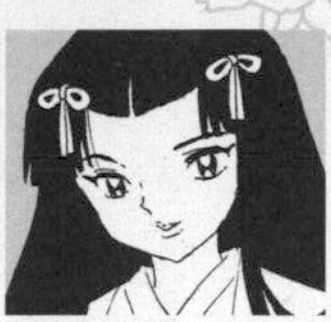

SANA
The master's daughter. Betrothed to Mao by her father.

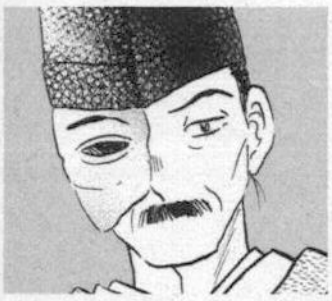

MASTER
The head of the Goko clan and Mao's former master. Wields forbidden spells and attempted to sacrifice Mao for his own ends.

OTOYA
Mao's hard-working shikigami.

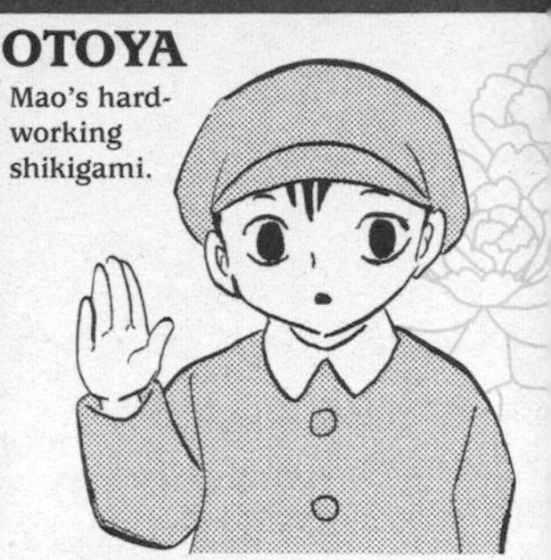

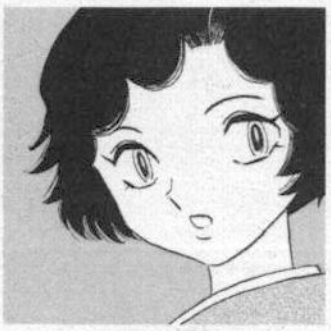

TENKO
Mao's informant, an ayakashi who works at Milk House.

PRESENT DAY

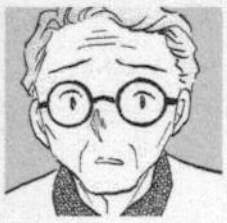

NANOKA'S GRANDFATHER
On his deathbed at the time of Nanoka's accident, it seems his life is being extended by Byoki.

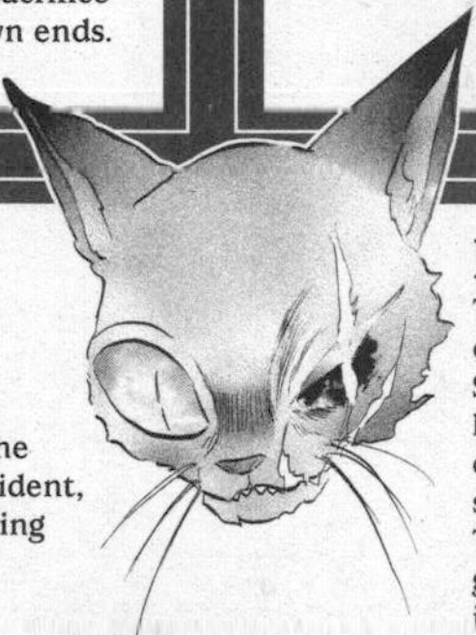

BYOKI
The kodoku cat who cursed Mao and Nanoka. Survives by possessing human bodies. After eating the forbidden scroll containing the Taizanfukun spell, he gained the ability to use it to control life spans.

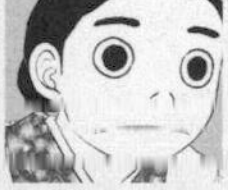

UOZUMI
Mao's shikigami and the housekeeper living in Nanoka's home.

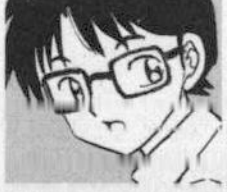

SHIRAHA
Nanoka's classmate. He's very good at researching.

Story thus far...

When Nanoka Kiba was seven years old, she was orphaned in a violent accident. Now she is a third-year student in middle school. One day she passes the spot where the accident occurred and is miraculously transported to the Taisho Era. There she meets an exorcist named Mao. When they realize they have both been cursed by Byoki, a cat demon, they join forces to find him and free themselves.

Mao continues to meet resurrected members of the Goko clan with whom he trained hundreds of years ago, including Sana, his fiancée and master's daughter. Did Mao kill her in the past or not? And why is she calling herself Yurako and working for senior apprentice Shiranui? Before these questions are answered, an assassin attacks wielding powerful metal spells. And then Shiranui himself arrives on the scene...

CONTENTS

Chapter 1:
White Bone Cave

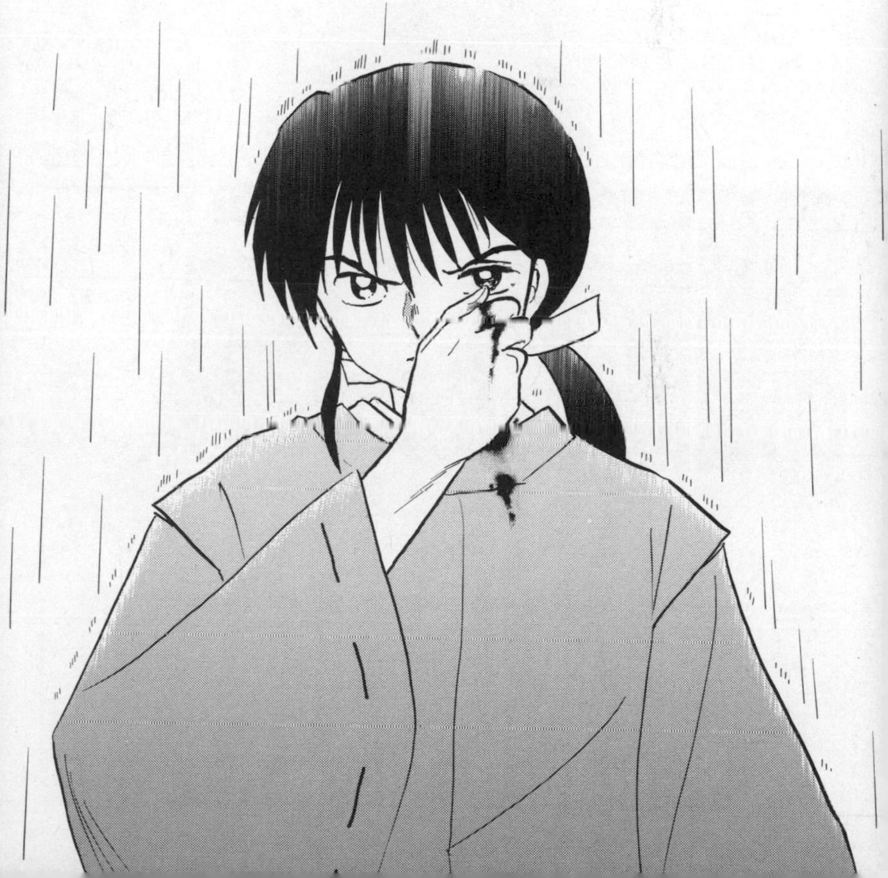

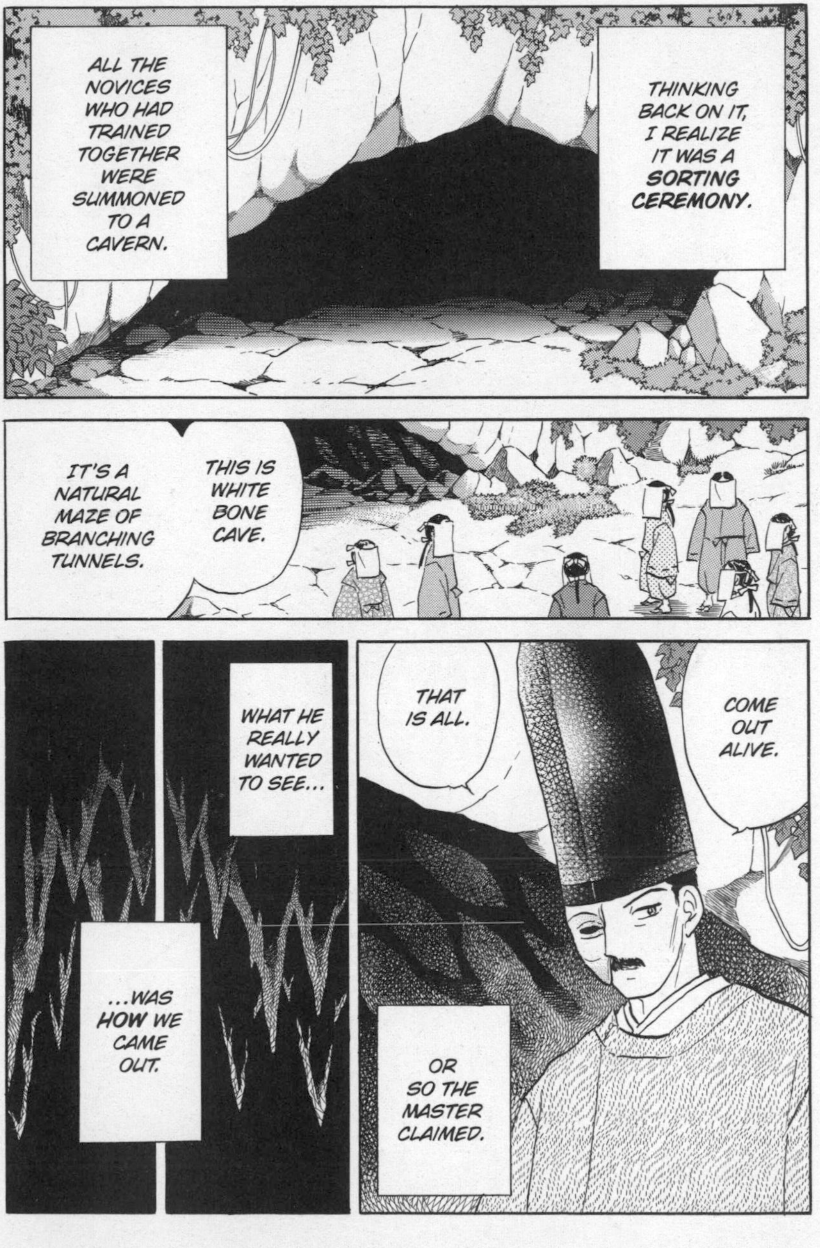
THINKING BACK ON IT, I REALIZE IT WAS A SORTING CEREMONY.
ALL THE NOVICES WHO HAD TRAINED TOGETHER WERE SUMMONED TO A CAVERN.
THIS IS WHITE BONE CAVE.
IT'S A NATURAL MAZE OF BRANCHING TUNNELS.
COME OUT ALIVE.
THAT IS ALL.
OR SO THE MASTER CLAIMED.
WHAT HE REALLY WANTED TO SEE...
...WAS HOW WE CAME OUT.

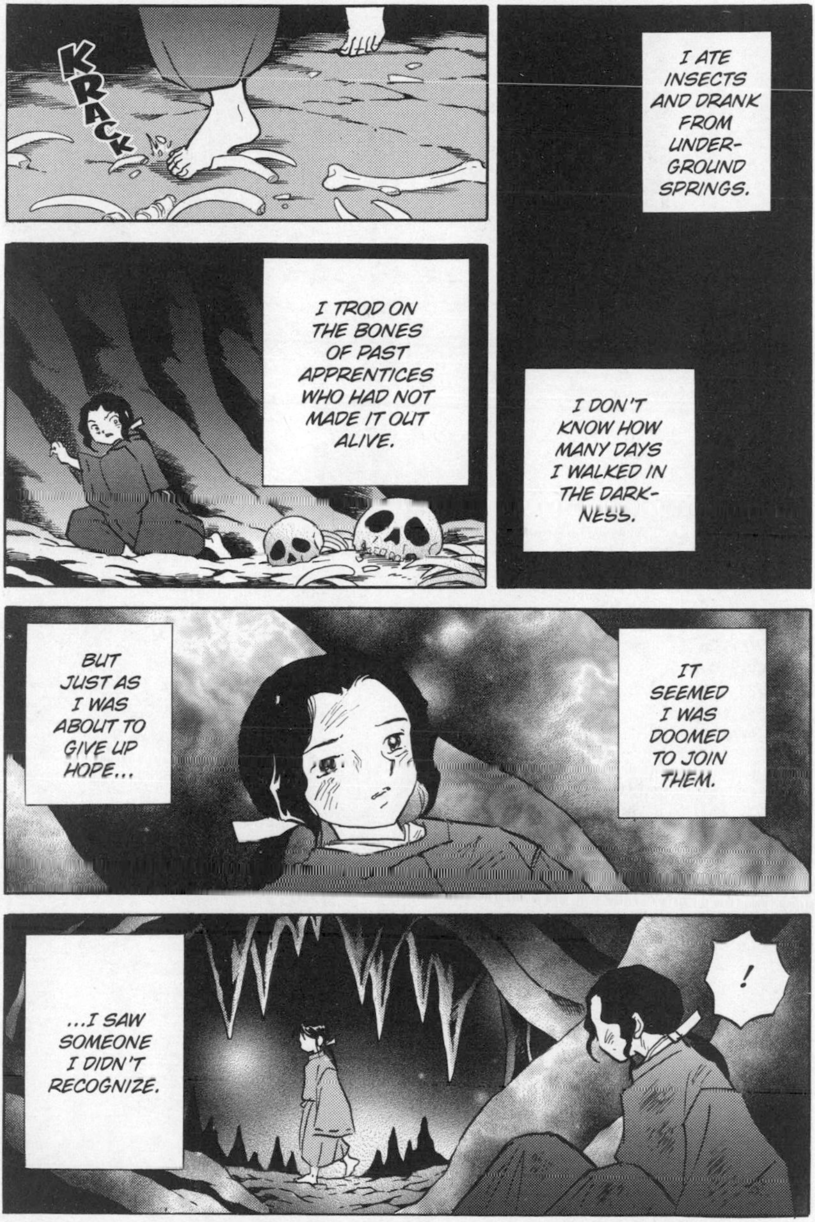
I ATE INSECTS AND DRANK FROM UNDER-GROUND SPRINGS.
I DON'T KNOW HOW MANY DAYS I WALKED IN THE DARK-NESS.
KRACK
I TROD ON THE BONES OF PAST APPRENTICES WHO HAD NOT MADE IT OUT ALIVE.
IT SEEMED I WAS DOOMED TO JOIN THEM.
BUT JUST AS I WAS ABOUT TO GIVE UP HOPE...
!
...I SAW SOMEONE I DIDN'T RECOGNIZE.

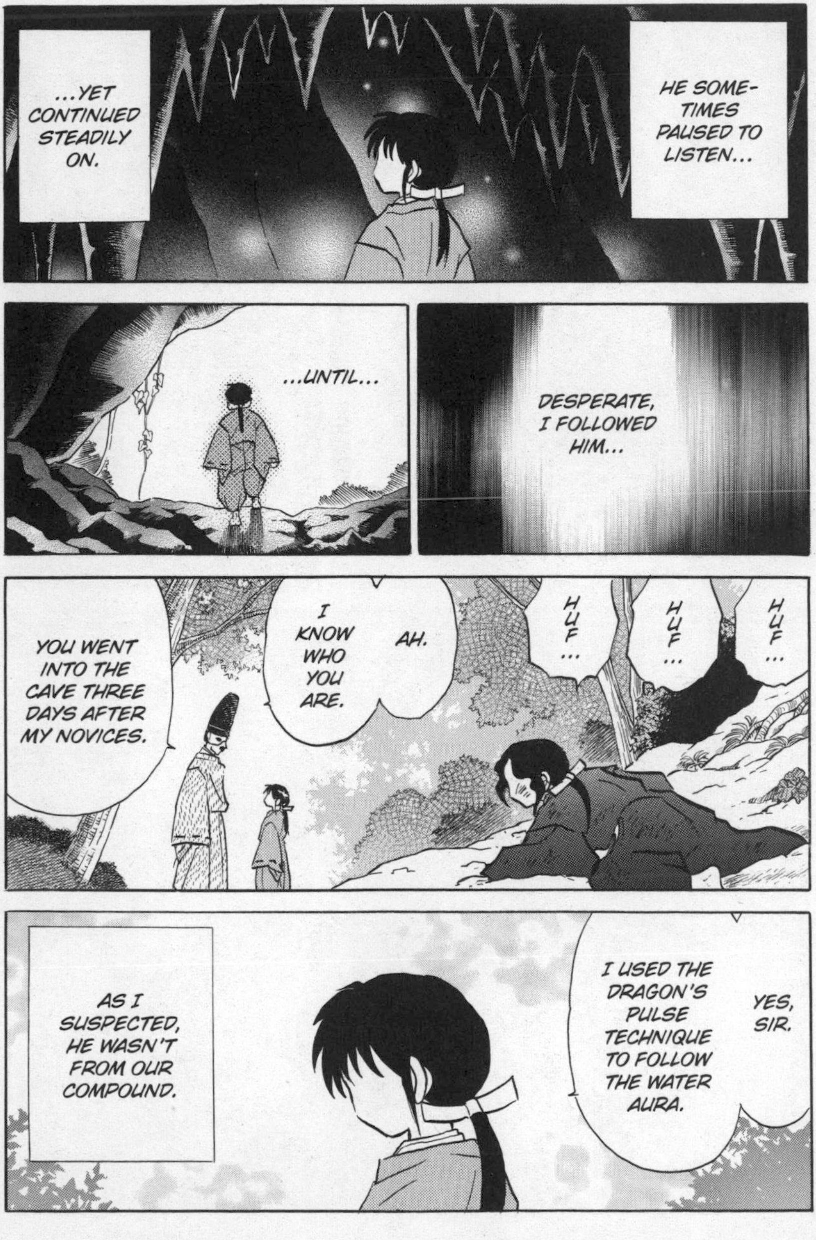
HE SOMETIMES PAUSED TO LISTEN...
...YET CONTINUED STEADILY ON.
DESPERATE, I FOLLOWED HIM...
...UNTIL...
HUF...
HUF...
HUF...
AH.
I KNOW WHO YOU ARE.
YOU WENT INTO THE CAVE THREE DAYS AFTER MY NOVICES.
YES, SIR.
I USED THE DRAGON'S PULSE TECHNIQUE TO FOLLOW THE WATER AURA.
AS I SUSPECTED, HE WASN'T FROM OUR COMPOUND.

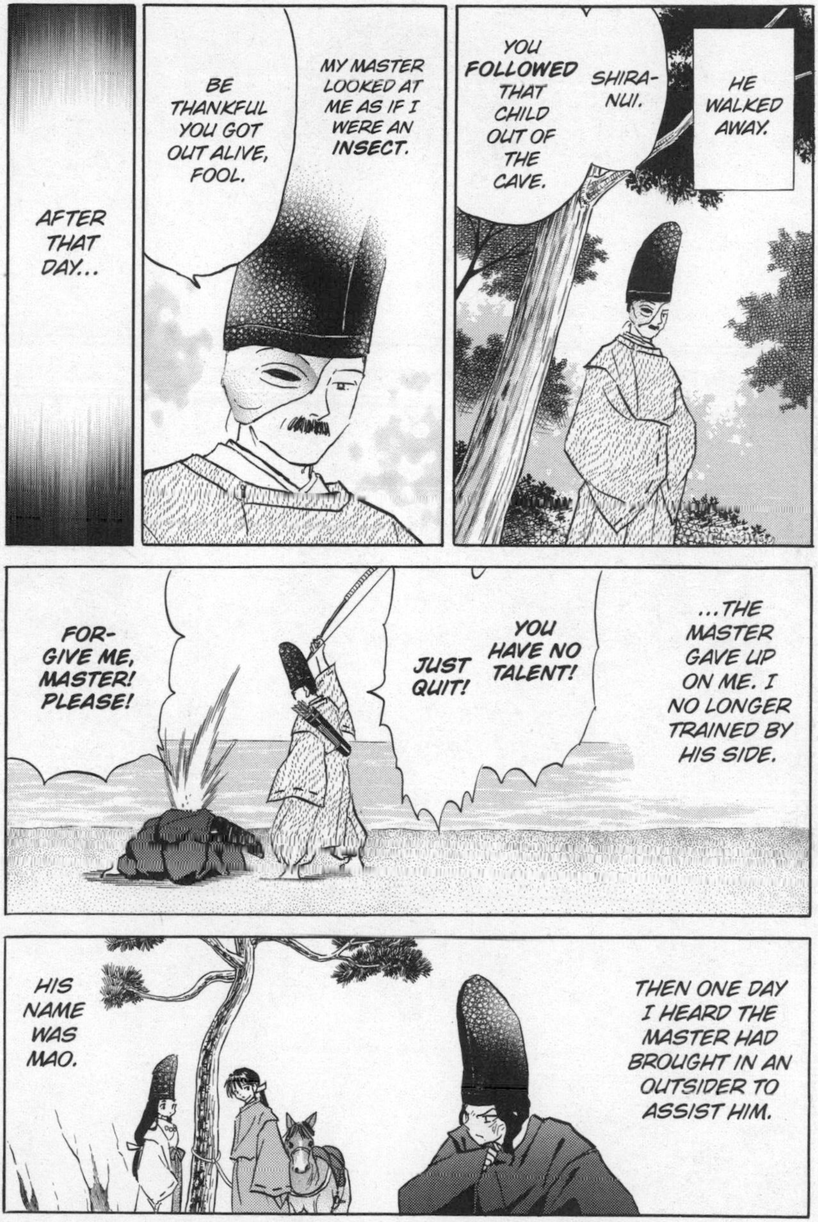
HE WALKED AWAY.
SHIRANUI.
YOU **FOLLOWED** THAT CHILD OUT OF THE CAVE.
MY MASTER LOOKED AT ME AS IF I WERE AN **INSECT**.
BE THANKFUL YOU GOT OUT ALIVE, FOOL.
AFTER THAT DAY...
...THE MASTER GAVE UP ON ME. I NO LONGER TRAINED BY HIS SIDE.
YOU HAVE NO TALENT!
JUST QUIT!
FORGIVE ME, MASTER! PLEASE!
THEN ONE DAY I HEARD THE MASTER HAD BROUGHT IN AN OUTSIDER TO ASSIST HIM.
HIS NAME WAS MAO.

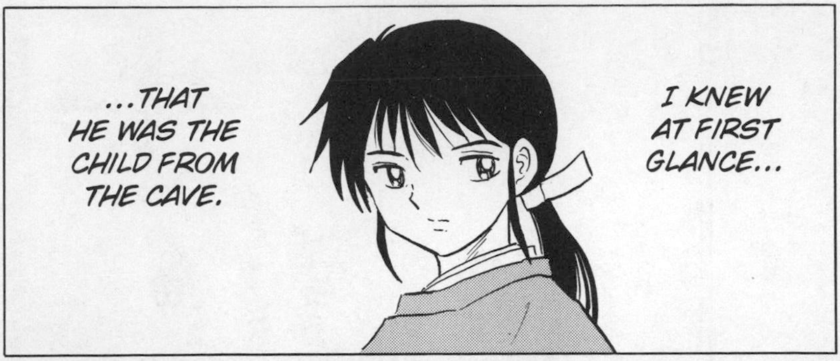
I KNEW AT FIRST GLANCE...
...THAT HE WAS THE CHILD FROM THE CAVE.

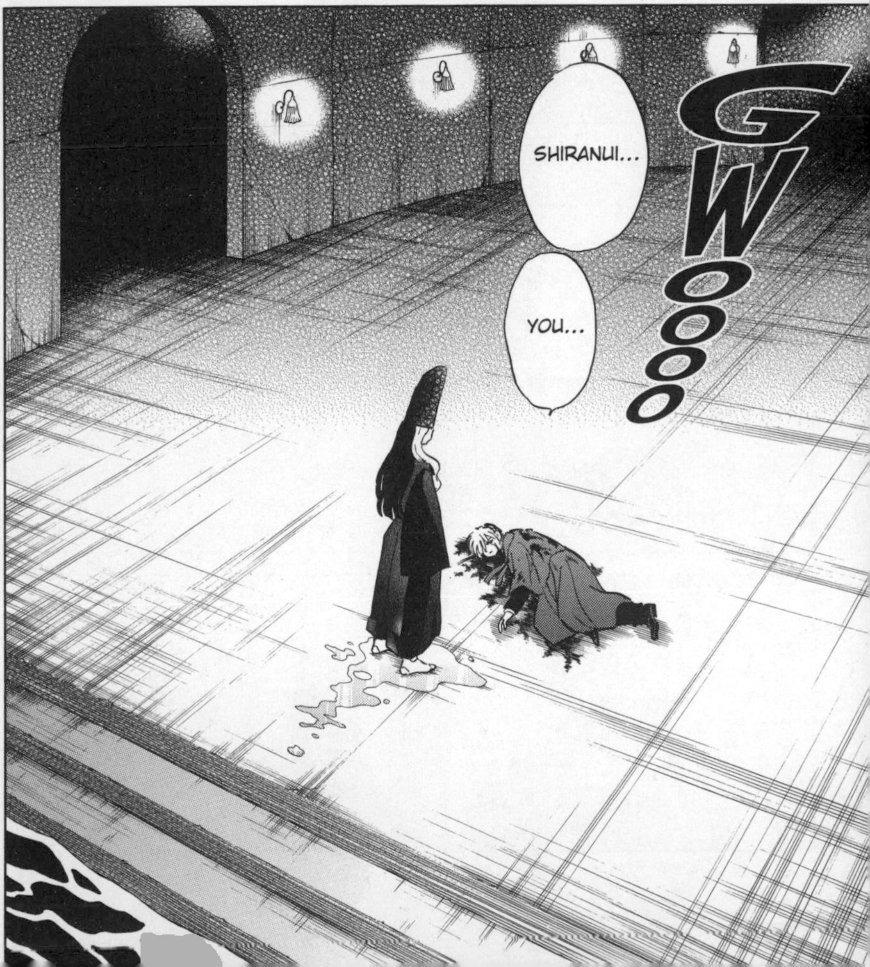
GWOOOO
SHIRANUI...
YOU...

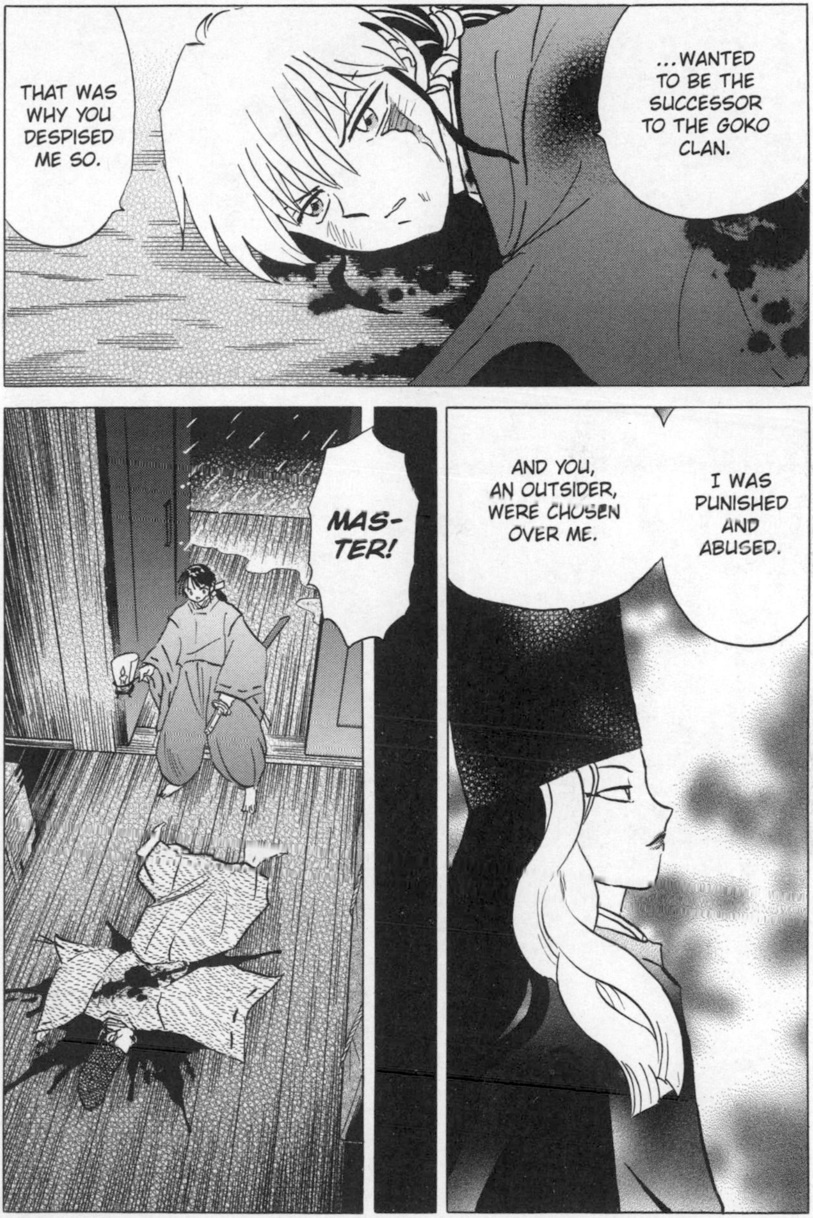
...WANTED TO BE THE SUCCESSOR TO THE GOKO CLAN.
THAT WAS WHY YOU DESPISED ME SO.
I WAS PUNISHED AND ABUSED.
AND YOU, AN OUTSIDER, WERE CHOSEN OVER ME.
MAS-TER!

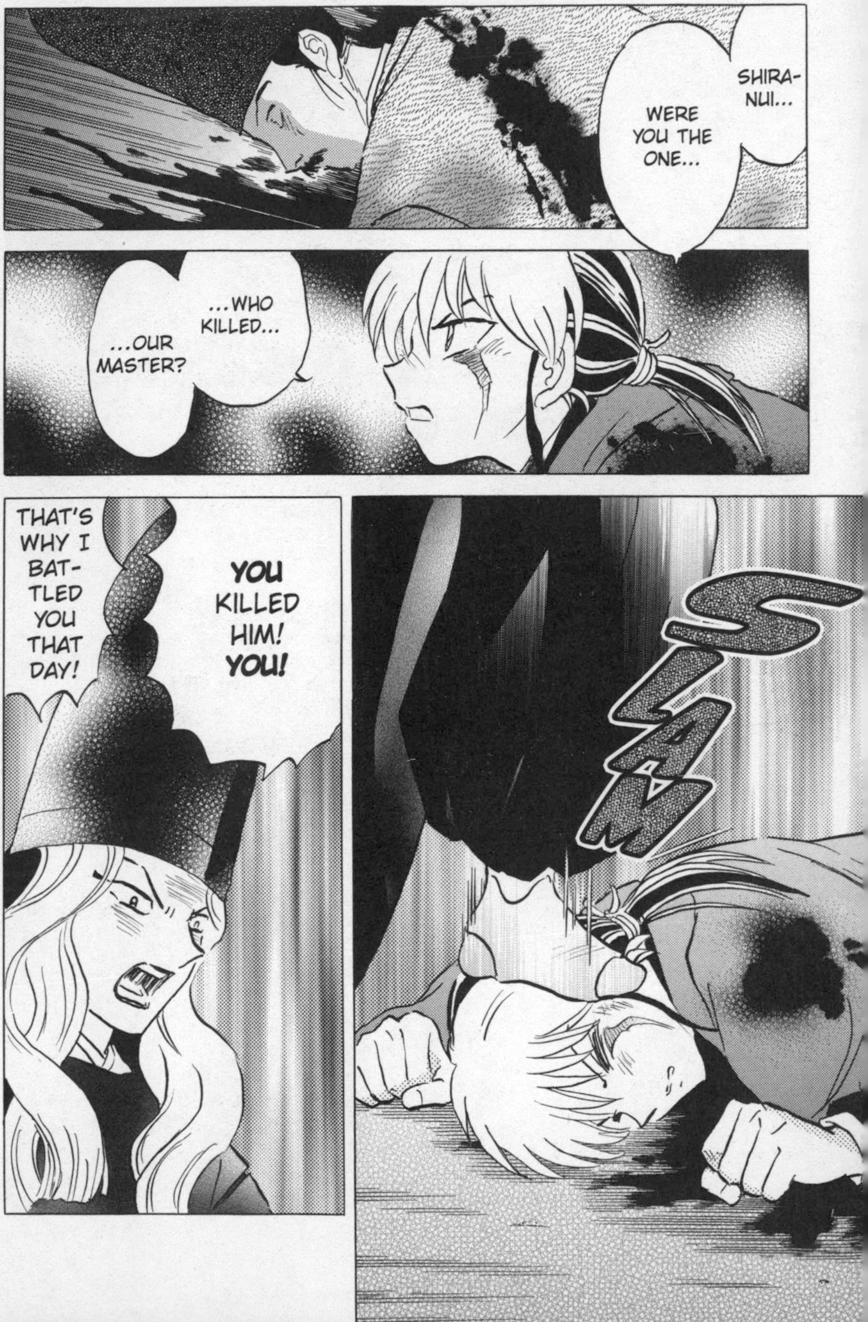
SHIRA-NUI...
WERE YOU THE ONE...
...WHO KILLED...
...OUR MASTER?
SLAM
YOU KILLED HIM! YOU!
THAT'S WHY I BATTLED YOU THAT DAY!

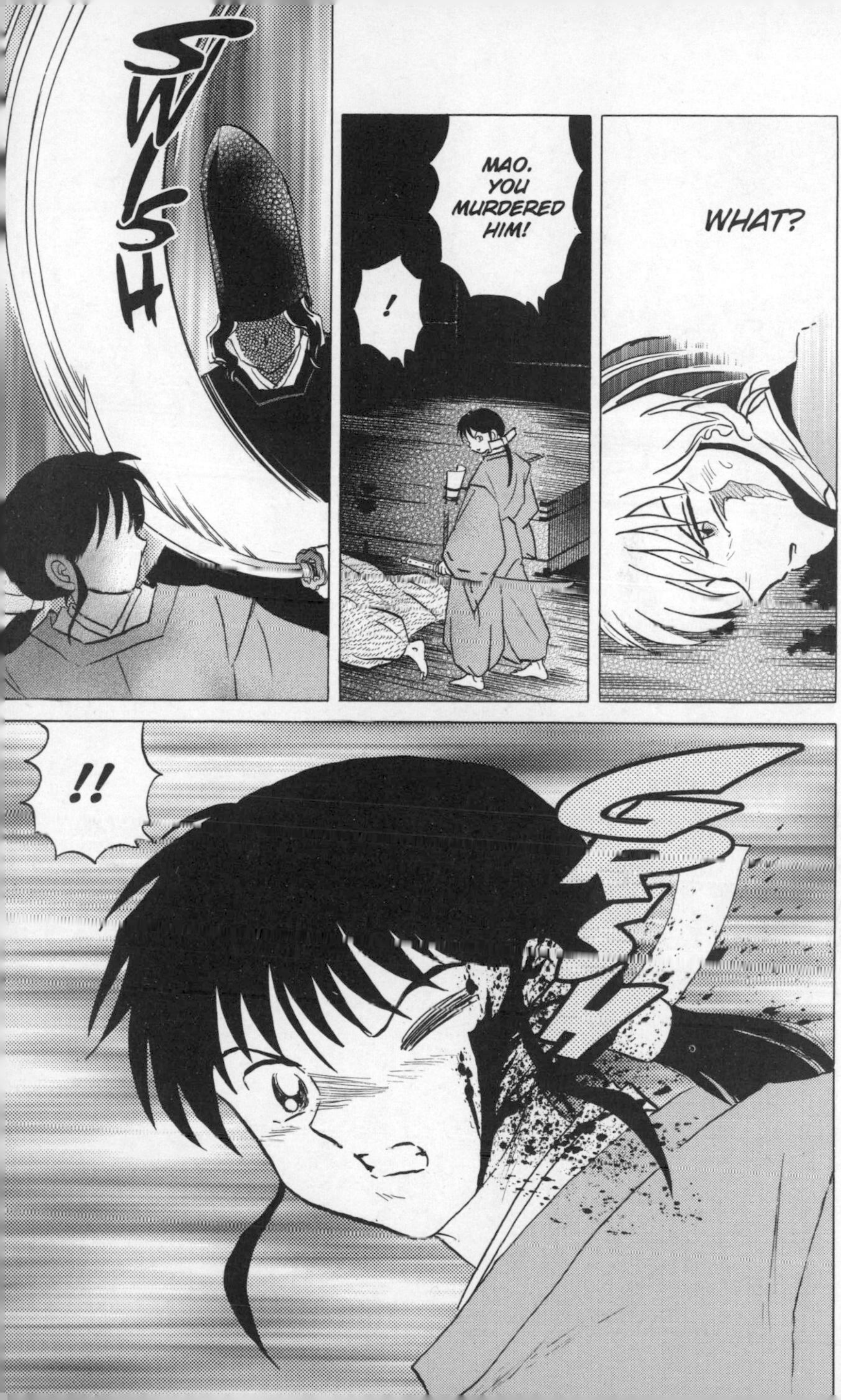
WHAT?
MAO. YOU MURDERED HIM!
!
SWISH
!!

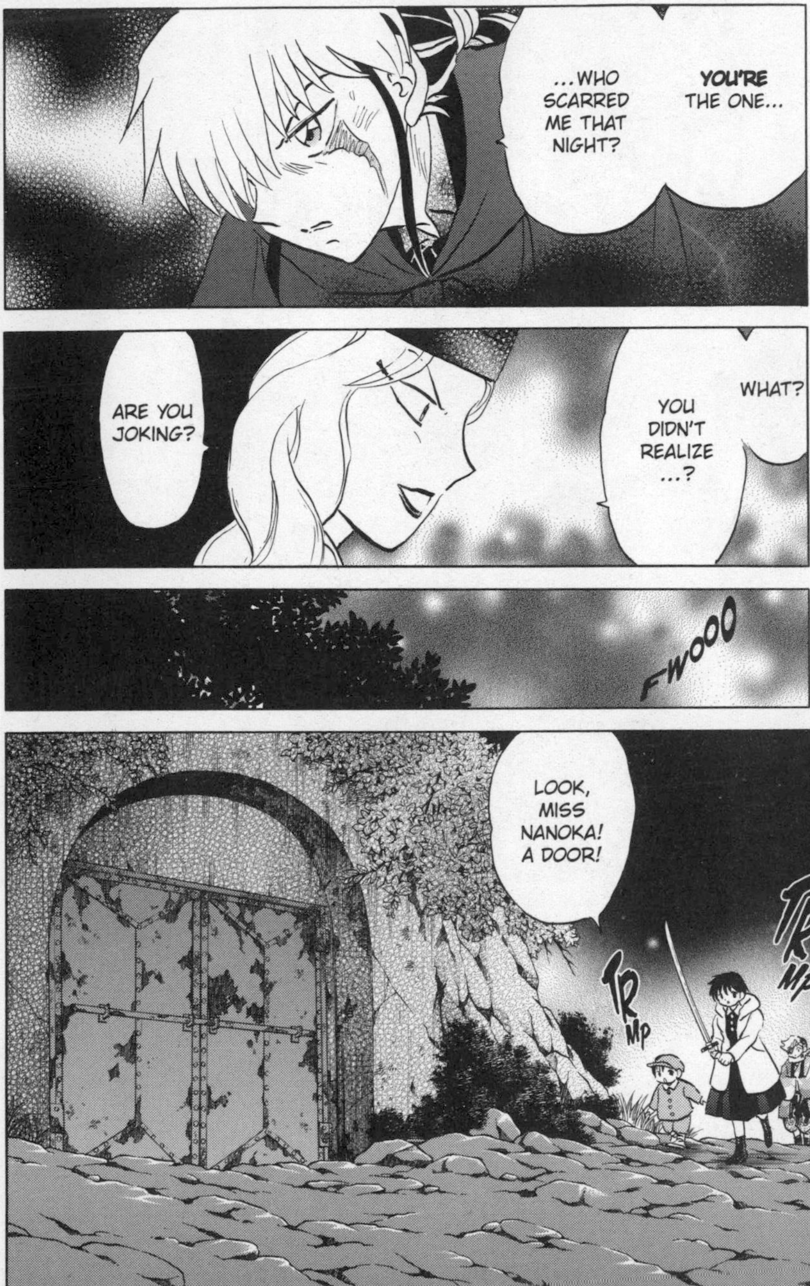
YOU'RE THE ONE...
...WHO SCARRED ME THAT NIGHT?
WHAT?
YOU DIDN'T REALIZE ...?
ARE YOU JOKING?
FWOOO
TRMP
LOOK, MISS NANOKA! A DOOR!
TRMP

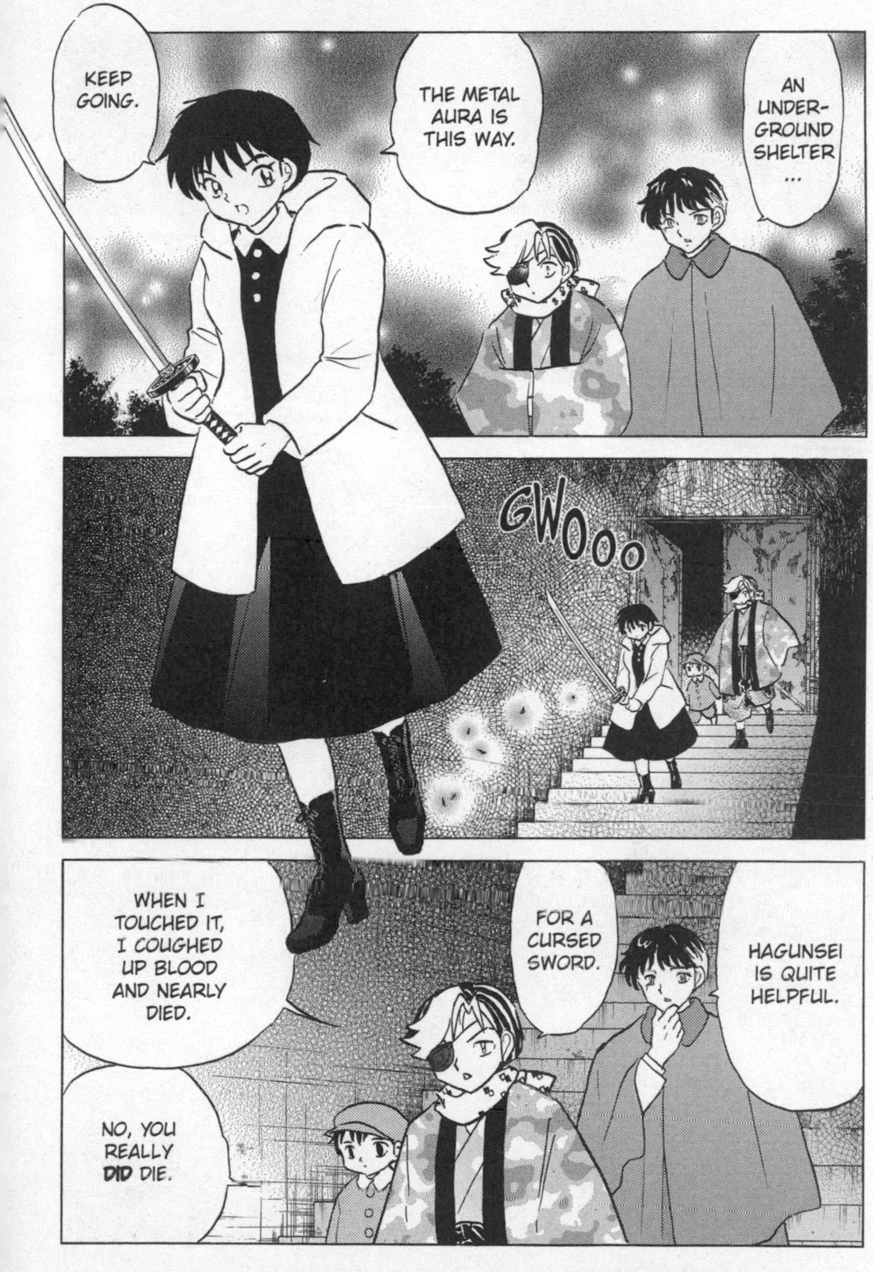
AN UNDER-GROUND SHELTER ...
THE METAL AURA IS THIS WAY.
KEEP GOING.
GWOOOO
HAGUNSEI IS QUITE HELPFUL.
FOR A CURSED SWORD.
WHEN I TOUCHED IT, I COUGHED UP BLOOD AND NEARLY DIED.
NO, YOU REALLY **DID** DIE.

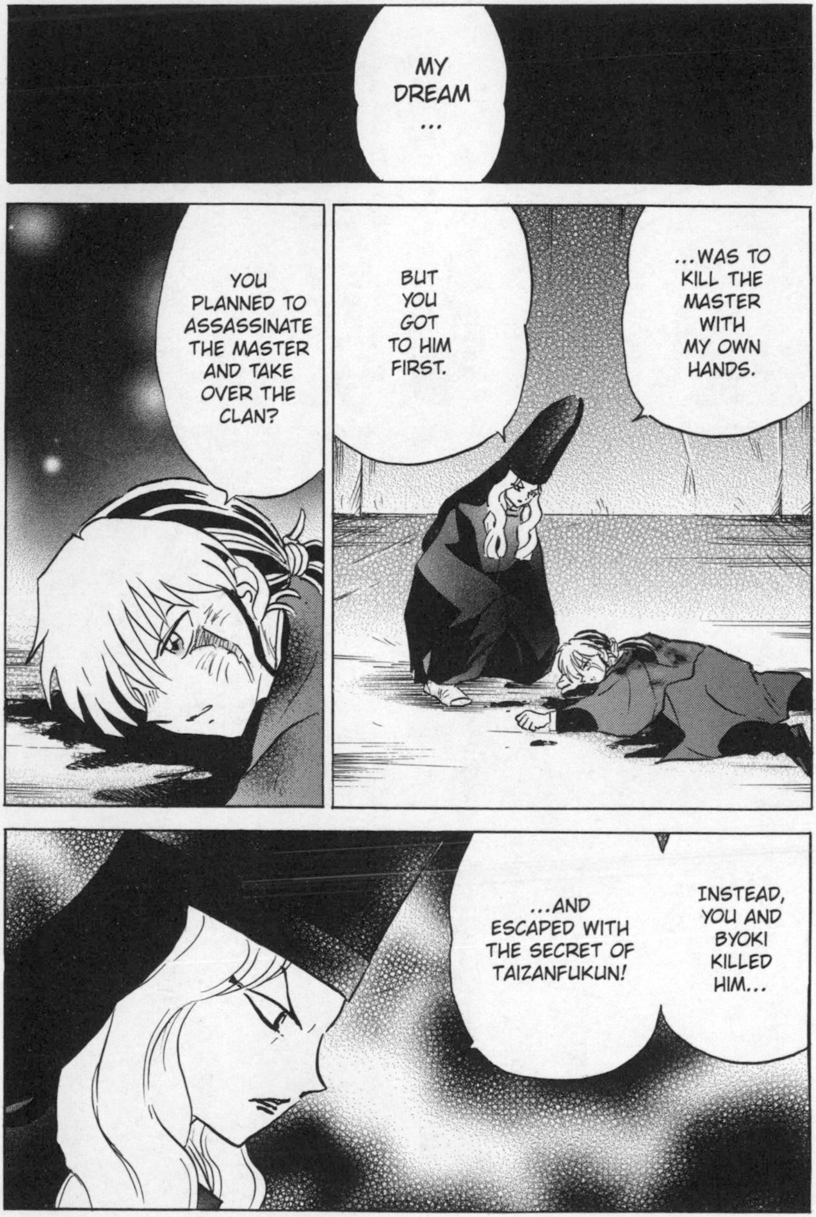
MY DREAM ...
...WAS TO KILL THE MASTER WITH MY OWN HANDS.
BUT YOU GOT TO HIM FIRST.
YOU PLANNED TO ASSASSINATE THE MASTER AND TAKE OVER THE CLAN?
INSTEAD, YOU AND BYOKI KILLED HIM...
...AND ESCAPED WITH THE SECRET OF TAIZANFUKUN!

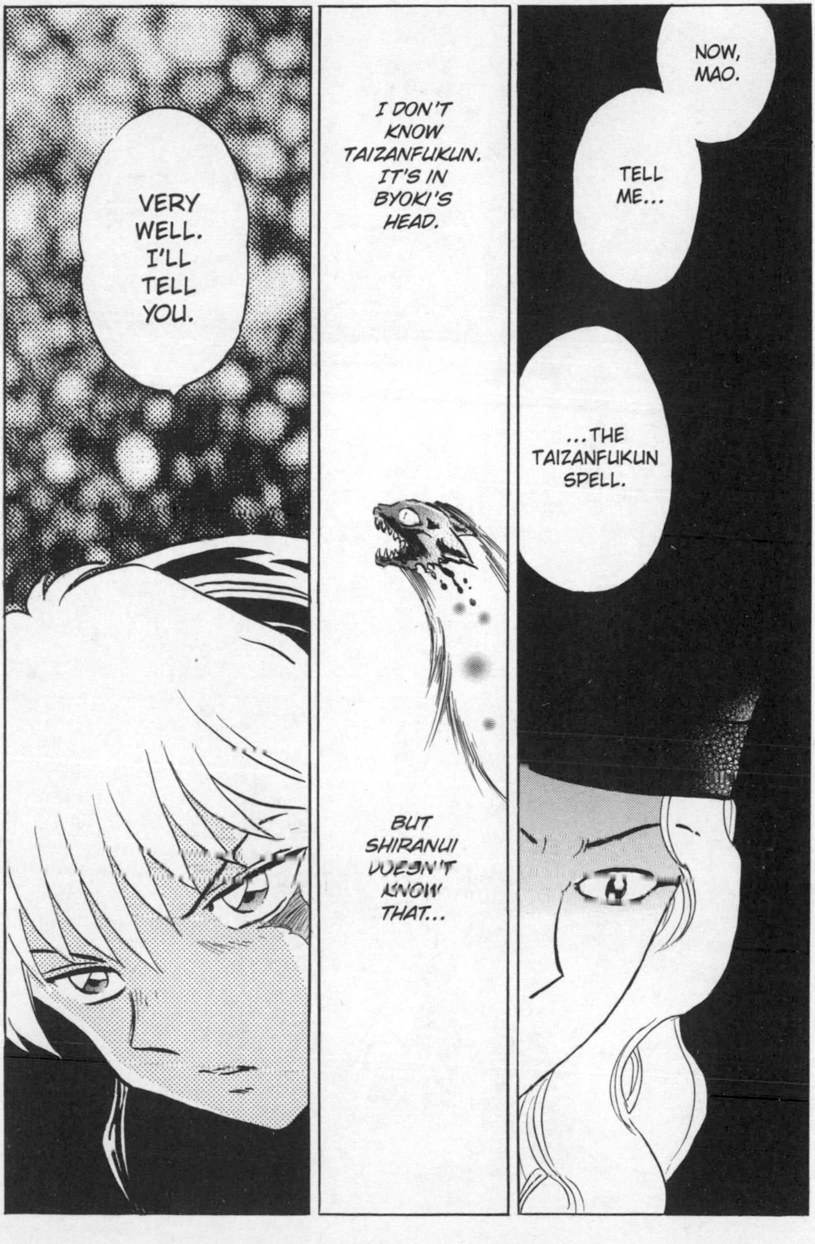
NOW, MAO.
TELL ME...
...THE TAIZANFUKUN SPELL.
I DON'T KNOW TAIZANFUKUN. IT'S IN BYOKI'S HEAD.
BUT SHIRANUI DOESN'T KNOW THAT...
VERY WELL. I'LL TELL YOU.

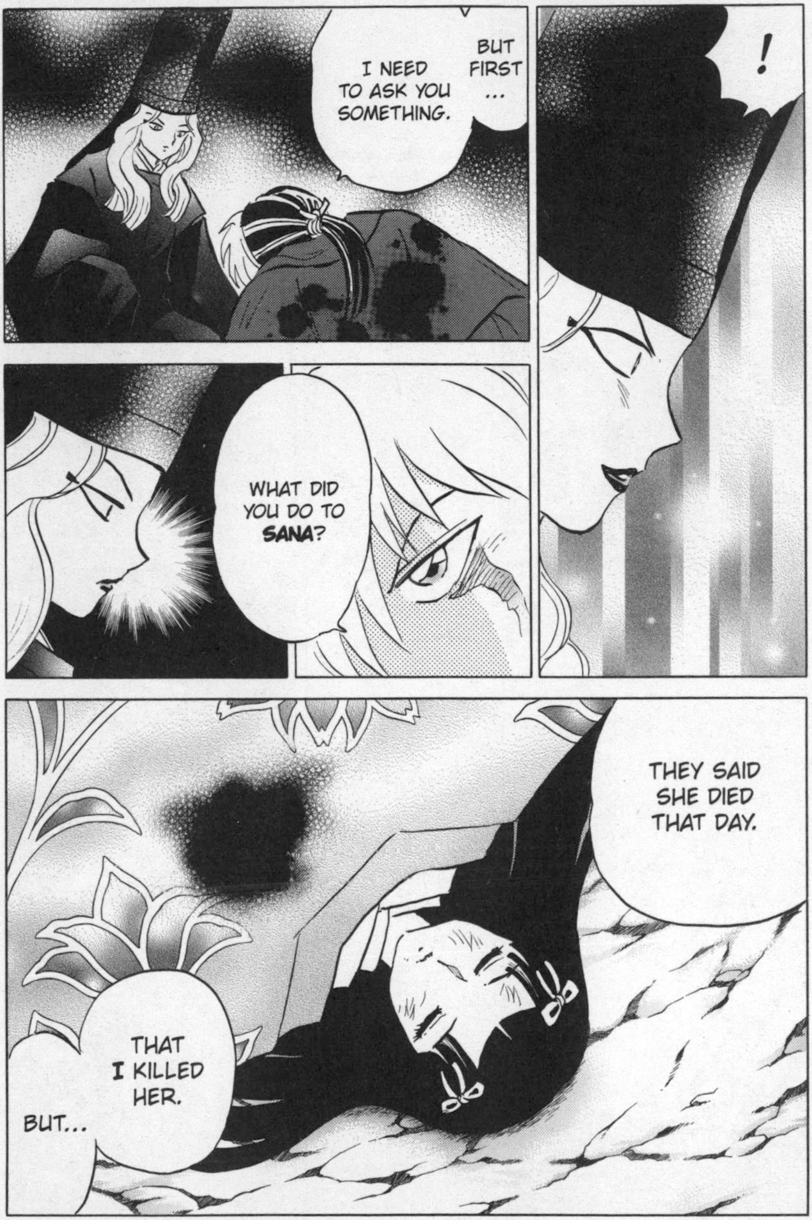
!
BUT FIRST...
I NEED TO ASK YOU SOMETHING.
WHAT DID YOU DO TO **SANA**?
THEY SAID SHE DIED THAT DAY.
THAT **I** KILLED HER.
BUT...

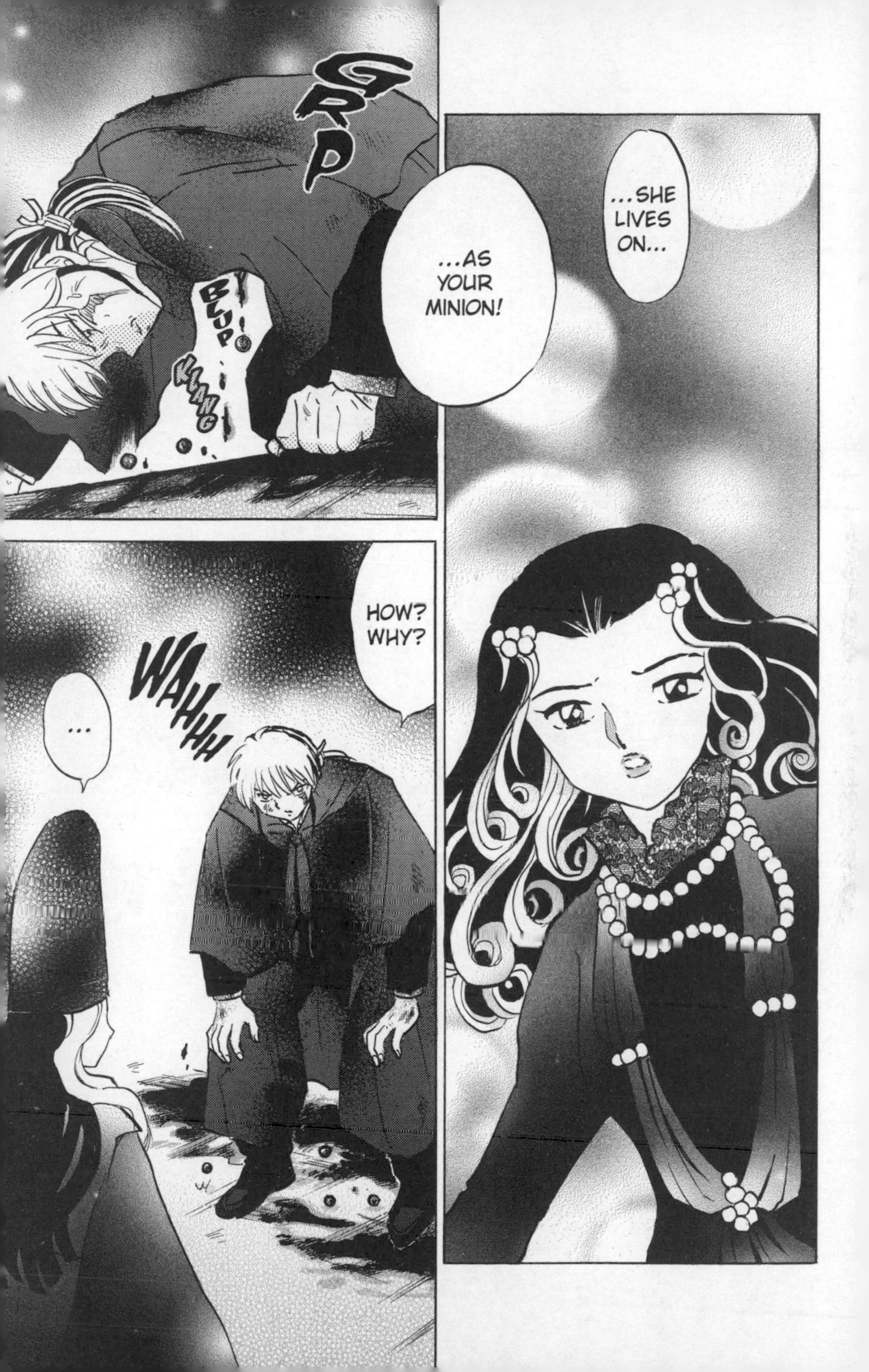
...SHE LIVES ON...
...AS YOUR MINION!
GRP
BLUP
KLANG
HOW? WHY?
WAHHH
...

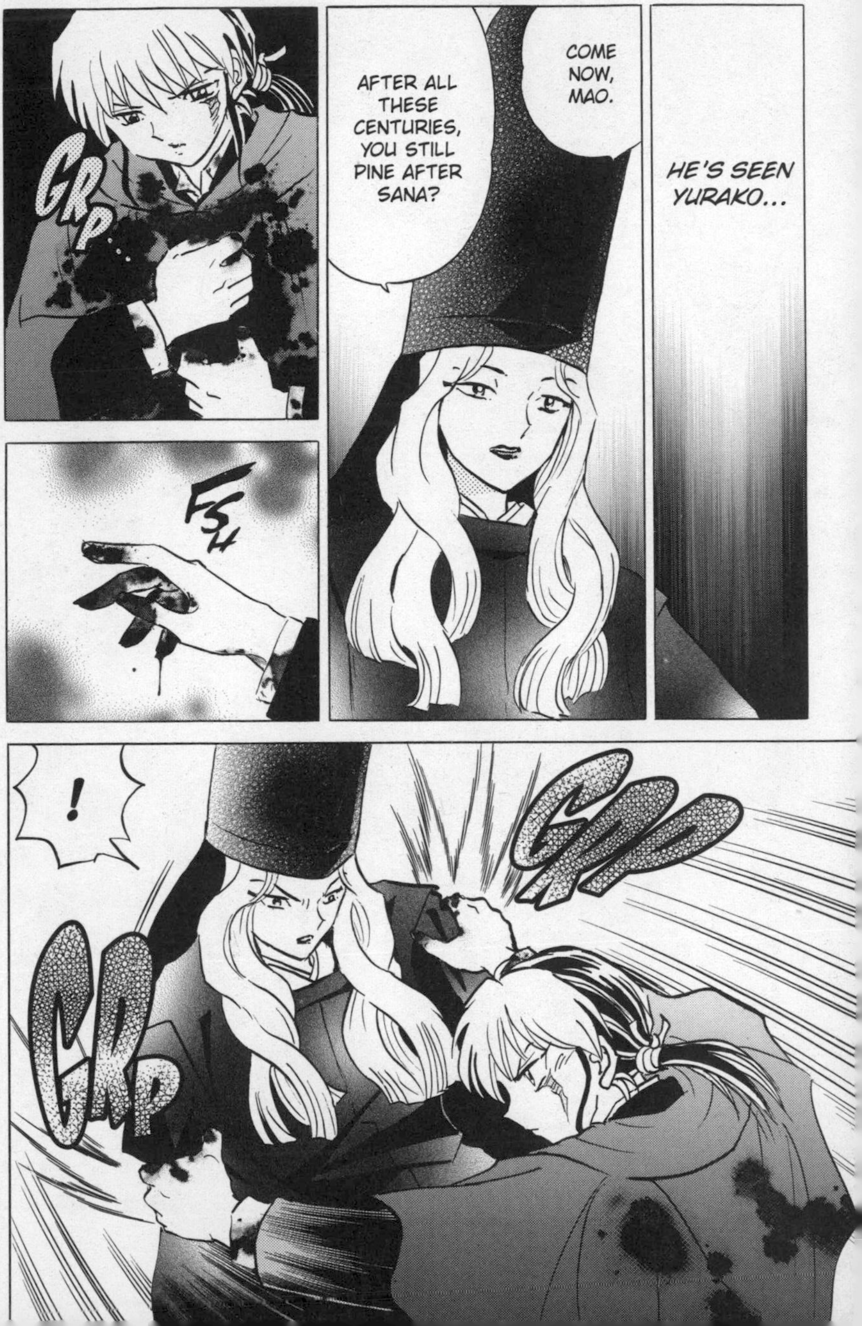
HE'S SEEN YURAKO...
COME NOW, MAO.
AFTER ALL THESE CENTURIES, YOU STILL PINE AFTER SANA?
GRP
FSH
GRP
!
GRP

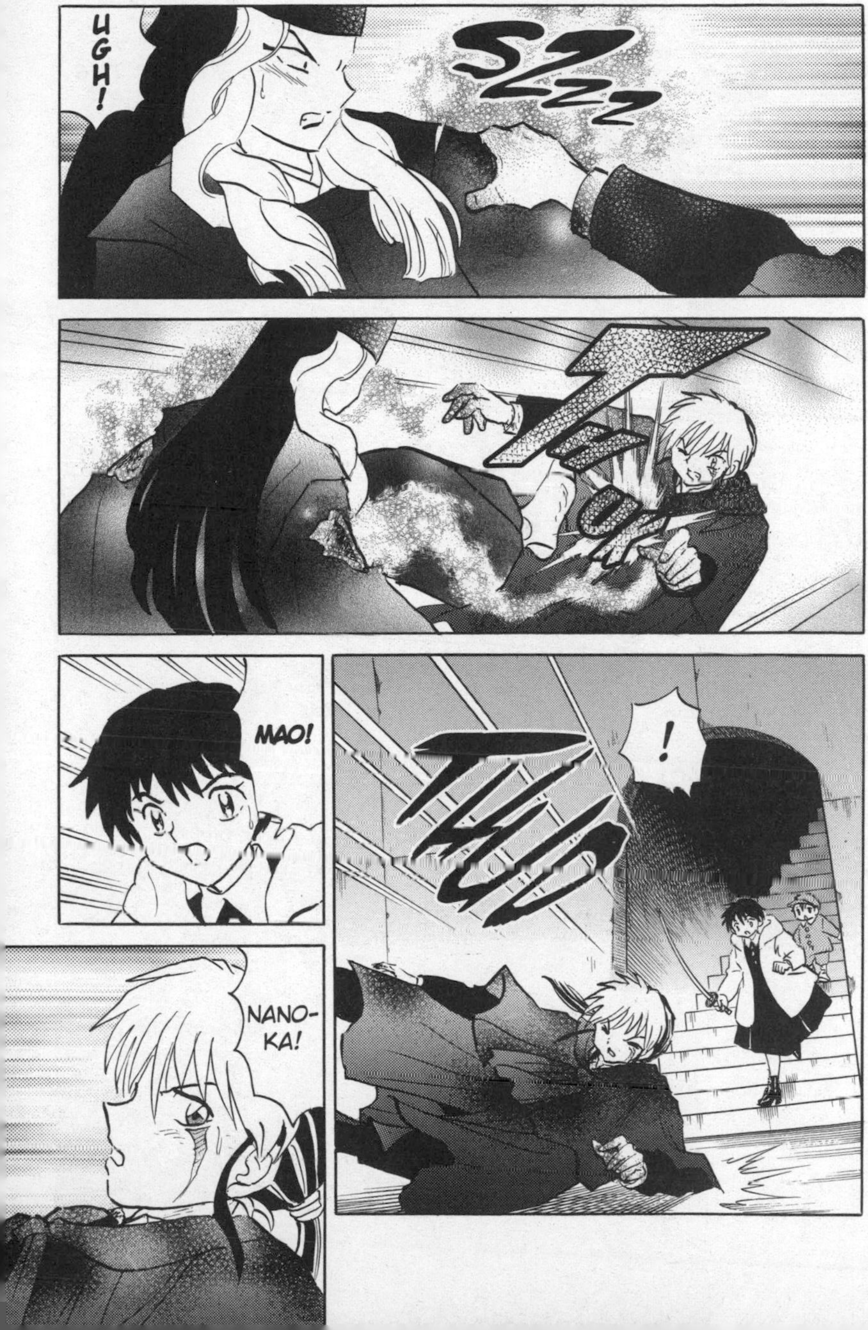
SZZZ
UGH!
!
THUD
MAO!
NANO-KA!

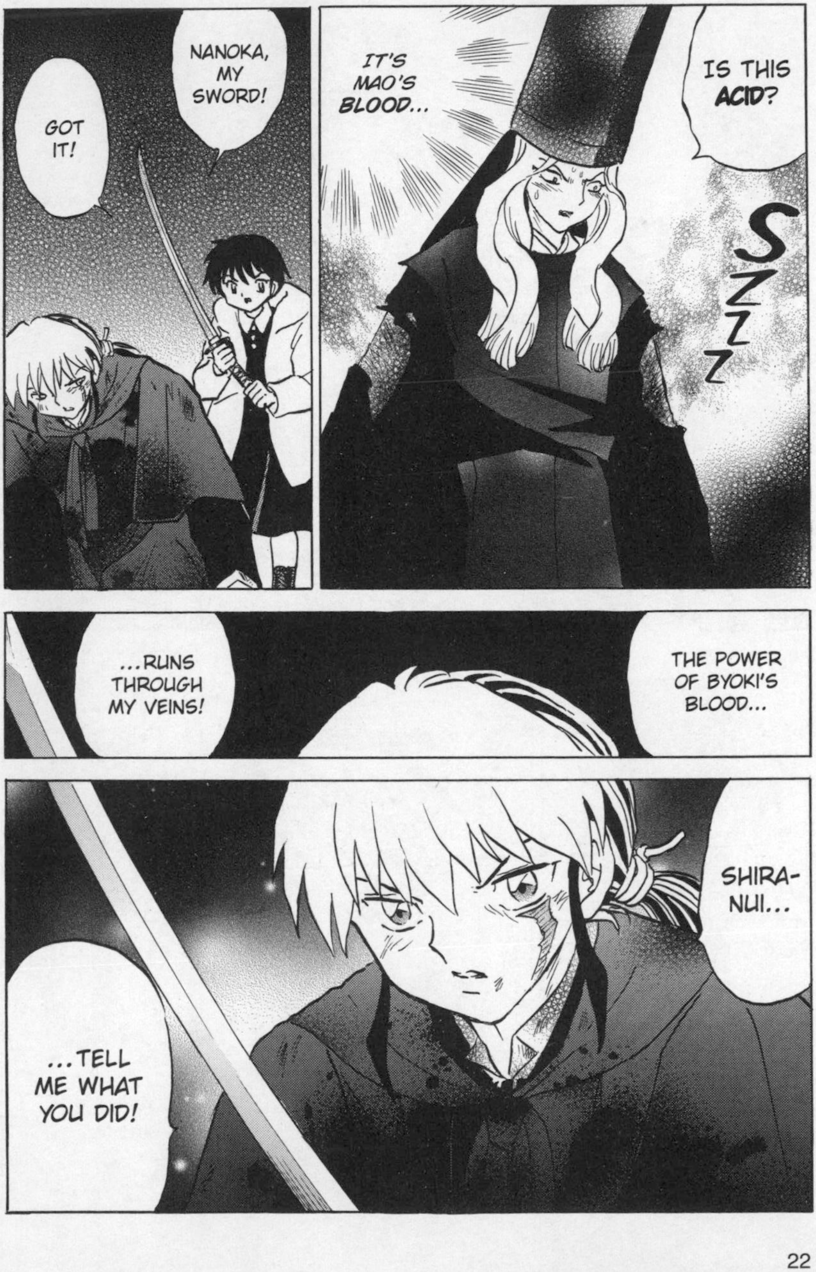
IS THIS ACID?
IT'S MAO'S BLOOD...
SZZZ
NANOKA, MY SWORD!
GOT IT!
THE POWER OF BYOKI'S BLOOD...
...RUNS THROUGH MY VEINS!
SHIRA-NUI...
...TELL ME WHAT YOU DID!

Chapter 2:
Shiranui's Legs

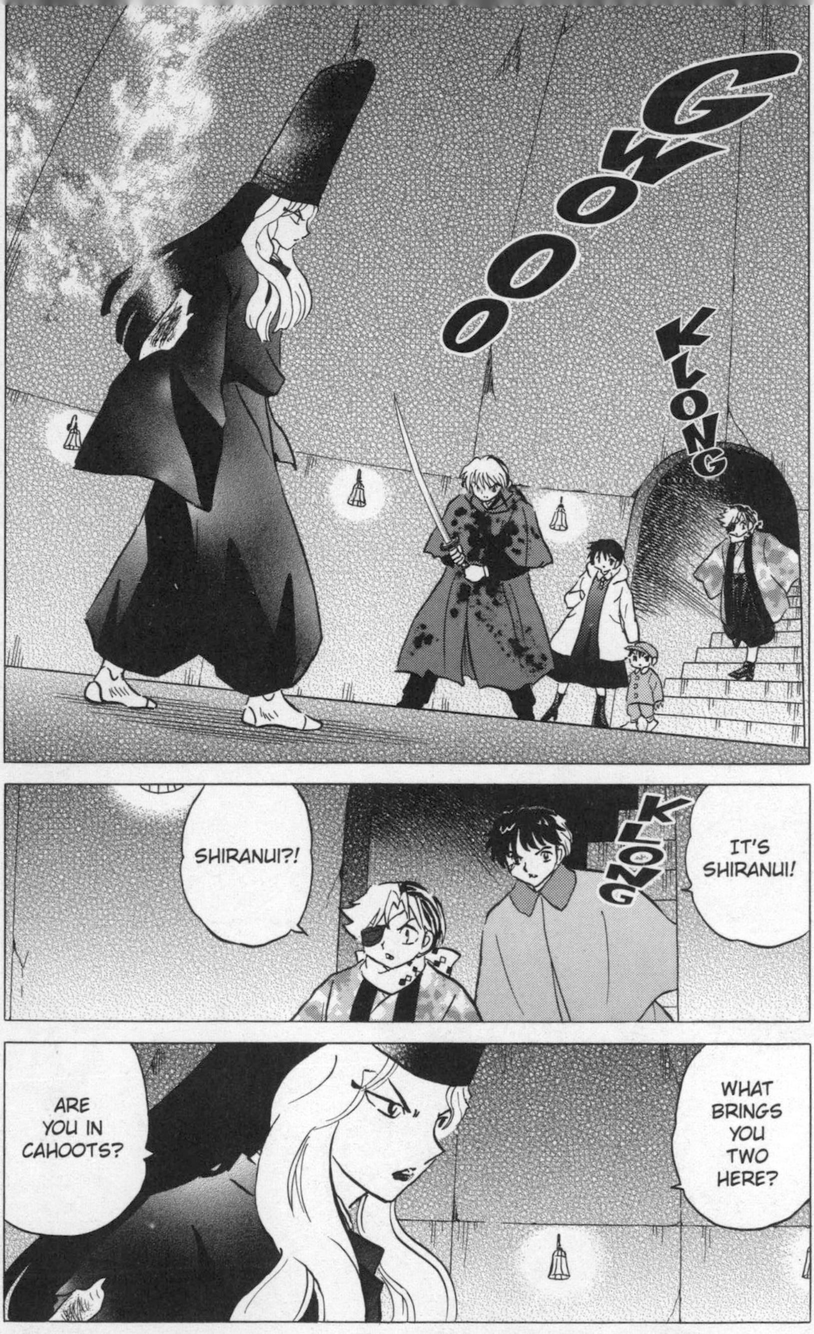
GWOOOOO
KLONG
IT'S SHIRANUI!
KLONG
SHIRANUI?!
WHAT BRINGS YOU TWO HERE?
ARE YOU IN CAHOOTS?

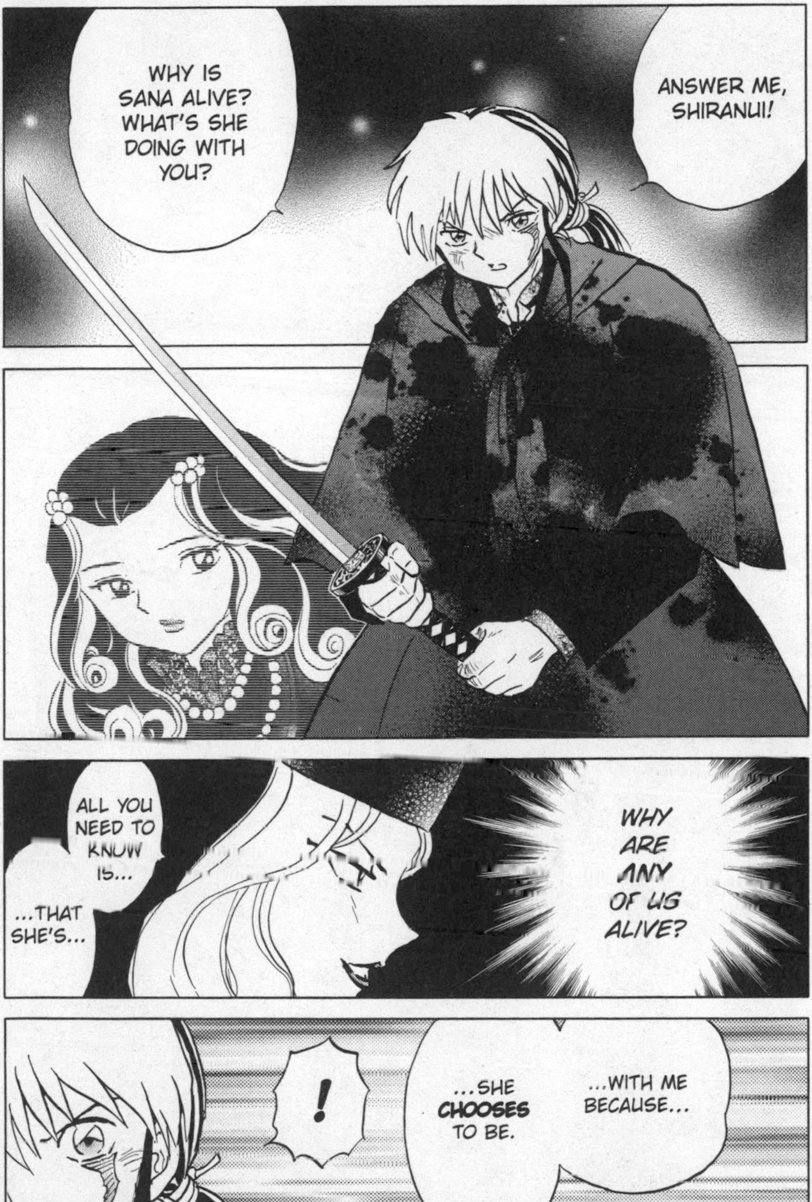
ANSWER ME, SHIRANUI!
WHY IS SANA ALIVE? WHAT'S SHE DOING WITH YOU?
WHY ARE ANY OF US ALIVE?
ALL YOU NEED TO KNOW IS...
...THAT SHE'S...
...WITH ME BECAUSE...
...SHE **CHOOSES** TO BE.
!

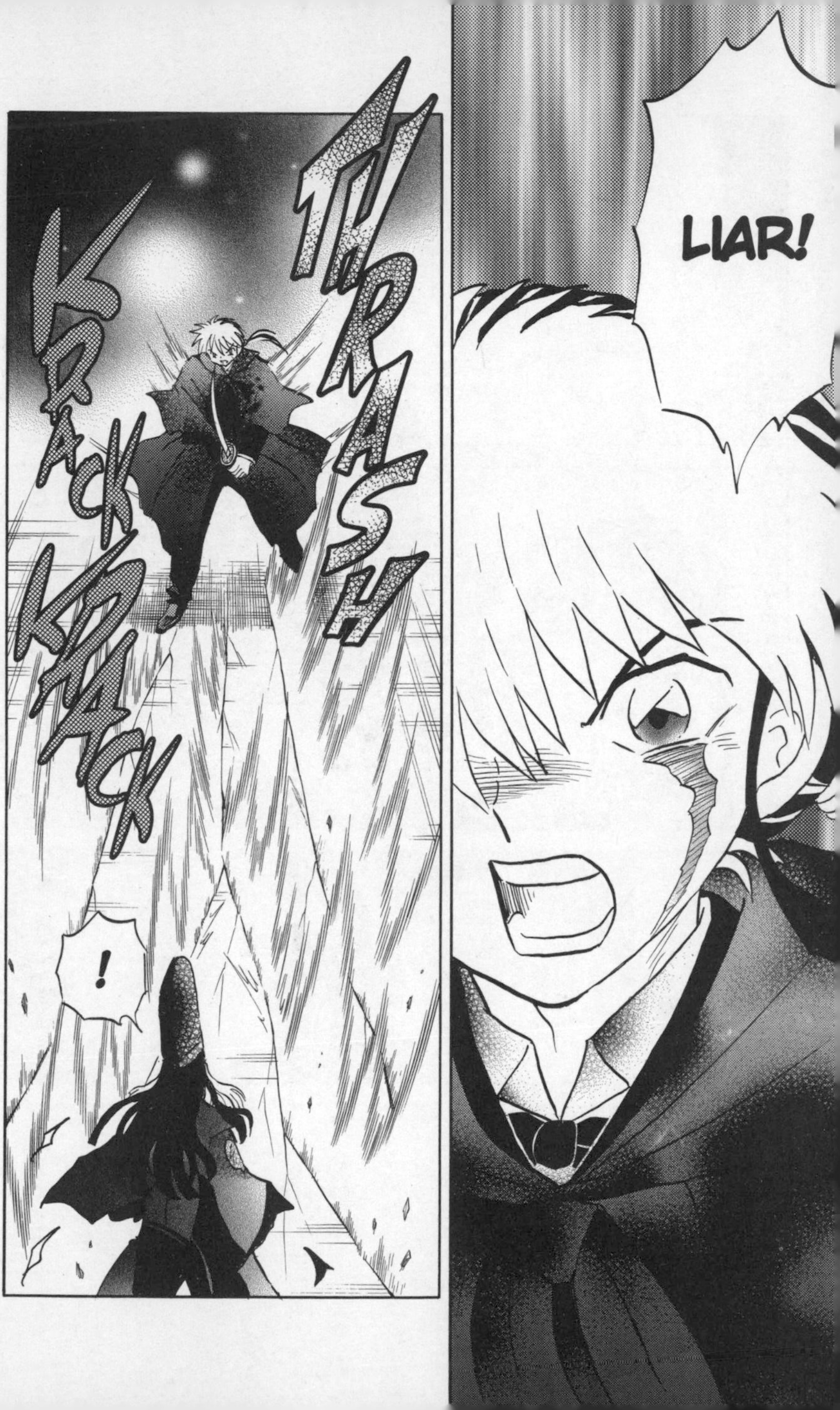
LIAR!
THRASH
KRACK KRACK
!

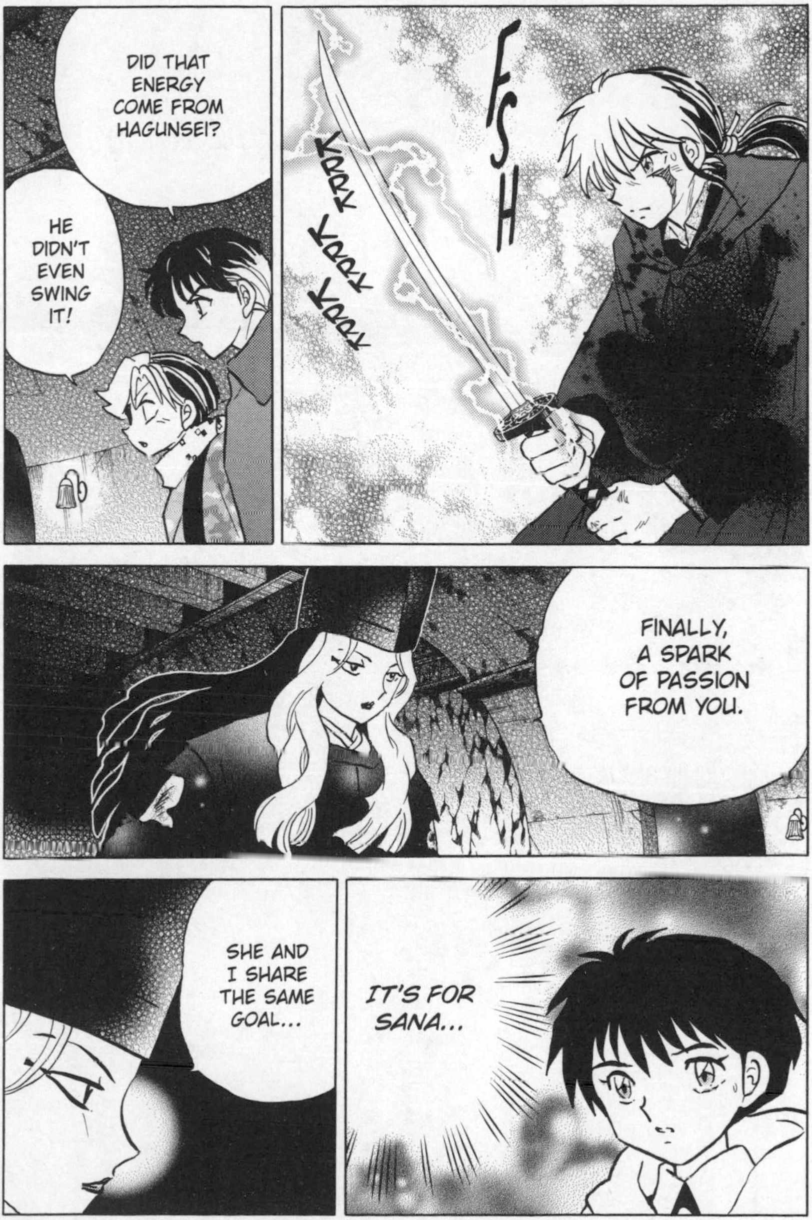
FSH
KRRK KRRK KRRK
DID THAT ENERGY COME FROM HAGUNSEI?
HE DIDN'T EVEN SWING IT!
FINALLY, A SPARK OF PASSION FROM YOU.
IT'S FOR SANA...
SHE AND I SHARE THE SAME GOAL...

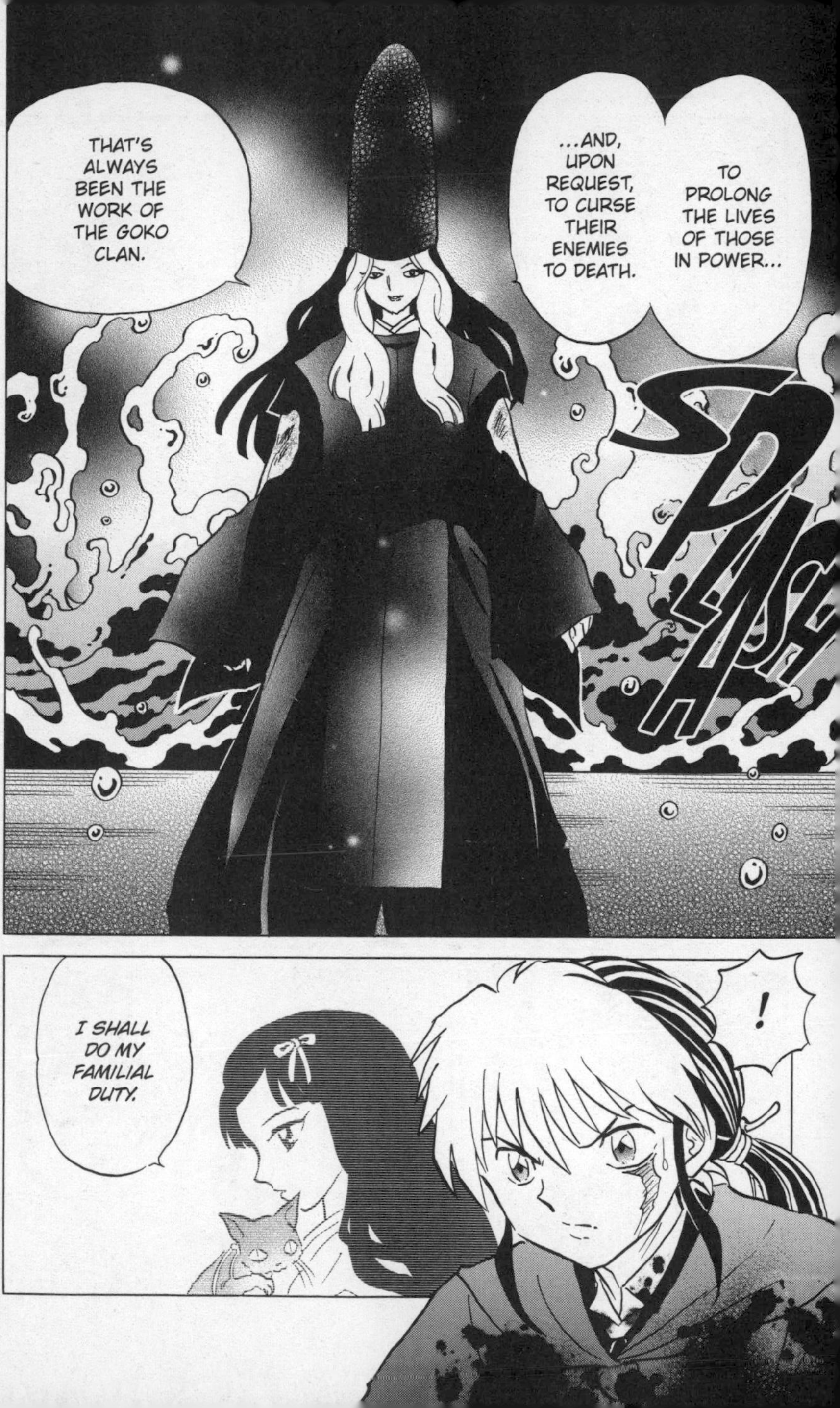
TO PROLONG THE LIVES OF THOSE IN POWER...
...AND, UPON REQUEST, TO CURSE THEIR ENEMIES TO DEATH.
THAT'S ALWAYS BEEN THE WORK OF THE GOKO CLAN.
SPLASH
!
I SHALL DO MY FAMILIAL DUTY.

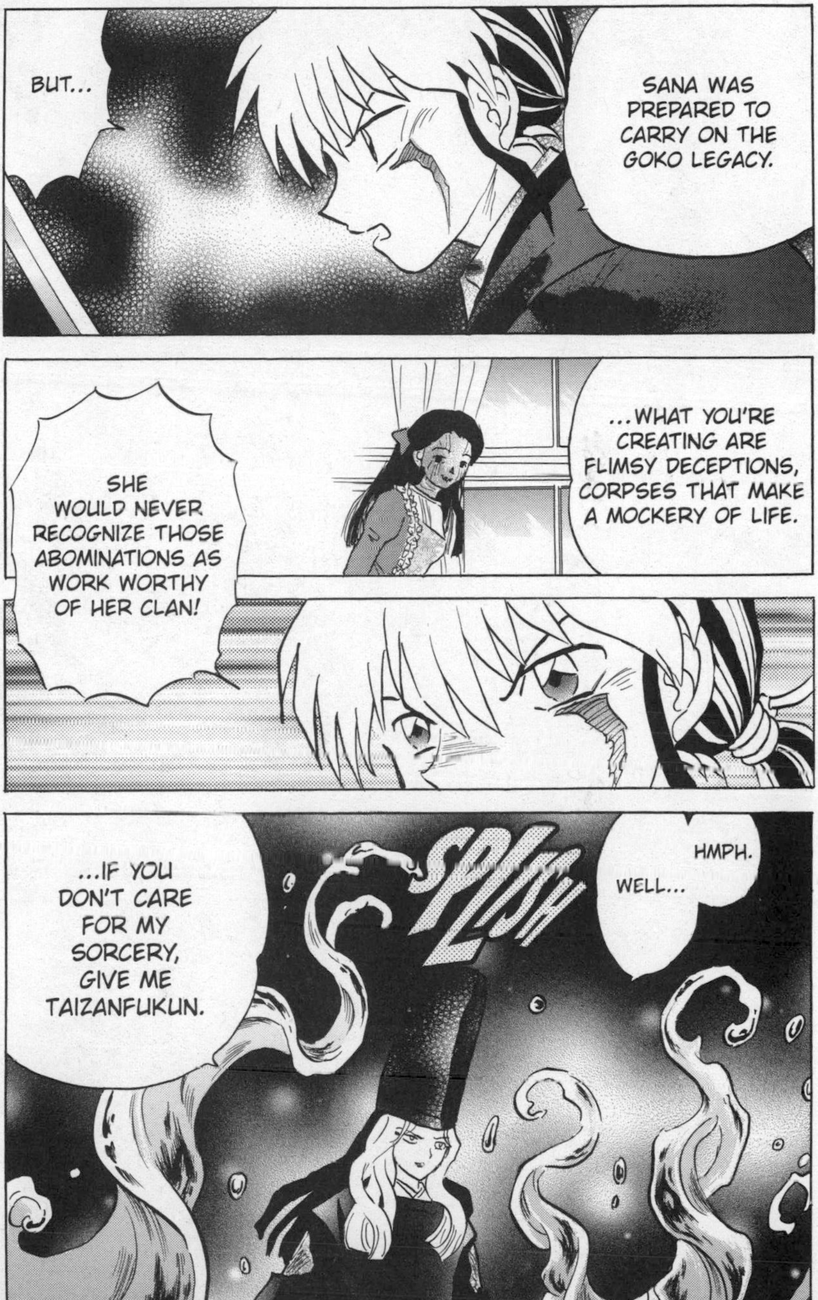
SANA WAS PREPARED TO CARRY ON THE GOKO LEGACY.
BUT...
...WHAT YOU'RE CREATING ARE FLIMSY DECEPTIONS, CORPSES THAT MAKE A MOCKERY OF LIFE.
SHE WOULD NEVER RECOGNIZE THOSE ABOMINATIONS AS WORK WORTHY OF HER CLAN!
HMPH.
WELL...
SPLISH
...IF YOU DON'T CARE FOR MY SORCERY, GIVE ME TAIZANFUKUN.

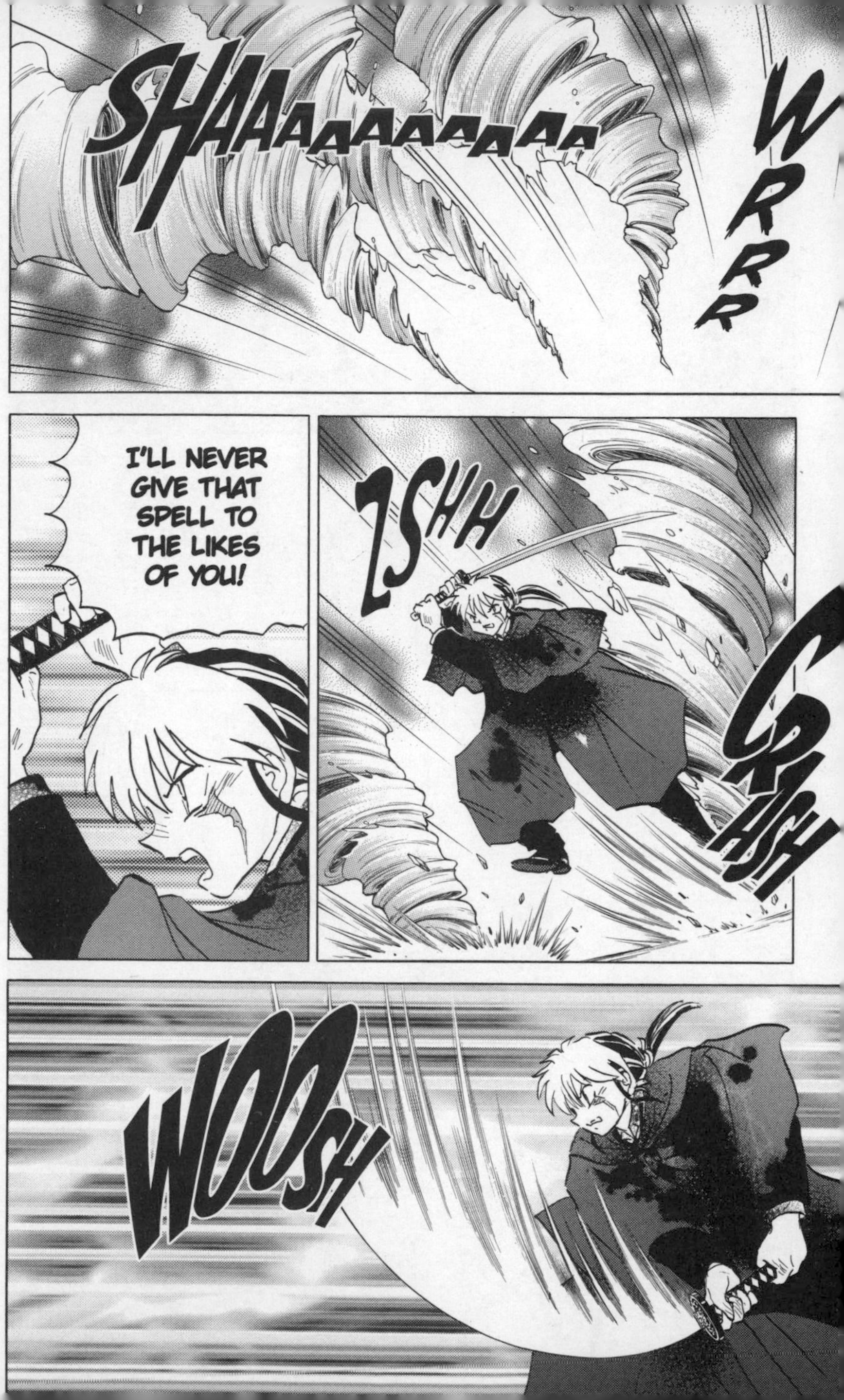
WRRR
SHAAAAAAAAAA
ZSHH
CRASH
I'LL NEVER GIVE THAT SPELL TO THE LIKES OF YOU!
WOOSH

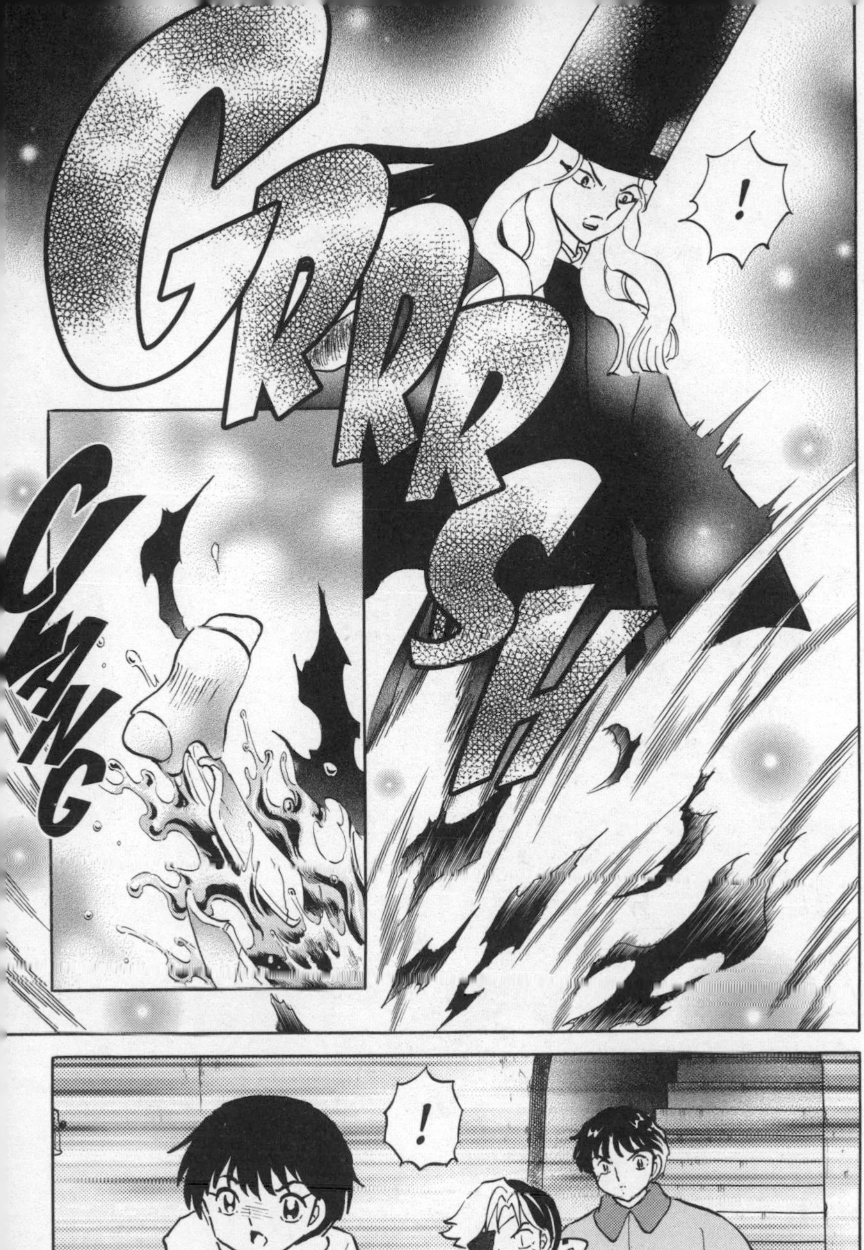
!
GRRRSH
CLANG
!

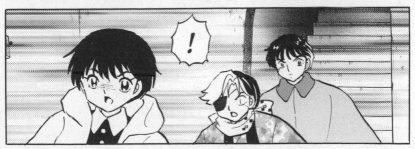

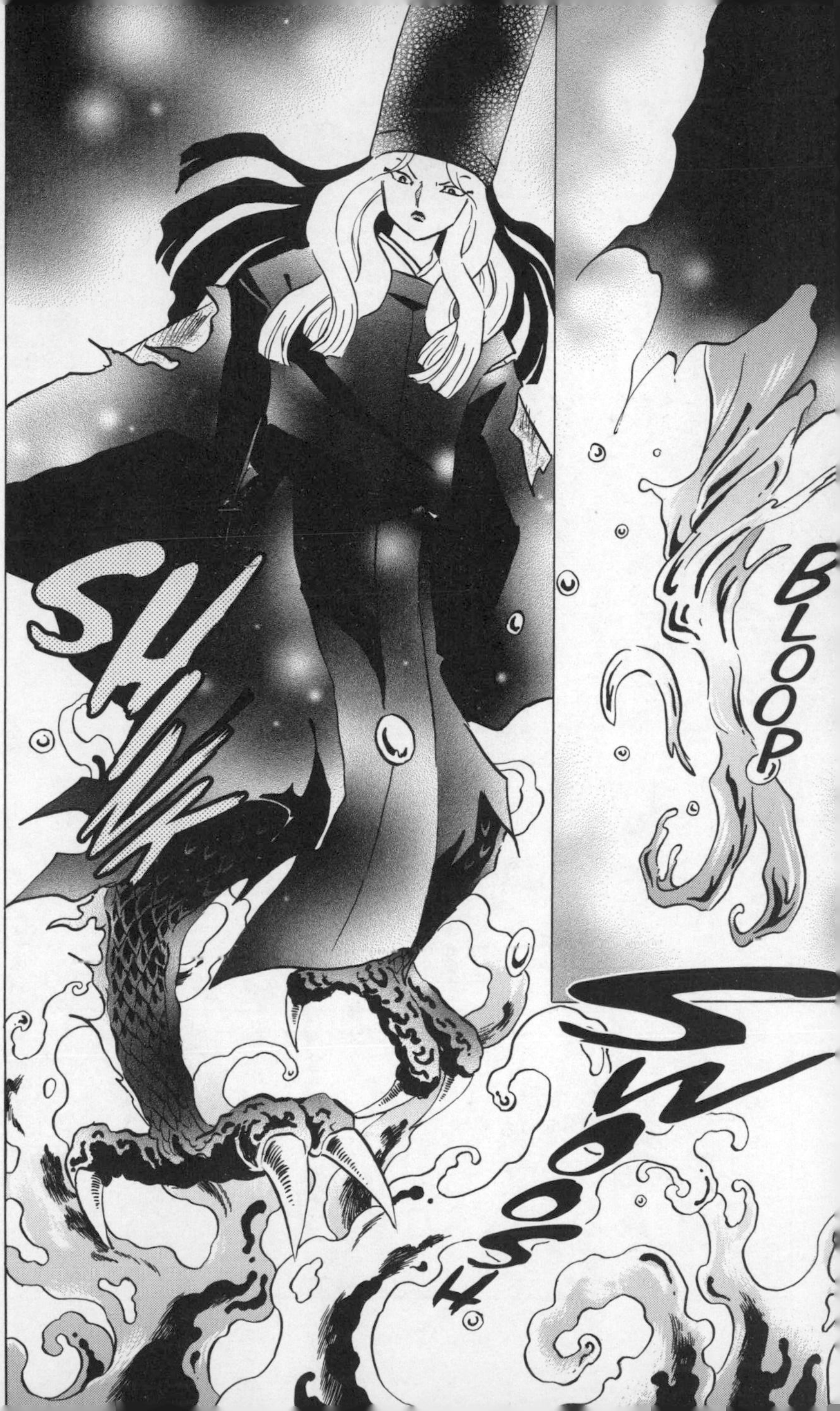
BLOOOP
SWOOSH
SHINK

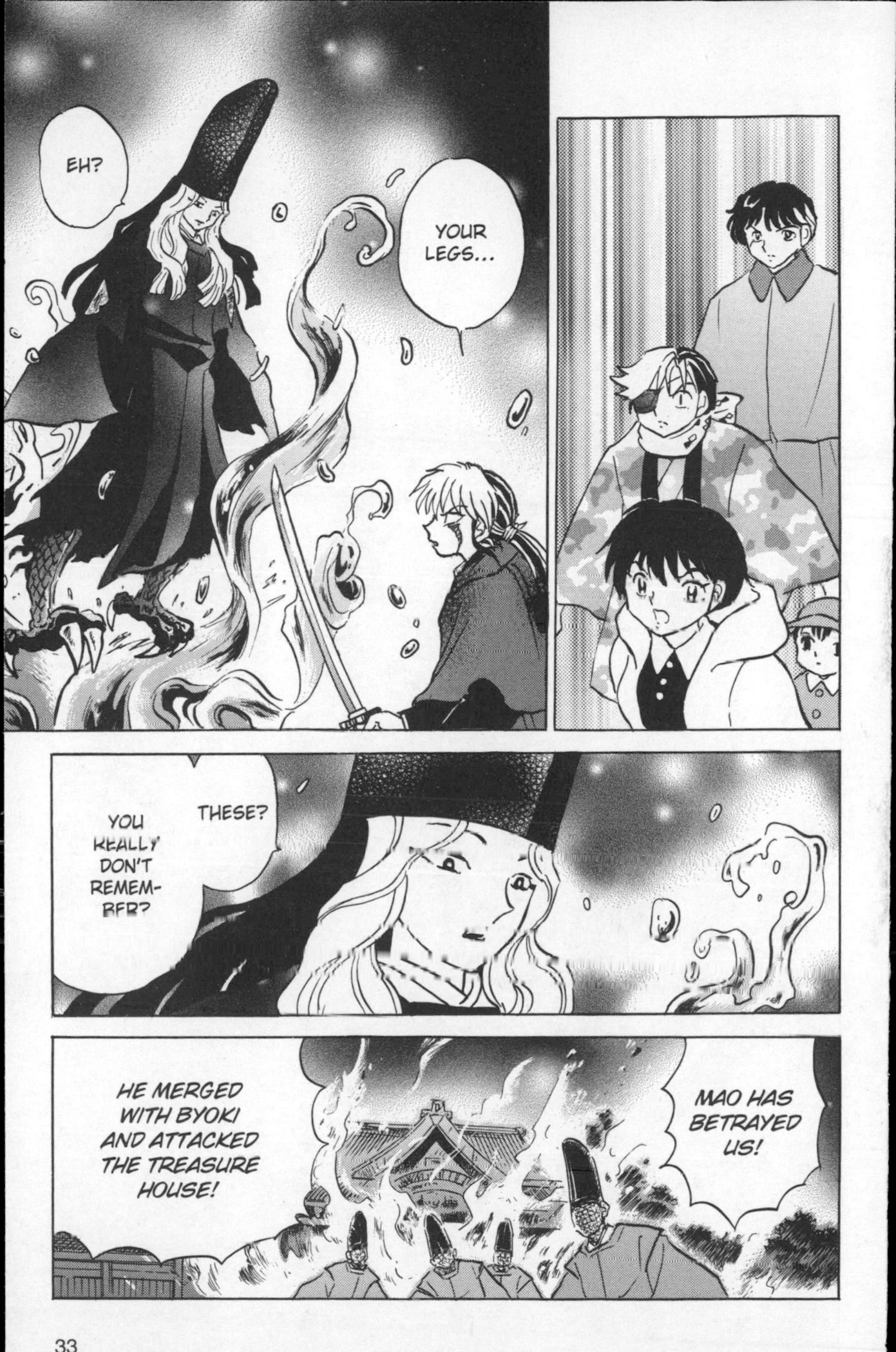
YOUR LEGS...
EH?
THESE?
YOU REALLY DON'T REMEMBER?
MAO HAS BETRAYED US!
HE MERGED WITH BYOKI AND ATTACKED THE TREASURE HOUSE!

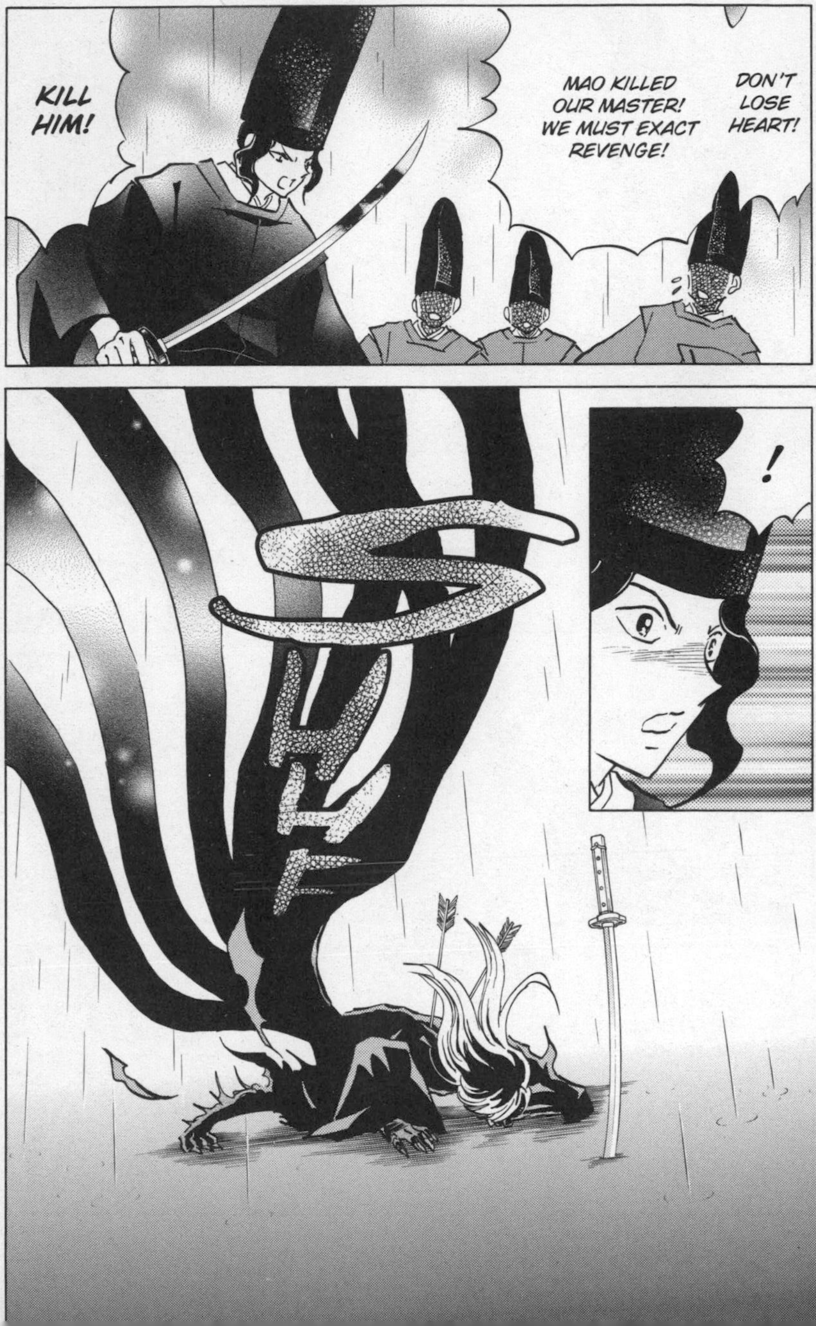
DON'T LOSE HEART!
MAO KILLED OUR MASTER! WE MUST EXACT REVENGE!
KILL HIM!
!

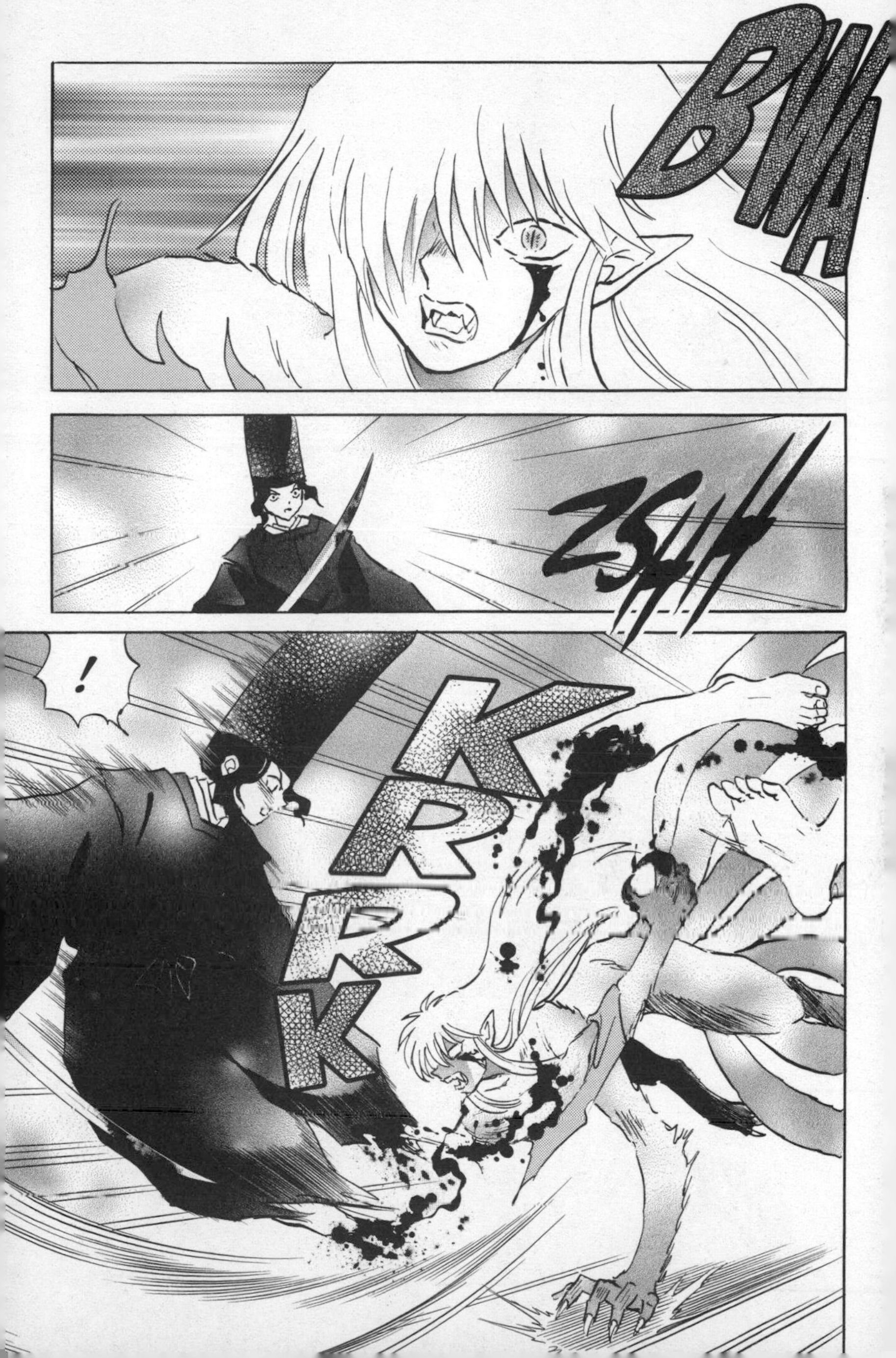
BWA
ZSHH
!
KRRK

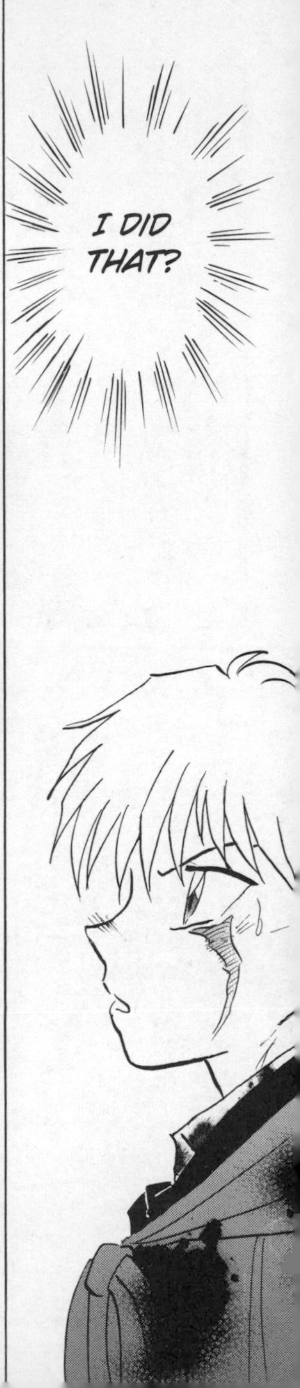
I DID THAT?

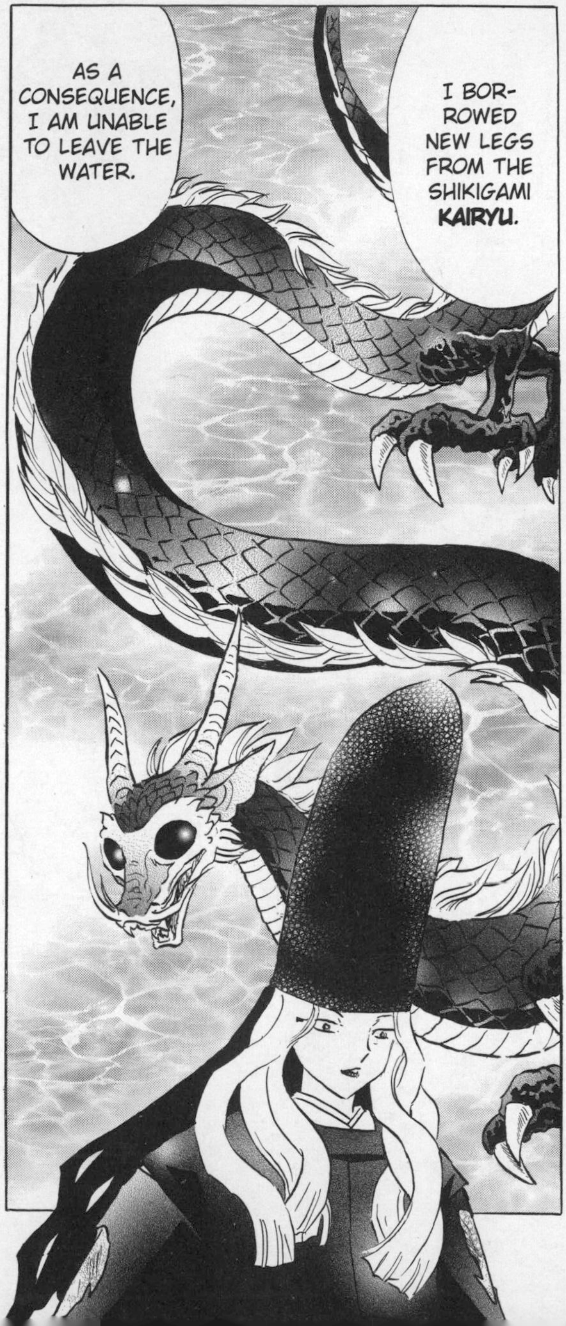
I BOR-ROWED NEW LEGS FROM THE SHIKIGAMI **KAIRYU.**
AS A CONSEQUENCE, I AM UNABLE TO LEAVE THE WATER.

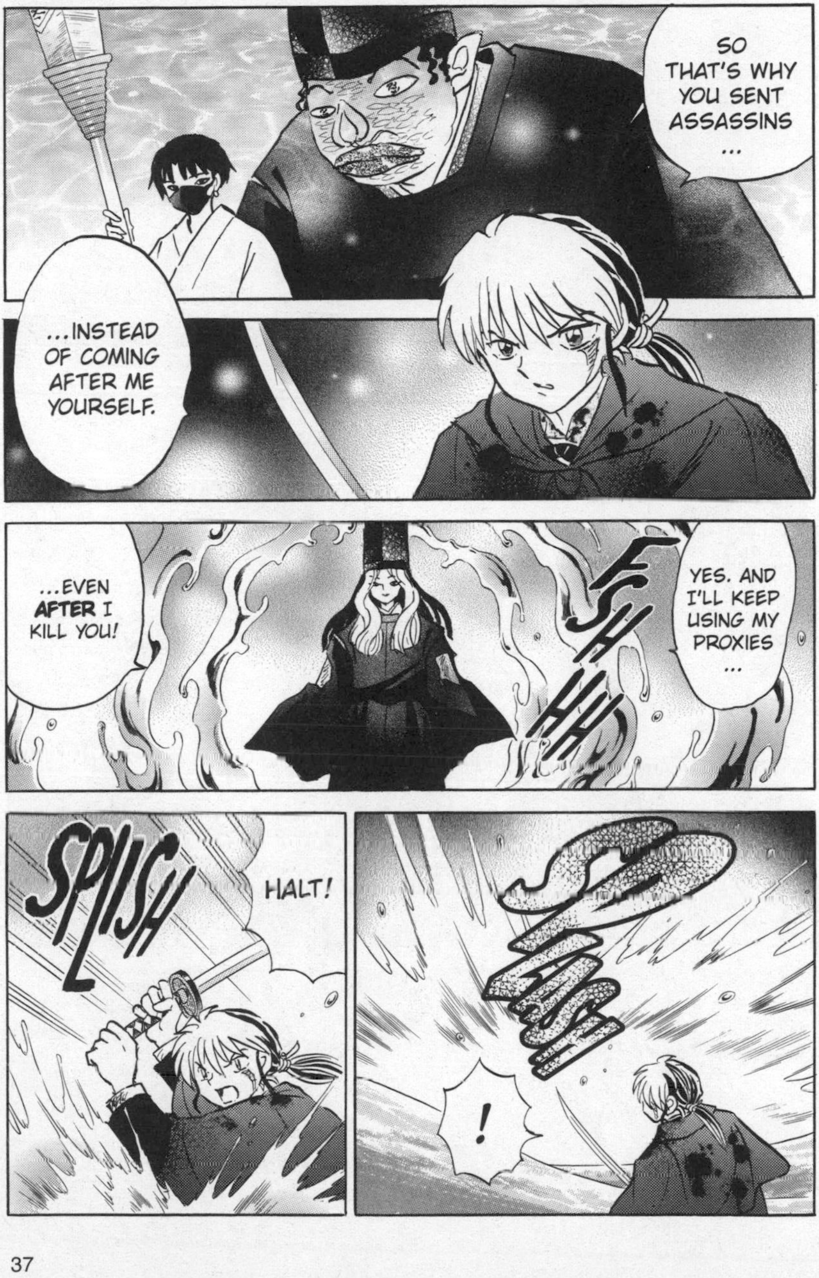
SO THAT'S WHY YOU SENT ASSASSINS ...
...INSTEAD OF COMING AFTER ME YOURSELF.
YES. AND I'LL KEEP USING MY PROXIES ...
FSHHH
...EVEN **AFTER** I KILL YOU!
SPLASH
!
SPLISH
HALT!

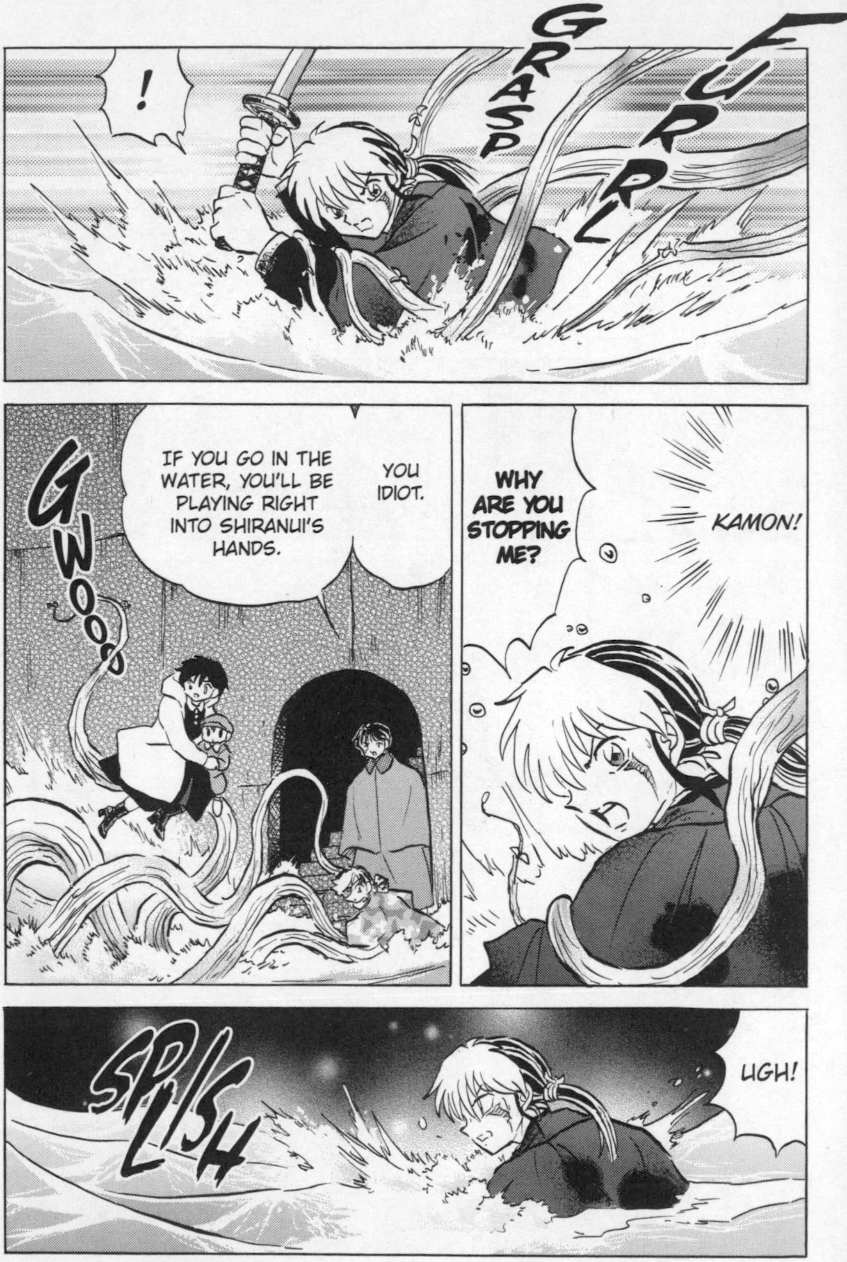
FURRL
GRASP
!
KAMON!
WHY ARE YOU STOPPING ME?
YOU IDIOT.
IF YOU GO IN THE WATER, YOU'LL BE PLAYING RIGHT INTO SHIRANUI'S HANDS.
GWOO
UGH!
SPLISH

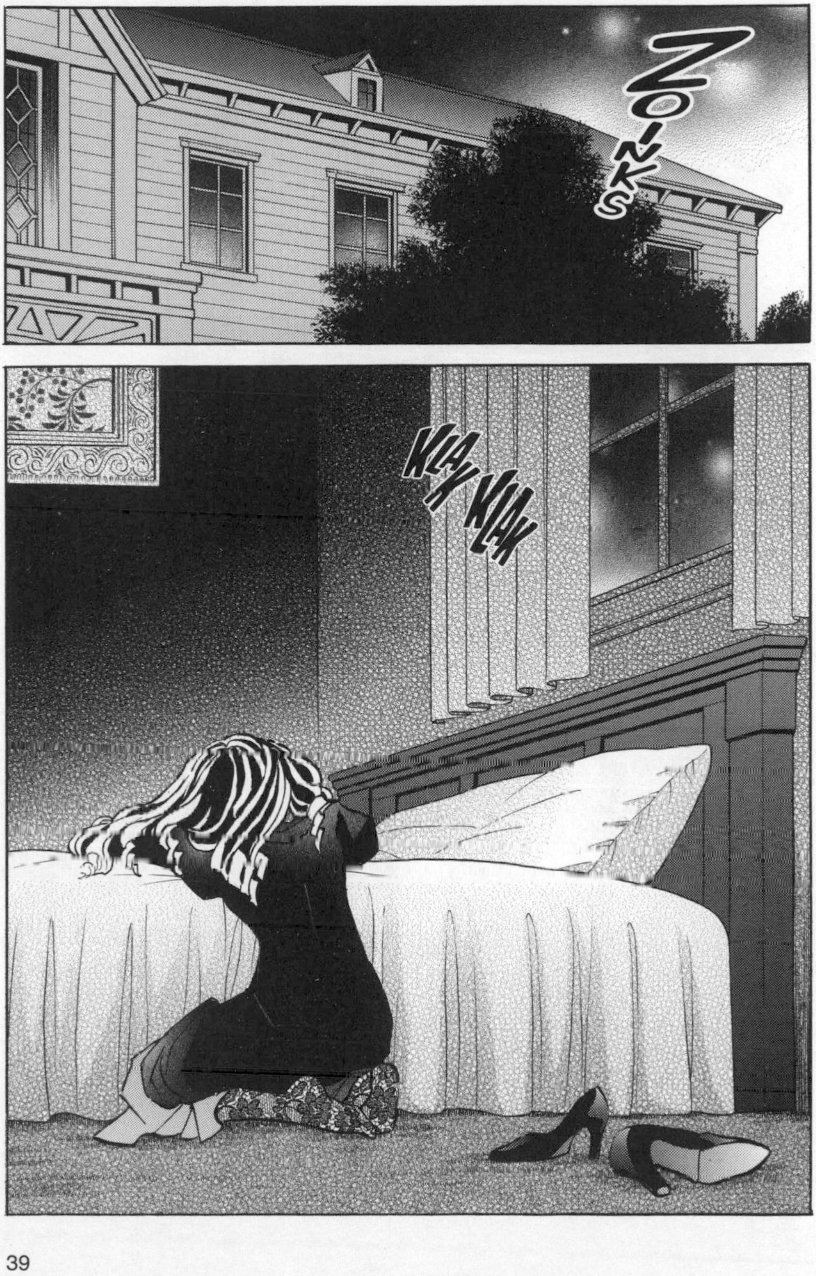
ZOINKS
KLAK KLAK

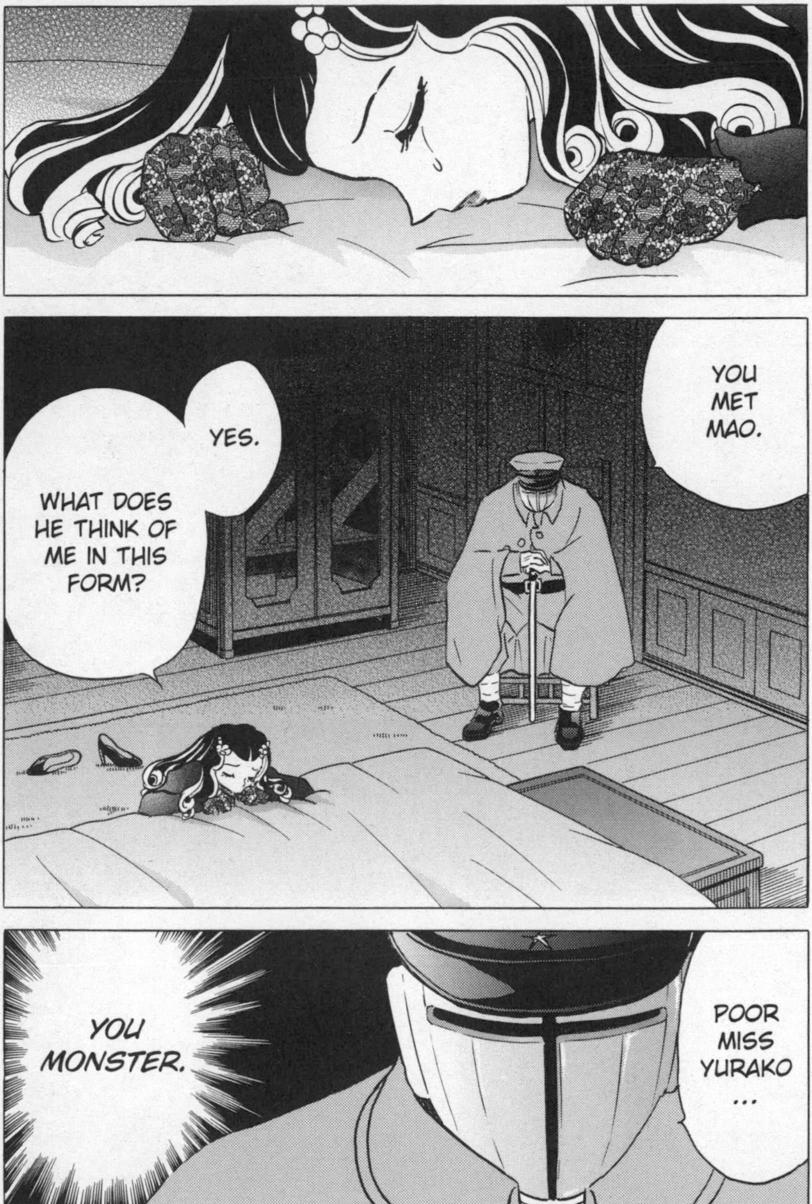
YOU MET MAO.
YES.
WHAT DOES HE THINK OF ME IN THIS FORM?
POOR MISS YURAKO ...
YOU MONSTER.

Chapter 3:
Nanoka's Suspicions

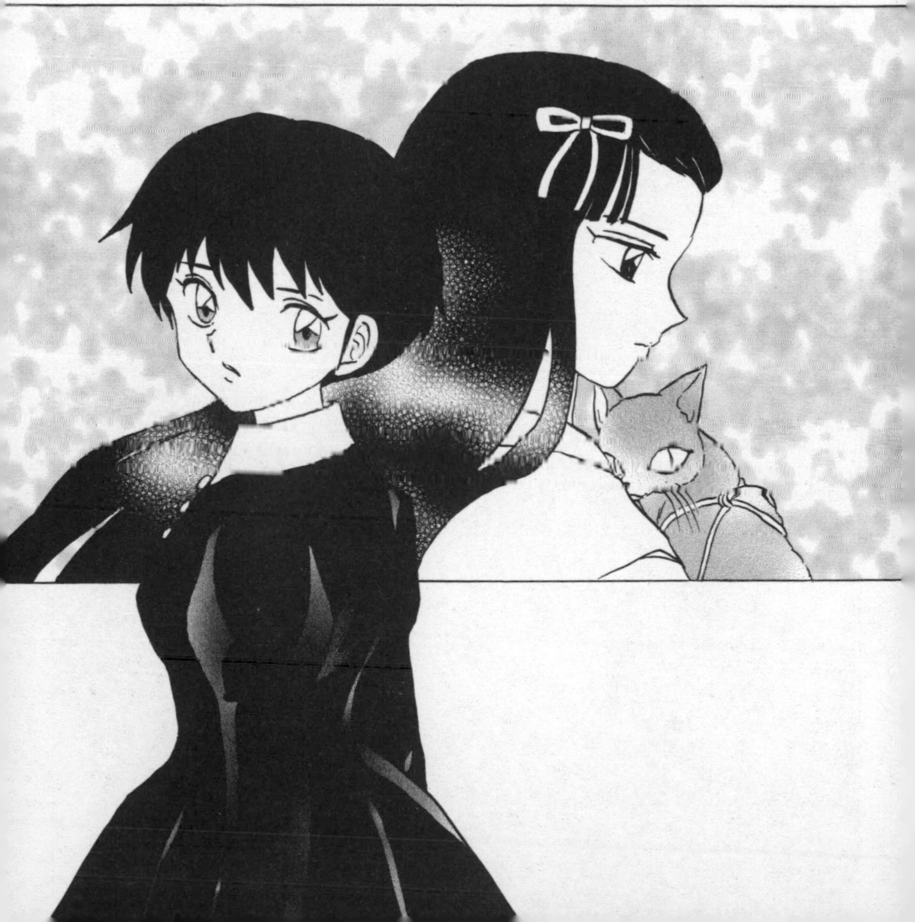

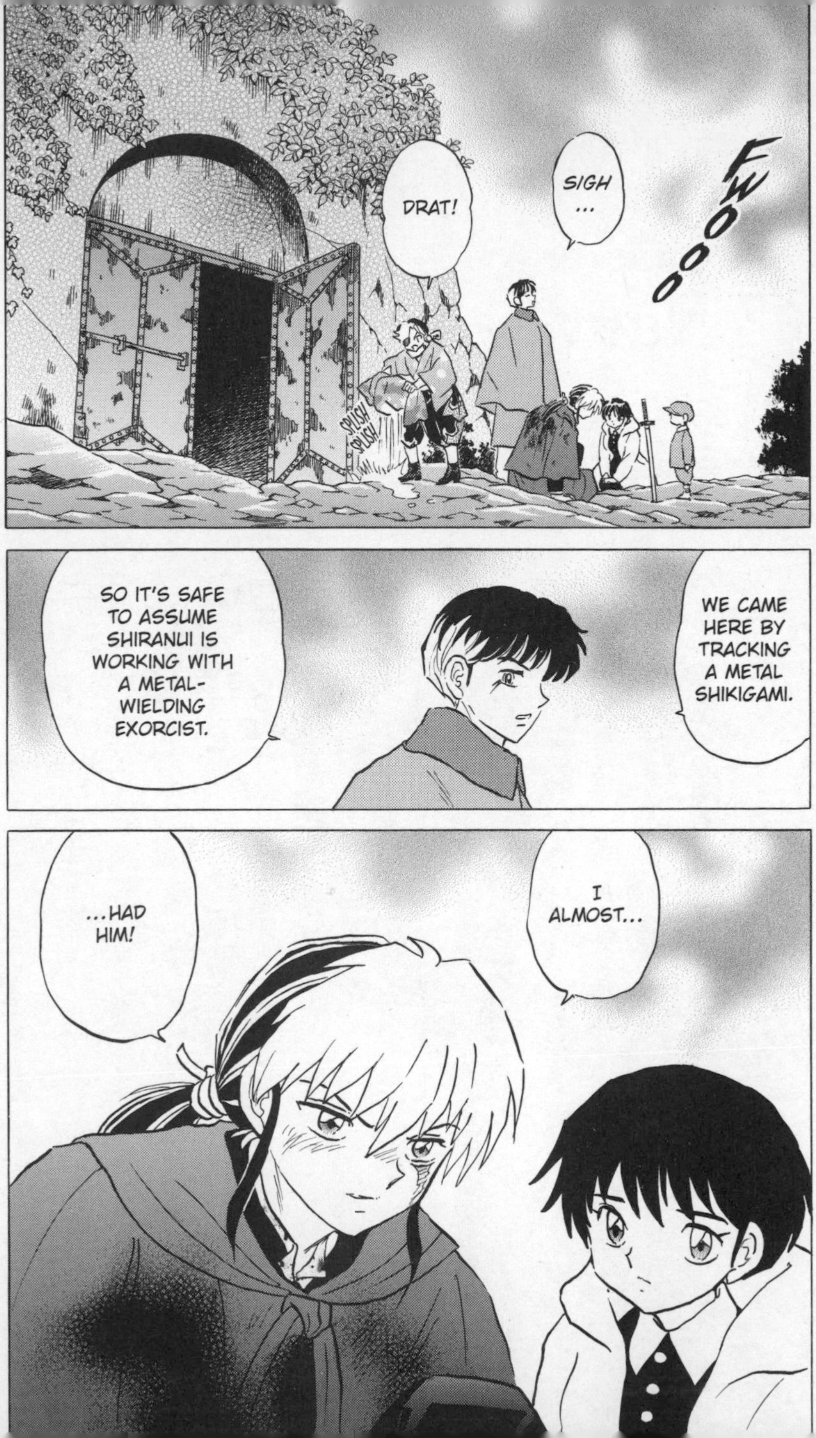
FWOOOOO
SIGH ...
DRAT!
SPLISH SPLISH
WE CAME HERE BY TRACKING A METAL SHIKIGAMI.
SO IT'S SAFE TO ASSUME SHIRANUI IS WORKING WITH A METAL-WIELDING EXORCIST.
I ALMOST...
...HAD HIM!

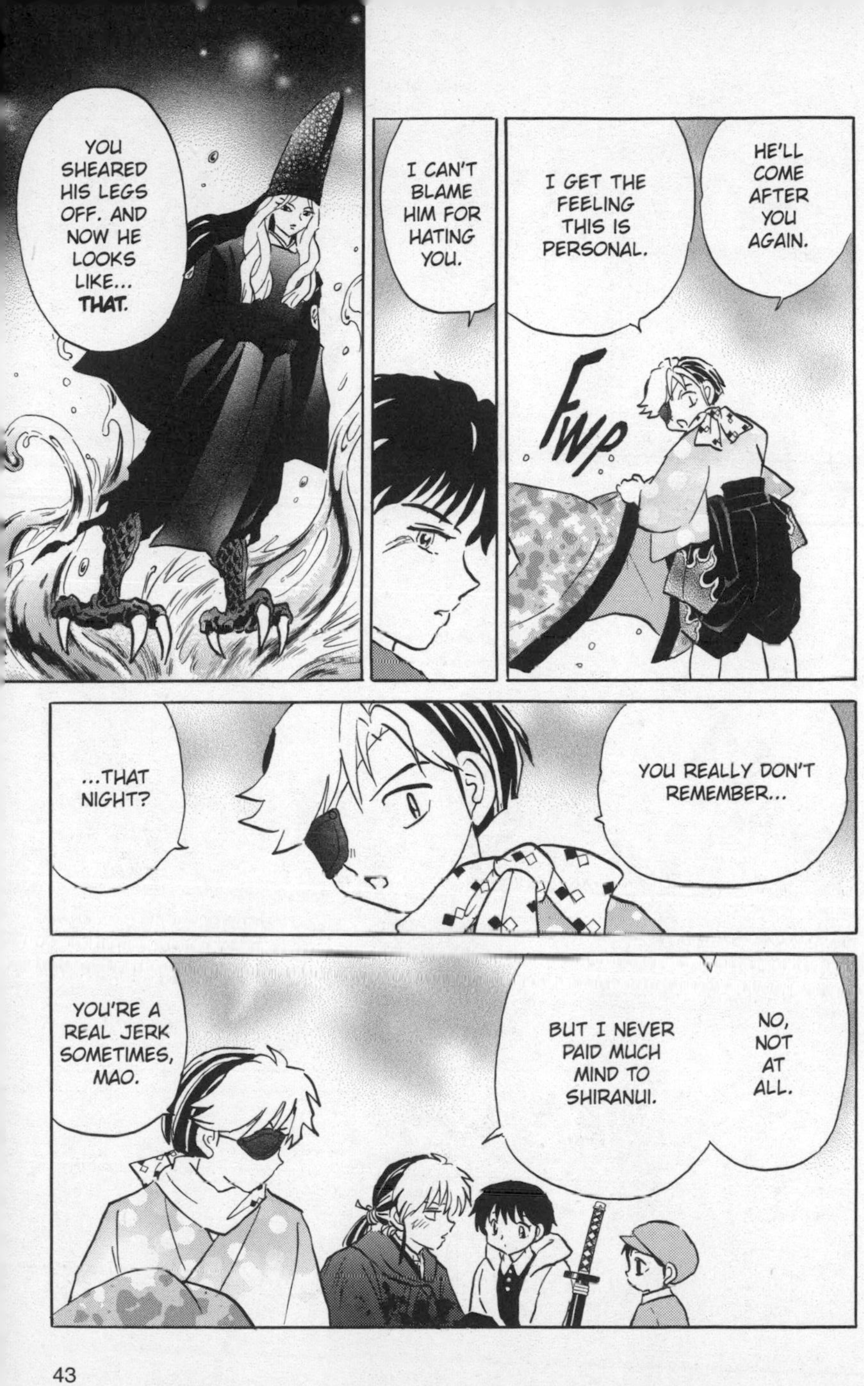
HE'LL COME AFTER YOU AGAIN.
I GET THE FEELING THIS IS PERSONAL.
FWP
I CAN'T BLAME HIM FOR HATING YOU.
YOU SHEARED HIS LEGS OFF. AND NOW HE LOOKS LIKE... **THAT.**
YOU REALLY DON'T REMEMBER...
...THAT NIGHT?
NO, NOT AT ALL.
BUT I NEVER PAID MUCH MIND TO SHIRANUI.
YOU'RE A REAL JERK SOMETIMES, MAO.

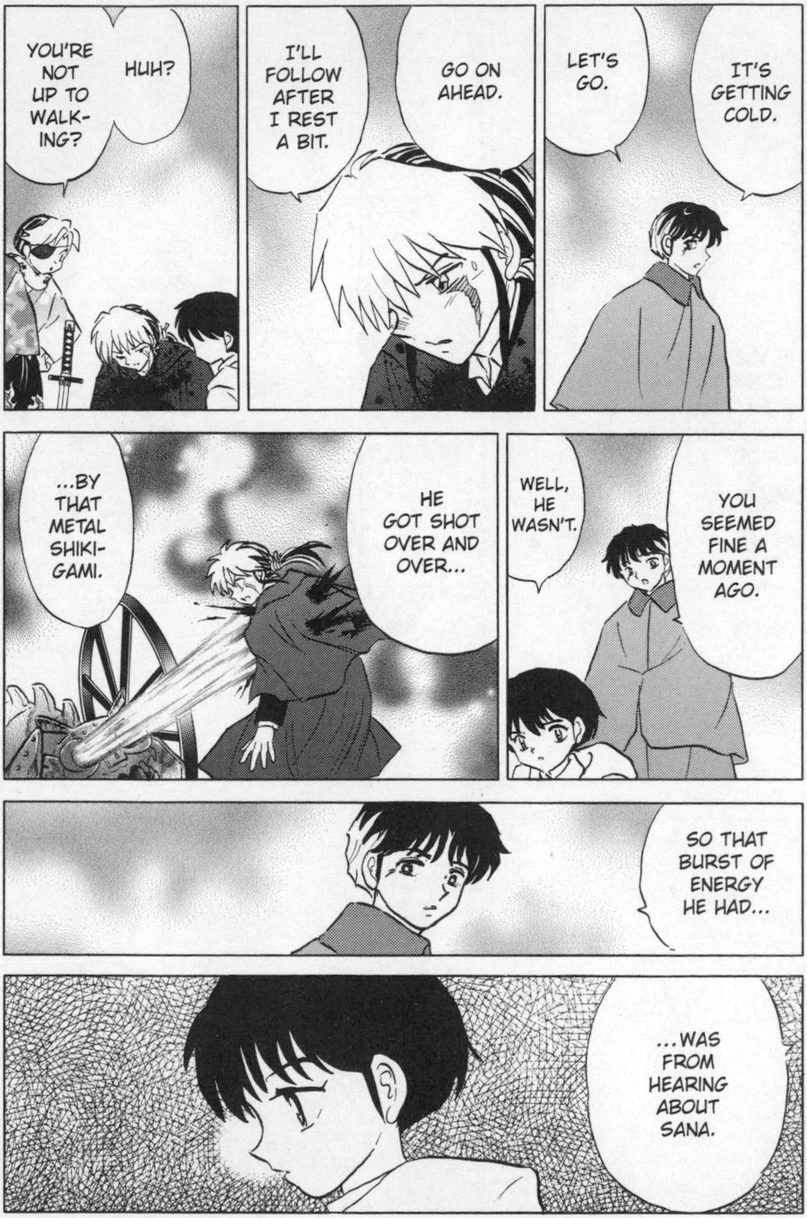
IT'S GETTING COLD.
LET'S GO.
GO ON AHEAD.
I'LL FOLLOW AFTER I REST A BIT.
HUH?
YOU'RE NOT UP TO WALK-ING?
YOU SEEMED FINE A MOMENT AGO.
WELL, HE WASN'T.
HE GOT SHOT OVER AND OVER...
...BY THAT METAL SHIKI-GAMI.
SO THAT BURST OF ENERGY HE HAD...
...WAS FROM HEARING ABOUT SANA.

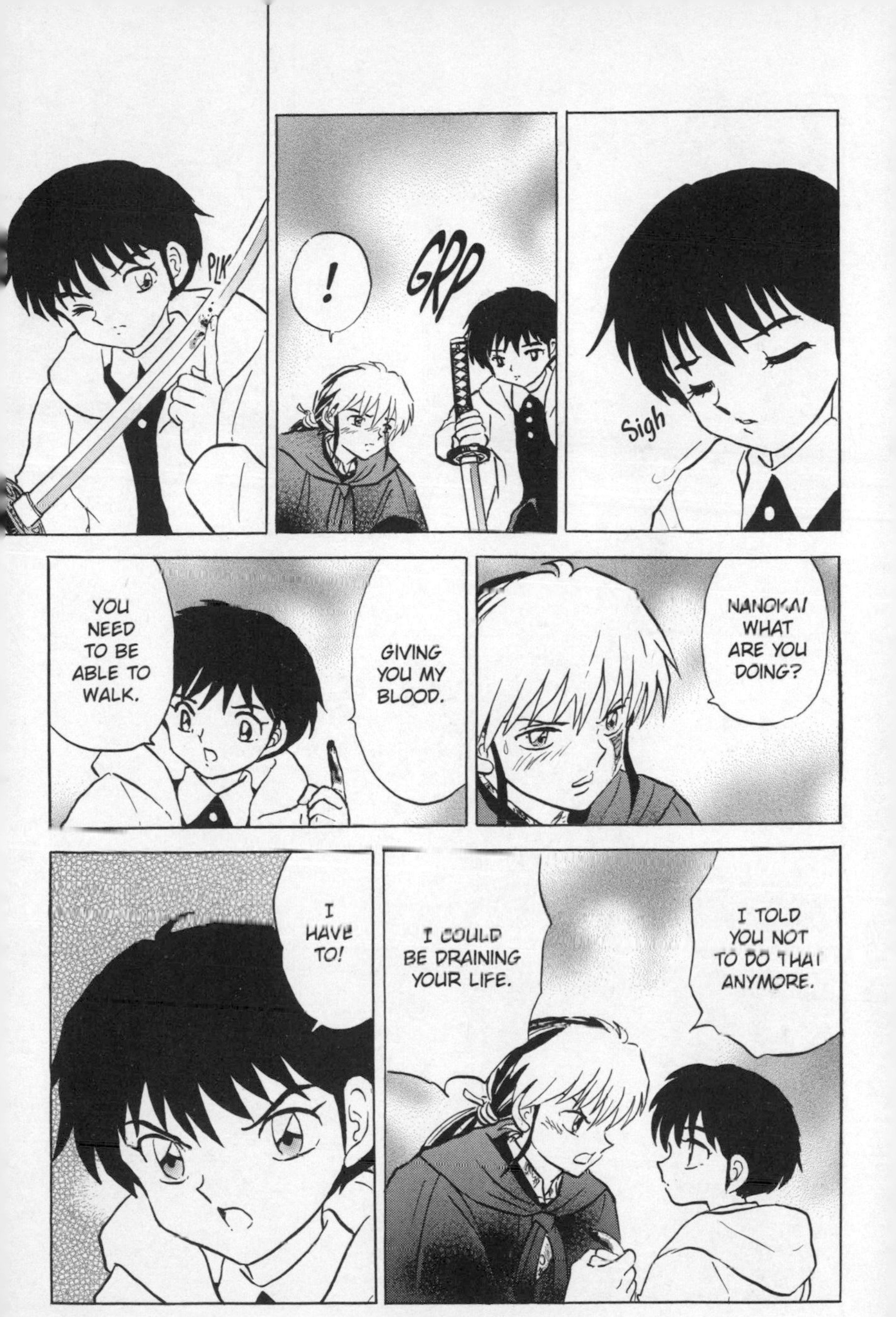
Sigh
!
GRP
PLK
NANOKA! WHAT ARE YOU DOING?
GIVING YOU MY BLOOD.
YOU NEED TO BE ABLE TO WALK.
I TOLD YOU NOT TO DO THAT ANYMORE.
I COULD BE DRAINING YOUR LIFE.
I HAVE TO!

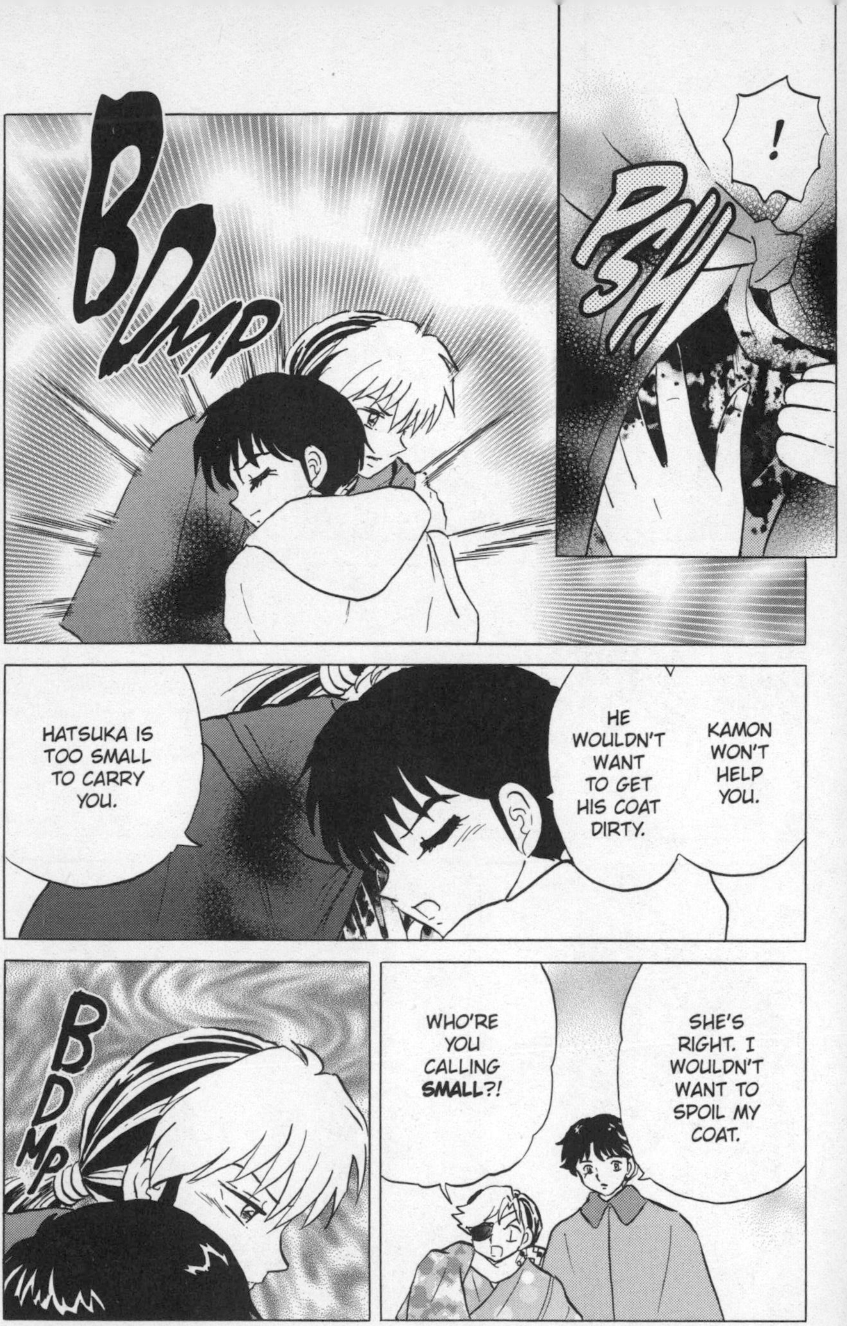
!
PASH
BDMP
KAMON WON'T HELP YOU.
HE WOULDN'T WANT TO GET HIS COAT DIRTY.
HATSUKA IS TOO SMALL TO CARRY YOU.
SHE'S RIGHT. I WOULDN'T WANT TO SPOIL MY COAT.
WHO'RE YOU CALLING **SMALL**?!
BDMP

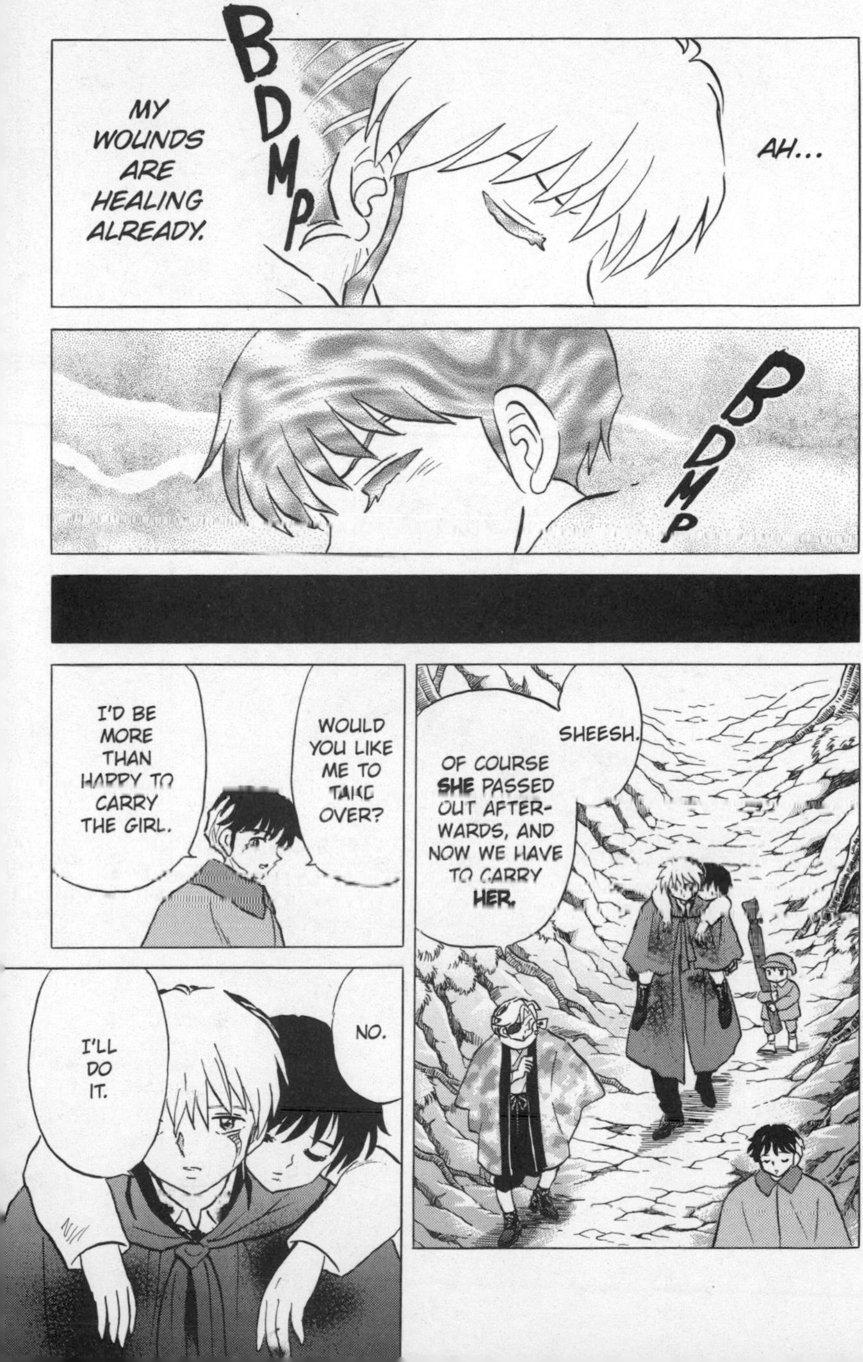
AH...
BDMP
MY WOUNDS ARE HEALING ALREADY.
BDMP
SHEESH.
OF COURSE SHE PASSED OUT AFTER-WARDS, AND NOW WE HAVE TO CARRY HER.
WOULD YOU LIKE ME TO TAKE OVER?
I'D BE MORE THAN HAPPY TO CARRY THE GIRL.
NO.
I'LL DO IT.

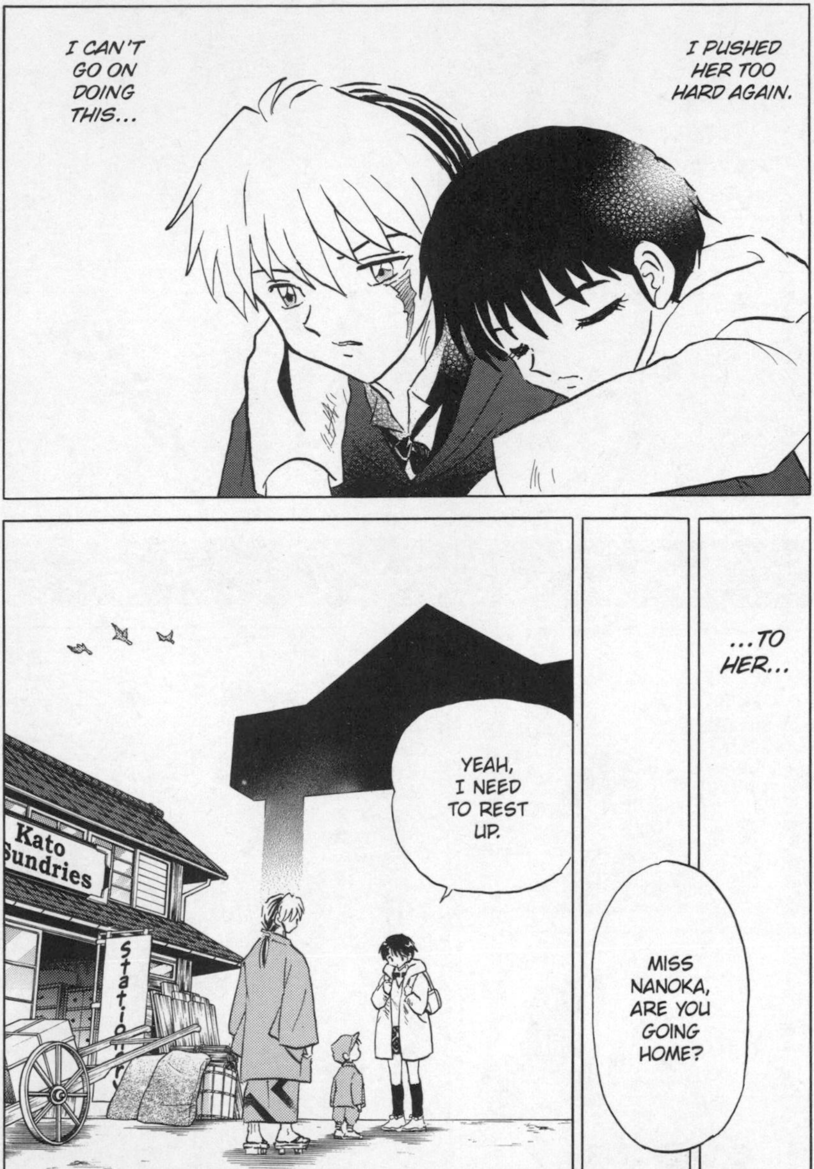
I PUSHED HER TOO HARD AGAIN.
I CAN'T GO ON DOING THIS...
...TO HER...
MISS NANOKA, ARE YOU GOING HOME?
YEAH, I NEED TO REST UP.
Kato Sundries

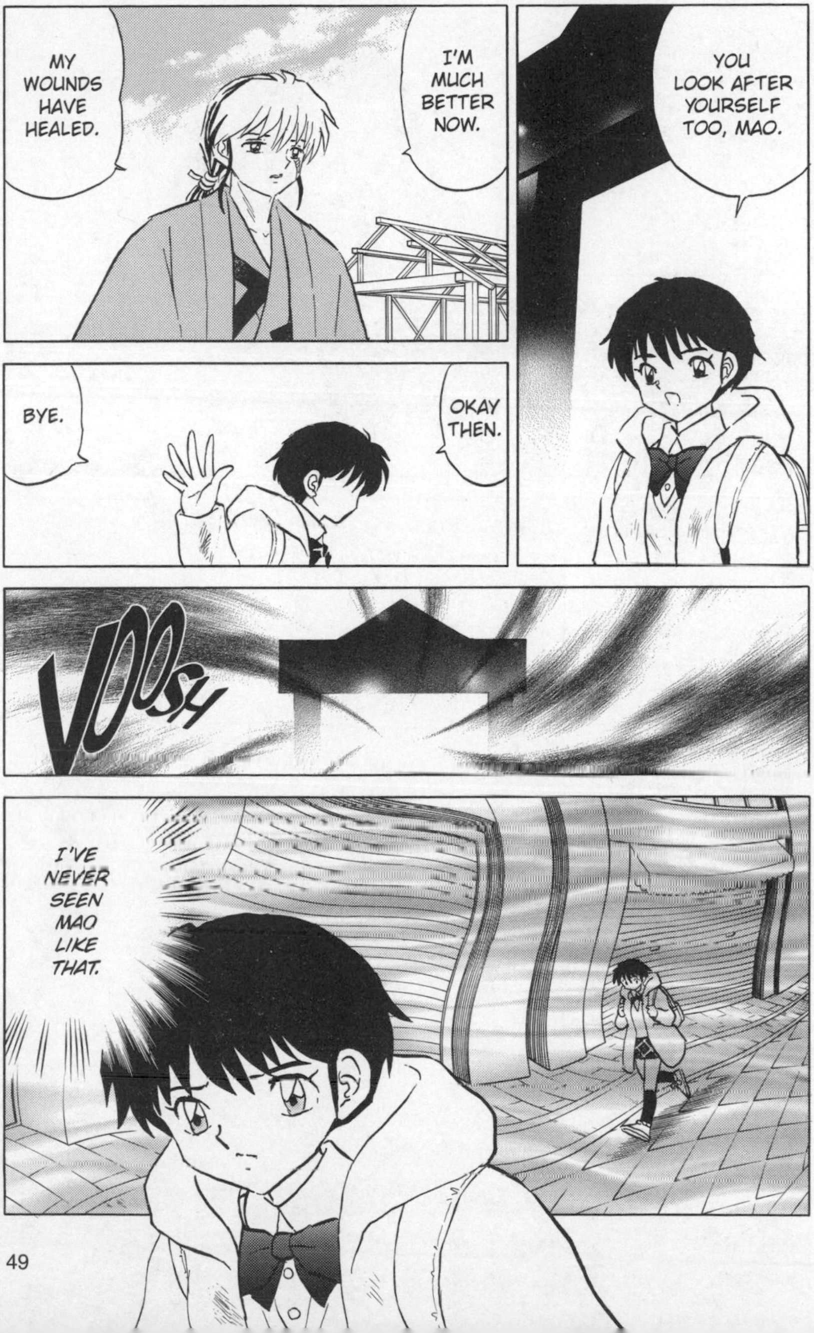
YOU LOOK AFTER YOURSELF TOO, MAO.
I'M MUCH BETTER NOW.
MY WOUNDS HAVE HEALED.
OKAY THEN.
BYE.
VOOSH
I'VE NEVER SEEN MAO LIKE THAT.

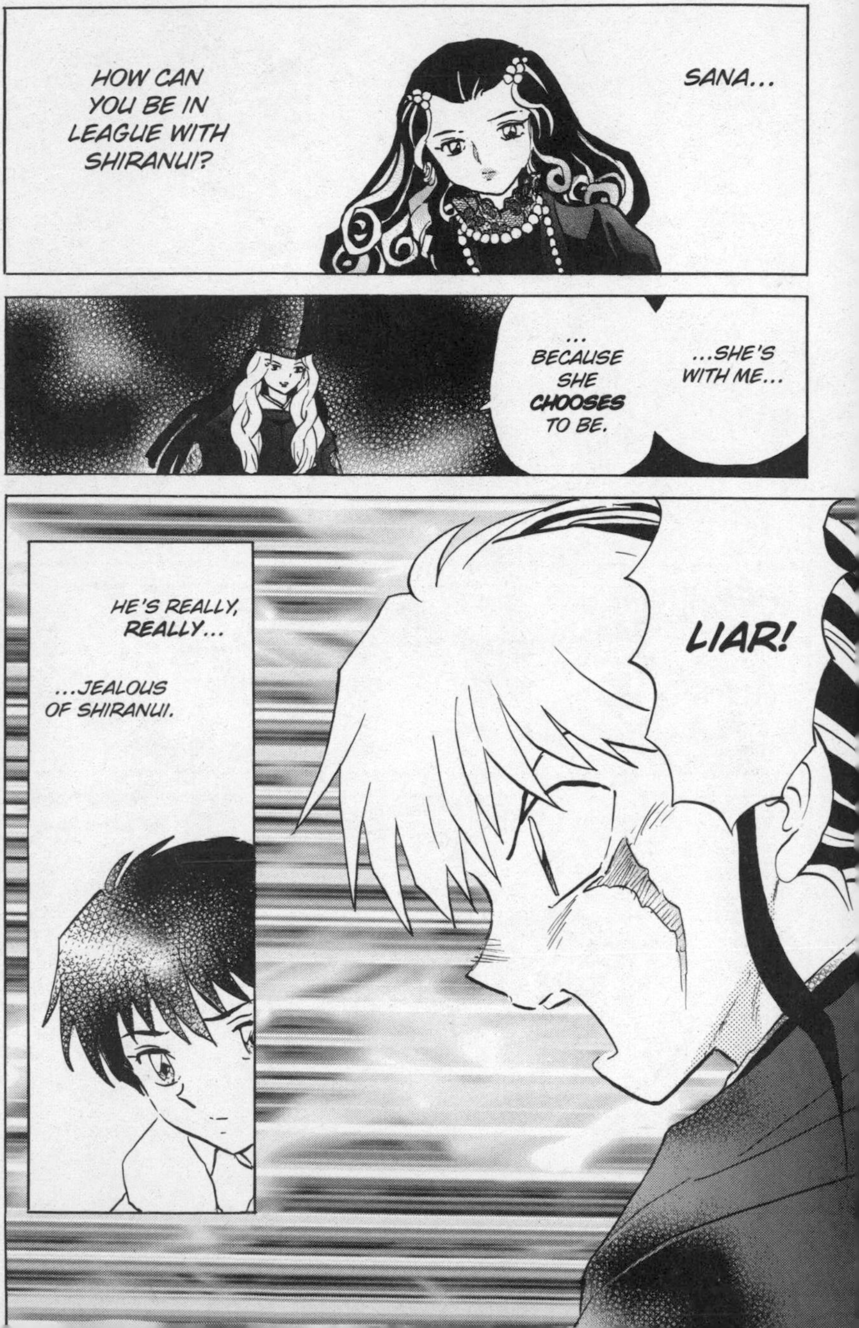
SANA...
HOW CAN YOU BE IN LEAGUE WITH SHIRANUI?
...SHE'S WITH ME...
...BECAUSE SHE CHOOSES TO BE.
LIAR!
HE'S REALLY, REALLY...
...JEALOUS OF SHIRANUI.

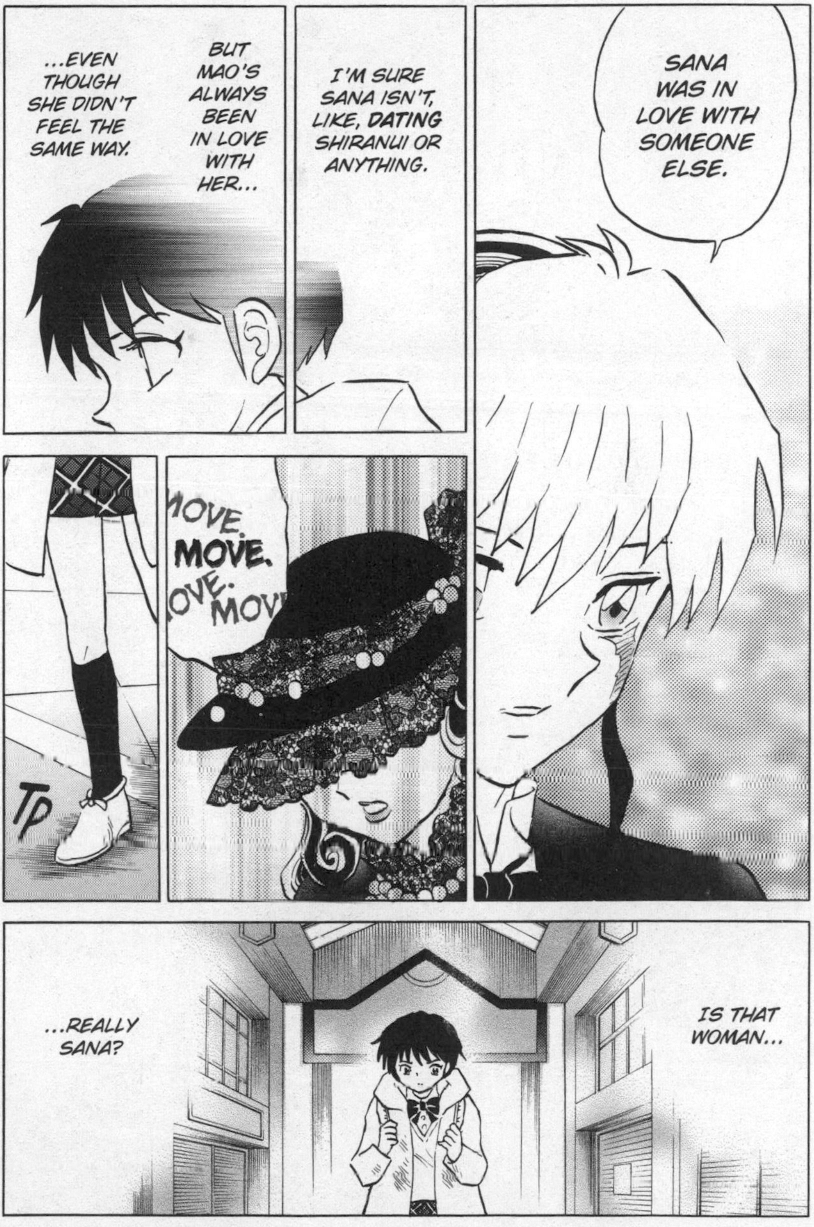
SANA WAS IN LOVE WITH SOMEONE ELSE.
I'M SURE SANA ISN'T, LIKE, DATING SHIRANUI OR ANYTHING.
BUT MAO'S ALWAYS BEEN IN LOVE WITH HER...
...EVEN THOUGH SHE DIDN'T FEEL THE SAME WAY.
OVE.
MOVE.
OVE.
MOV
TP
IS THAT WOMAN...
...REALLY SANA?

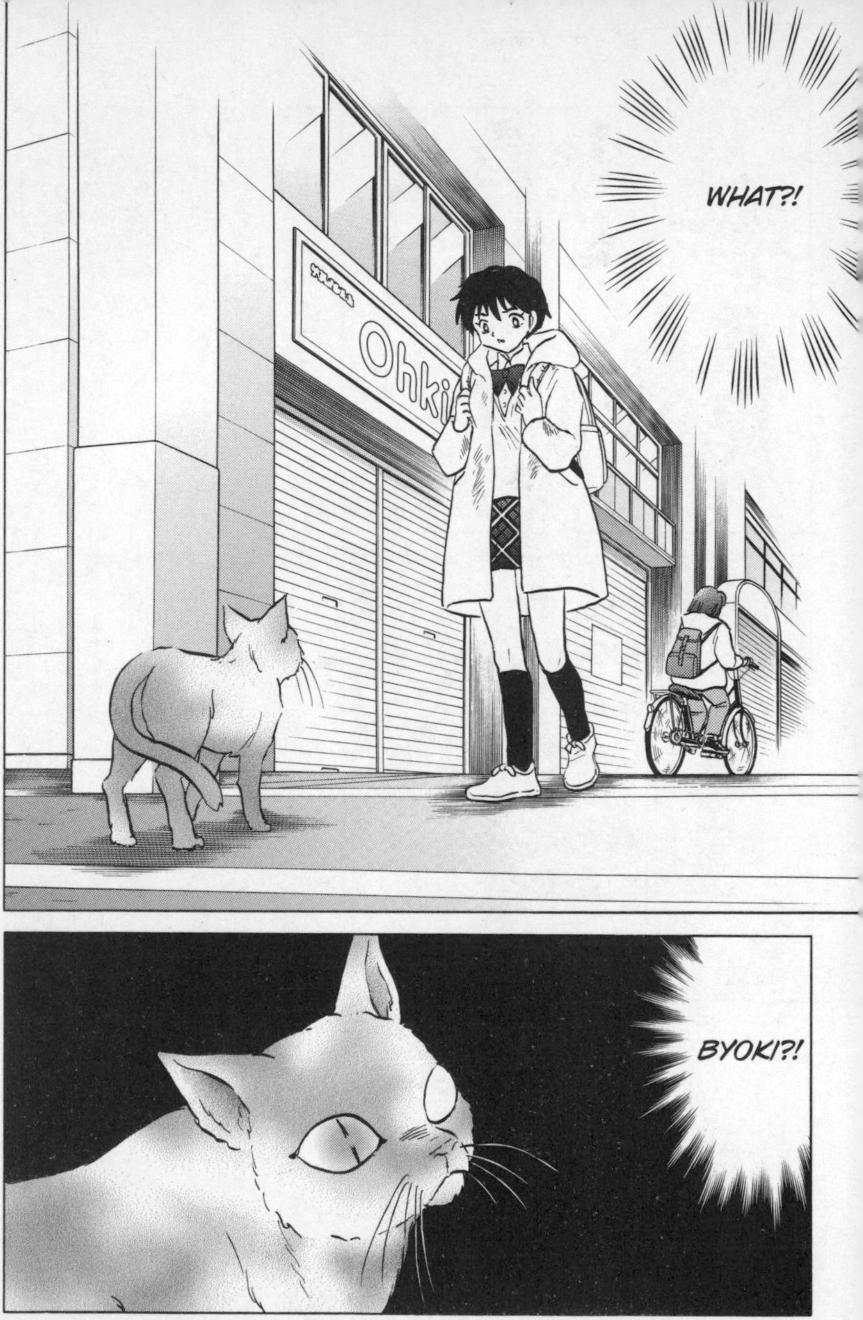
WHAT?!
Ohki
BYOKI?!

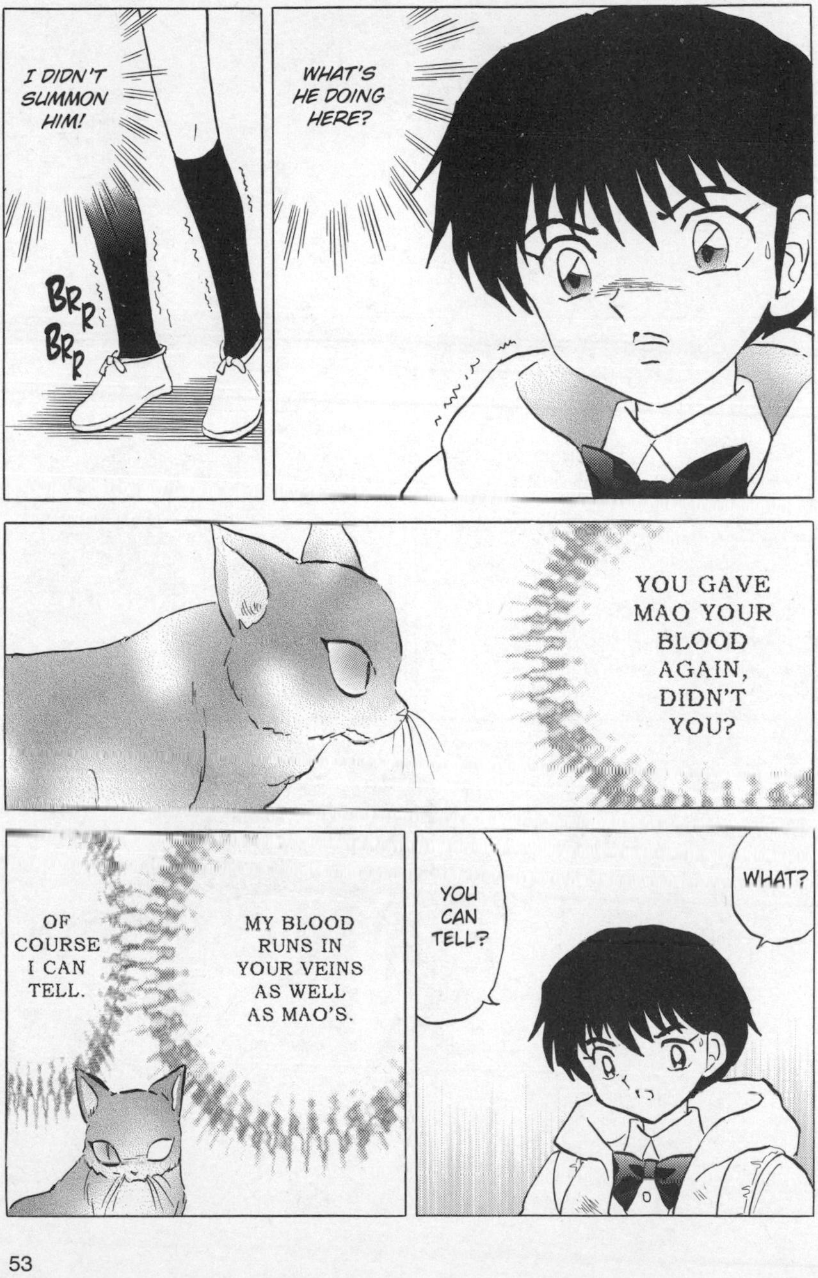
WHAT'S HE DOING HERE?
I DIDN'T SUMMON HIM!
BRR BRR
YOU GAVE MAO YOUR BLOOD AGAIN, DIDN'T YOU?
WHAT?
YOU CAN TELL?
OF COURSE I CAN TELL.
MY BLOOD RUNS IN YOUR VEINS AS WELL AS MAO'S.

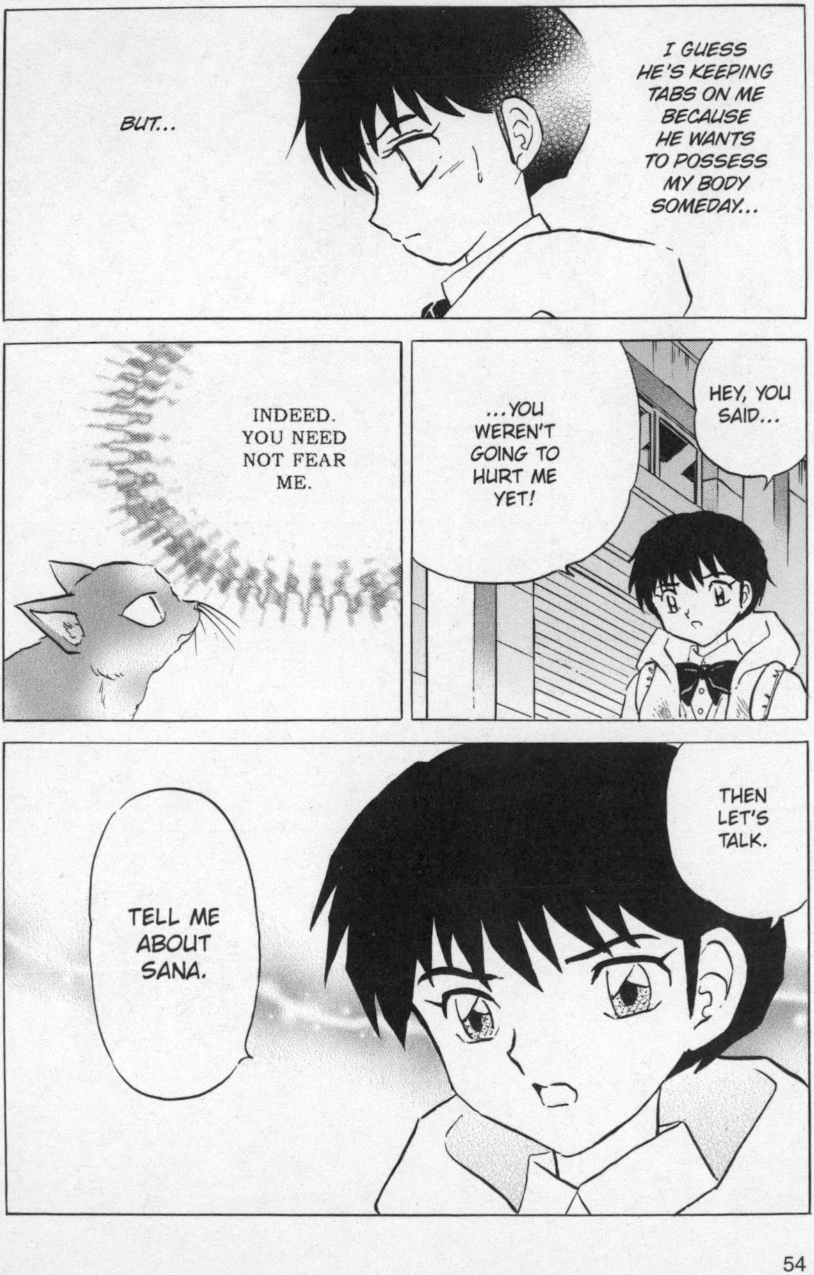
I GUESS HE'S KEEPING TABS ON ME BECAUSE HE WANTS TO POSSESS MY BODY SOMEDAY...
BUT...
HEY, YOU SAID...
...YOU WEREN'T GOING TO HURT ME YET!
INDEED. YOU NEED NOT FEAR ME.
THEN LET'S TALK.
TELL ME ABOUT SANA.

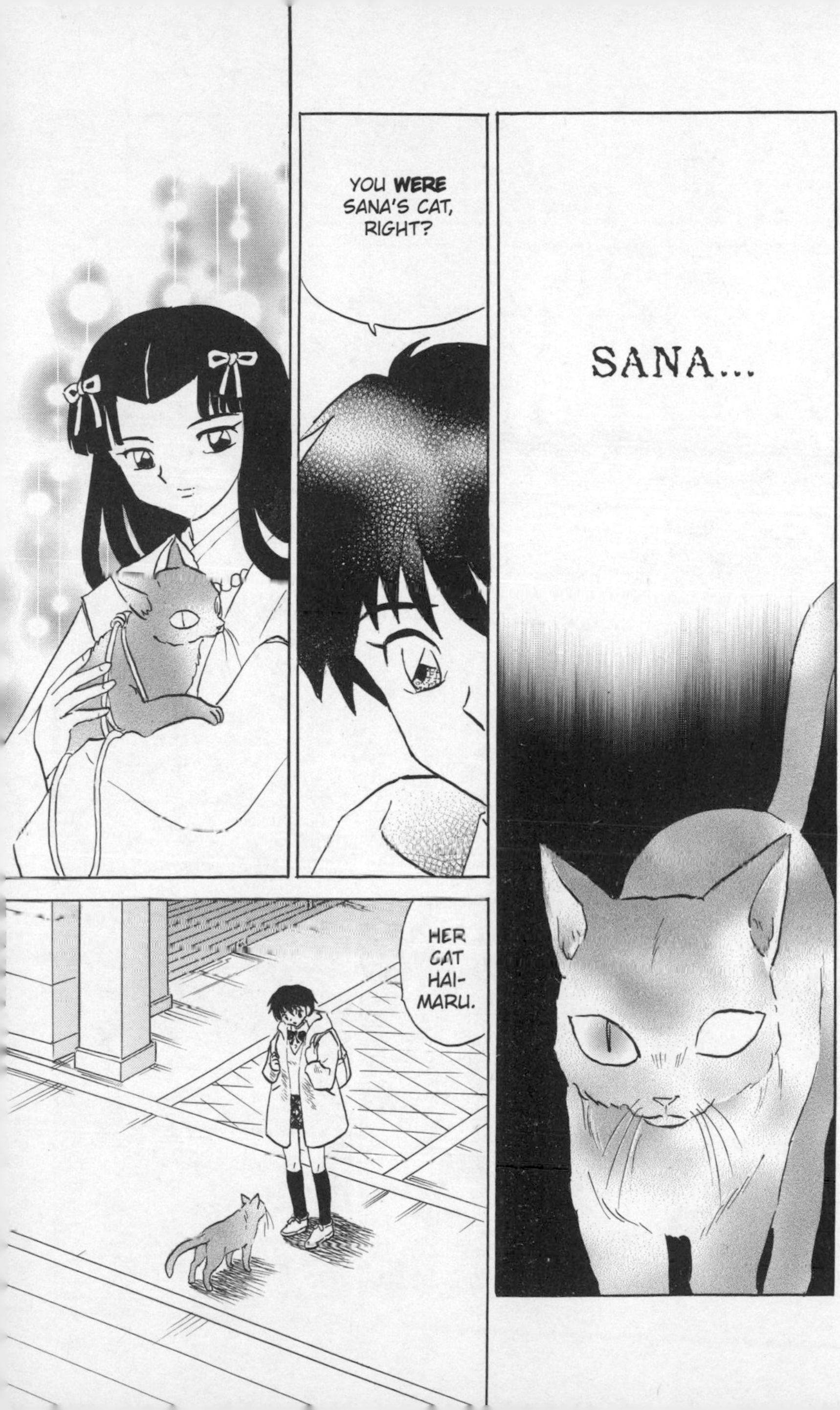
SANA...
YOU WERE SANA'S CAT, RIGHT?
HER CAT HAI-MARU.

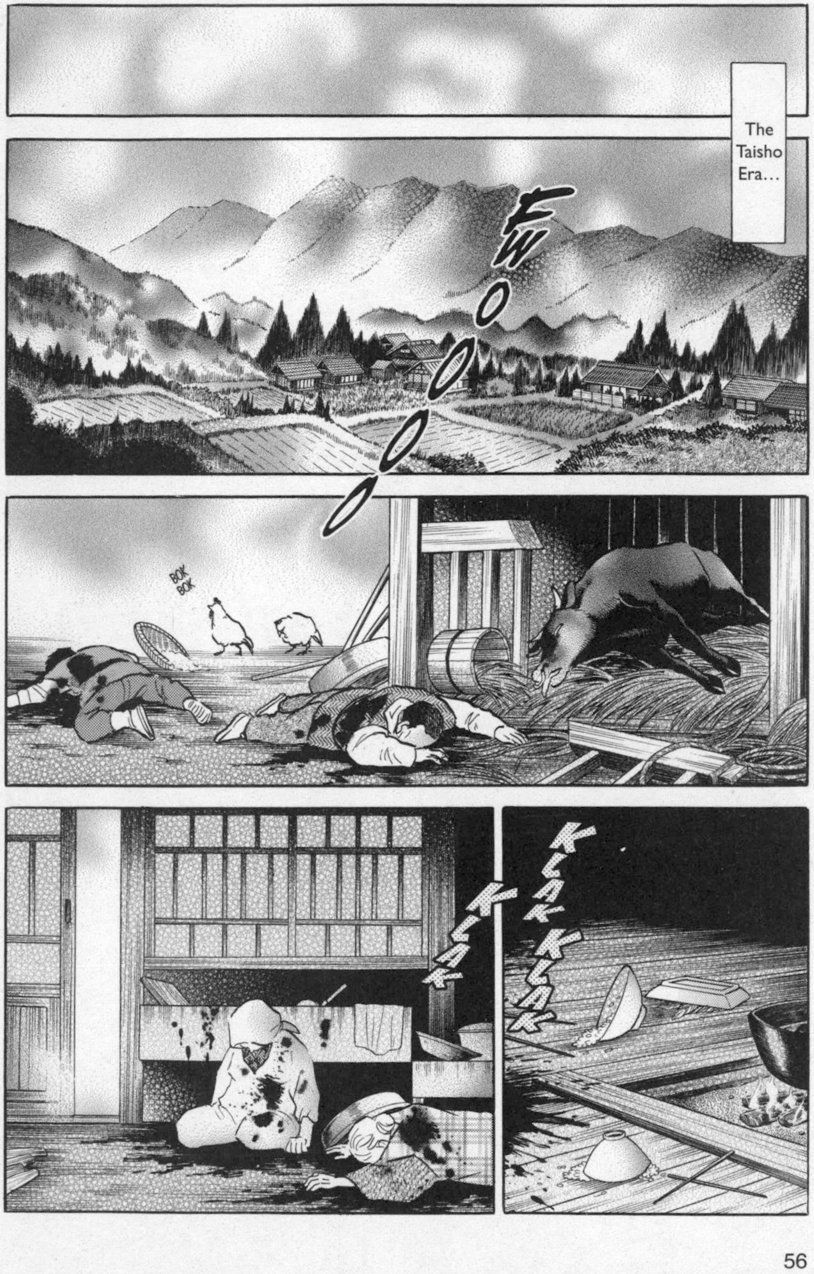
The Taisho Era…
FWOOOOOOO
BOK BOK
KLAK KLAK KLAK
KLAK KLAK

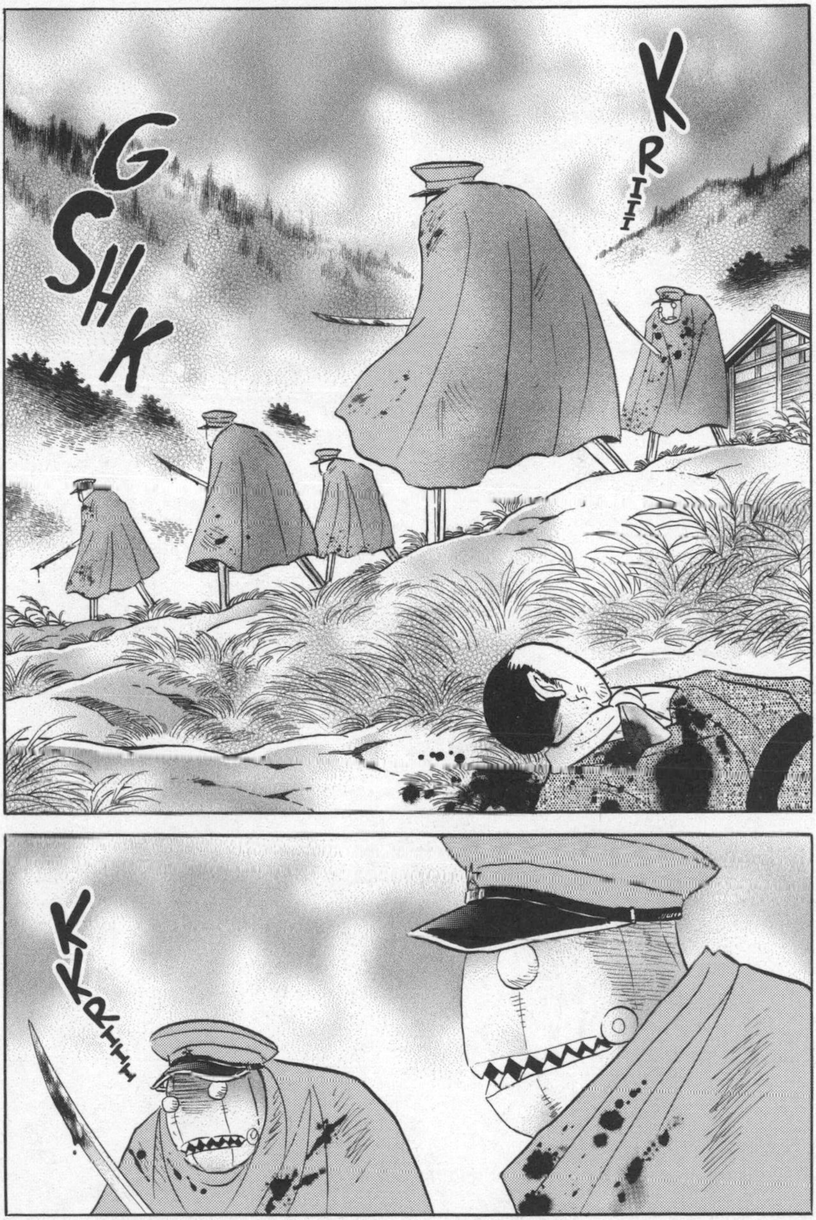
KRIII
GSHK
KKRIII

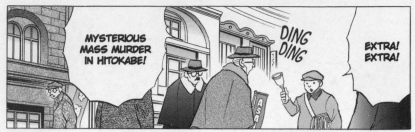

EXTRA! EXTRA!
DING DING
MYSTERIOUS MASS MURDER IN HITOKABE!
...
A DELIVERY MAN VISITING THE VILLAGE REPORTED A GRUESOME SCENE.
EVERY VILLAGER HAD BEEN SLAIN WITH A SINGLE BLOW FROM A SHARP WEAPON.
I SAW A SORT OF... METAL SCARECROW... LEAVING THE VILLAGE.
...THE WITNESS REPORTED.
METAL SCARECROW?
THAT SOUNDS FAMILIAR...

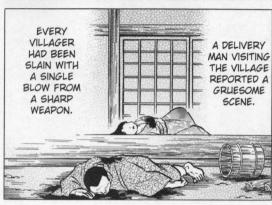

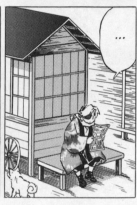

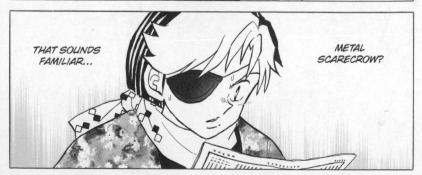

Chapter 4:
House of Curses

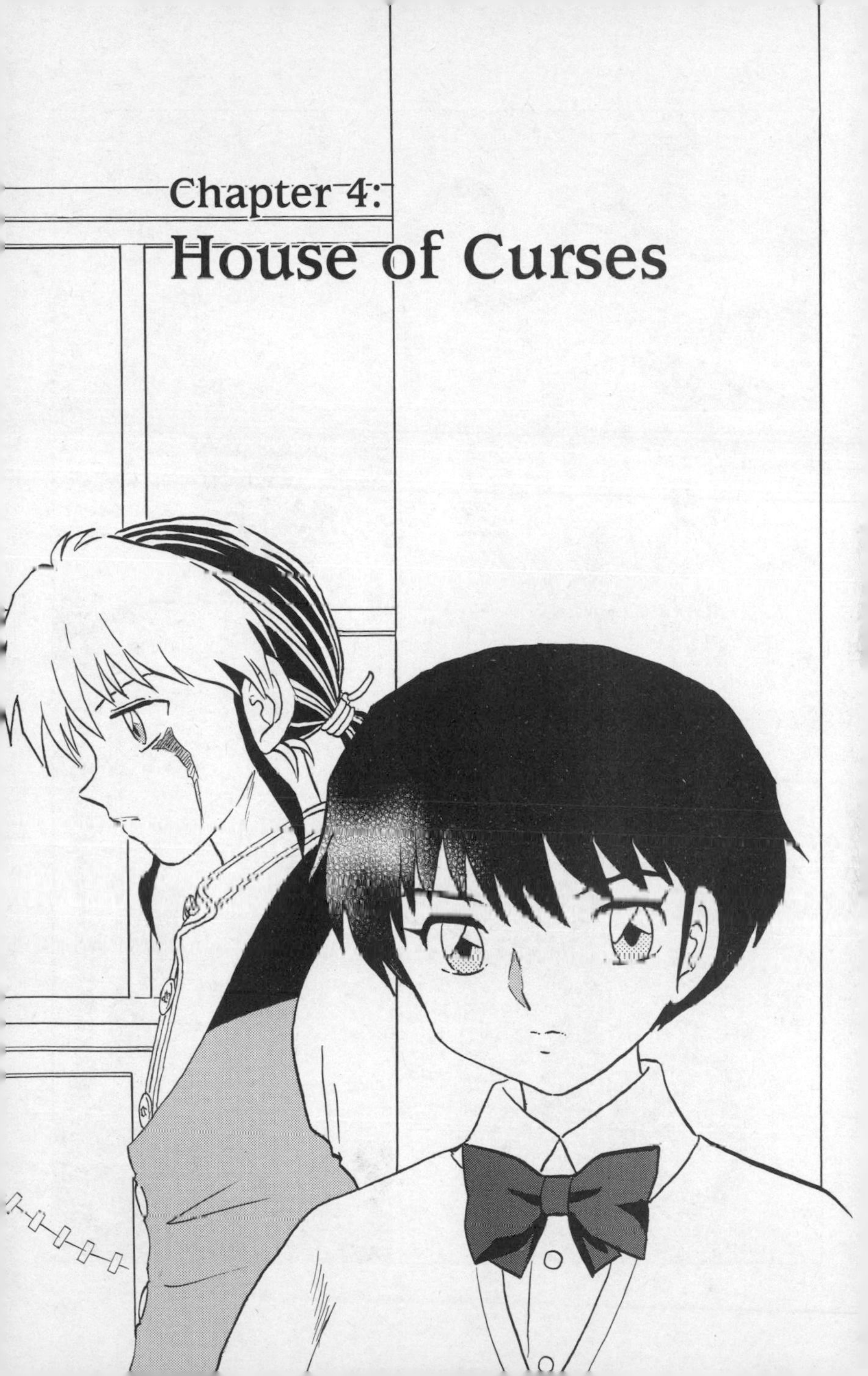

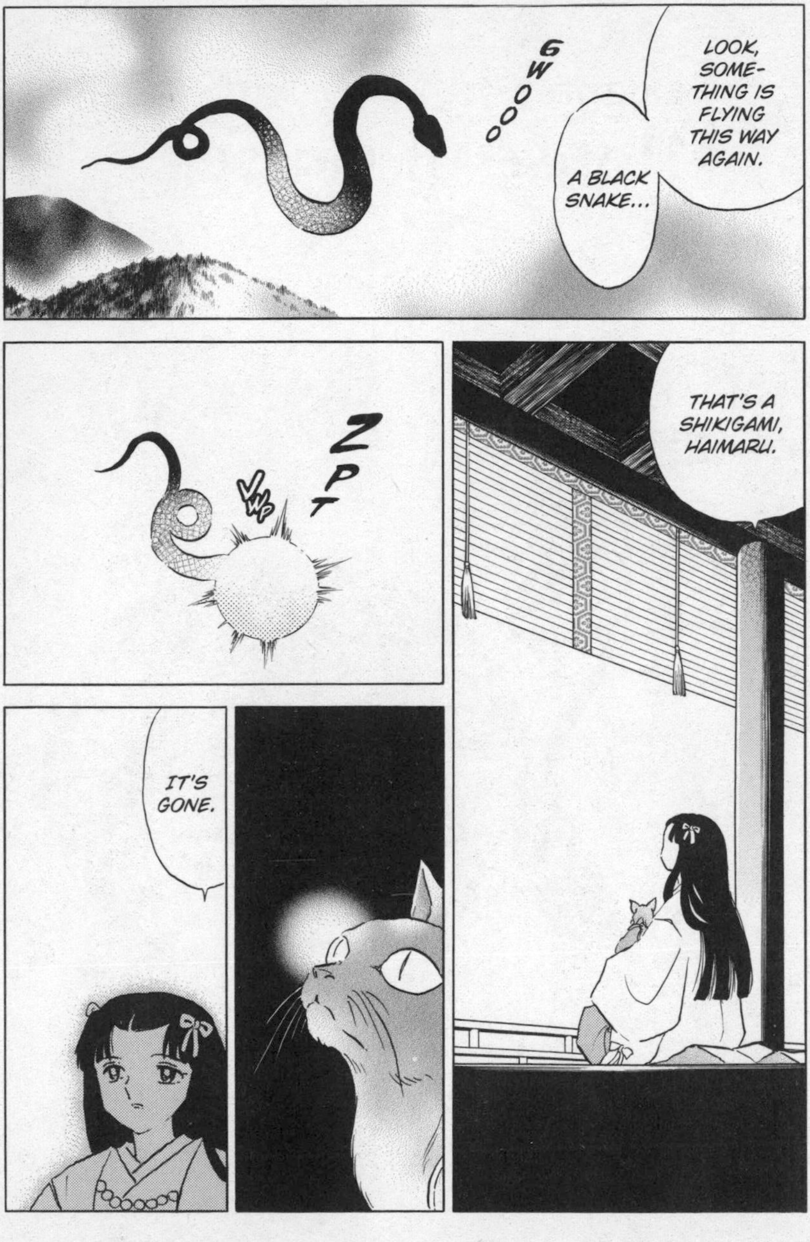
LOOK, SOME-THING IS FLYING THIS WAY AGAIN.
A BLACK SNAKE...
GWOOOO
THAT'S A SHIKIGAMI, HAIMARU.
ZPT
VWP
IT'S GONE.

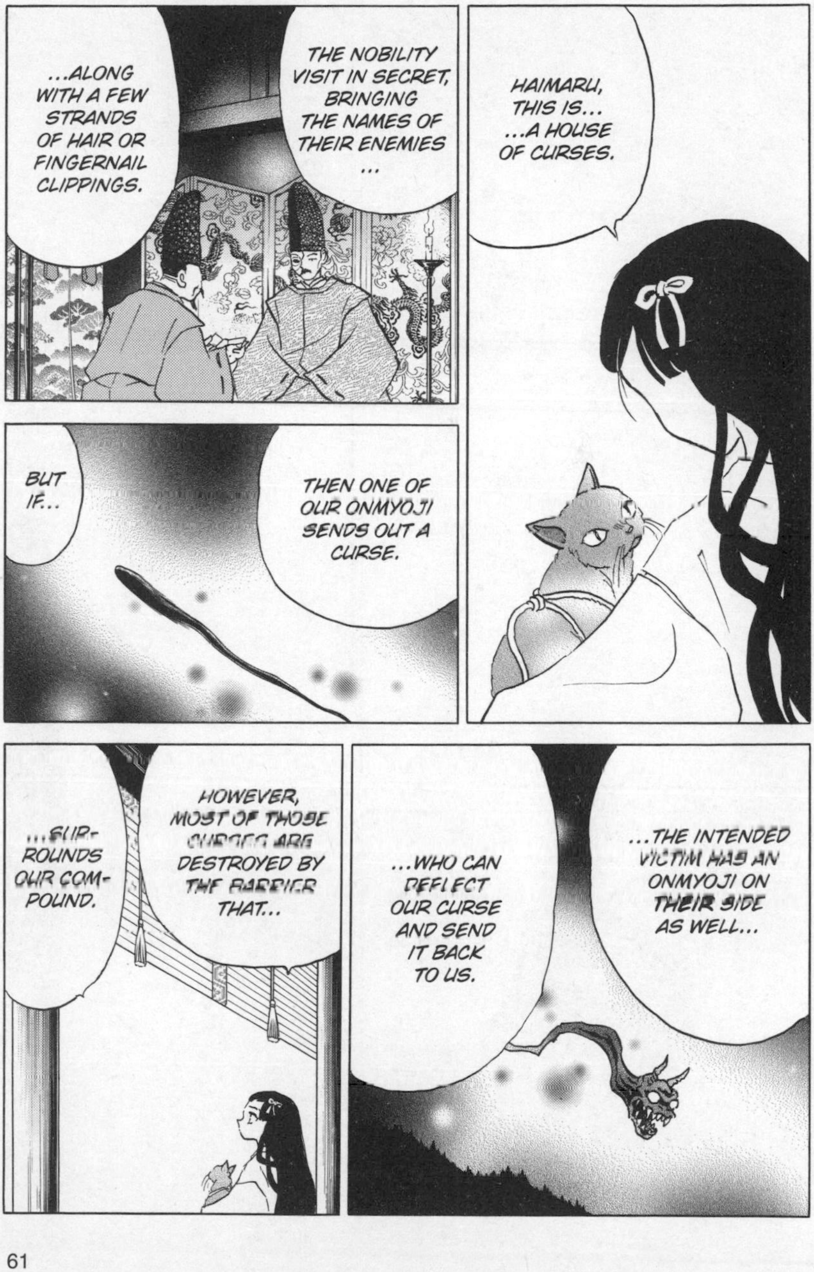
HAIMARU, THIS IS... ...A HOUSE OF CURSES.
THE NOBILITY VISIT IN SECRET, BRINGING THE NAMES OF THEIR ENEMIES ...
...ALONG WITH A FEW STRANDS OF HAIR OR FINGERNAIL CLIPPINGS.
THEN ONE OF OUR ONMYOJI SENDS OUT A CURSE.
BUT IF...
...THE INTENDED VICTIM HAS AN ONMYOJI ON THEIR SIDE AS WELL...
...WHO CAN DEFLECT OUR CURSE AND SEND IT BACK TO US.
HOWEVER, MOST OF THOSE CURSES ARE DESTROYED BY THE BARRIER THAT...
...SUR-ROUNDS OUR COM-POUND.

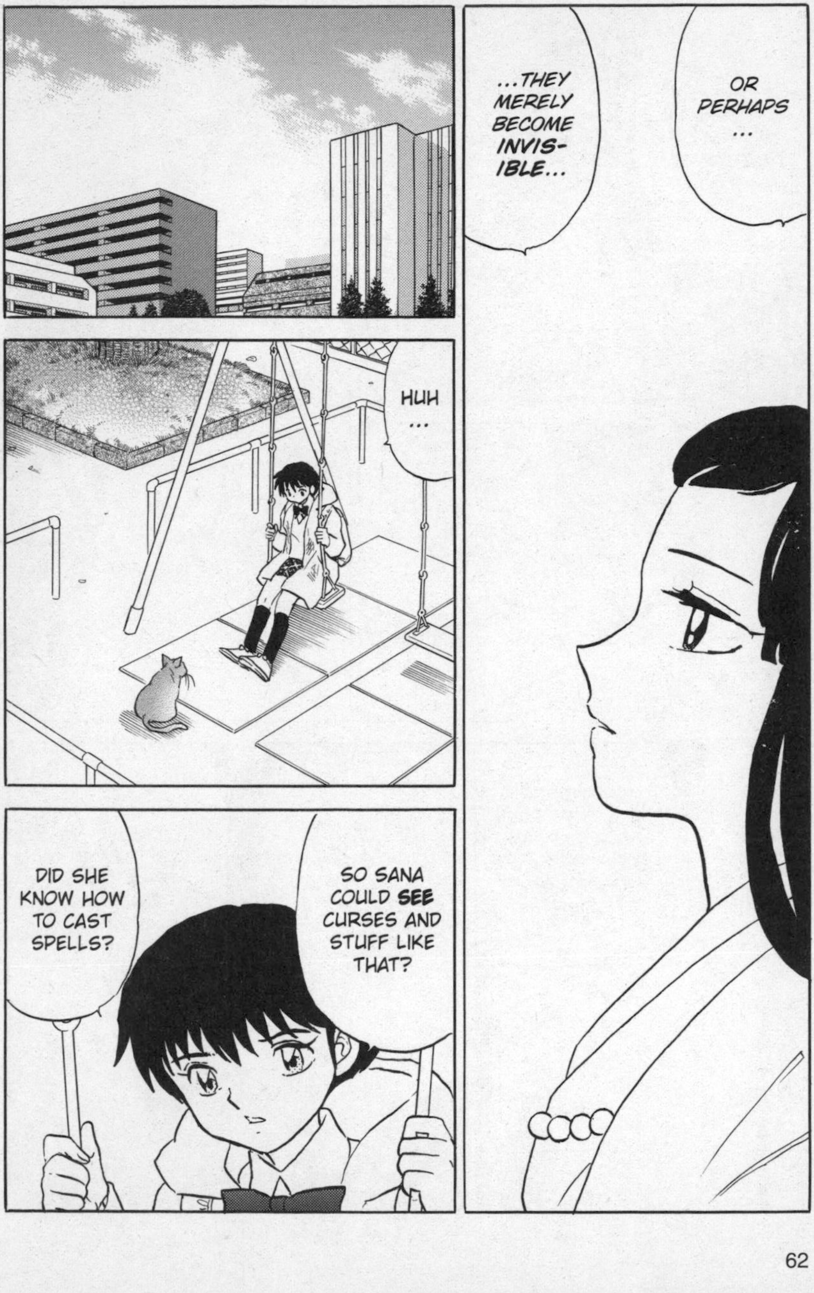
OR PERHAPS ...
...THEY MERELY BECOME INVISIBLE...
HUH ...
SO SANA COULD SEE CURSES AND STUFF LIKE THAT?
DID SHE KNOW HOW TO CAST SPELLS?

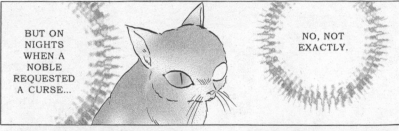

NO, NOT EXACTLY.
BUT ON NIGHTS WHEN A NOBLE REQUESTED A CURSE...
KREE
...SANA'S FATHER, THE MASTER, WOULD VISIT HER ROOM AS SHE SLEPT
SHP

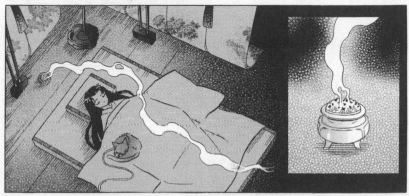

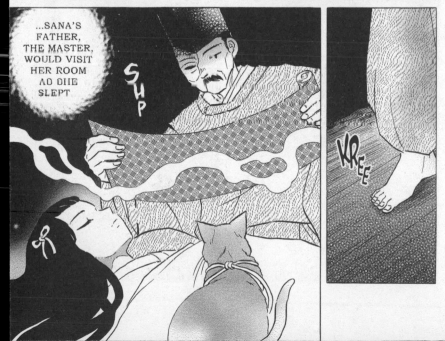

VWP

...ROLL THE BLACK VAPOR EMANATING FROM HER MOUTH INTO A SCROLL...

KOOOO

...AND GIVE IT TO AN ONMYOJI.

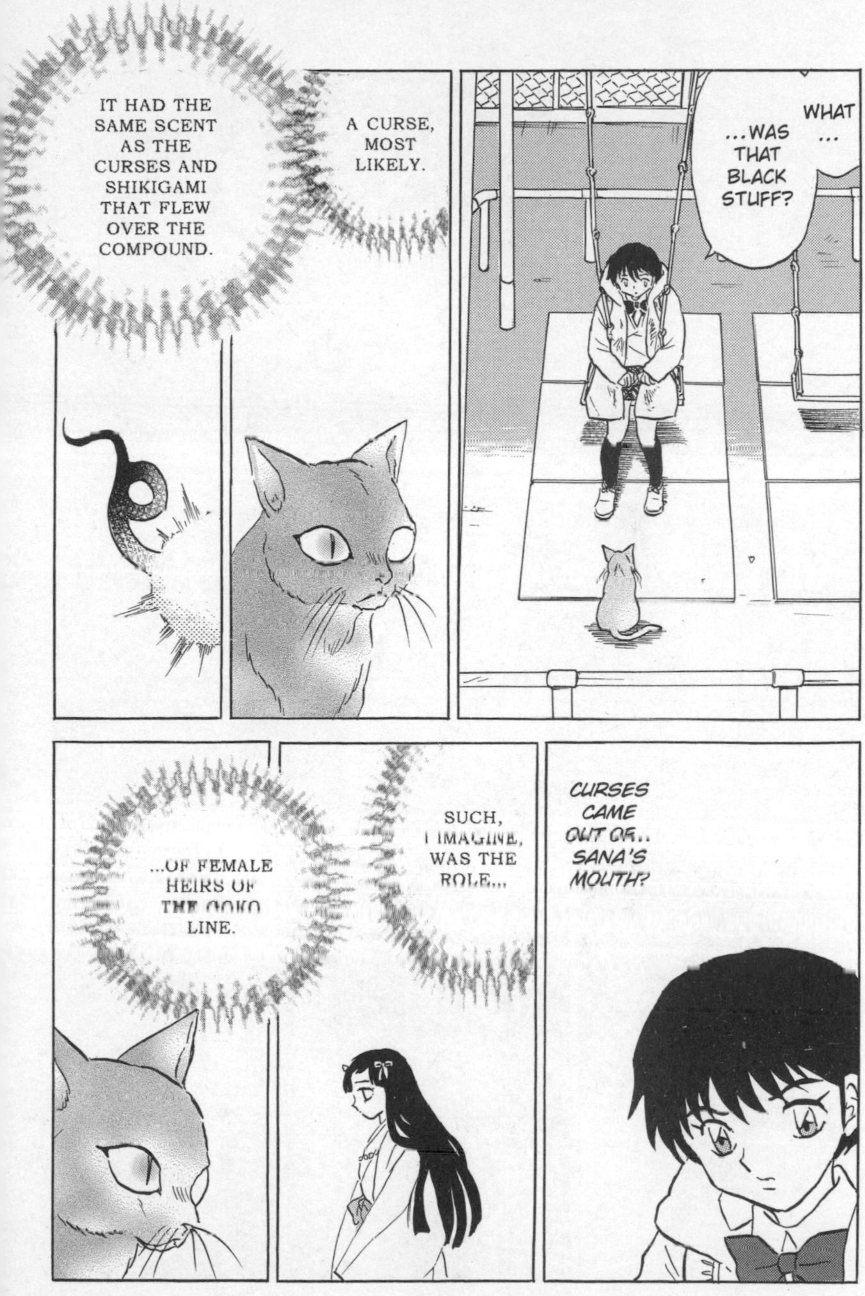
WHAT ...
...WAS THAT BLACK STUFF?
A CURSE, MOST LIKELY.
IT HAD THE SAME SCENT AS THE CURSES AND SHIKIGAMI THAT FLEW OVER THE COMPOUND.
CURSES CAME OUT OF... SANA'S MOUTH?
SUCH, I IMAGINE, WAS THE ROLE...
...OF FEMALE HEIRS OF THE OOKO LINE.

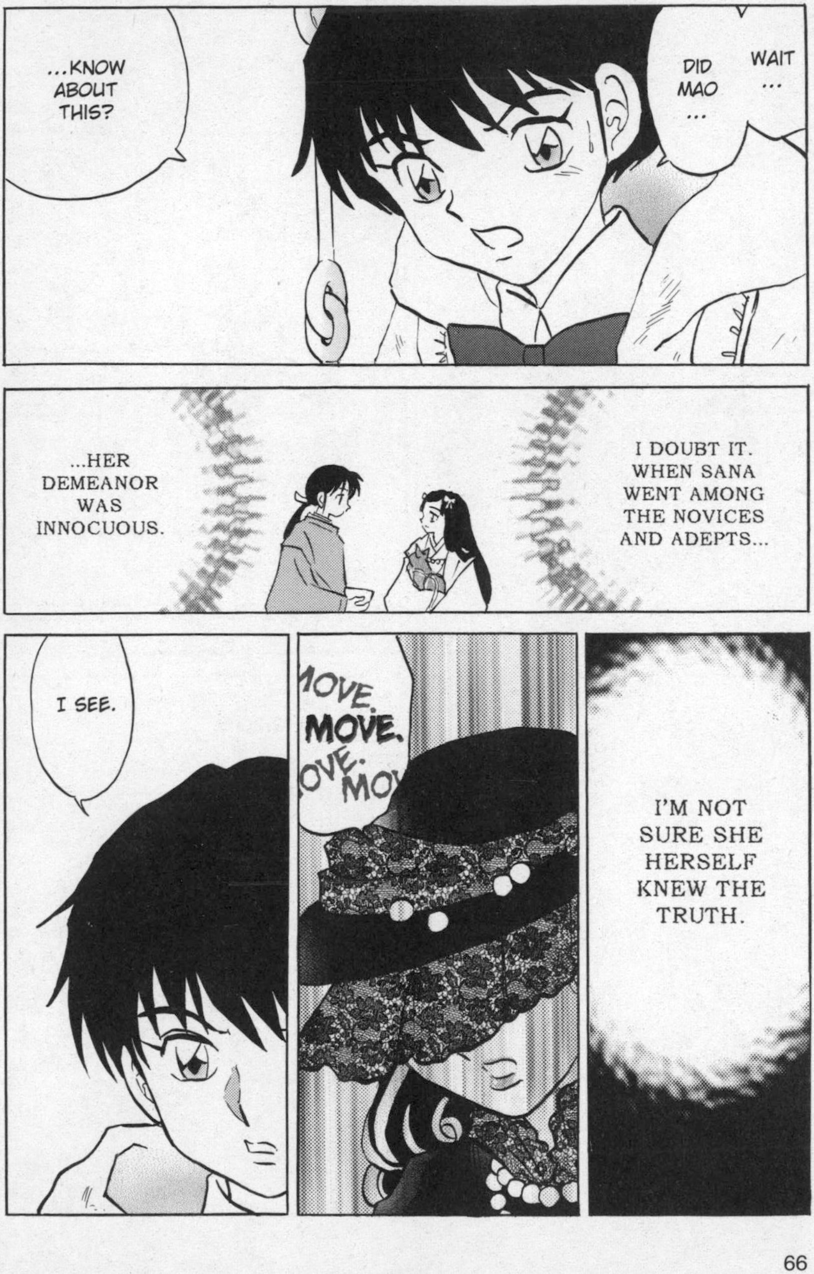
WAIT...
DID MAO...
...KNOW ABOUT THIS?
I DOUBT IT. WHEN SANA WENT AMONG THE NOVICES AND ADEPTS...
...HER DEMEANOR WAS INNOCUOUS.
I'M NOT SURE SHE HERSELF KNEW THE TRUTH.
MOVE.
I SEE.

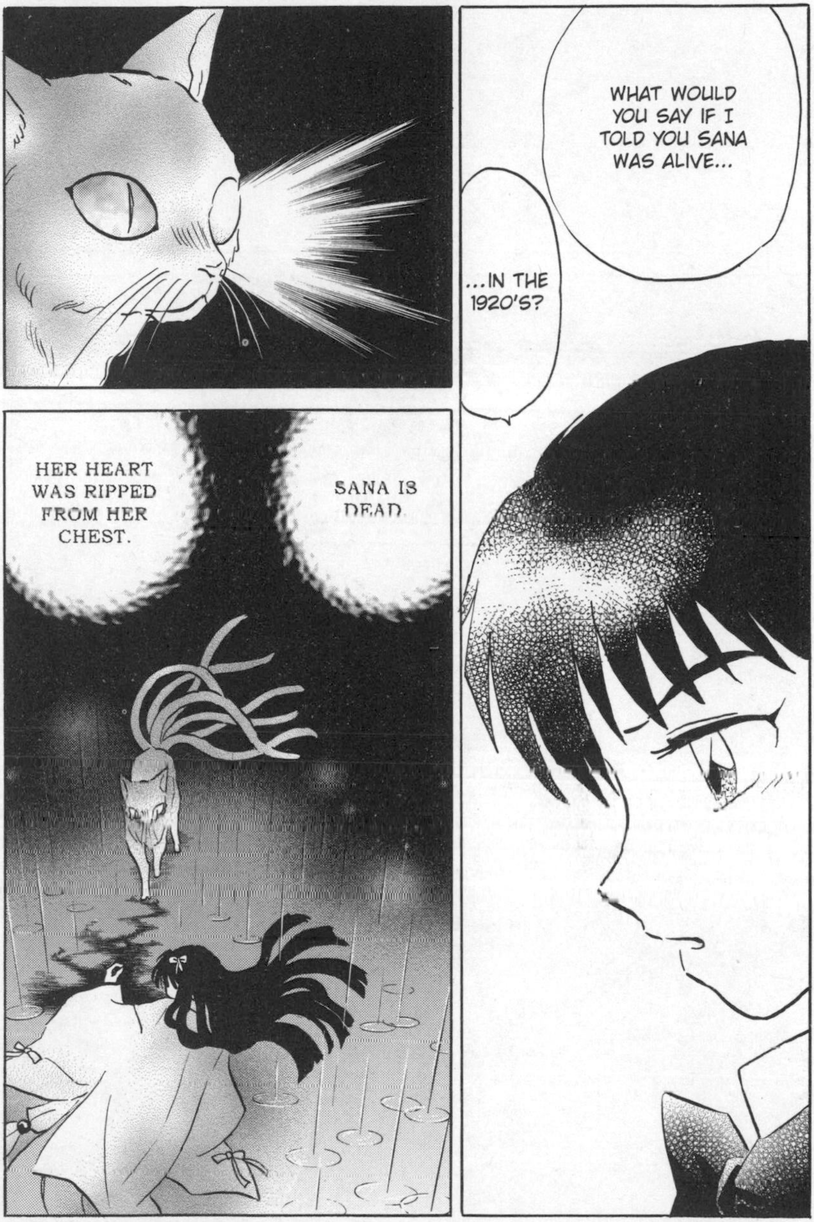
WHAT WOULD YOU SAY IF I TOLD YOU SANA WAS ALIVE...
...IN THE 1920'S?
SANA IS DEAD.
HER HEART WAS RIPPED FROM HER CHEST.

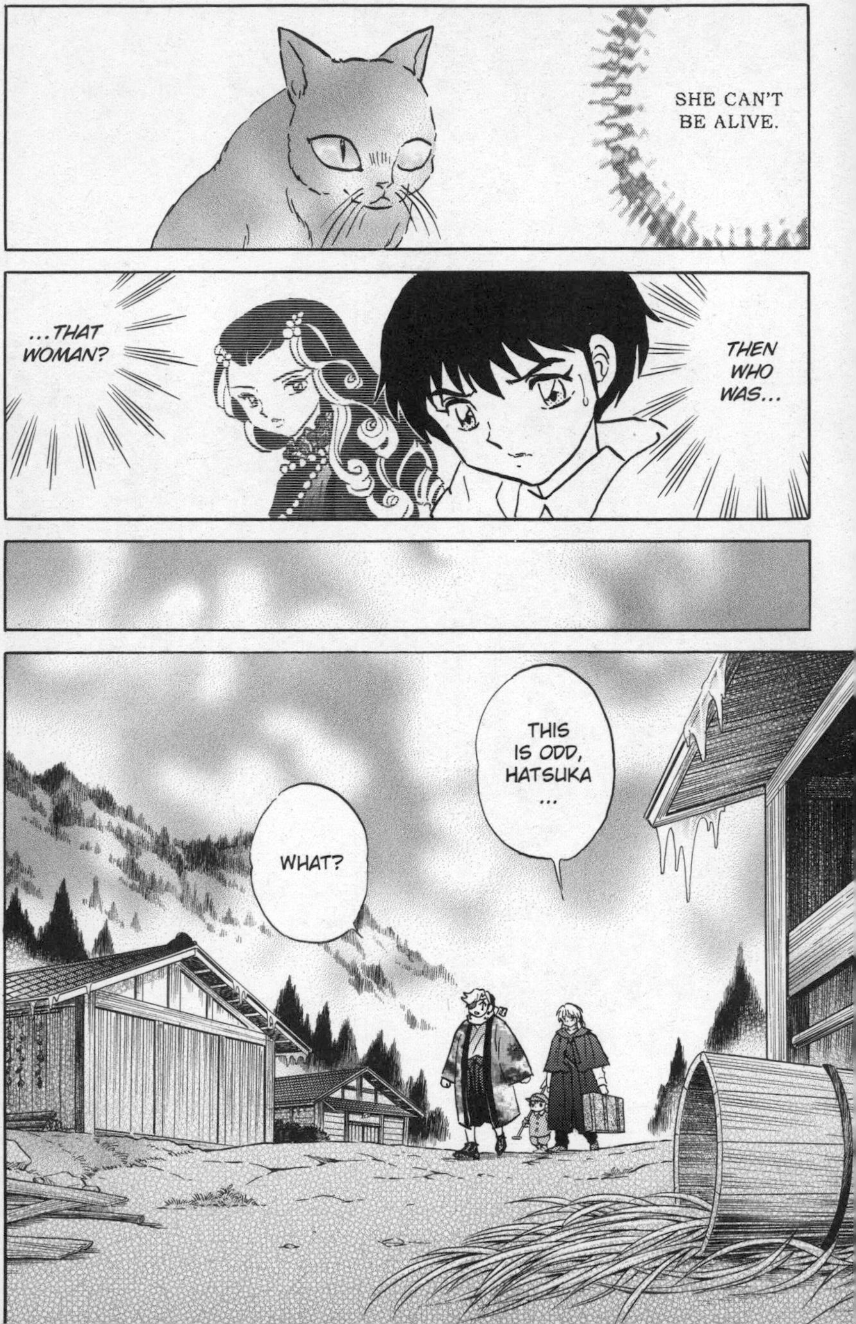
SHE CAN'T BE ALIVE.
THEN WHO WAS...
...THAT WOMAN?
THIS IS ODD, HATSUKA ...
WHAT?

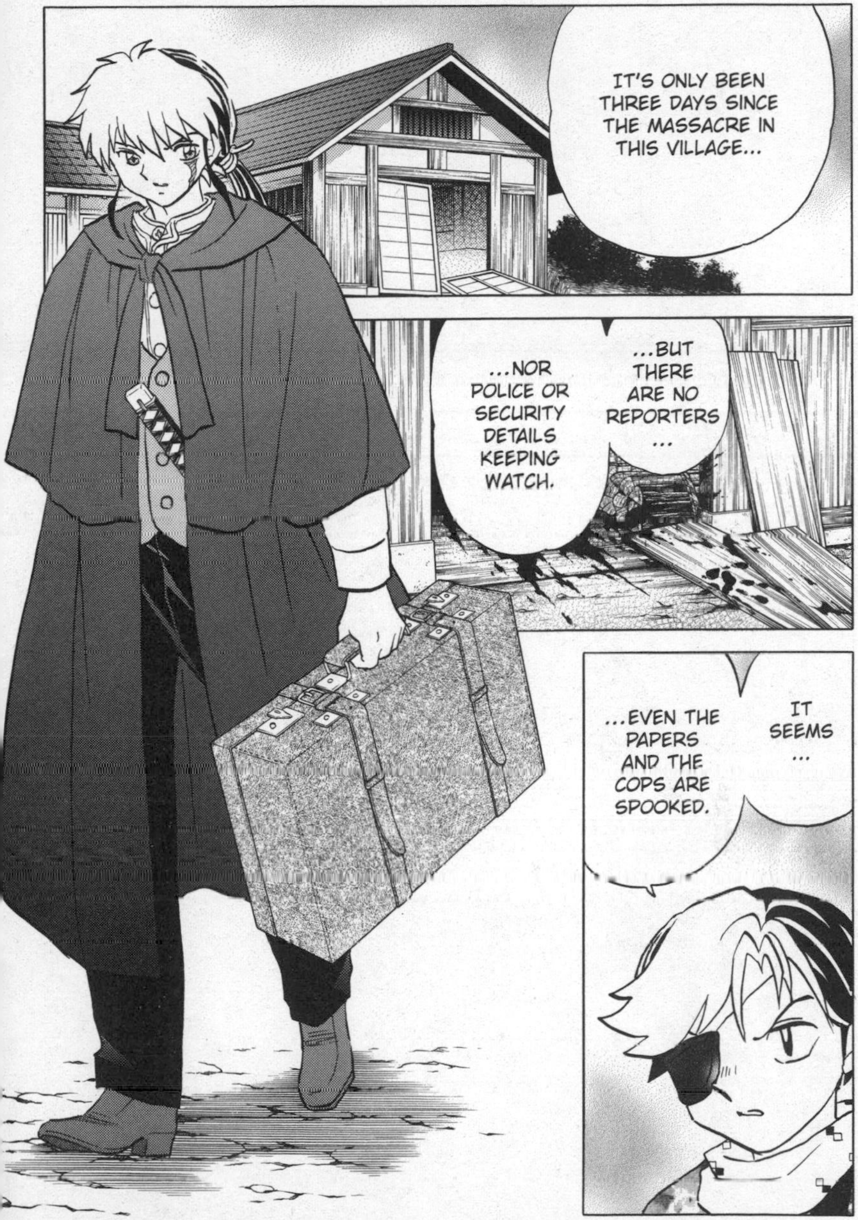
IT'S ONLY BEEN THREE DAYS SINCE THE MASSACRE IN THIS VILLAGE...
...BUT THERE ARE NO REPORTERS ...
...NOR POLICE OR SECURITY DETAILS KEEPING WATCH.
IT SEEMS ...
...EVEN THE PAPERS AND THE COPS ARE SPOOKED.

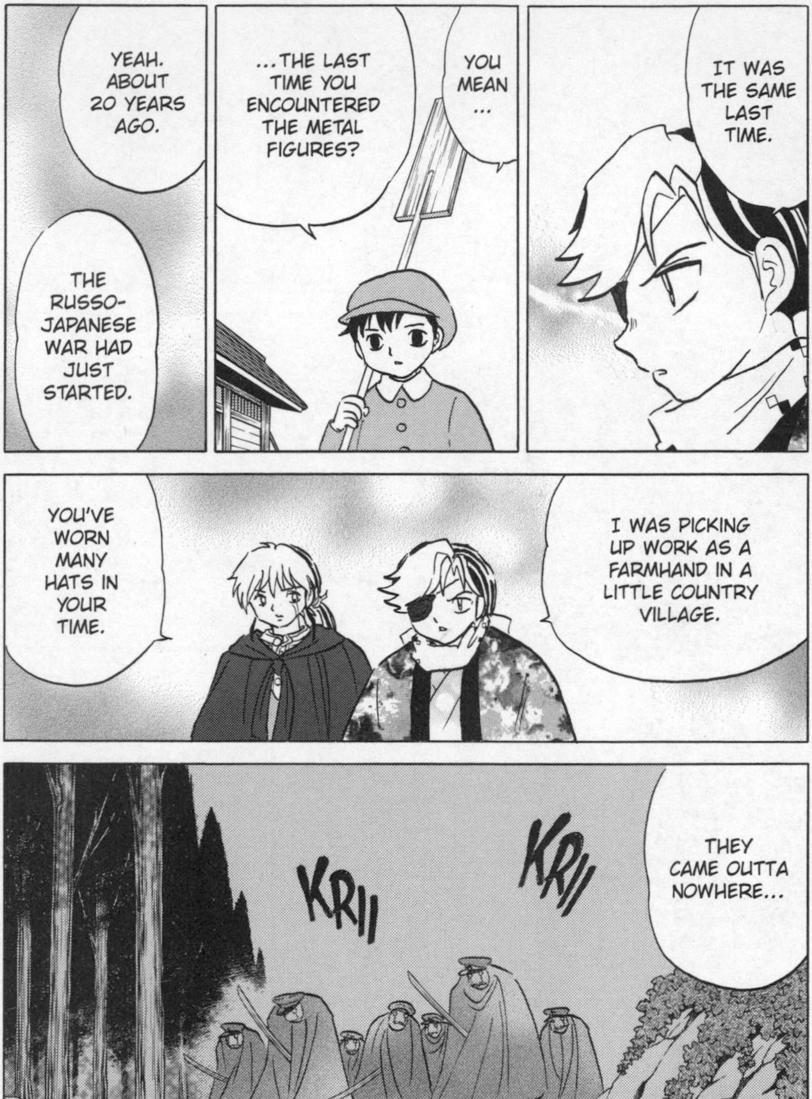
IT WAS THE SAME LAST TIME.
YOU MEAN ...
...THE LAST TIME YOU ENCOUNTERED THE METAL FIGURES?
YEAH. ABOUT 20 YEARS AGO.
THE RUSSO-JAPANESE WAR HAD JUST STARTED.
I WAS PICKING UP WORK AS A FARMHAND IN A LITTLE COUNTRY VILLAGE.
YOU'VE WORN MANY HATS IN YOUR TIME.
THEY CAME OUTTA NOWHERE...
KRII
KRII

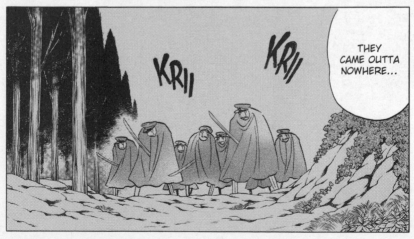

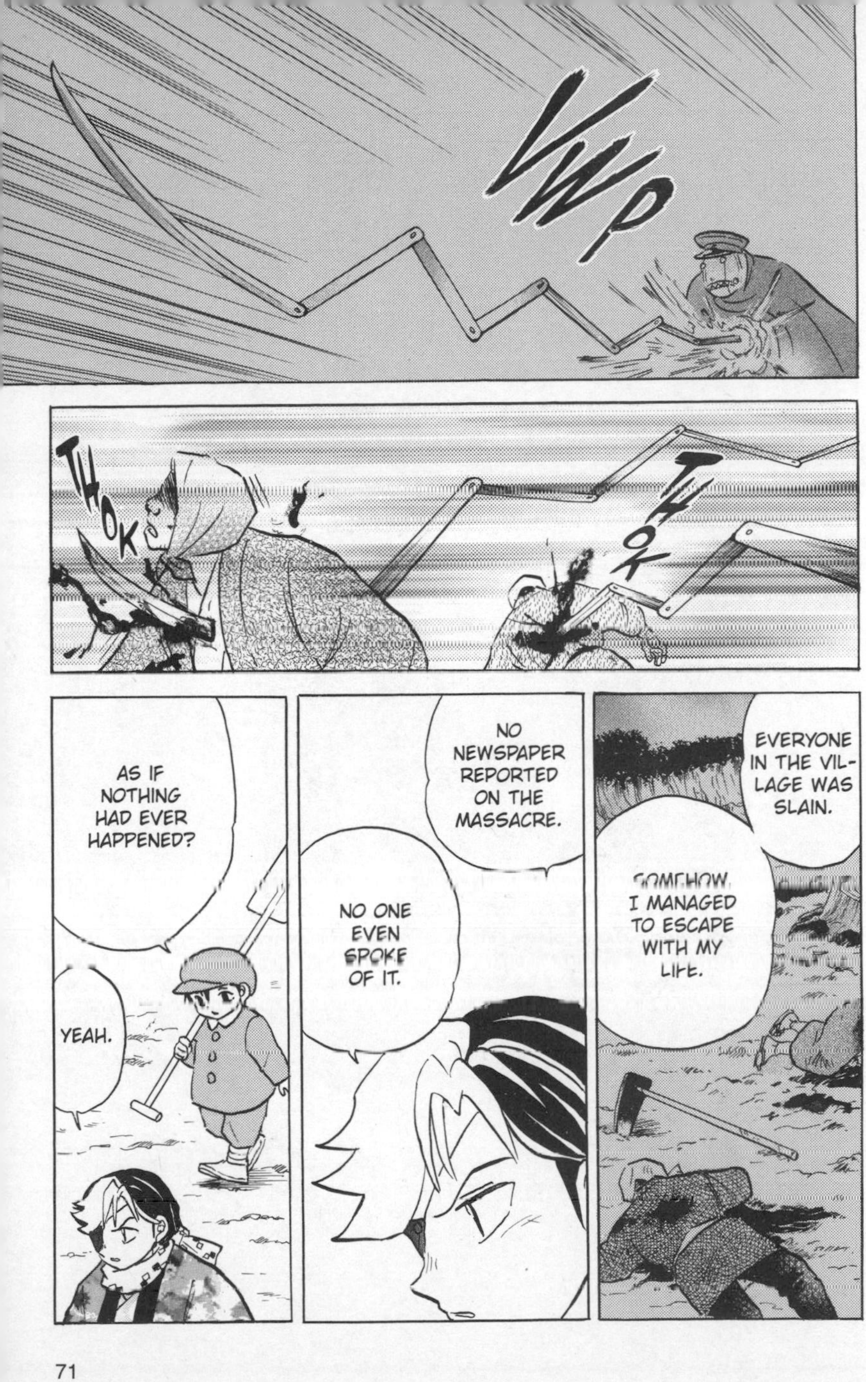
VWP
THOK
THOK
EVERYONE IN THE VIL-LAGE WAS SLAIN.
SOMEHOW, I MANAGED TO ESCAPE WITH MY LIFE.
NO NEWSPAPER REPORTED ON THE MASSACRE.
NO ONE EVEN SPOKE OF IT.
AS IF NOTHING HAD EVER HAPPENED?
YEAH.

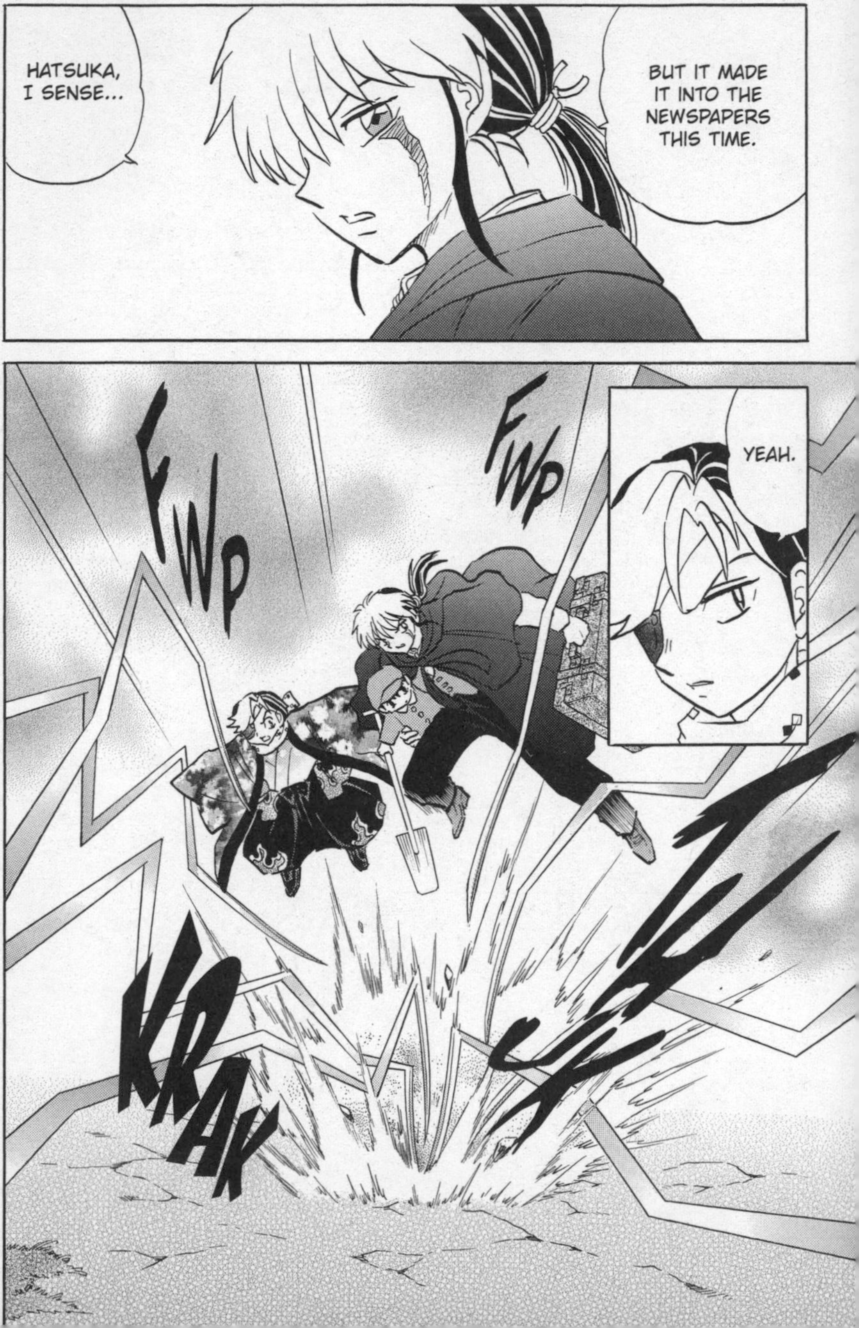
BUT IT MADE IT INTO THE NEWSPAPERS THIS TIME.
HATSUKA, I SENSE...
YEAH.
FWP
FWP
KRAK

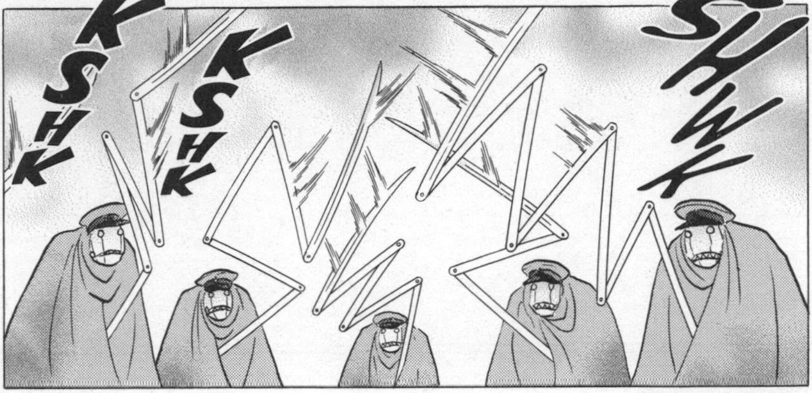
SHWK
KSHK
KSHK
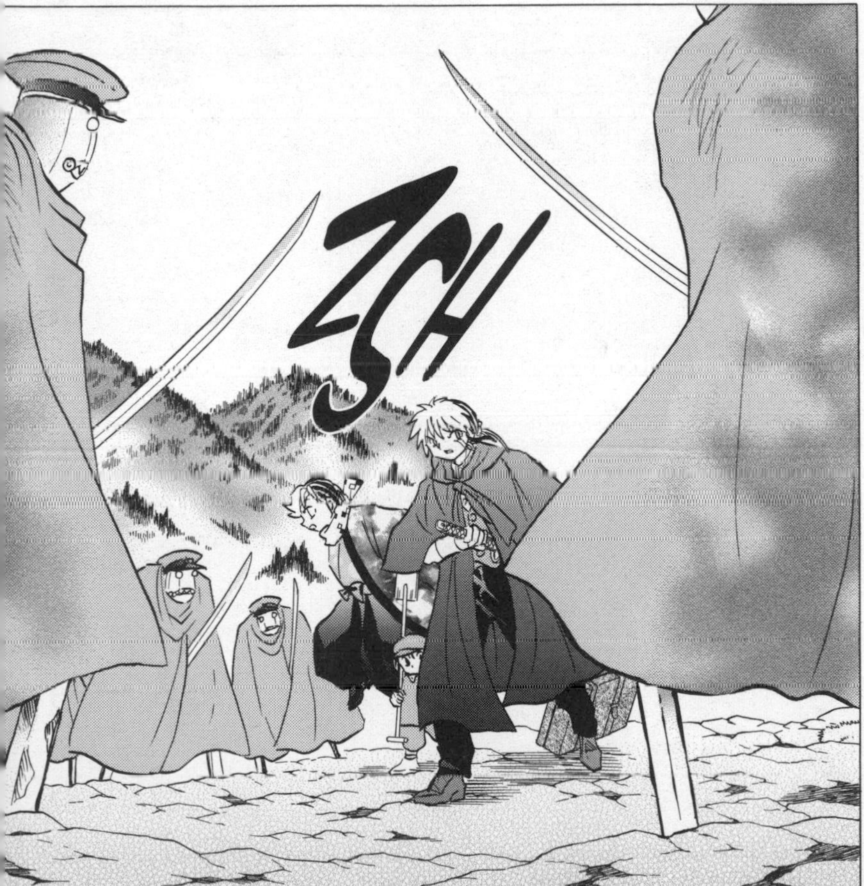
ZCH

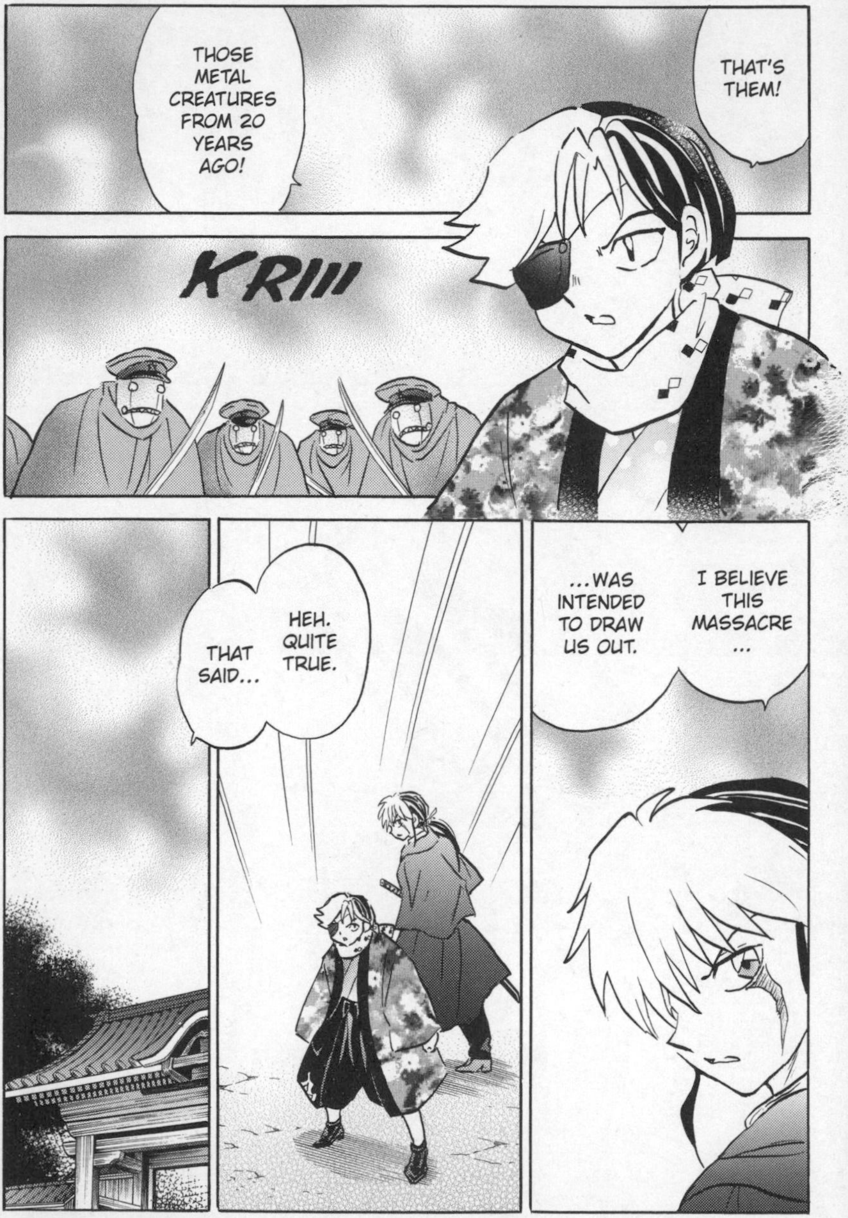
THAT'S THEM!
THOSE METAL CREATURES FROM 20 YEARS AGO!
KRIII
I BELIEVE THIS MASSACRE...
...WAS INTENDED TO DRAW US OUT.
HEH. QUITE TRUE.
THAT SAID...

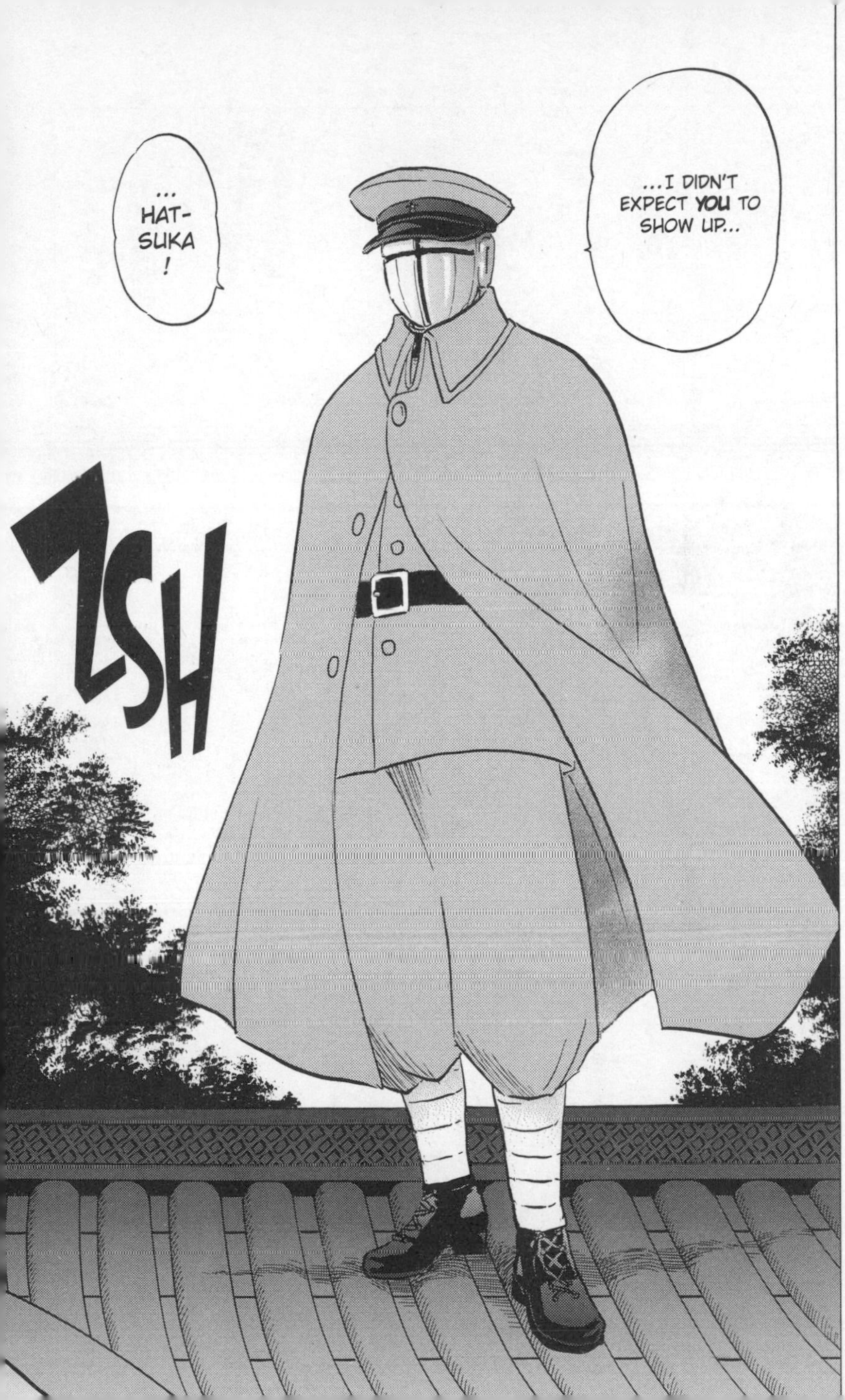
...I DIDN'T EXPECT **YOU** TO SHOW UP...
... HAT-SUKA !
ZSH

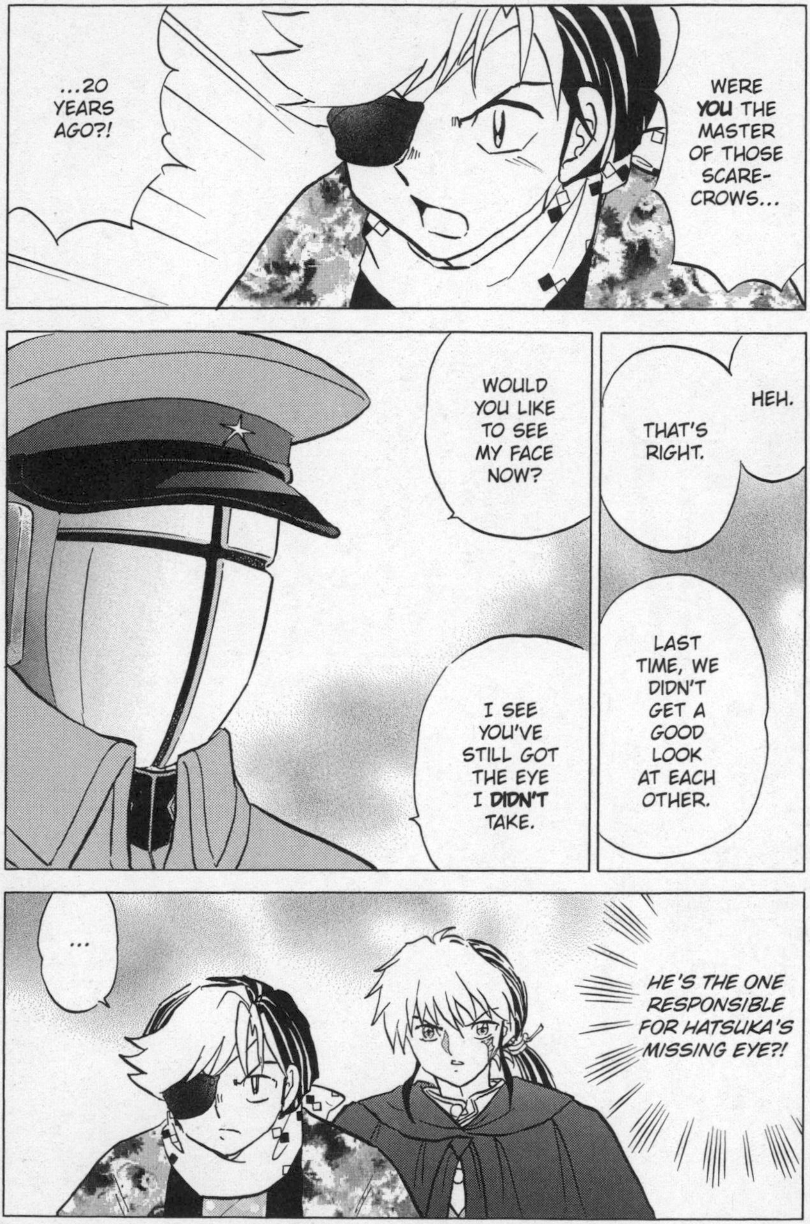
WERE YOU THE MASTER OF THOSE SCARE-CROWS...
...20 YEARS AGO?!
HEH.
THAT'S RIGHT.
LAST TIME, WE DIDN'T GET A GOOD LOOK AT EACH OTHER.
WOULD YOU LIKE TO SEE MY FACE NOW?
I SEE YOU'VE STILL GOT THE EYE I DIDN'T TAKE.
HE'S THE ONE RESPONSIBLE FOR HATSUKA'S MISSING EYE?!
...

Chapter 5: Under the Mask

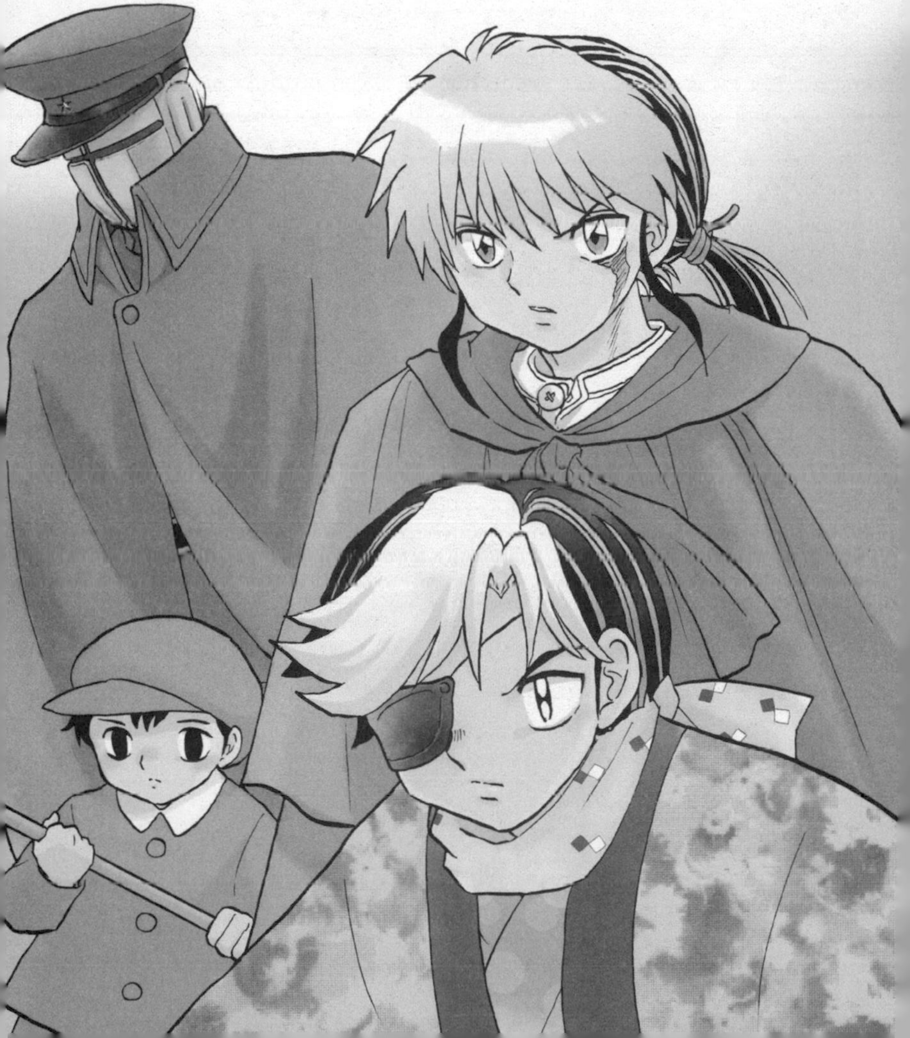

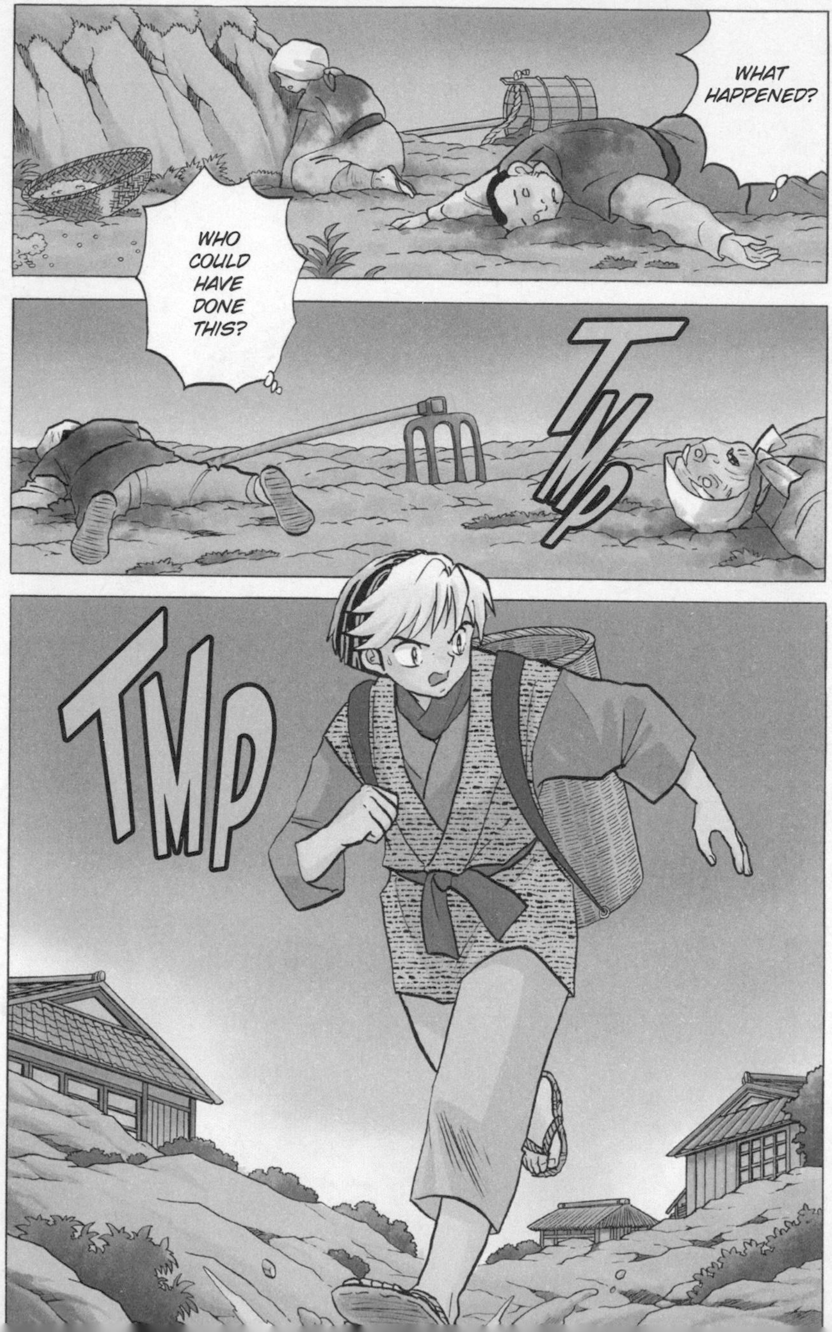
WHAT HAPPENED?
WHO COULD HAVE DONE THIS?
TMP
TMP

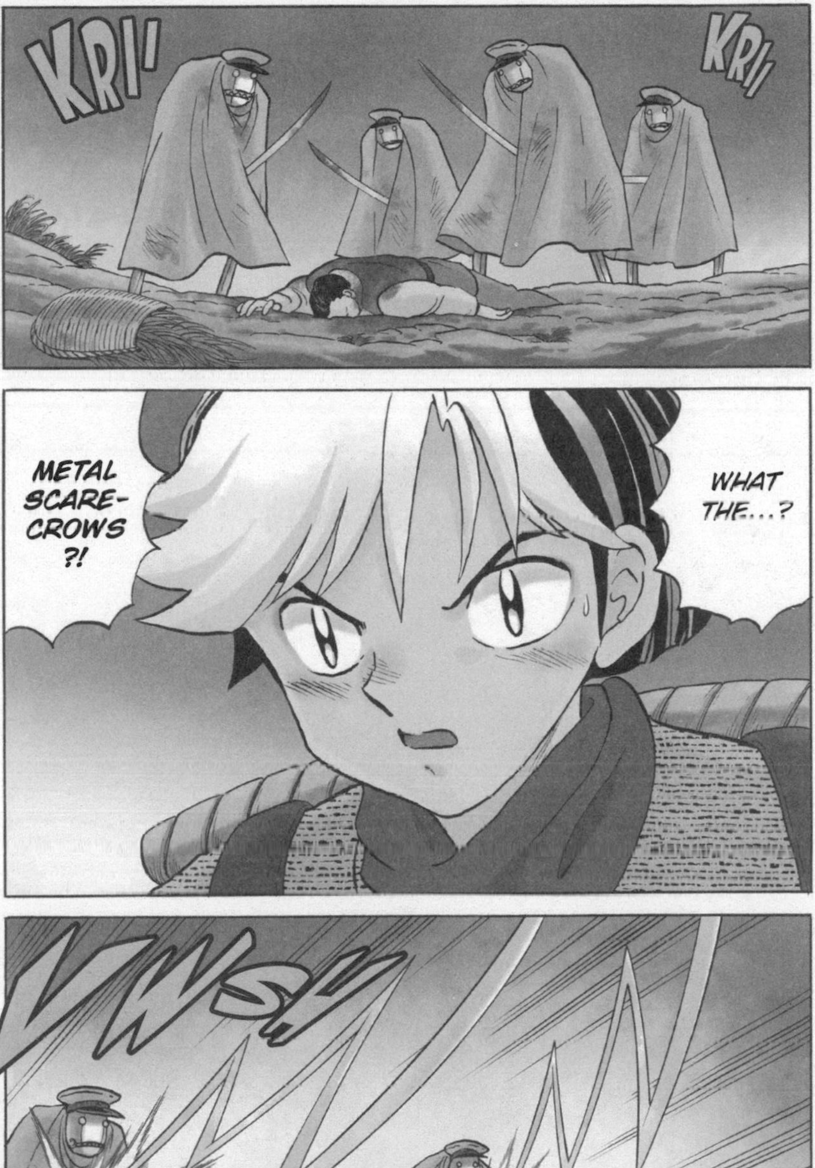
KRII
KRI'
WHAT THE...?
METAL SCARE-CROWS ?!
VWSH!

MAO

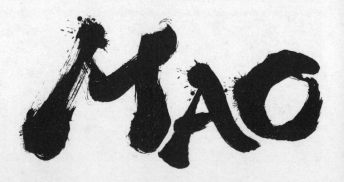

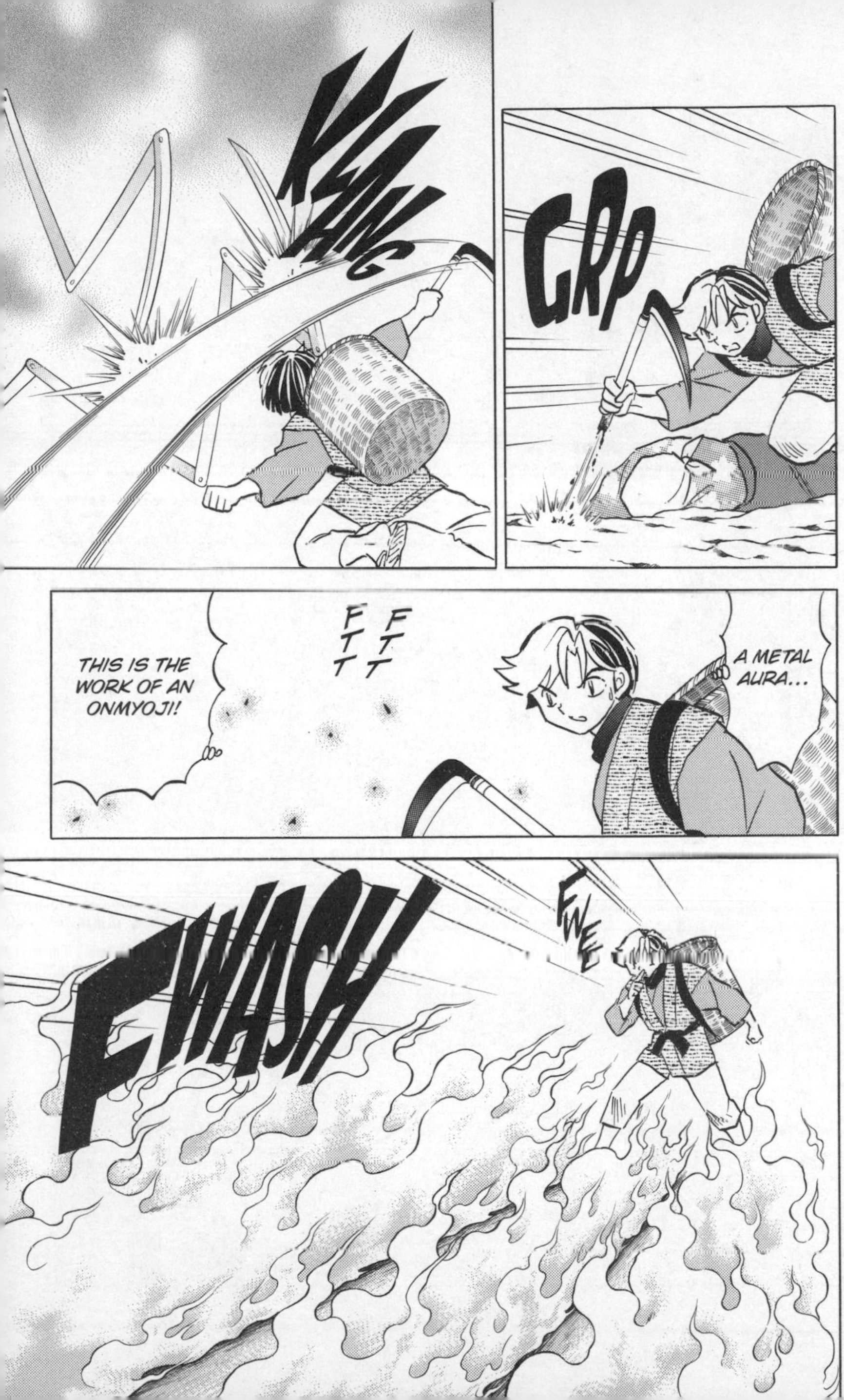
GRP
KWANG
A METAL AURA...
FTT FTT
THIS IS THE WORK OF AN ONMYOJI!
FWE
FWASH!

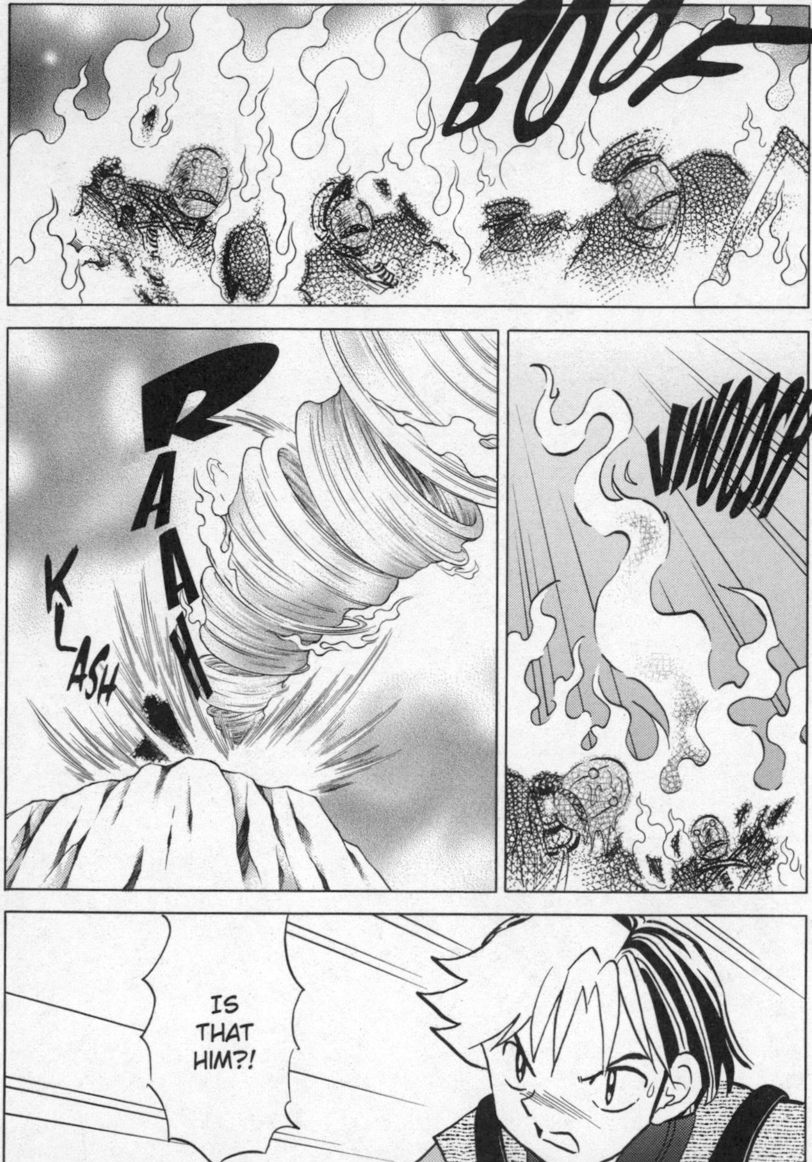
BOOF
JWOOSH
RAAAH
KLASH
IS THAT HIM?!

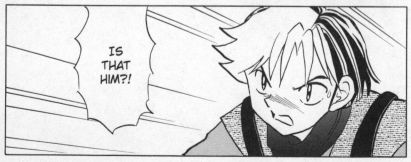

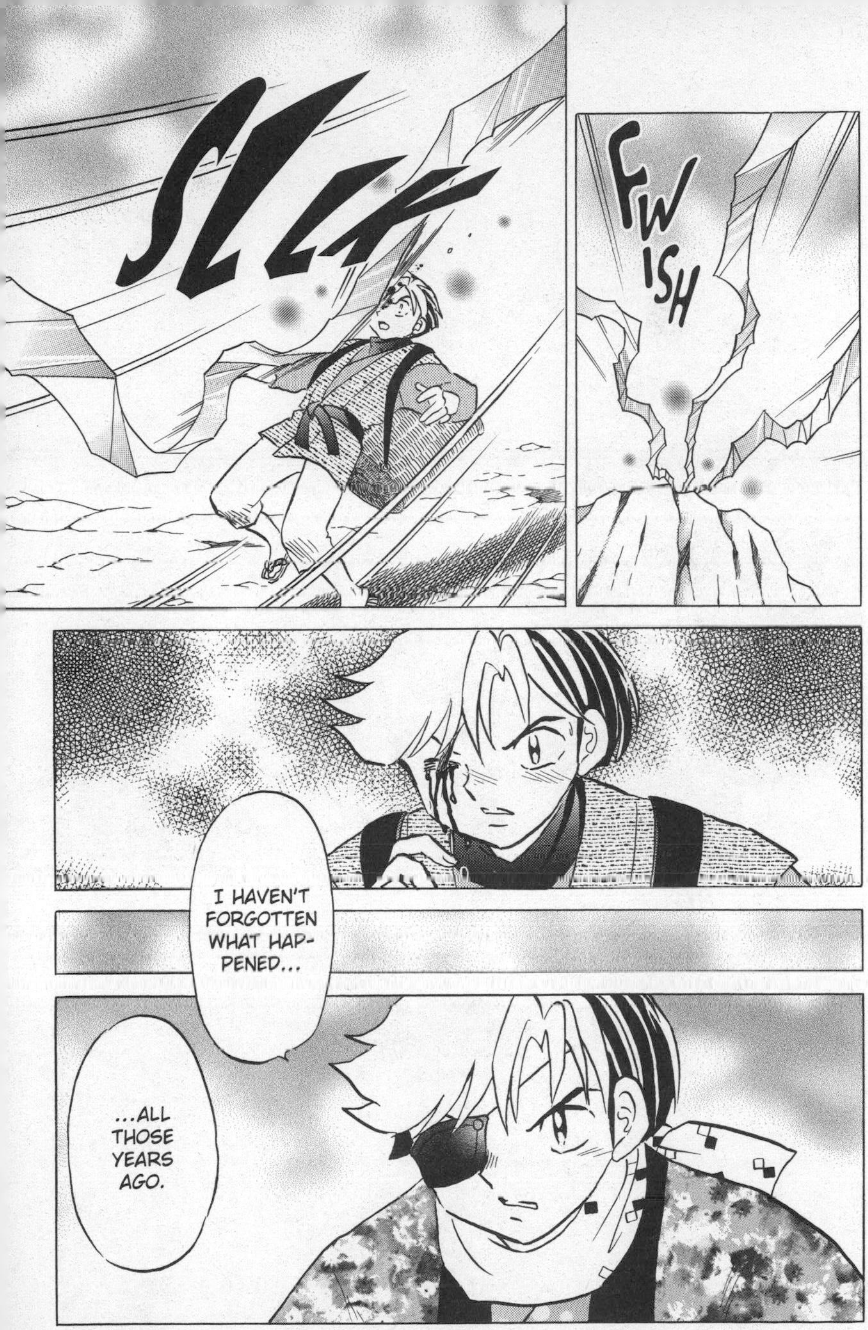
FWISH
SLCK
I HAVEN'T FORGOTTEN WHAT HAP-PENED...
...ALL THOSE YEARS AGO.

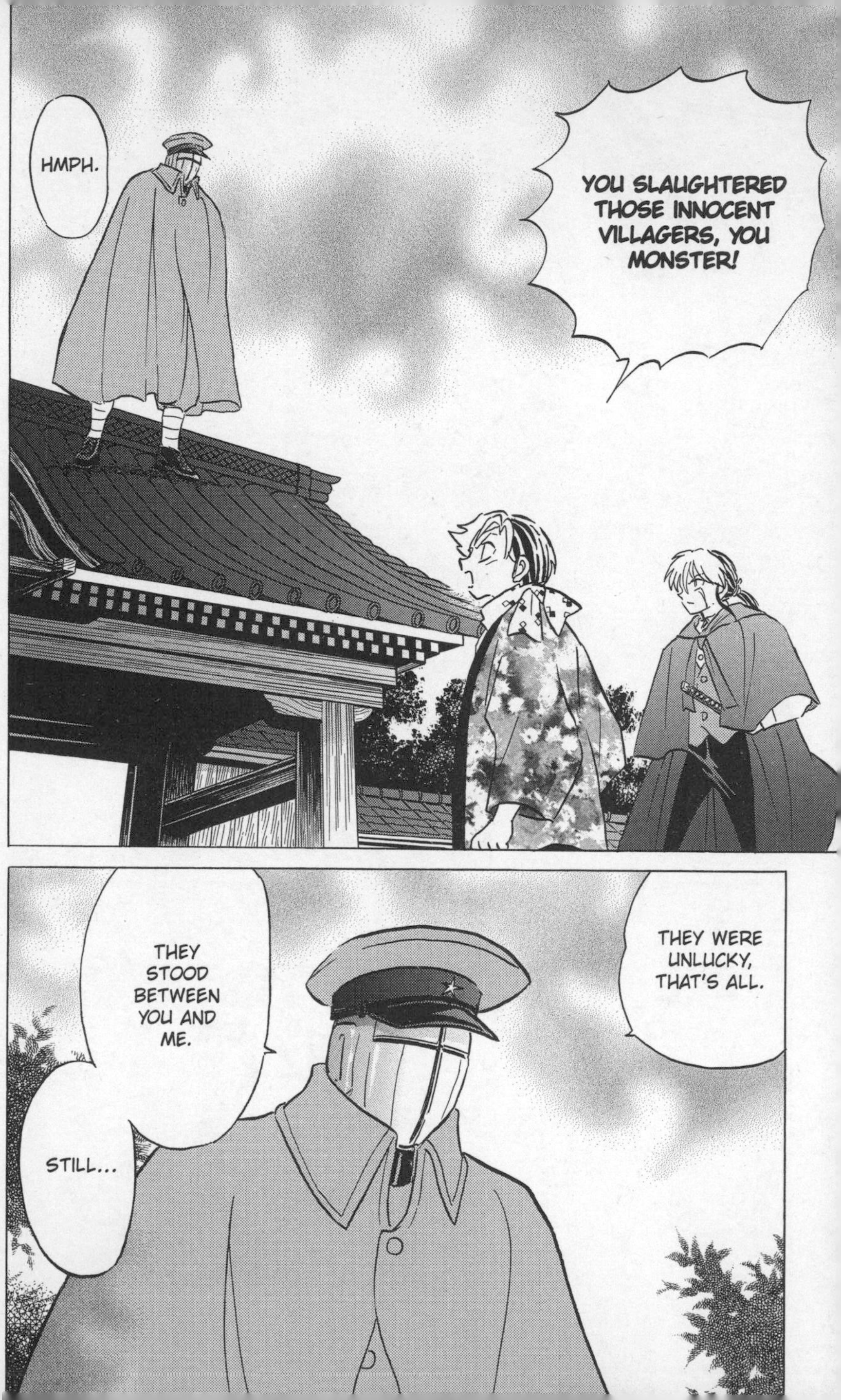
YOU SLAUGHTERED THOSE INNOCENT VILLAGERS, YOU MONSTER!
HMPH.
THEY WERE UNLUCKY, THAT'S ALL.
THEY STOOD BETWEEN YOU AND ME.
STILL...

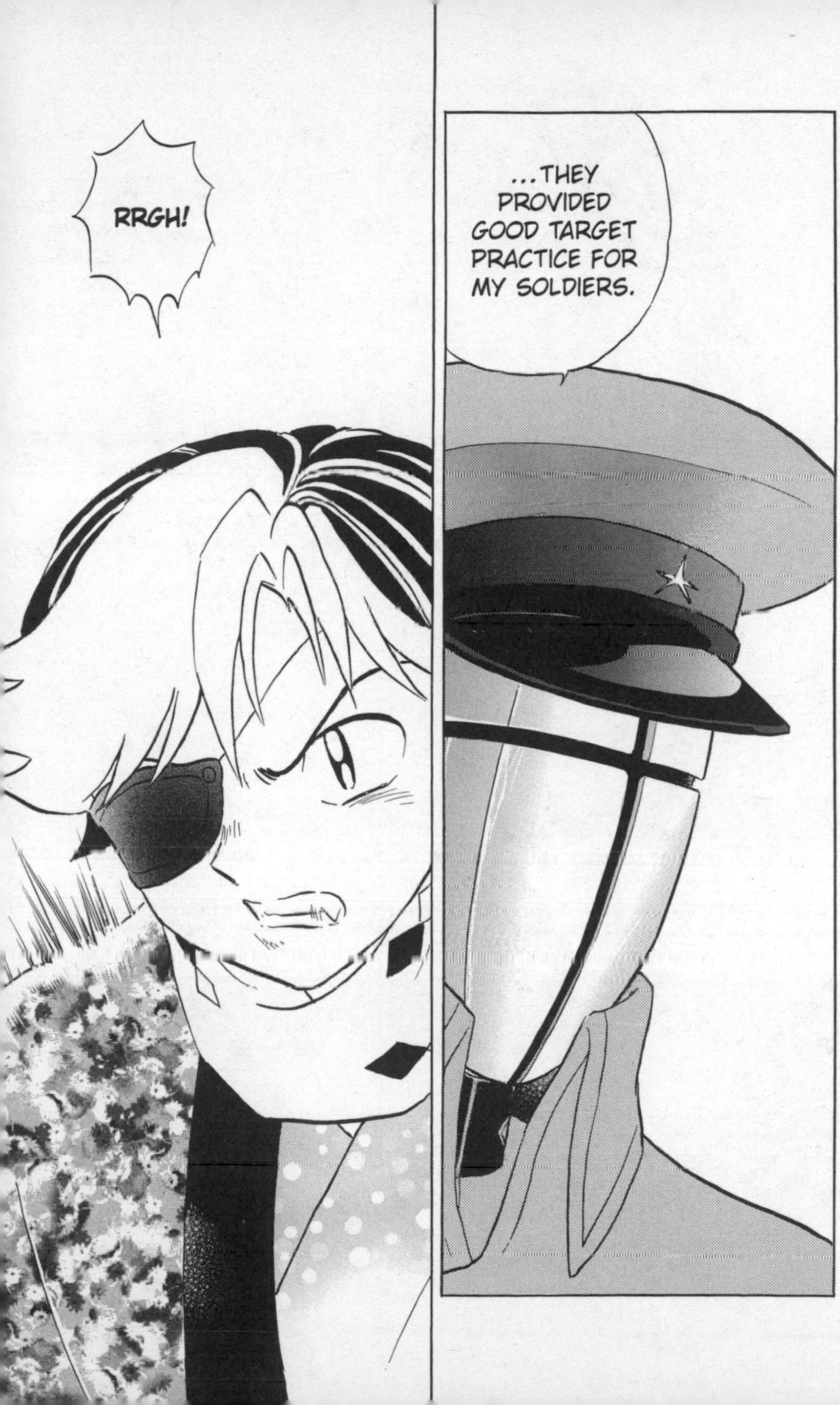
...THEY PROVIDED GOOD TARGET PRACTICE FOR MY SOLDIERS.
RRGH!

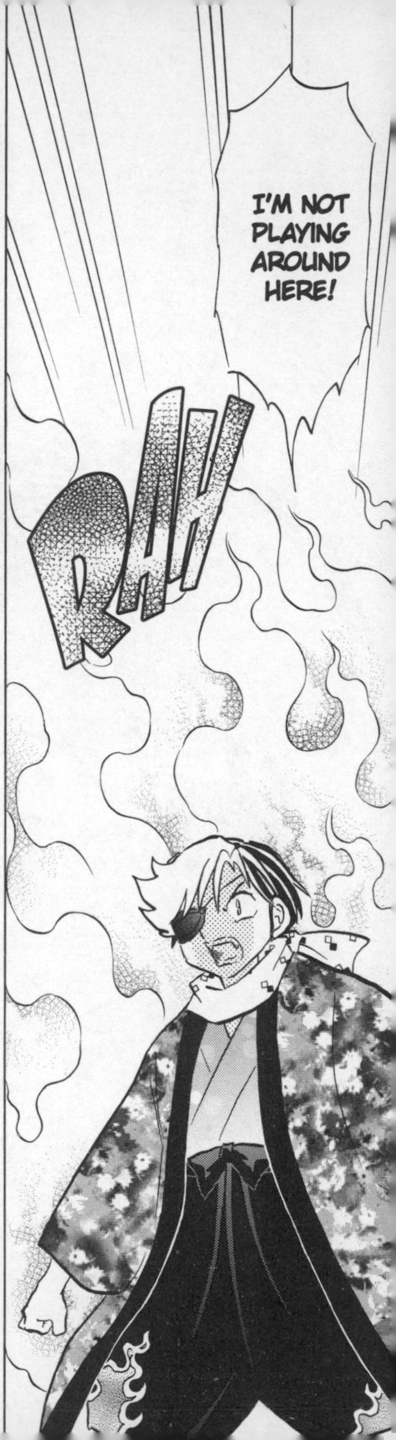
I'M NOT PLAYING AROUND HERE!
RAH

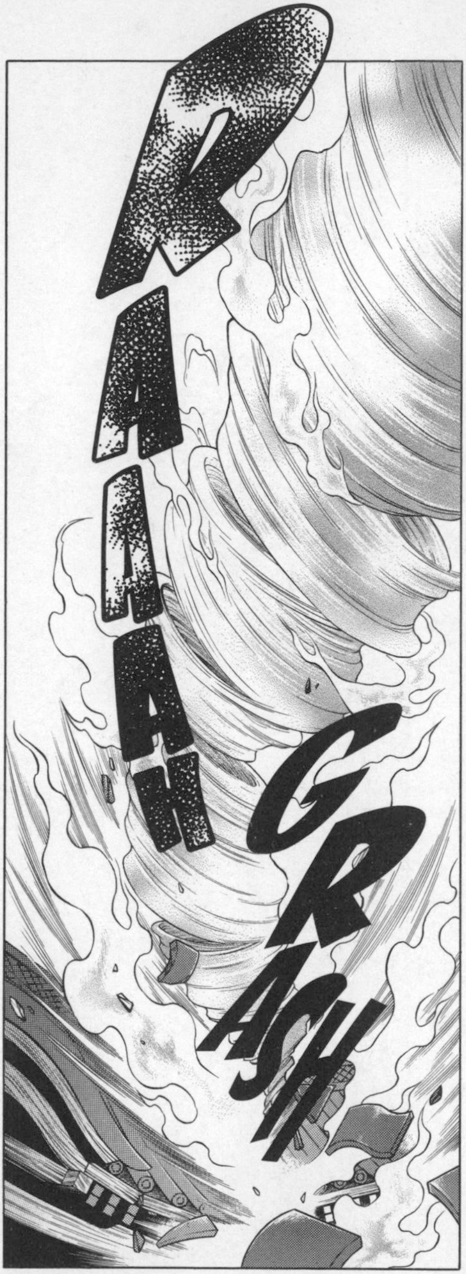
RAAAH
CRASH

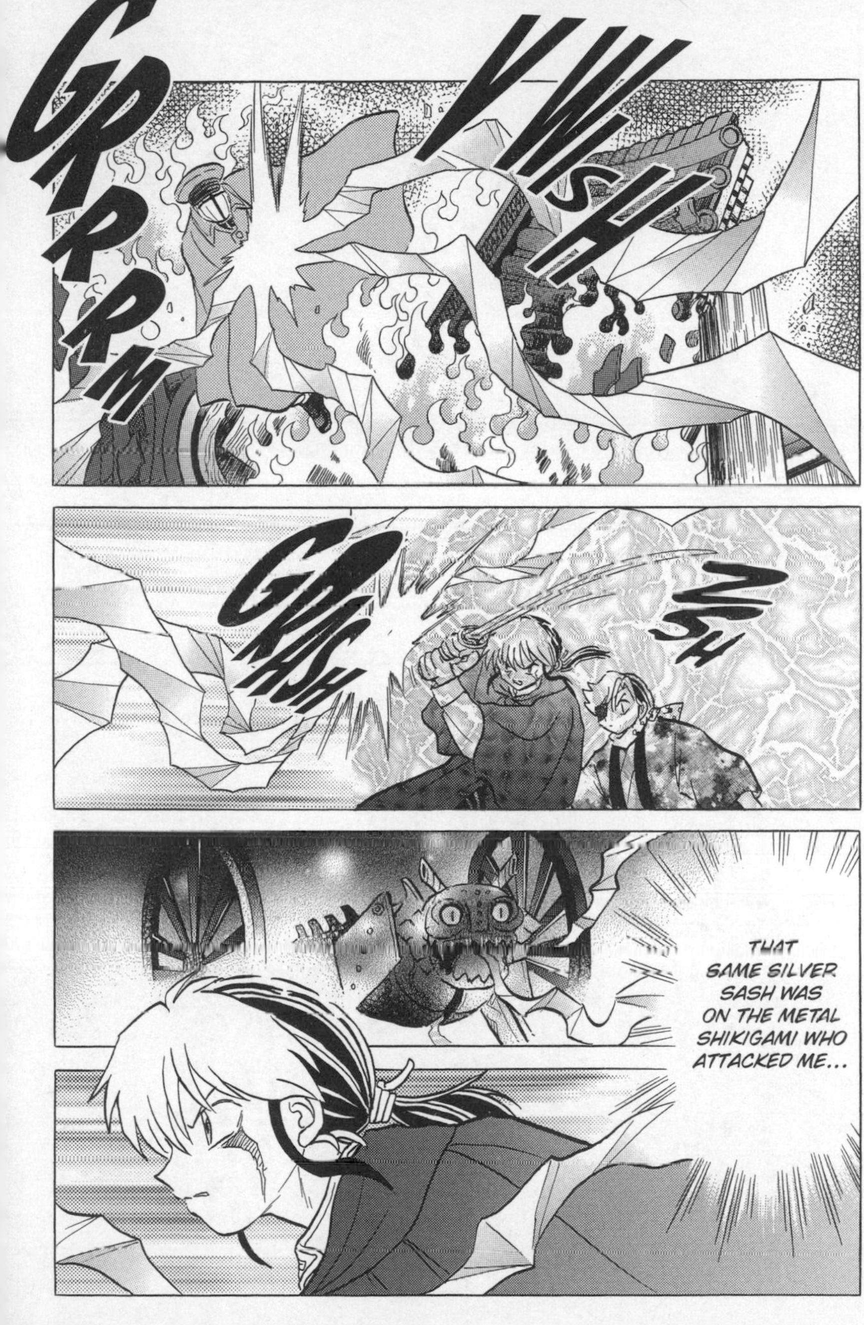
VWISH
GRRRM
ZASH
GNASH
THAT SAME SILVER SASH WAS ON THE METAL SHIKIGAMI WHO ATTACKED ME...

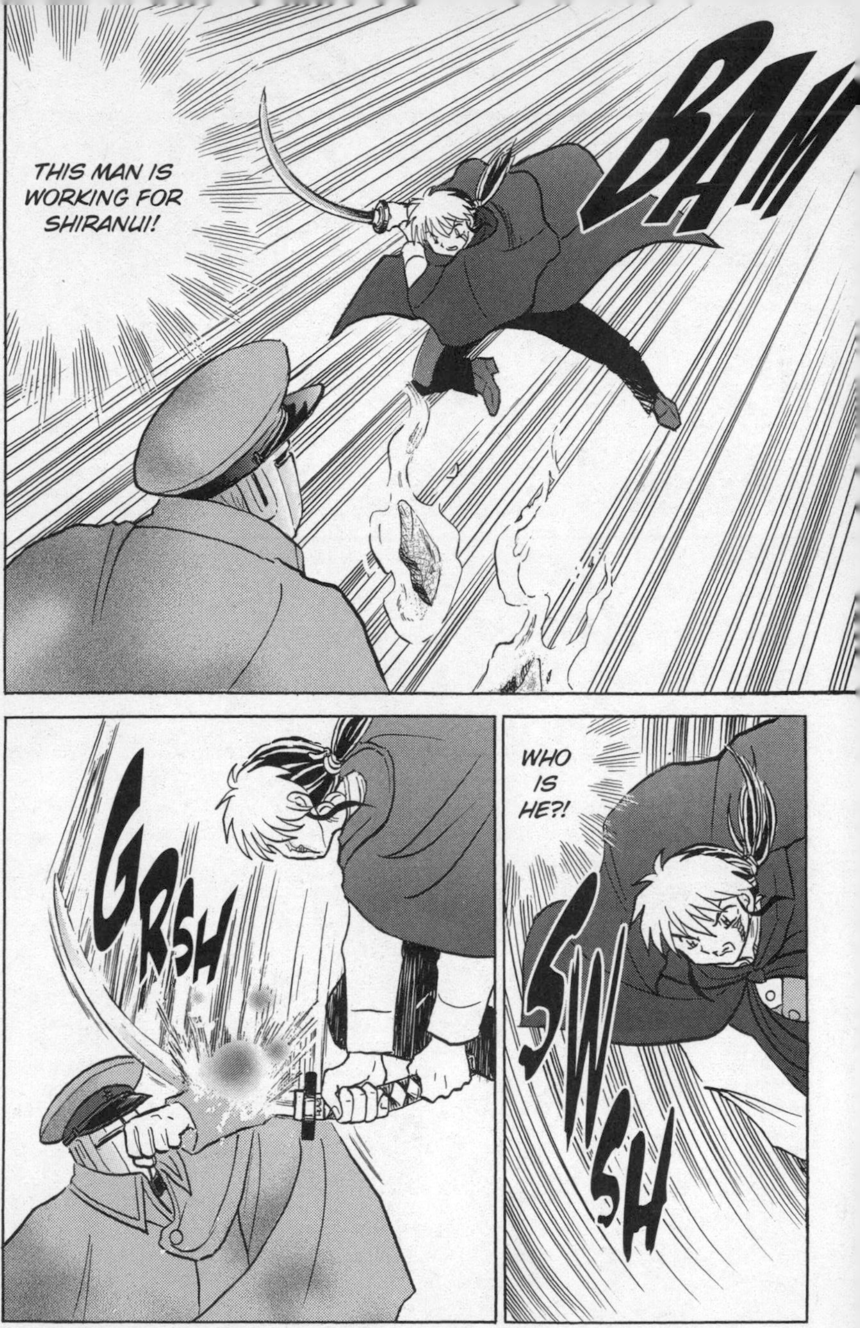
BAM
THIS MAN IS WORKING FOR SHIRANUI!
WHO IS HE?!
SWISH
GRSH

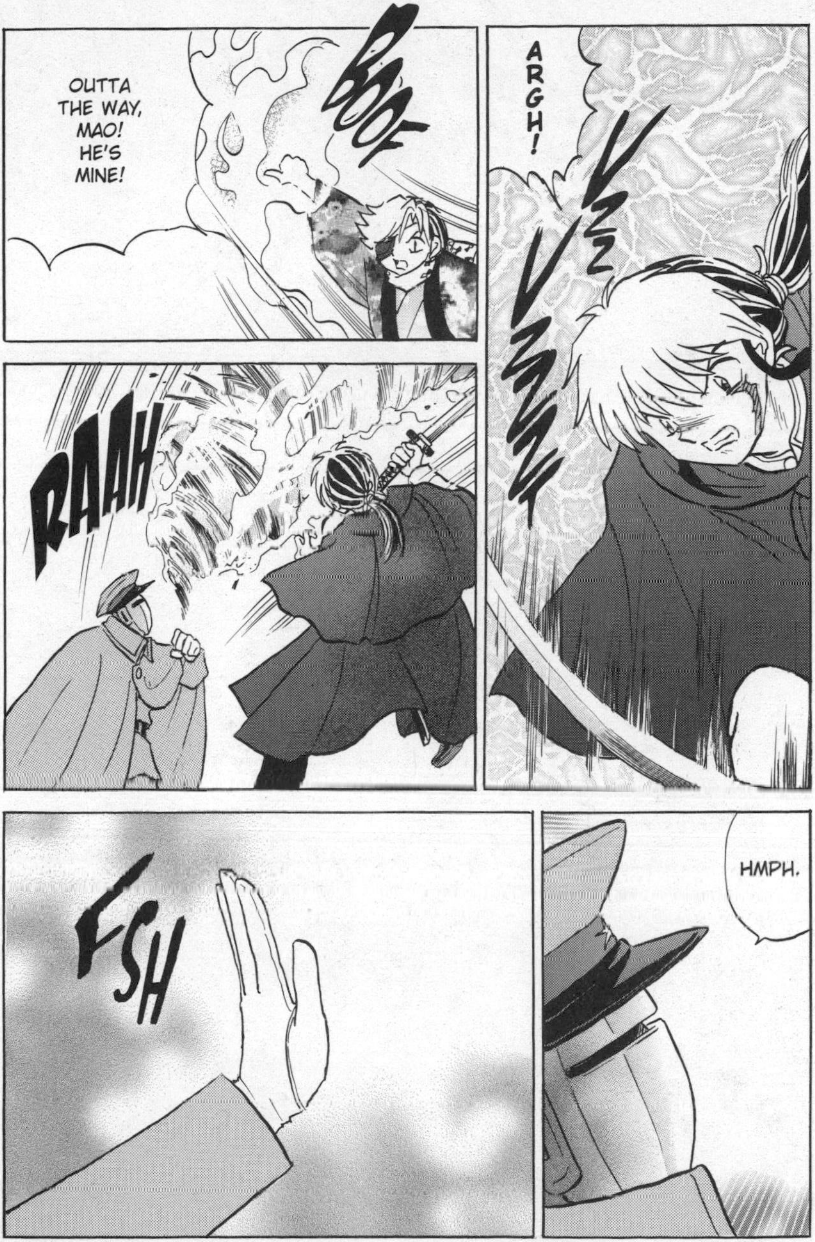
ARGH!
VZZZ
VZZZZZT
OUTTA THE WAY, MAO! HE'S MINE!
BOOOF
RAAH
HMPH.
FSH

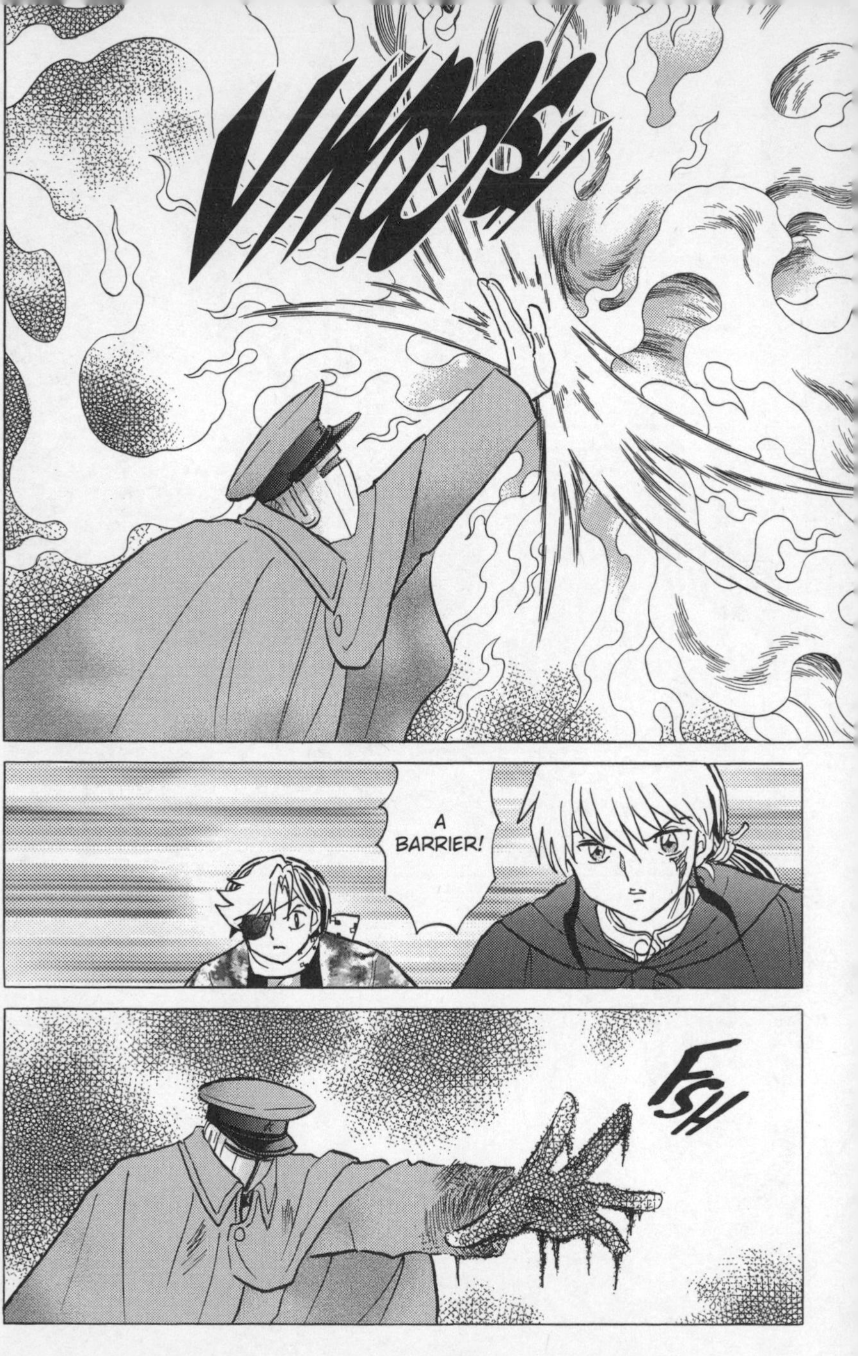
VWOOSH
A BARRIER!
FSH

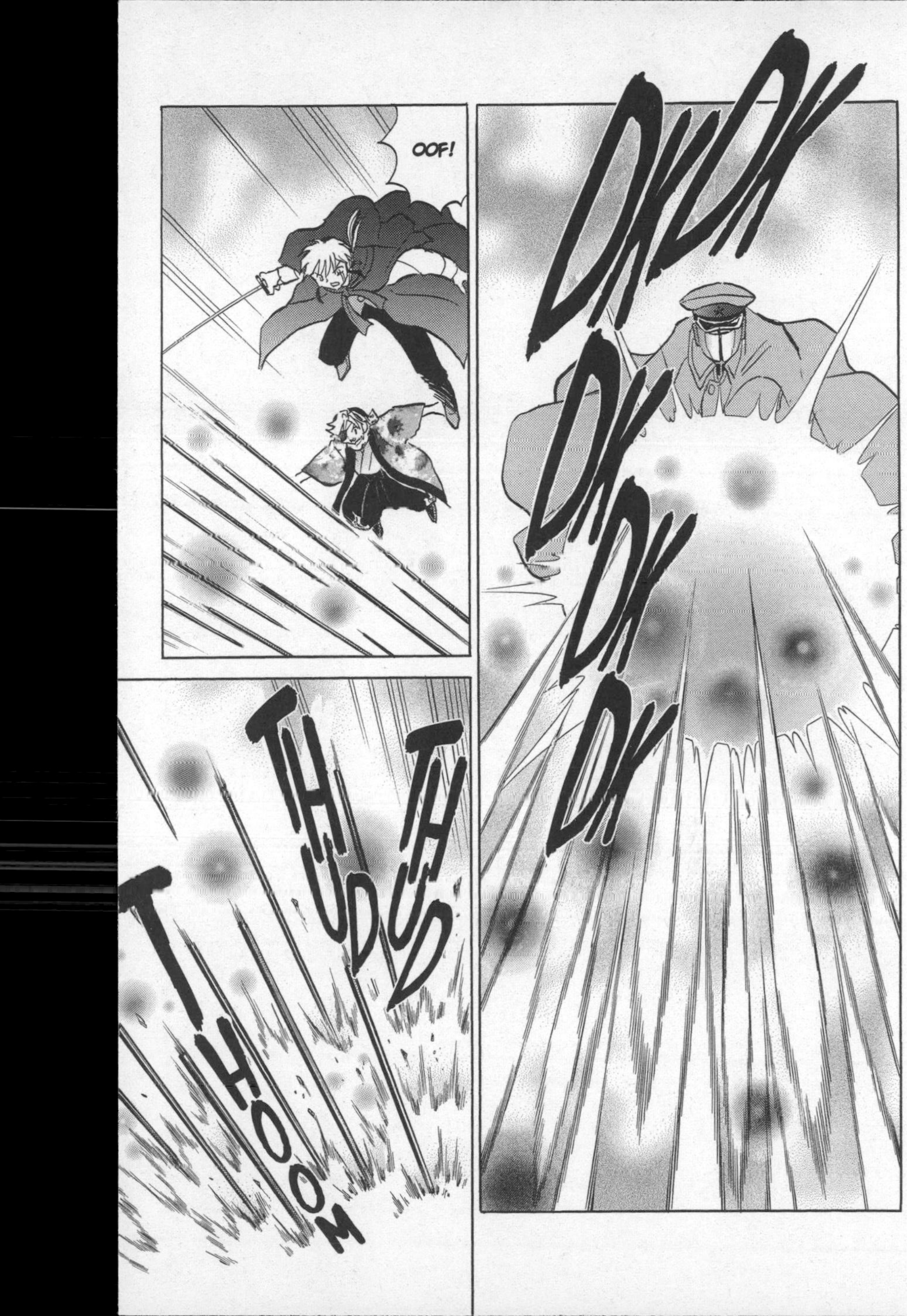
DKDK DK DK DK DK DK
OOF!
THUD
THUD
THOOM

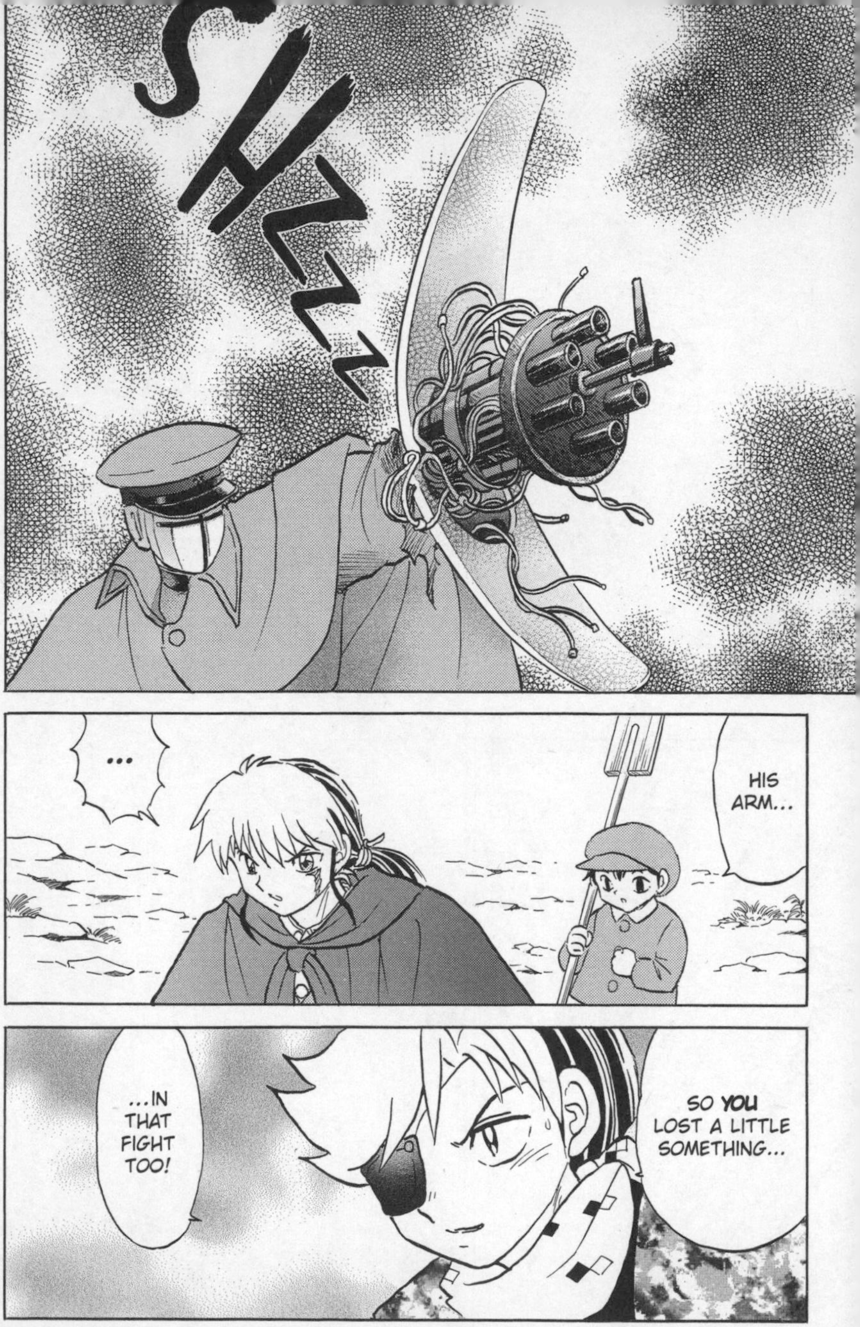
SHZZZ
HIS ARM...
...
SO YOU LOST A LITTLE SOMETHING...
...IN THAT FIGHT TOO!

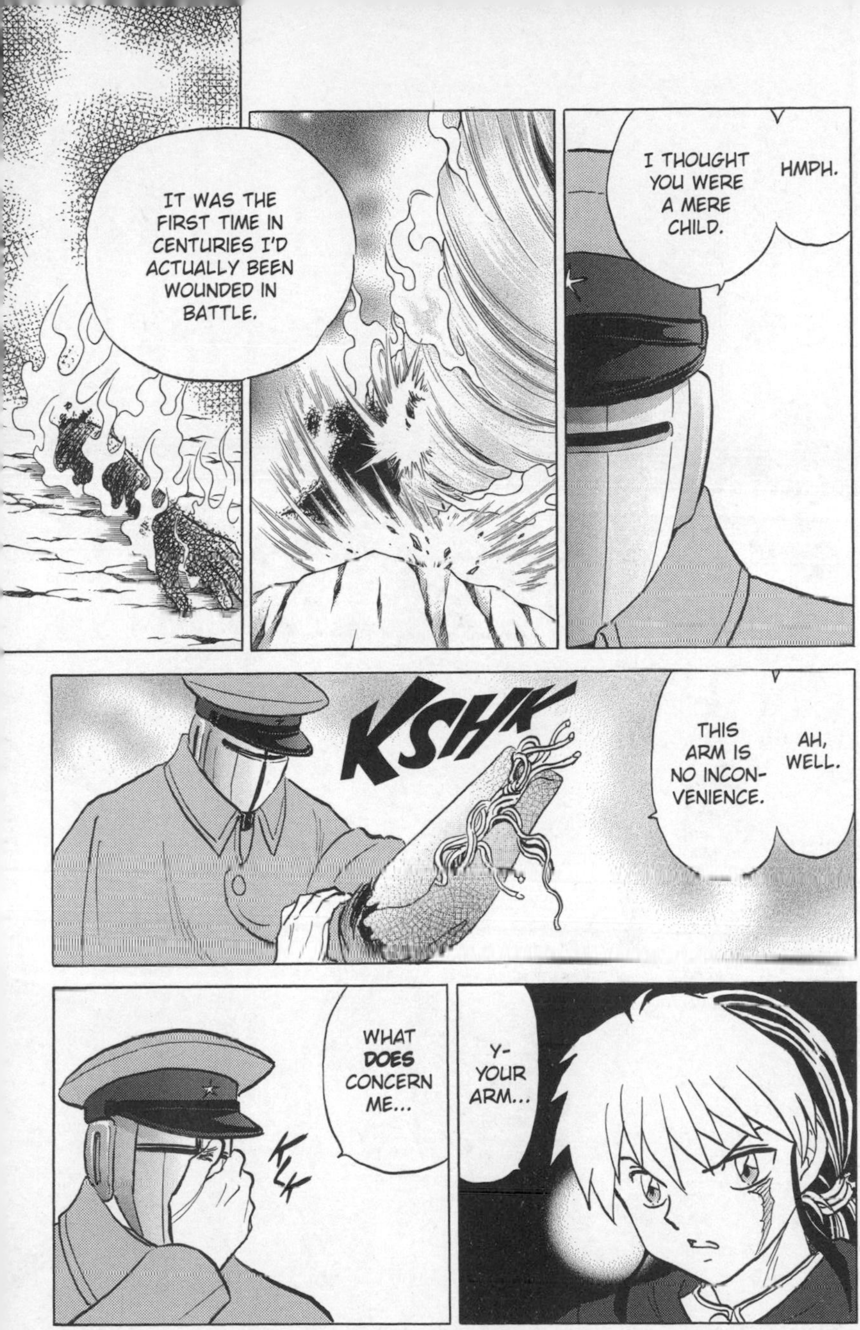
HMPH.
I THOUGHT YOU WERE A MERE CHILD.
IT WAS THE FIRST TIME IN CENTURIES I'D ACTUALLY BEEN WOUNDED IN BATTLE.
AH, WELL.
THIS ARM IS NO INCON-VENIENCE.
KSHK
Y- YOUR ARM...
WHAT **DOES** CONCERN ME...
KLK

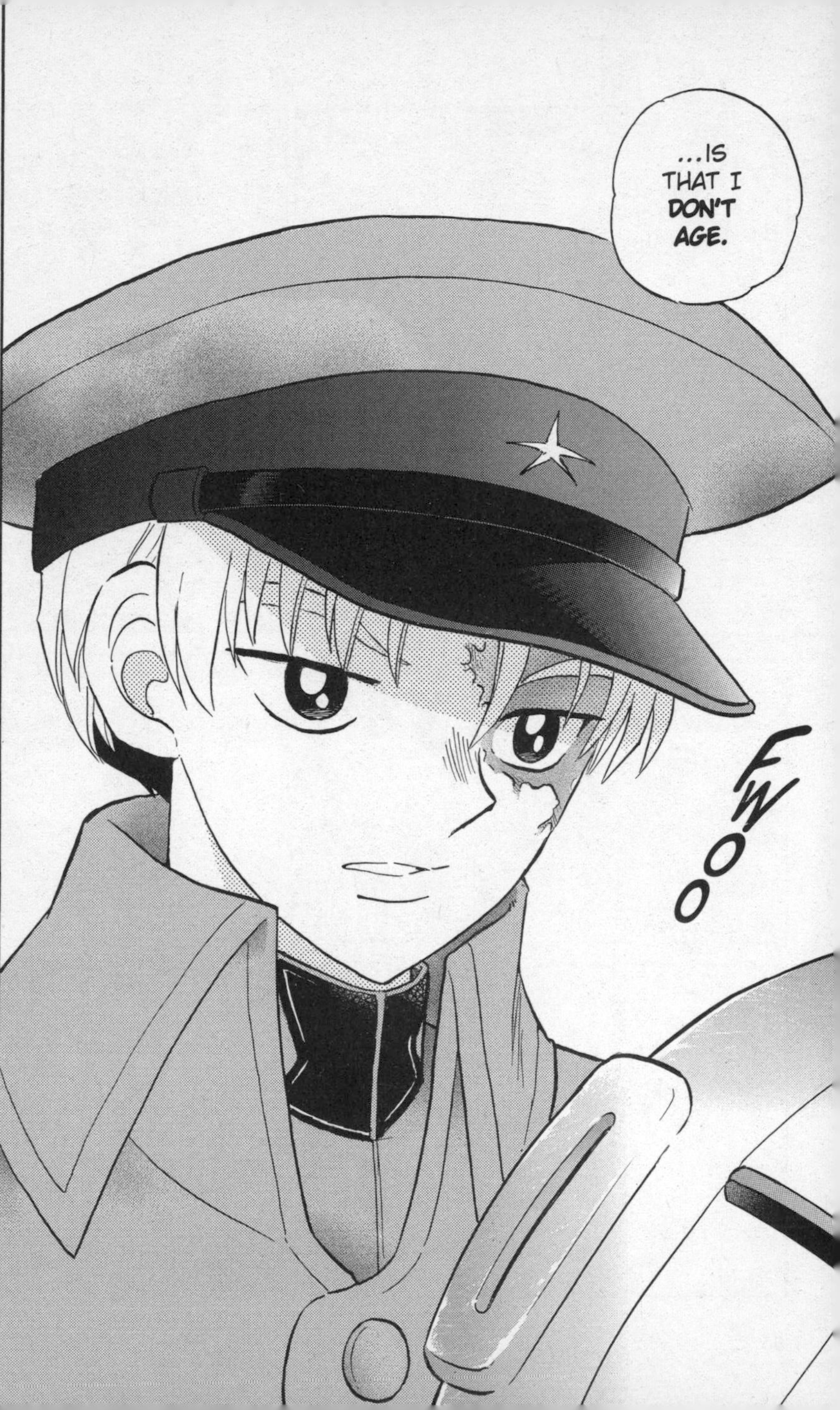
...IS THAT I **DON'T AGE.**
FWOOO

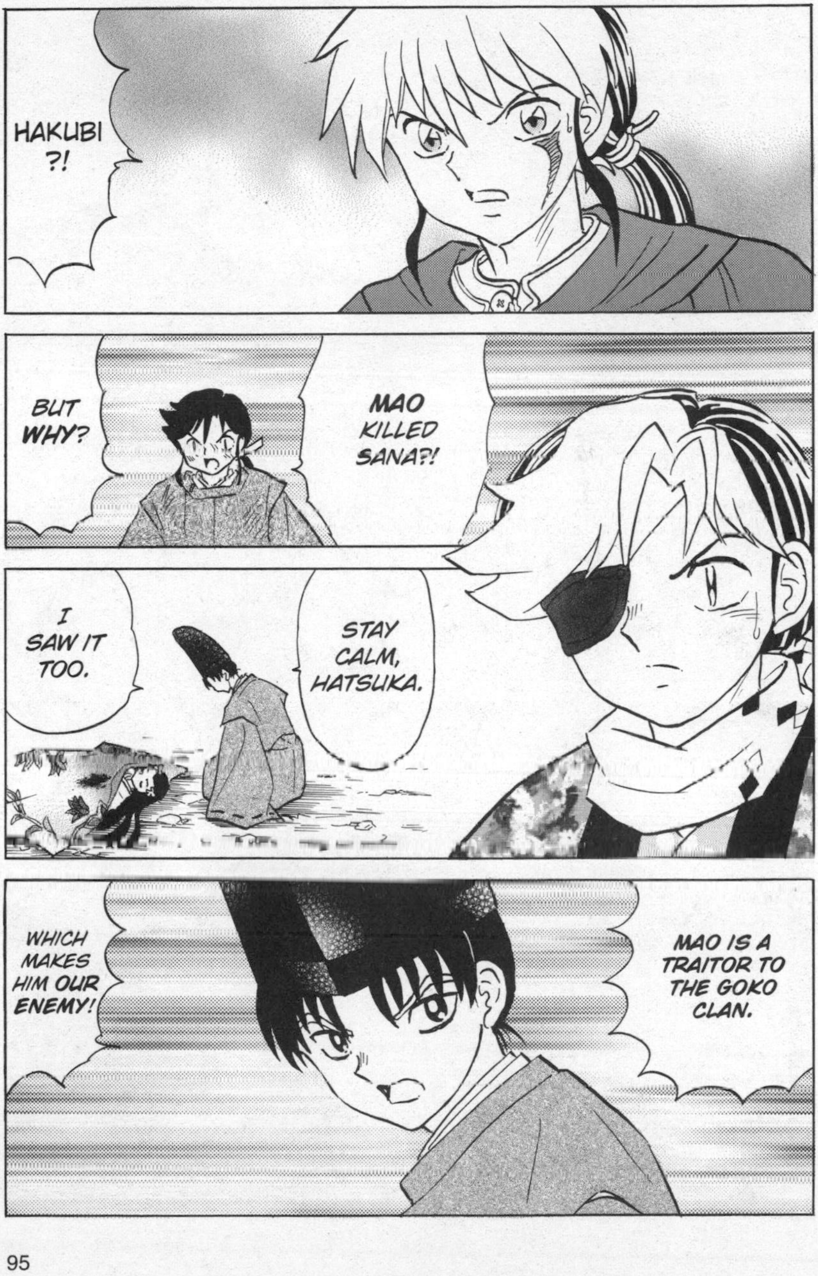
HAKUBI ?!
MAO KILLED SANA?!
BUT WHY?
STAY CALM, HATSUKA.
I SAW IT TOO.
MAO IS A TRAITOR TO THE GOKO CLAN.
WHICH MAKES HIM OUR ENEMY!

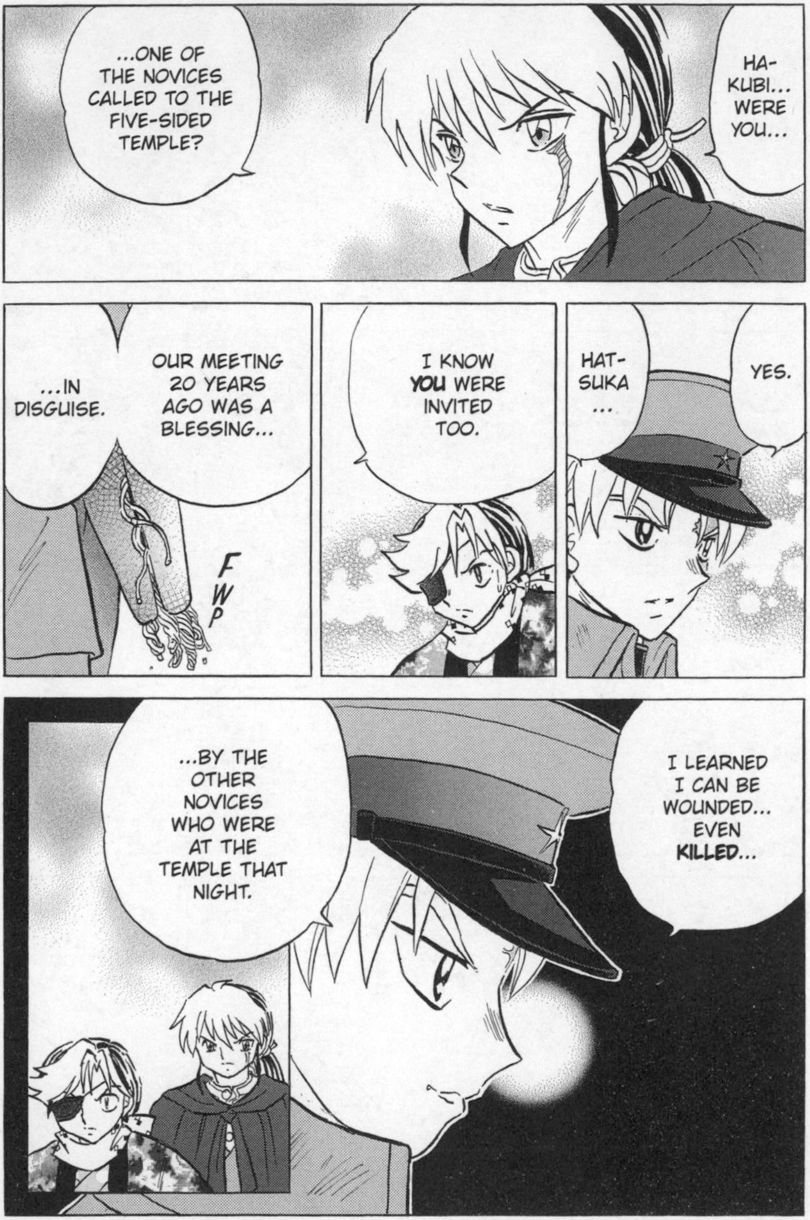
HA-KUBI... WERE YOU...
...ONE OF THE NOVICES CALLED TO THE FIVE-SIDED TEMPLE?
YES.
HAT-SUKA ...
I KNOW YOU WERE INVITED TOO.
OUR MEETING 20 YEARS AGO WAS A BLESSING...
...IN DISGUISE.
FWP
I LEARNED I CAN BE WOUNDED... EVEN KILLED...
...BY THE OTHER NOVICES WHO WERE AT THE TEMPLE THAT NIGHT.

Chapter 6: Hakubi

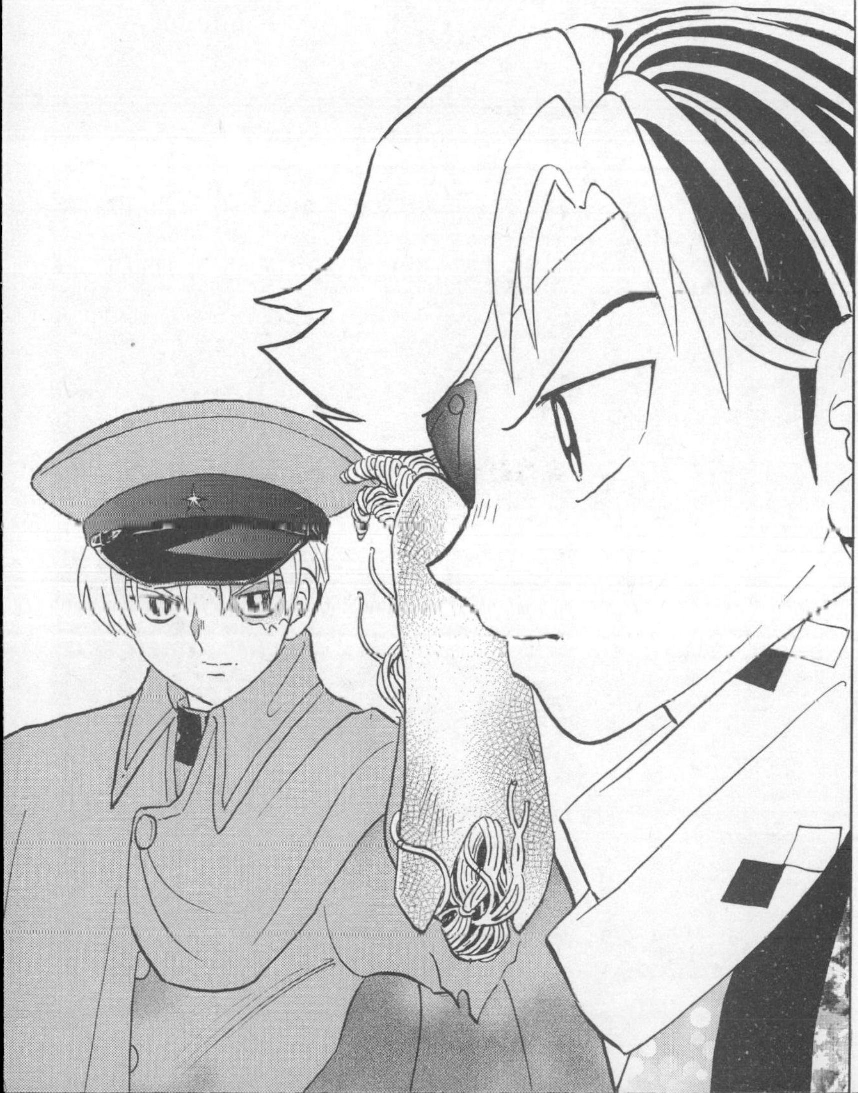

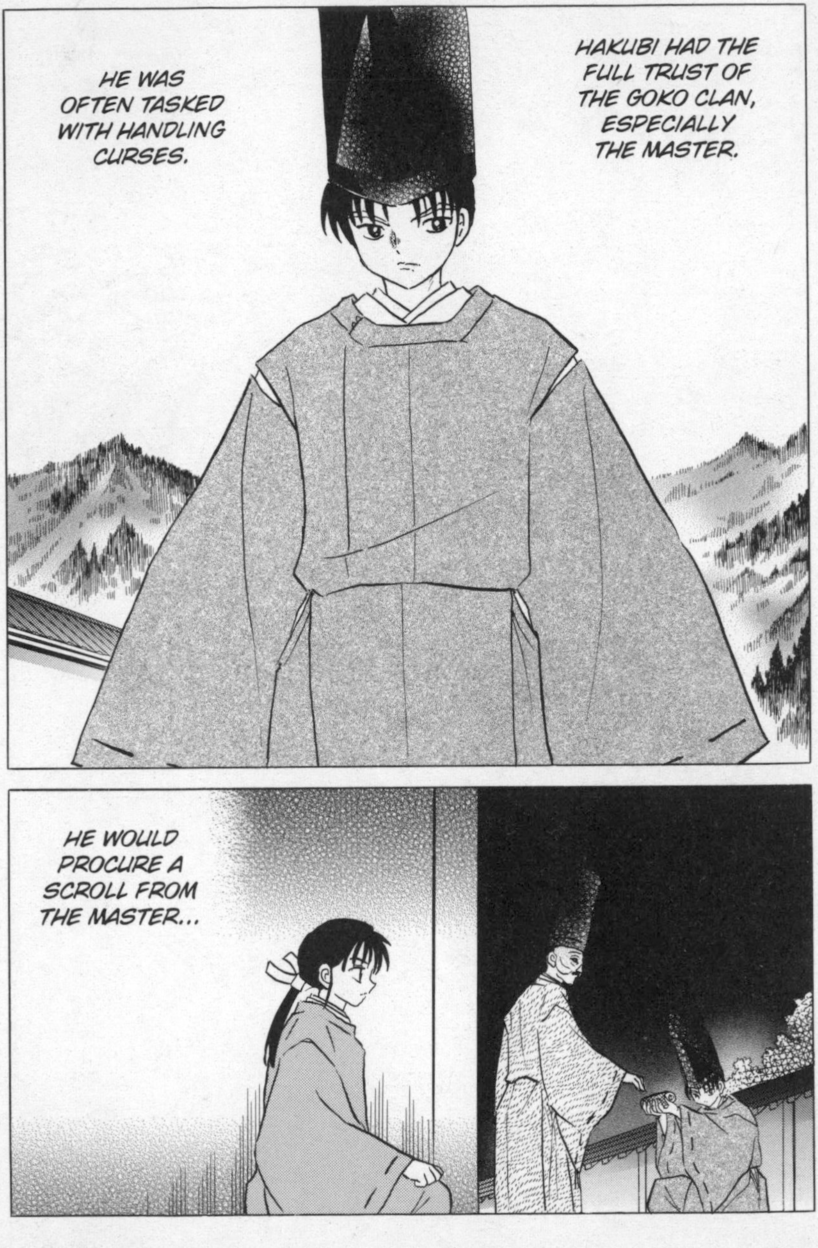
HAKUBI HAD THE FULL TRUST OF THE GOKO CLAN, ESPECIALLY THE MASTER.
HE WAS OFTEN TASKED WITH HANDLING CURSES.
HE WOULD PROCURE A SCROLL FROM THE MASTER...

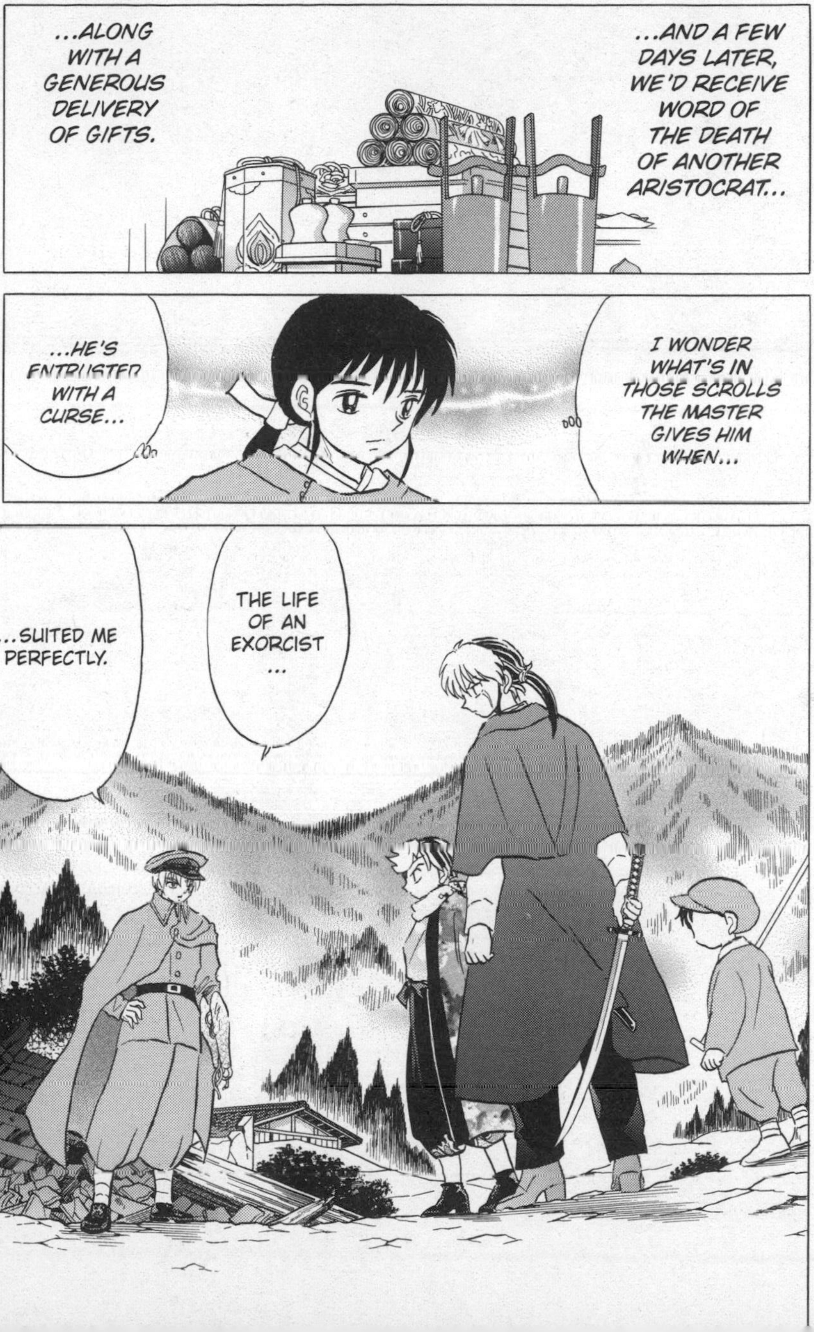
...AND A FEW DAYS LATER, WE'D RECEIVE WORD OF THE DEATH OF ANOTHER ARISTOCRAT...
...ALONG WITH A GENEROUS DELIVERY OF GIFTS.
I WONDER WHAT'S IN THOSE SCROLLS THE MASTER GIVES HIM WHEN...
...HE'S ENTRUSTED WITH A CURSE...
THE LIFE OF AN EXORCIST ...
...SUITED ME PERFECTLY.

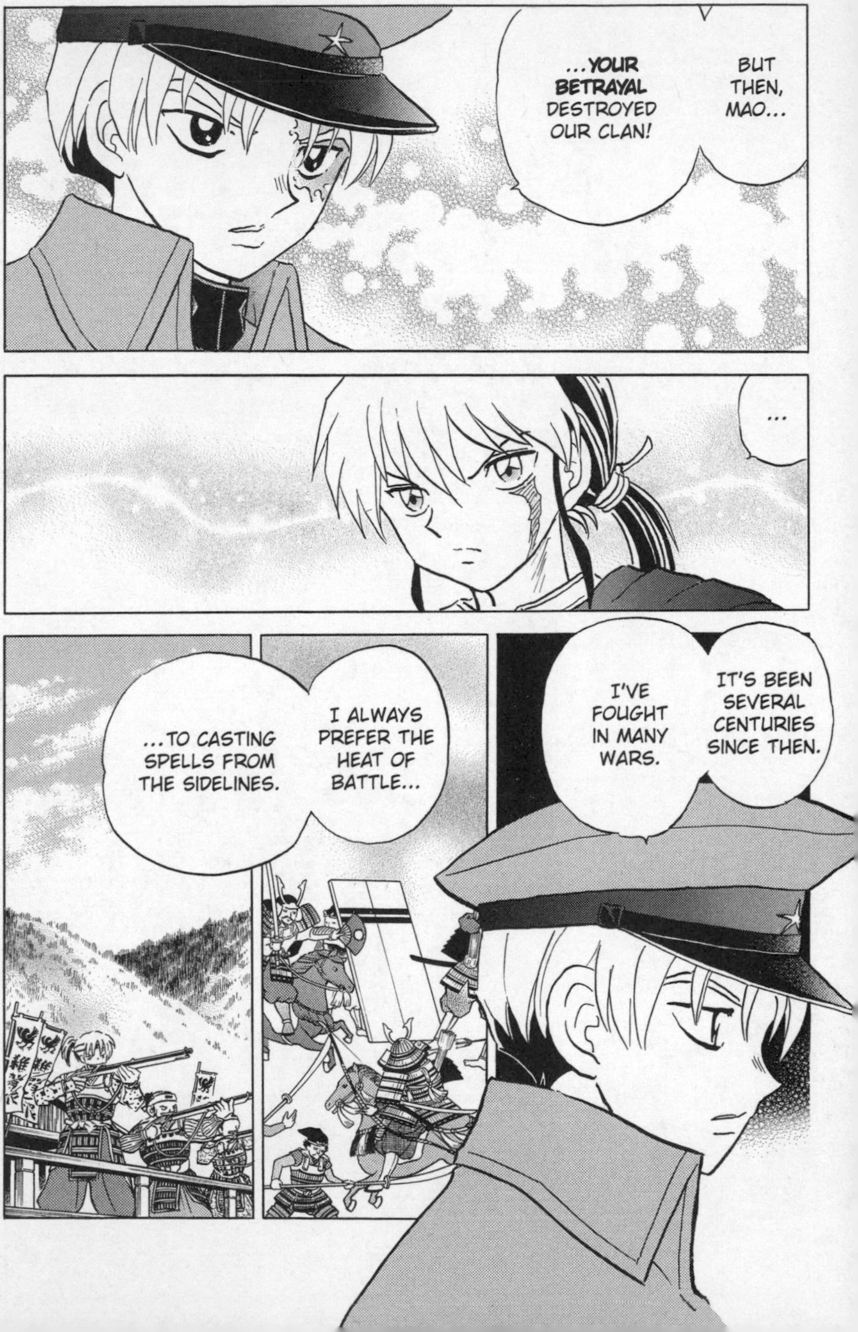
BUT THEN, MAO...
...**YOUR BETRAYAL** DESTROYED OUR CLAN!
...
IT'S BEEN SEVERAL CENTURIES SINCE THEN.
I'VE FOUGHT IN MANY WARS.
I ALWAYS PREFER THE HEAT OF BATTLE...
...TO CASTING SPELLS FROM THE SIDELINES.

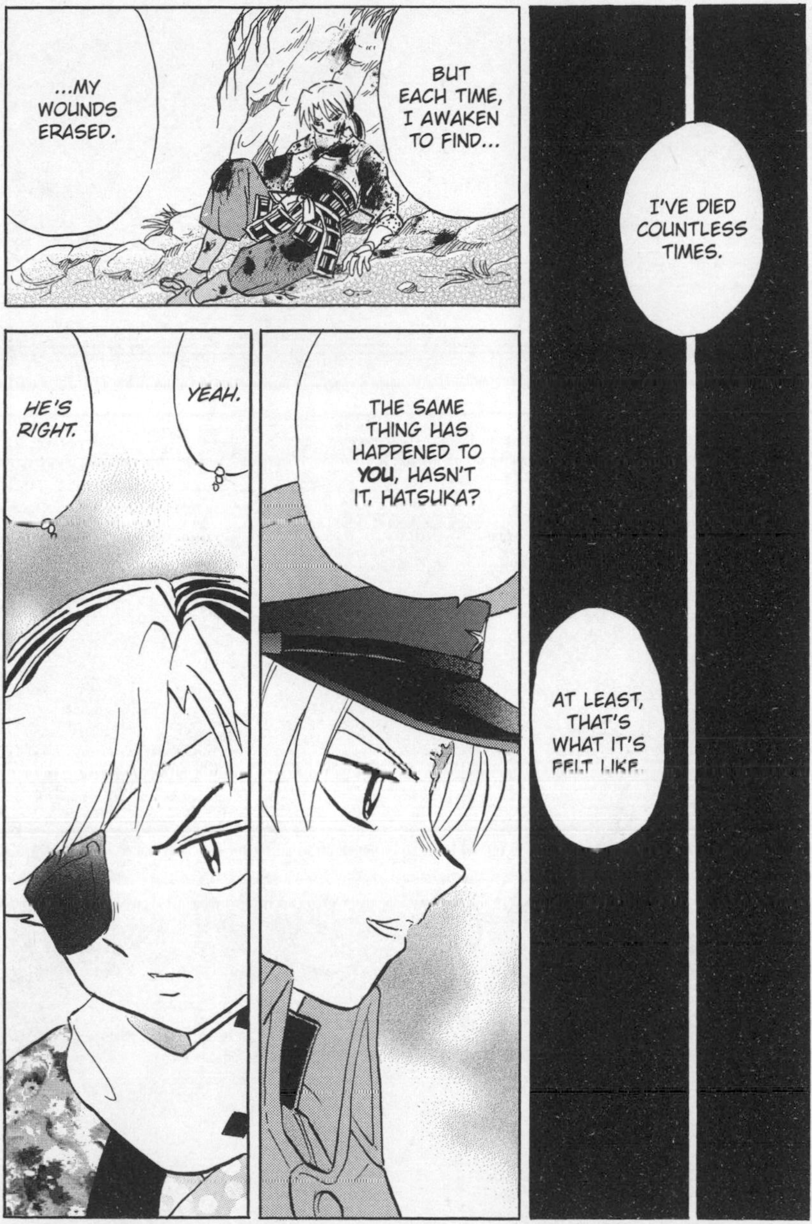
I'VE DIED COUNTLESS TIMES.
AT LEAST, THAT'S WHAT IT'S FELT LIKE.
BUT EACH TIME, I AWAKEN TO FIND...
...MY WOUNDS ERASED.
THE SAME THING HAS HAPPENED TO **YOU**, HASN'T IT, HATSUKA?
YEAH.
HE'S RIGHT.

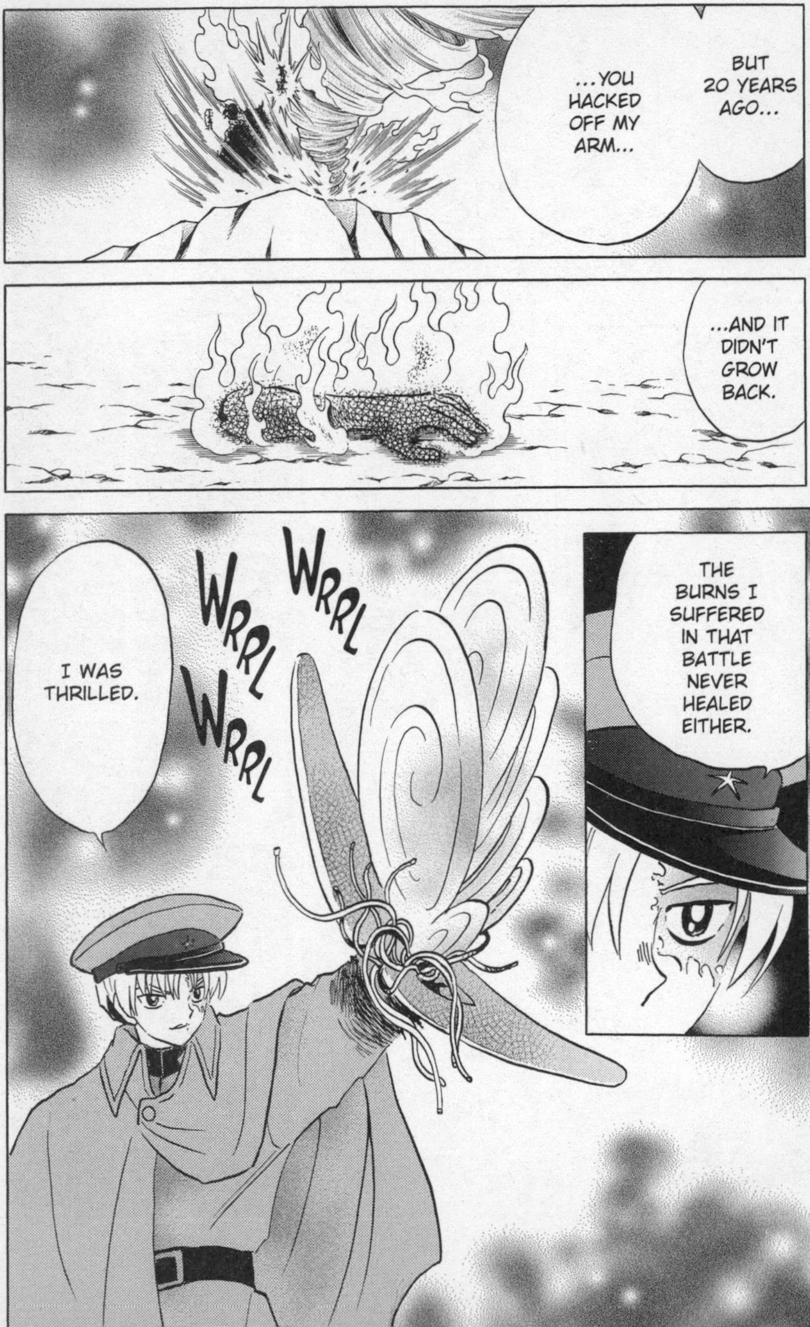
BUT 20 YEARS AGO...
...YOU HACKED OFF MY ARM...
...AND IT DIDN'T GROW BACK.
THE BURNS I SUFFERED IN THAT BATTLE NEVER HEALED EITHER.
WRRL
WRRL
WRRL
I WAS THRILLED.

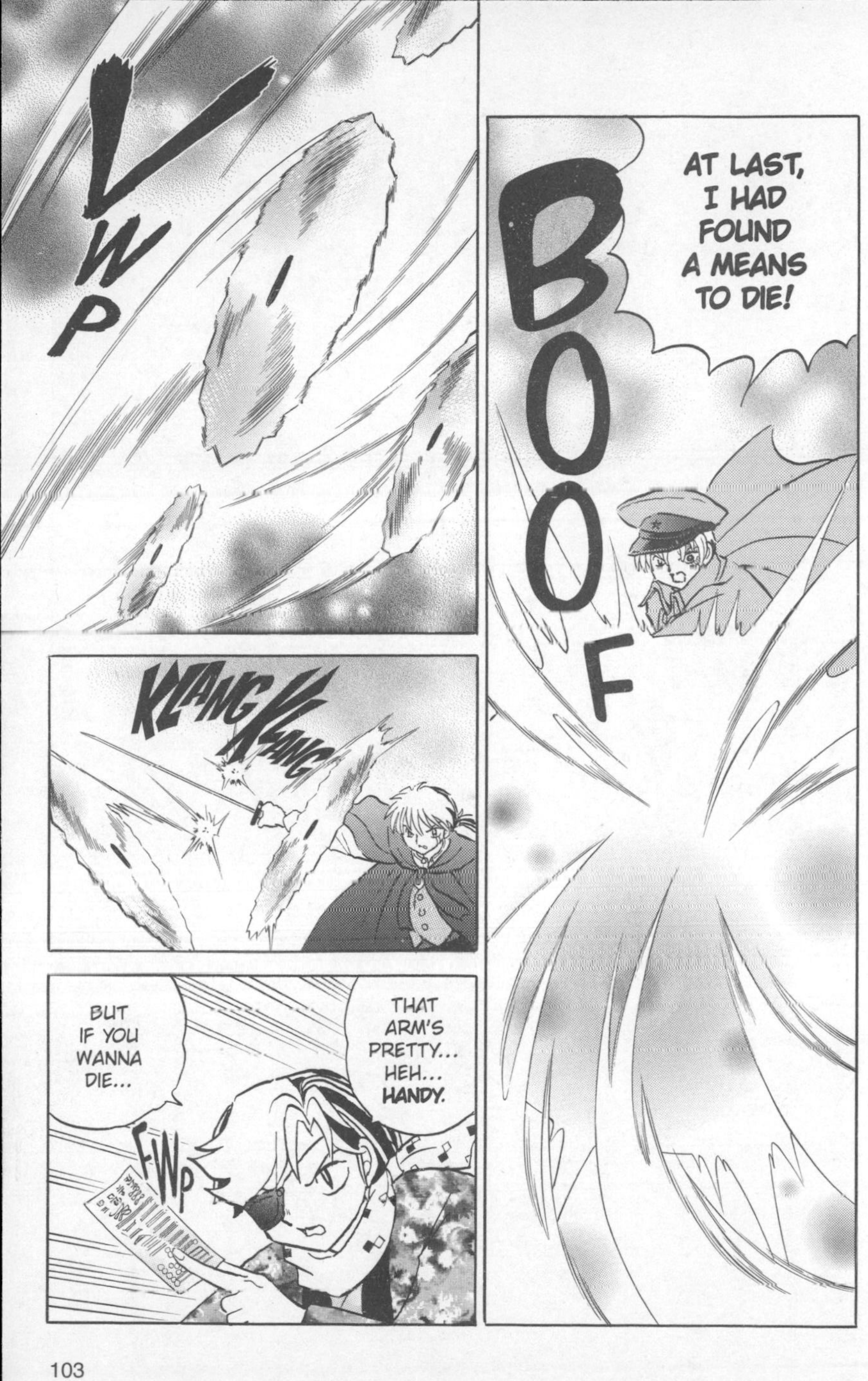
AT LAST, I HAD FOUND A MEANS TO DIE!
BOOOF
VWP
KLANG KLANG
THAT ARM'S PRETTY... HEH... **HANDY.**
BUT IF YOU WANNA DIE...
FWP

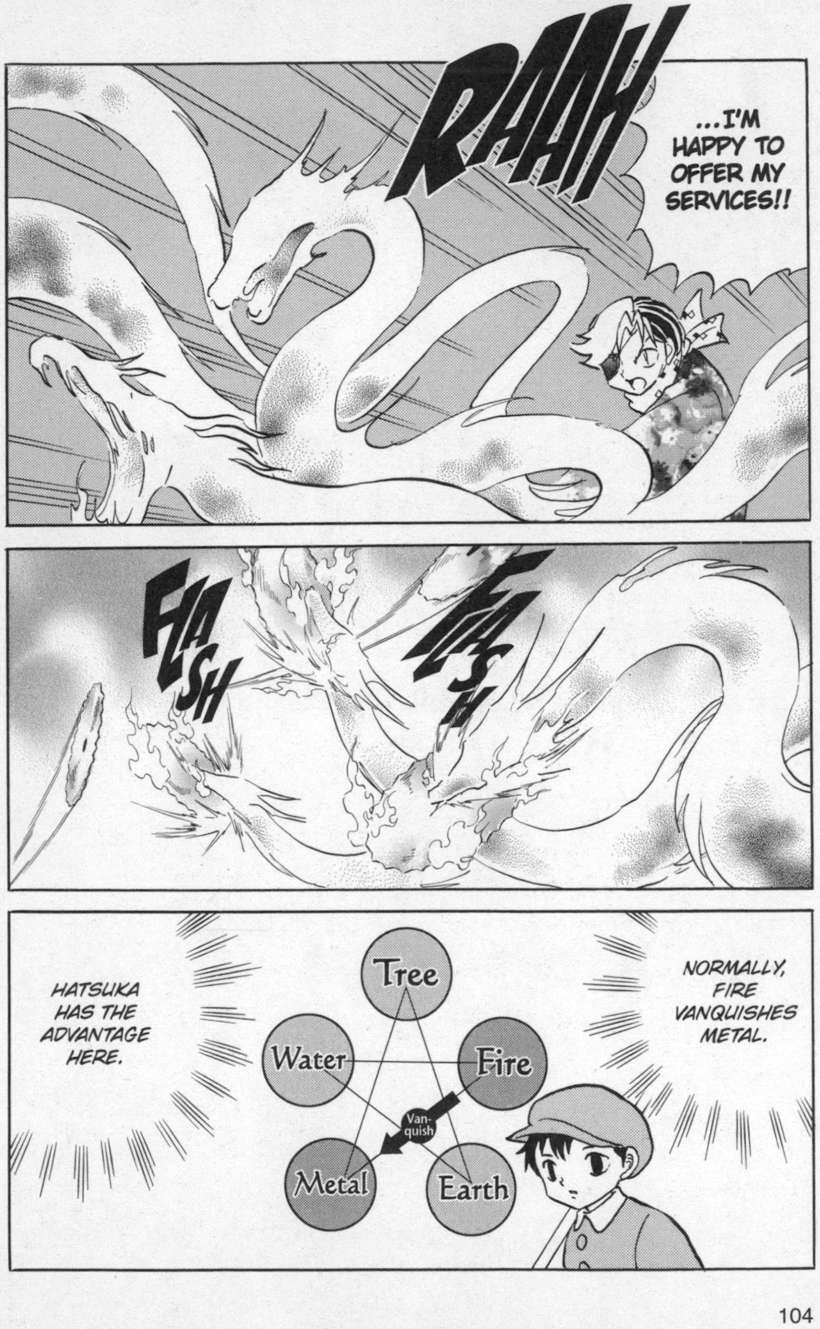
RAAH
...I'M HAPPY TO OFFER MY SERVICES!!
FLASH
FLASH
NORMALLY, FIRE VANQUISHES METAL.
HATSUKA HAS THE ADVANTAGE HERE.
Tree
Water
Fire
Van-quish
Metal
Earth

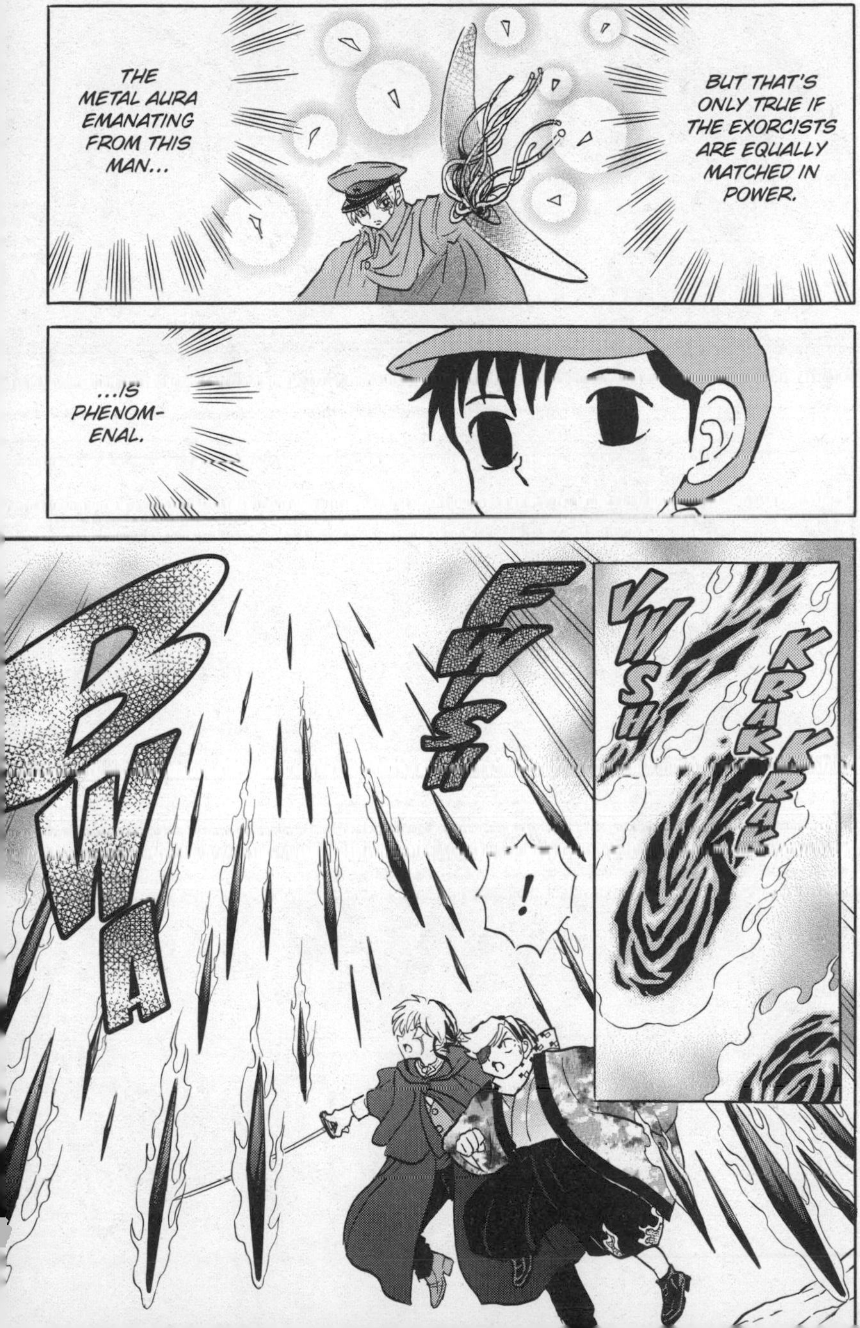
BUT THAT'S ONLY TRUE IF THE EXORCISTS ARE EQUALLY MATCHED IN POWER.
THE METAL AURA EMANATING FROM THIS MAN...
...IS PHENOM-ENAL.
KRAK KRAK
VWSH
FWSH
!
BWA

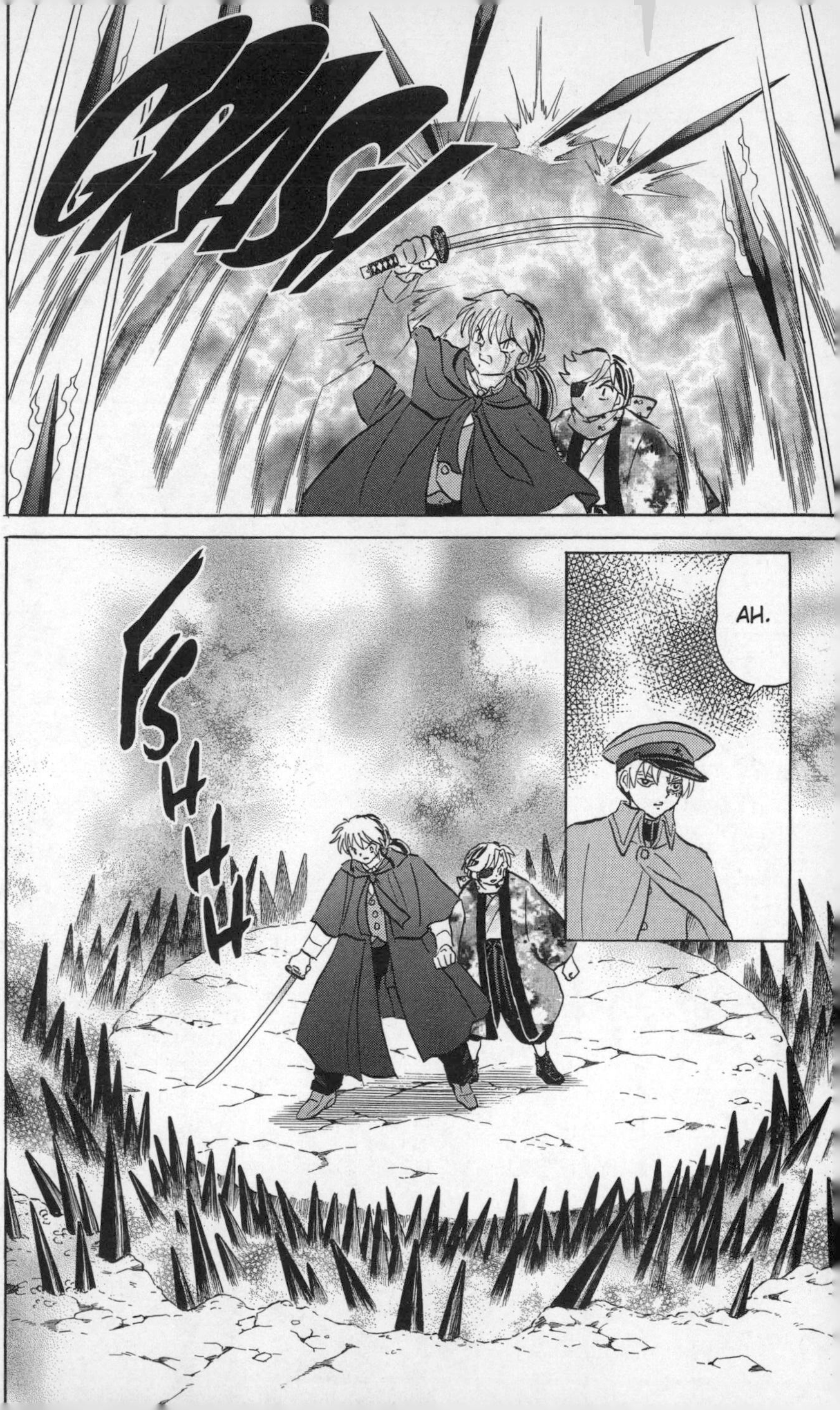
CRASH!
AH.
FSHHHH

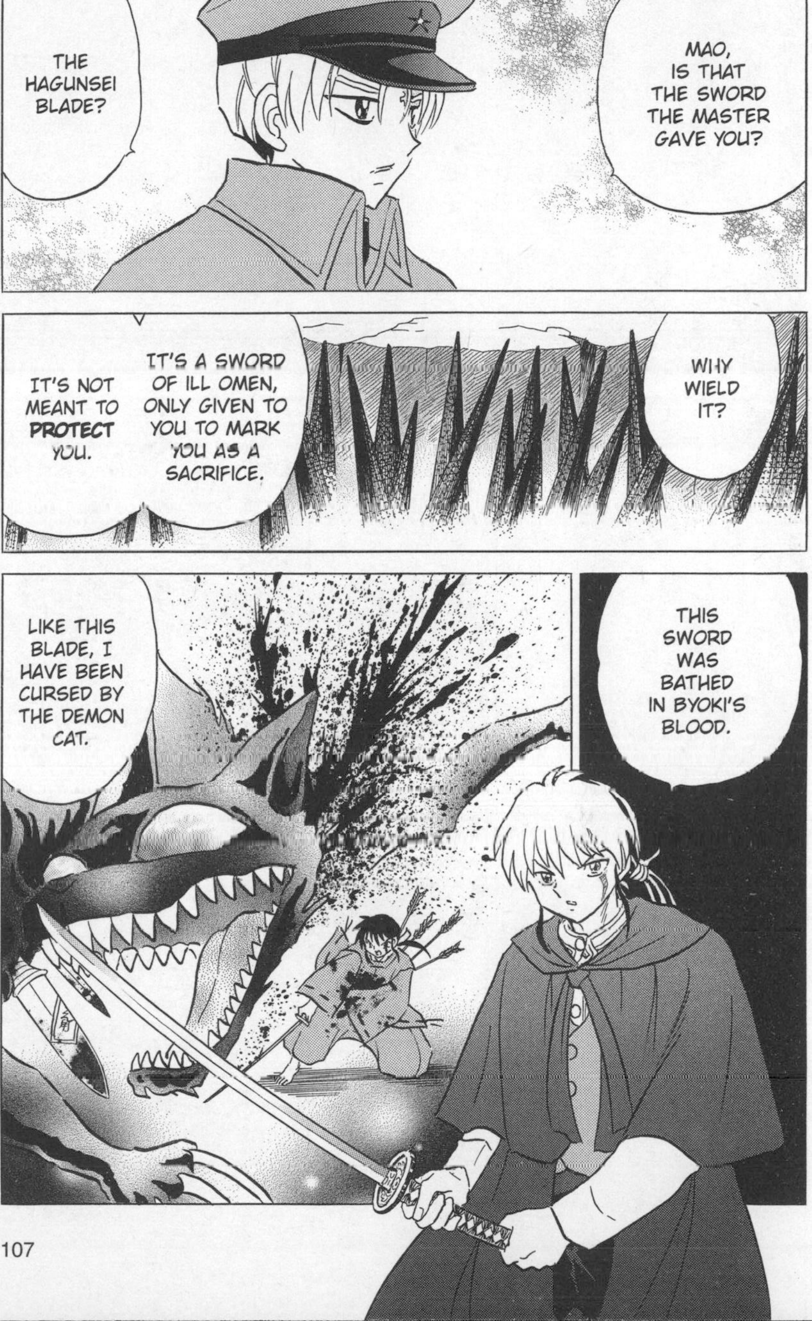
MAO, IS THAT THE SWORD THE MASTER GAVE YOU?
THE HAGUNSEI BLADE?
WHY WIELD IT?
IT'S A SWORD OF ILL OMEN, ONLY GIVEN TO YOU TO MARK YOU AS A SACRIFICE.
IT'S NOT MEANT TO **PROTECT** YOU.
THIS SWORD WAS BATHED IN BYOKI'S BLOOD.
LIKE THIS BLADE, I HAVE BEEN CURSED BY THE DEMON CAT.

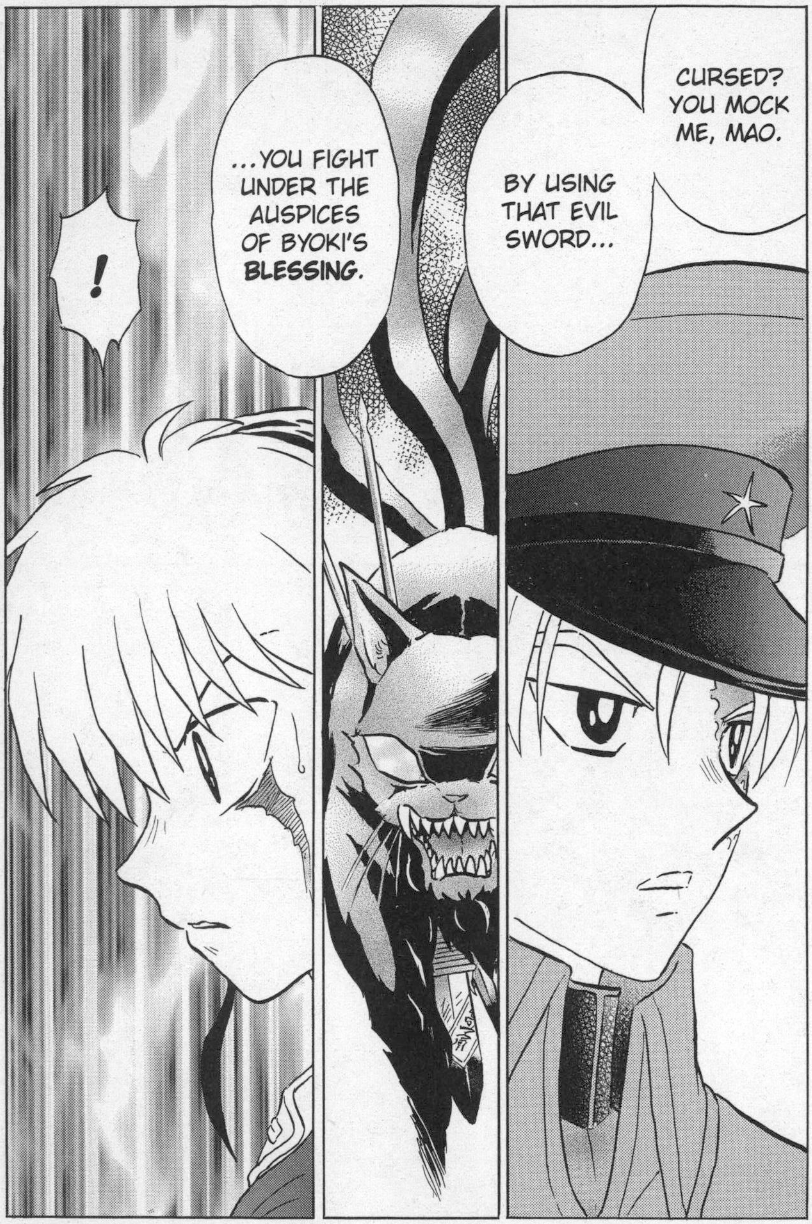
CURSED? YOU MOCK ME, MAO.
BY USING THAT EVIL SWORD...
...YOU FIGHT UNDER THE AUSPICES OF BYOKI'S **BLESSING.**
!

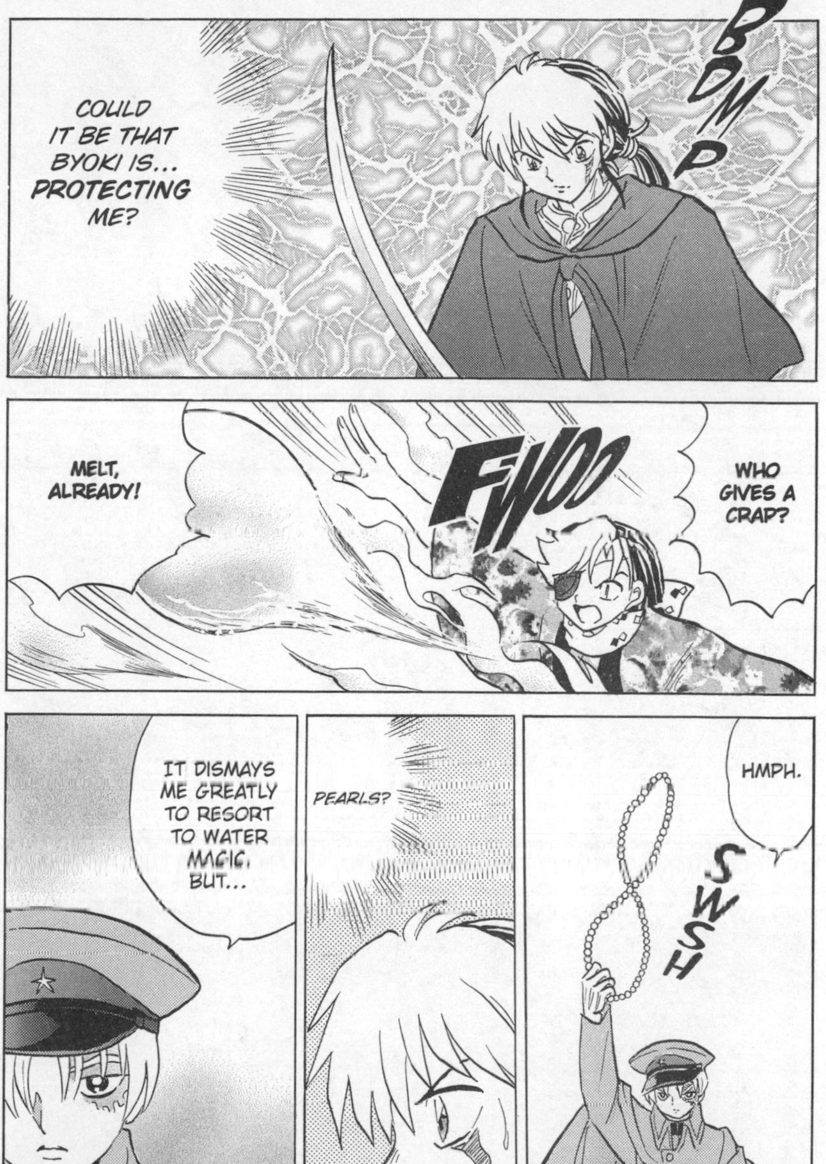
BDMP
COULD IT BE THAT BYOKI IS... PROTECTING ME?
WHO GIVES A CRAP?
FWOO
MELT, ALREADY!
HMPH.
SWSH
PEARLS?
IT DISMAYS ME GREATLY TO RESORT TO WATER MAGIC, BUT...

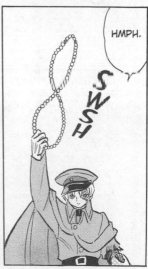

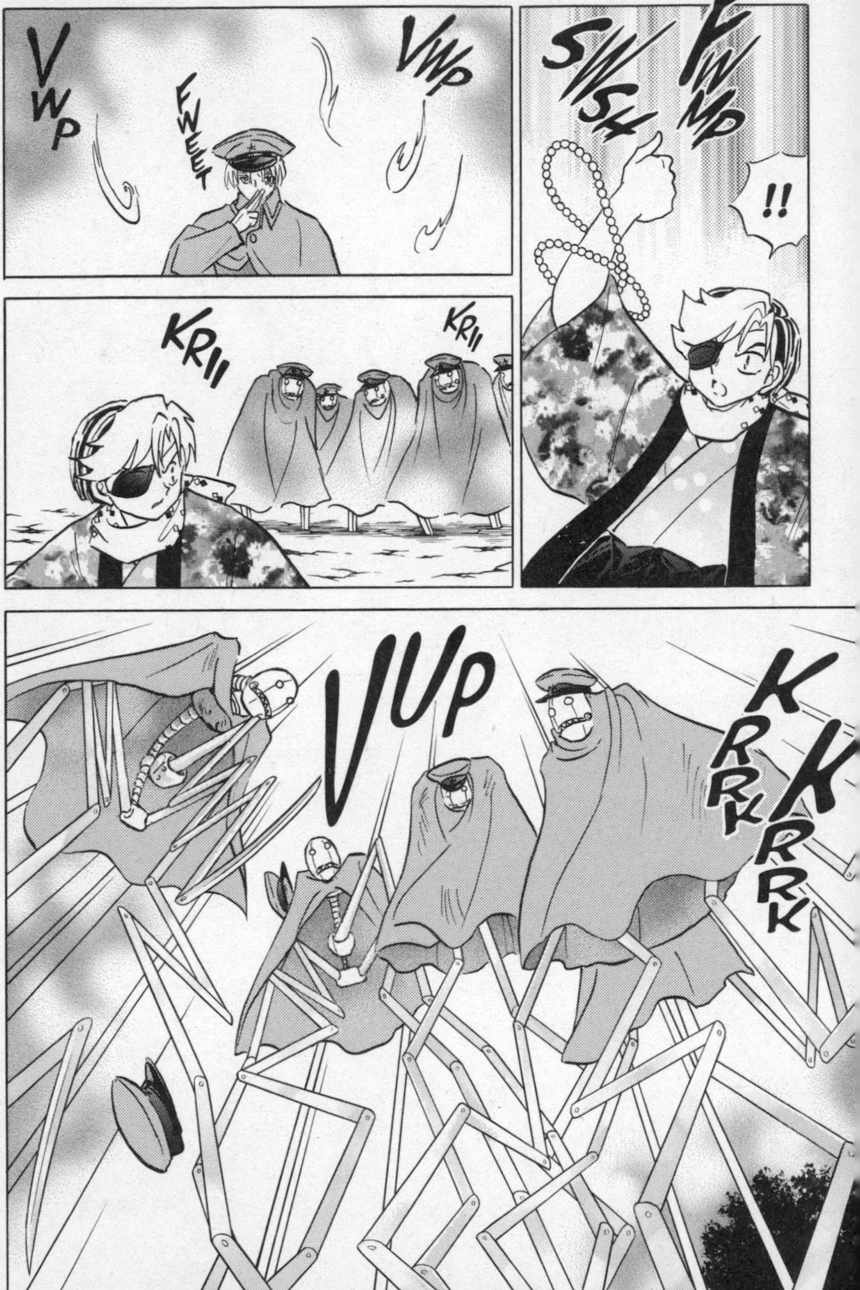
FWMP
SWISH
!!
VWP
FWEET
VWP
KRII
KRII
KRRRK
KRRRK
VUP

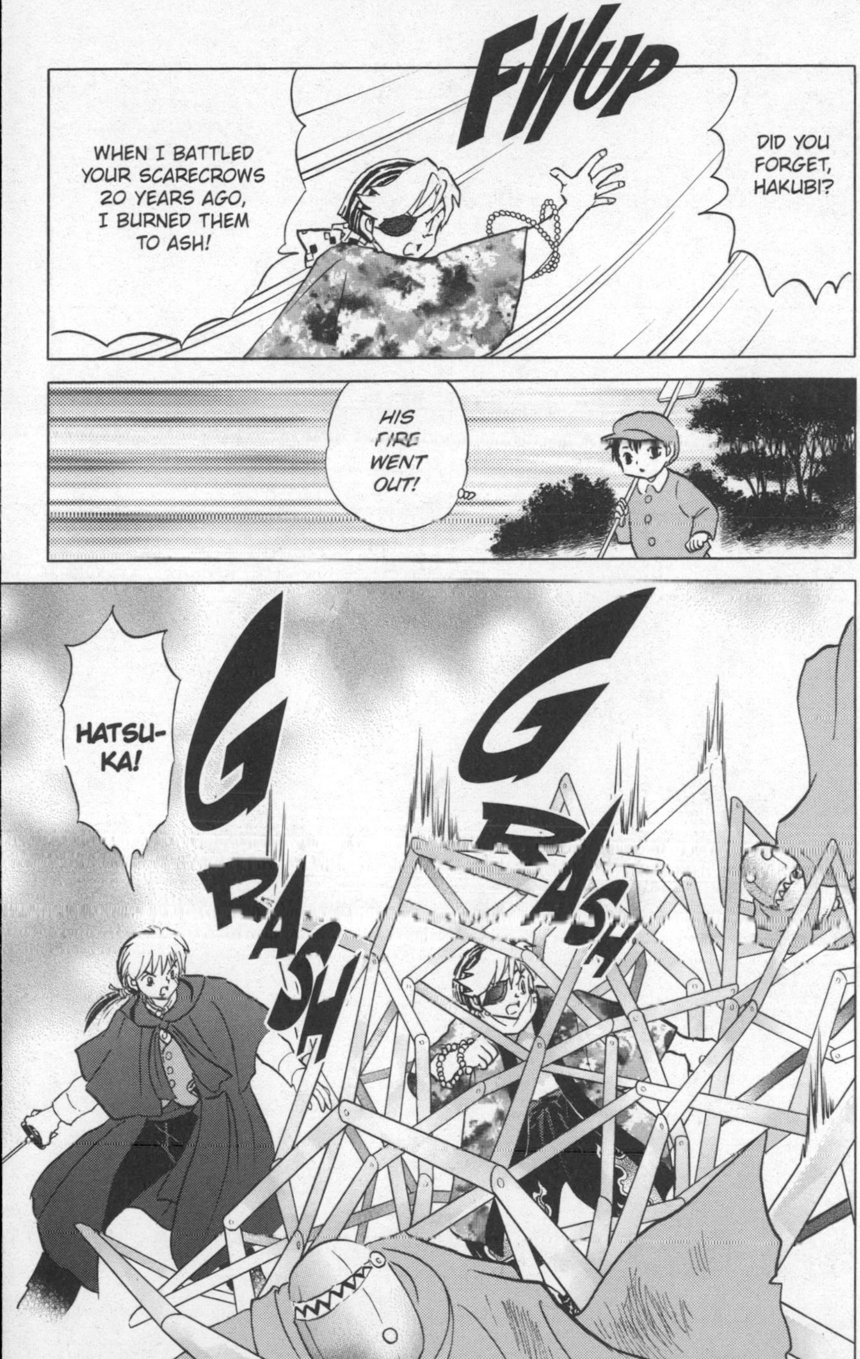
FWUP
DID YOU FORGET, HAKUBI?
WHEN I BATTLED YOUR SCARECROWS 20 YEARS AGO, I BURNED THEM TO ASH!
HIS FIRE WENT OUT!
GRASH
GRASH
HATSU-KA!

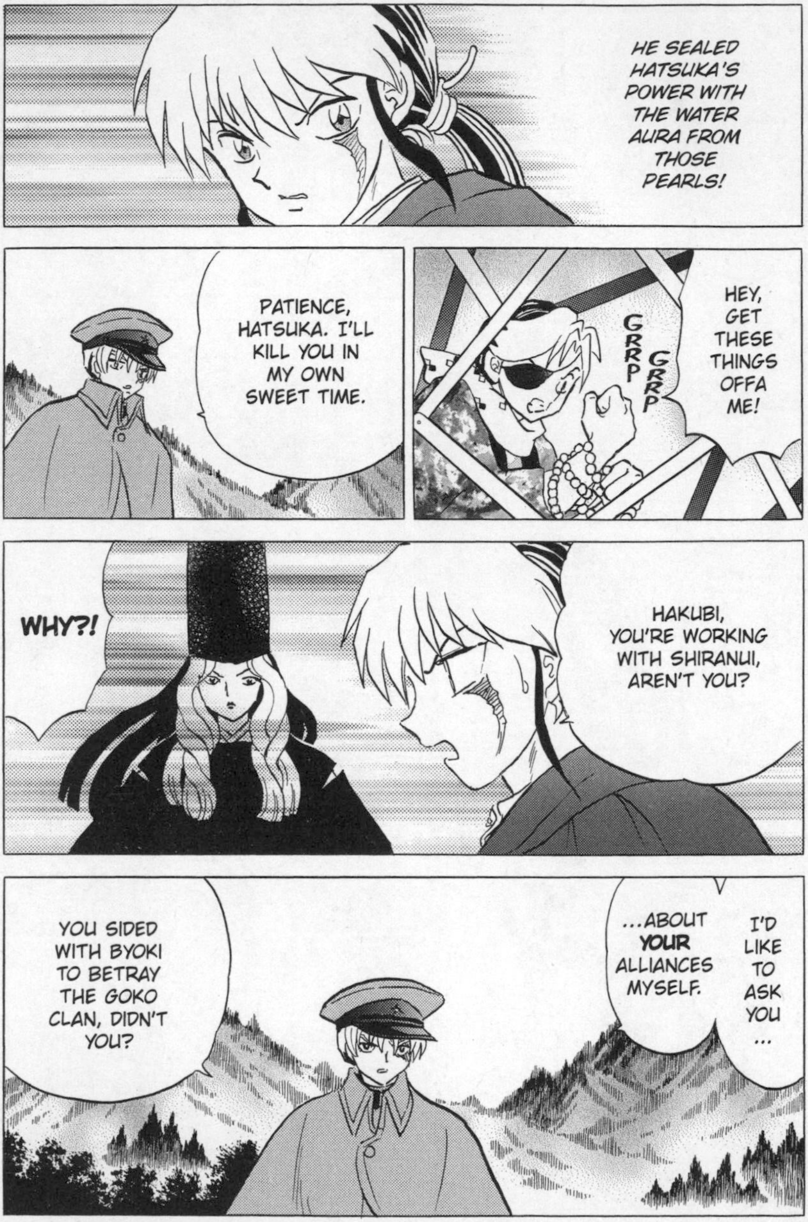
HE SEALED HATSUKA'S POWER WITH THE WATER AURA FROM THOSE PEARLS!
HEY, GET THESE THINGS OFFA ME!
GRRP GRRP
PATIENCE, HATSUKA. I'LL KILL YOU IN MY OWN SWEET TIME.
HAKUBI, YOU'RE WORKING WITH SHIRANUI, AREN'T YOU?
WHY?!
I'D LIKE TO ASK YOU ...
...ABOUT **YOUR** ALLIANCES MYSELF.
YOU SIDED WITH BYOKI TO BETRAY THE GOKO CLAN, DIDN'T YOU?

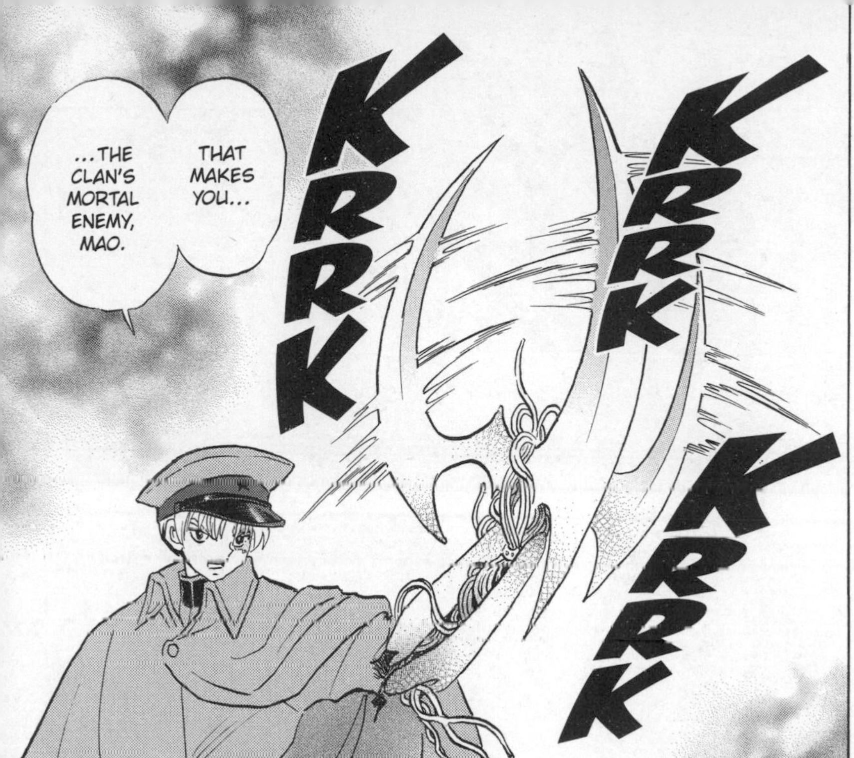
KRRK
KRRK
KRRK
THAT MAKES YOU...
...THE CLAN'S MORTAL ENEMY, MAO.

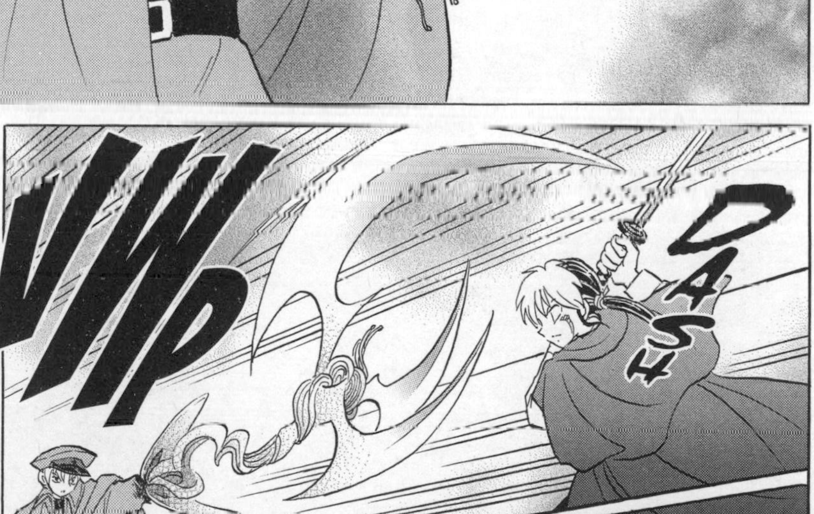
DASH
VWIP

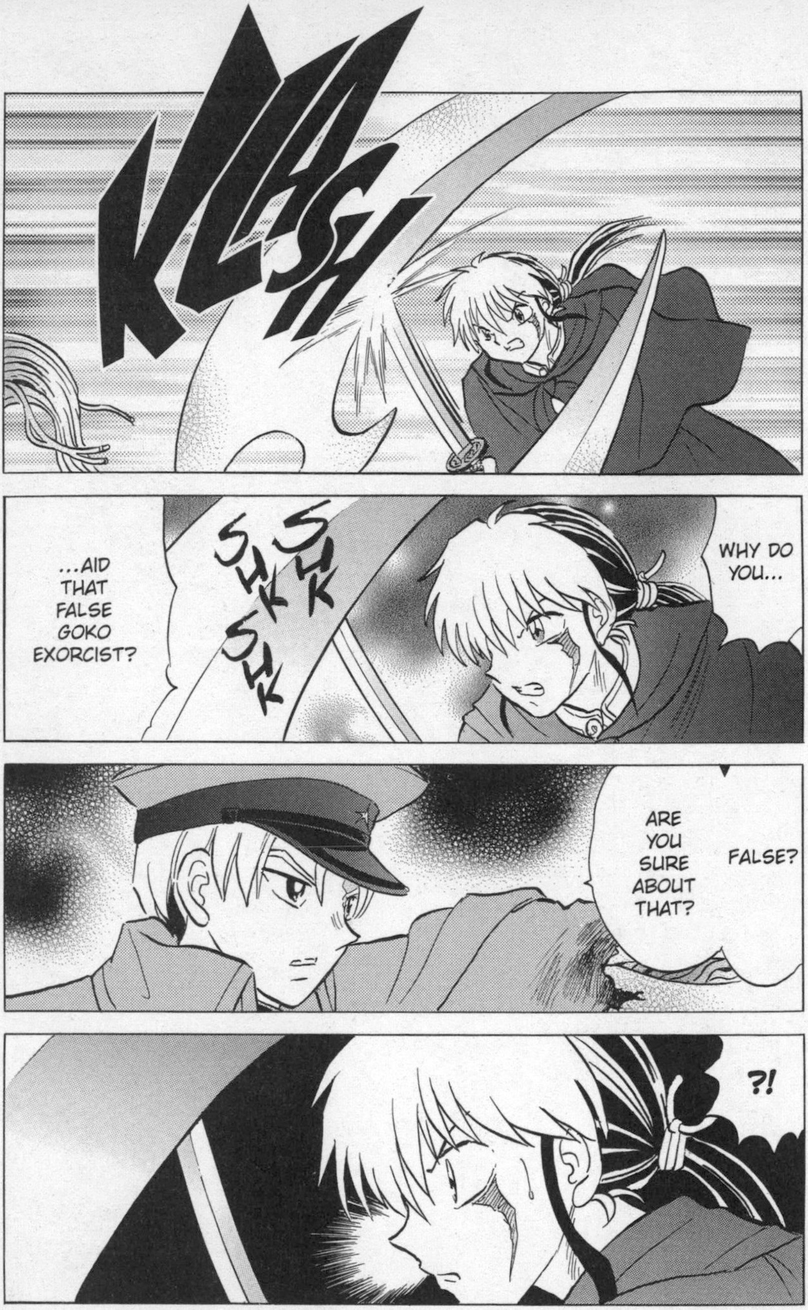
KLASH
WHY DO YOU...
SHK SHK
SHK
...AID THAT FALSE GOKO EXORCIST?
FALSE?
ARE YOU SURE ABOUT THAT?
?!

Chapter 7:
A Woman of the Goko Clan

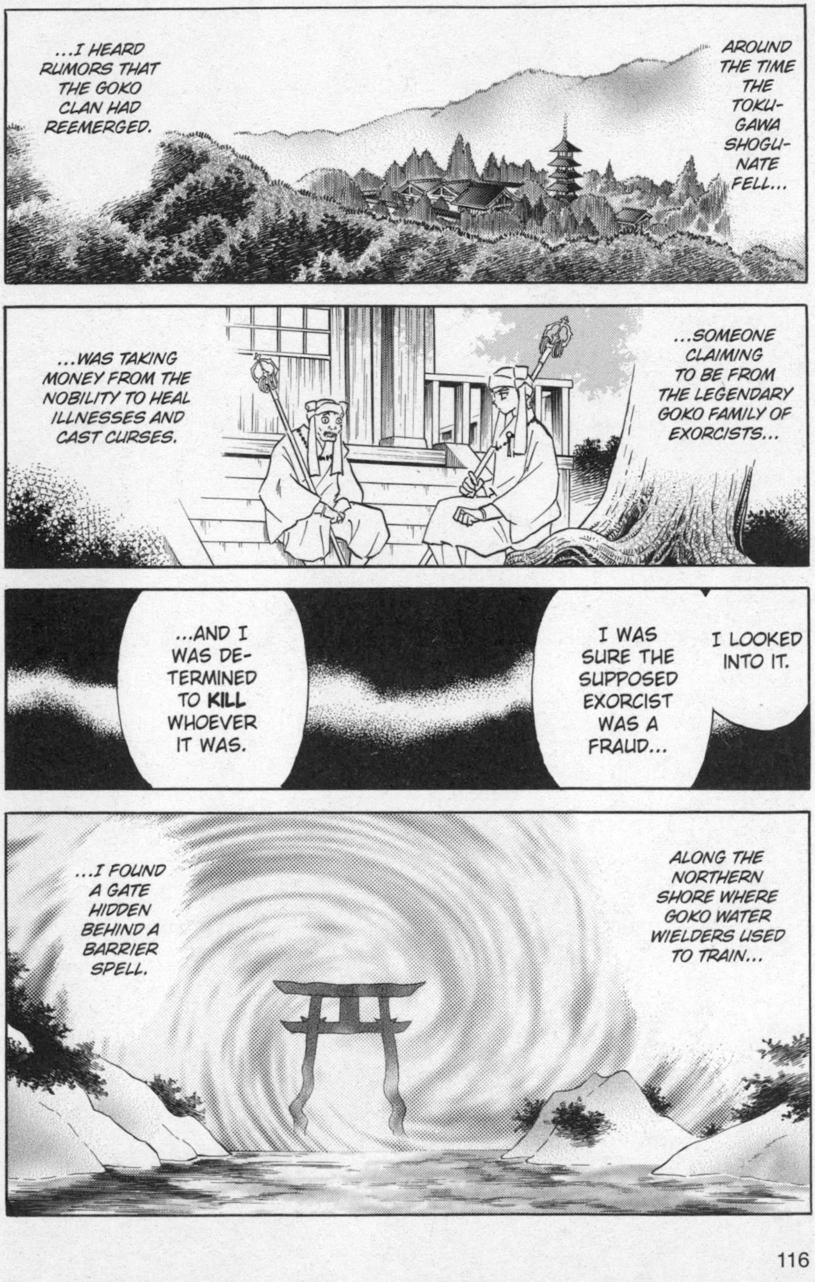
AROUND THE TIME THE TOKU-GAWA SHOGU-NATE FELL...
...I HEARD RUMORS THAT THE GOKO CLAN HAD REEMERGED.
...SOMEONE CLAIMING TO BE FROM THE LEGENDARY GOKO FAMILY OF EXORCISTS...
...WAS TAKING MONEY FROM THE NOBILITY TO HEAL ILLNESSES AND CAST CURSES.
I LOOKED INTO IT.
I WAS SURE THE SUPPOSED EXORCIST WAS A FRAUD...
...AND I WAS DE-TERMINED TO **KILL** WHOEVER IT WAS.
ALONG THE NORTHERN SHORE WHERE GOKO WATER WIELDERS USED TO TRAIN...
...I FOUND A GATE HIDDEN BEHIND A BARRIER SPELL.

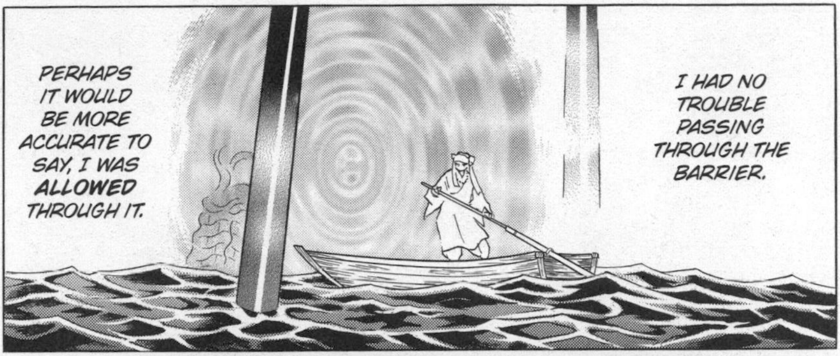
I HAD NO TROUBLE PASSING THROUGH THE BARRIER.
PERHAPS IT WOULD BE MORE ACCURATE TO SAY, I WAS **ALLOWED** THROUGH IT.
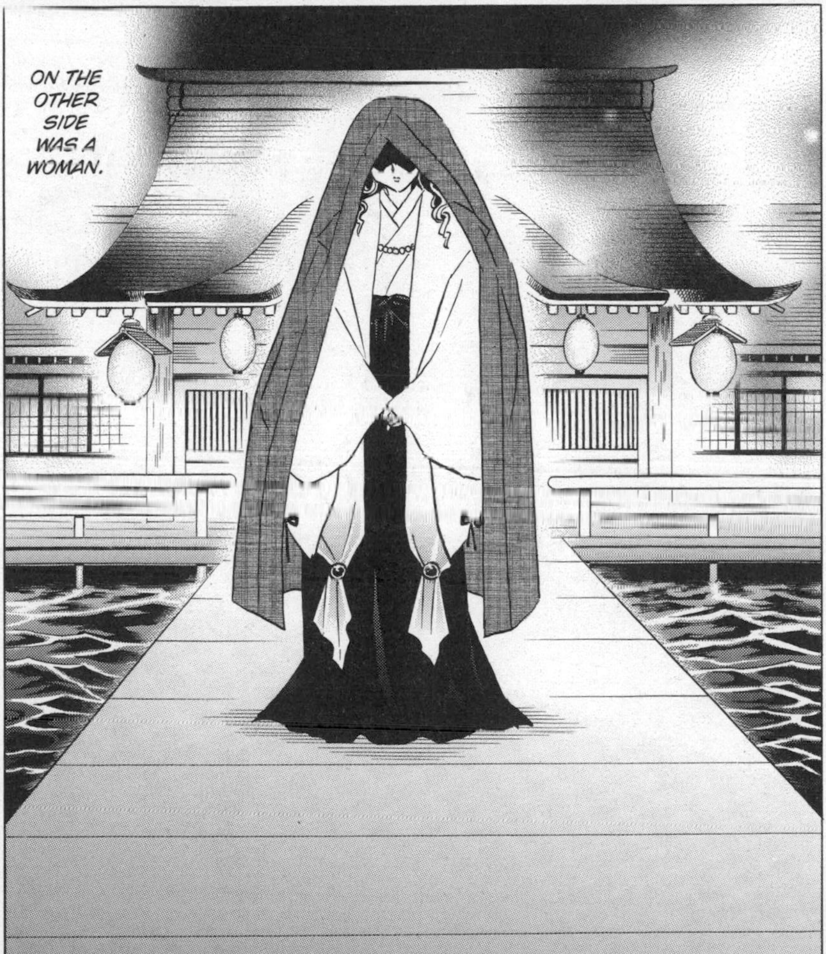
ON THE OTHER SIDE WAS A WOMAN.

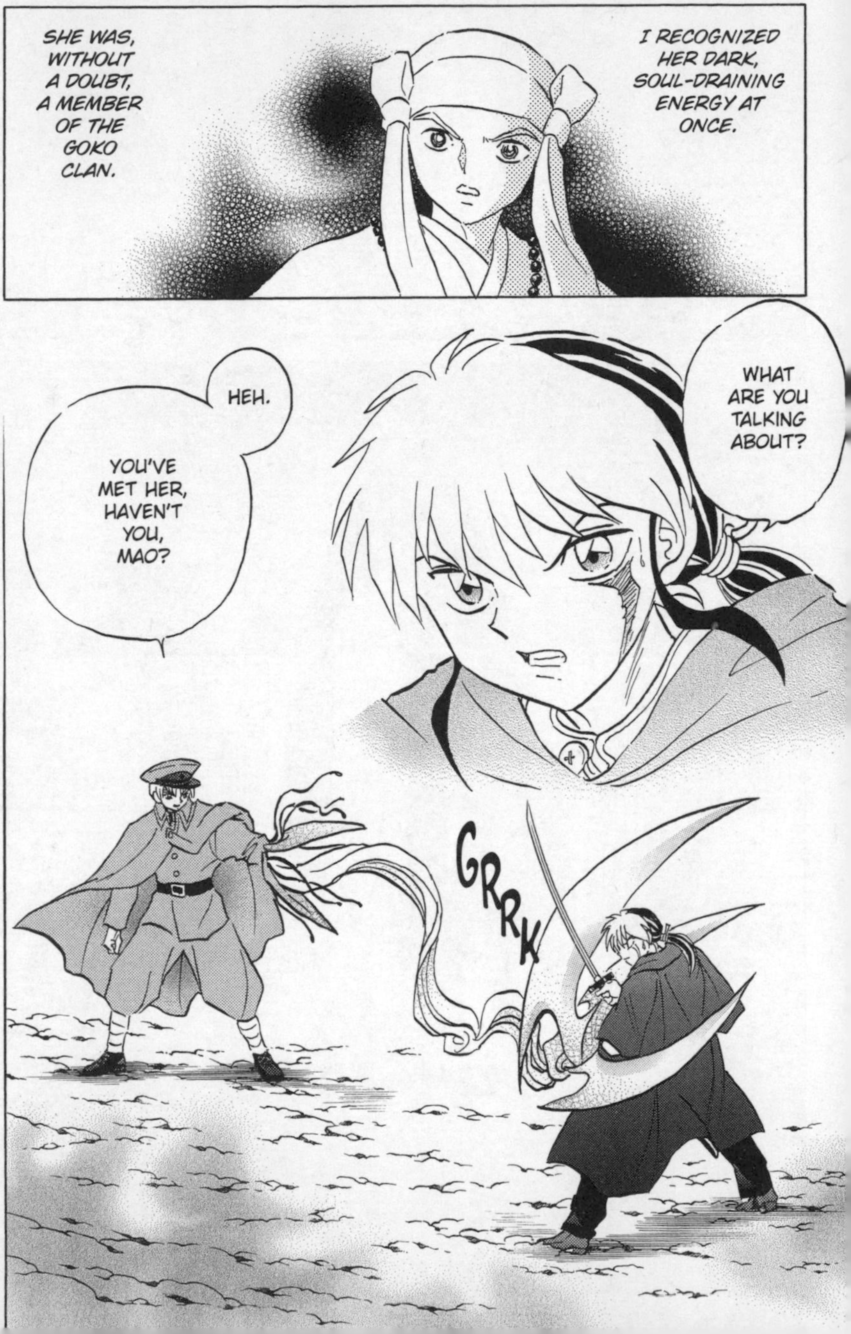
I RECOGNIZED HER DARK, SOUL-DRAINING ENERGY AT ONCE.
SHE WAS, WITHOUT A DOUBT, A MEMBER OF THE GOKO CLAN.
WHAT ARE YOU TALKING ABOUT?
HEH.
YOU'VE MET HER, HAVEN'T YOU, MAO?
GRRK

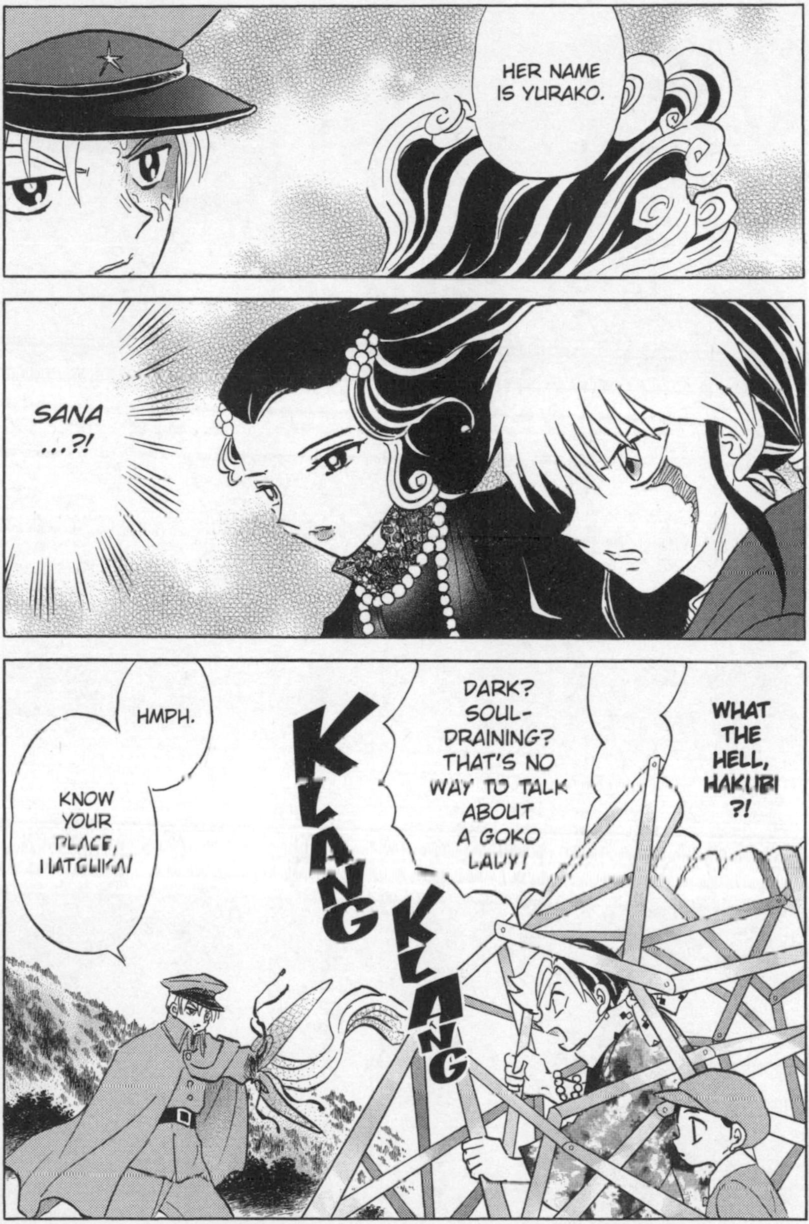
HER NAME IS YURAKO.
SANA ...?!
WHAT THE HELL, HAKUBI?!
DARK? SOUL-DRAINING? THAT'S NO WAY TO TALK ABOUT A GOKO LADY!
KLANG
KLANG
HMPH.
KNOW YOUR PLACE, HATSUKA!

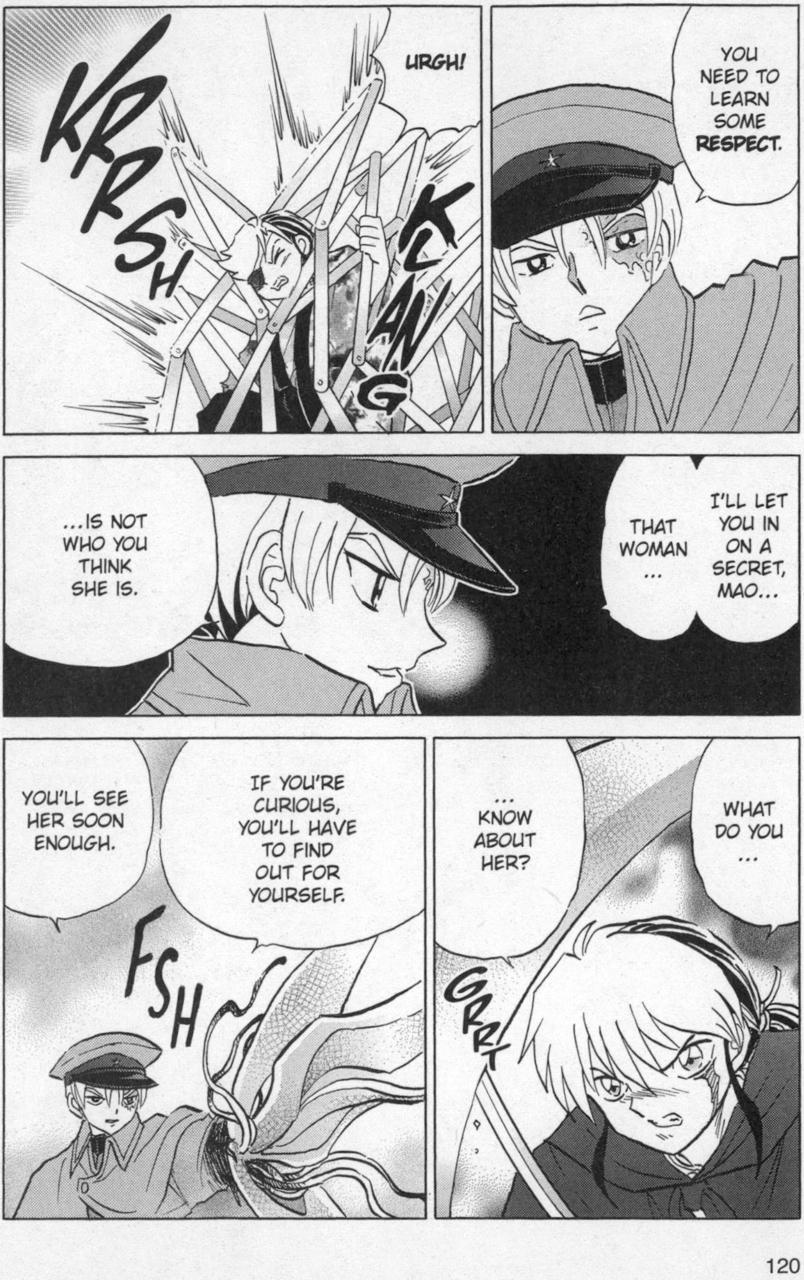
YOU NEED TO LEARN SOME **RESPECT.**
URGH!
KCLANG
KRRSH
I'LL LET YOU IN ON A SECRET, MAO...
THAT WOMAN ...
...IS NOT WHO YOU THINK SHE IS.
WHAT DO YOU ...
... KNOW ABOUT HER?
GRRT
IF YOU'RE CURIOUS, YOU'LL HAVE TO FIND OUT FOR YOURSELF.
YOU'LL SEE HER SOON ENOUGH.
FSH

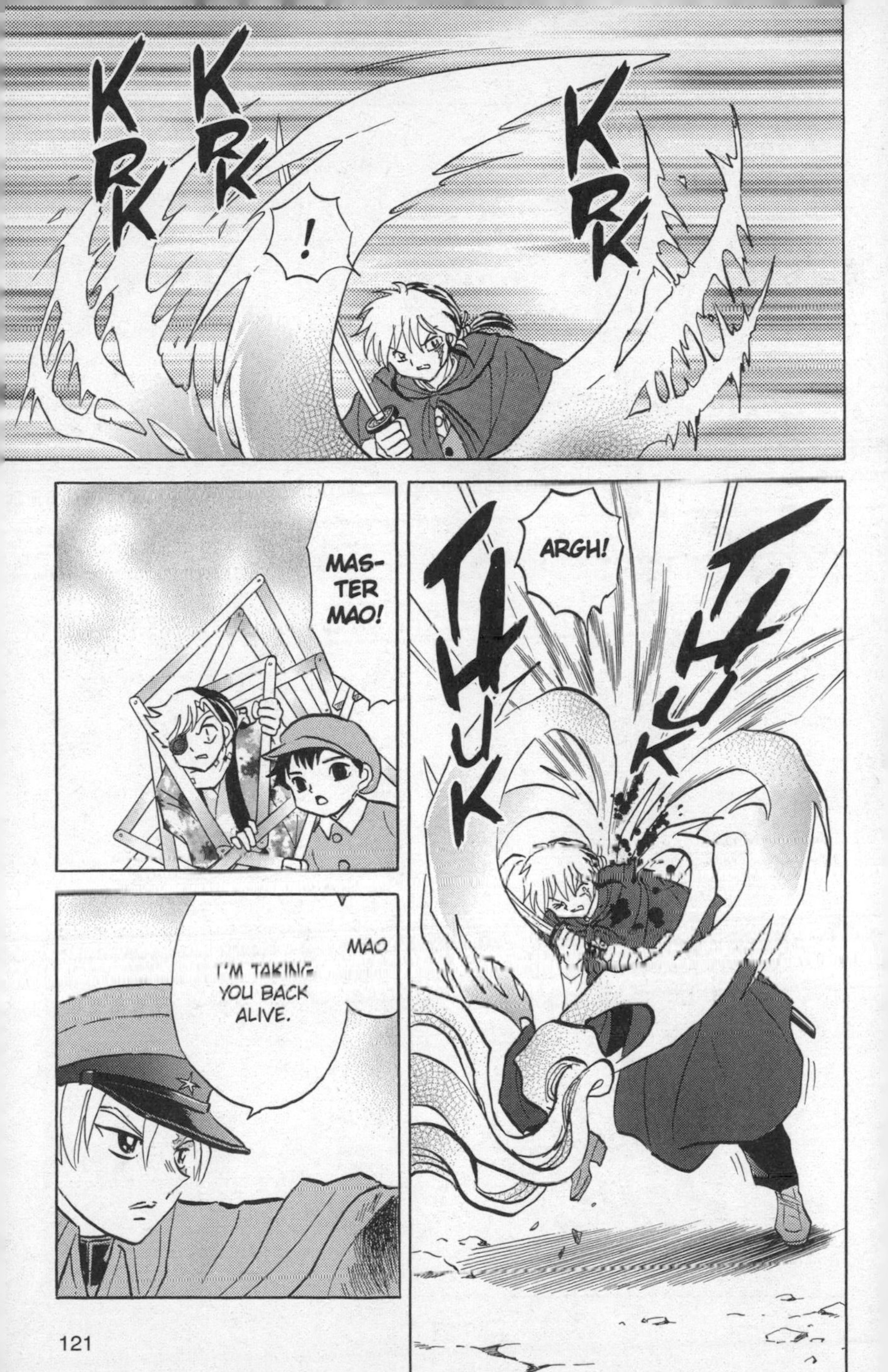
KRK
!
KRK
KRK
ARGH!
THUK
THUK
MAS-
TER
MAO!
MAO
I'M TAKING
YOU BACK
ALIVE.

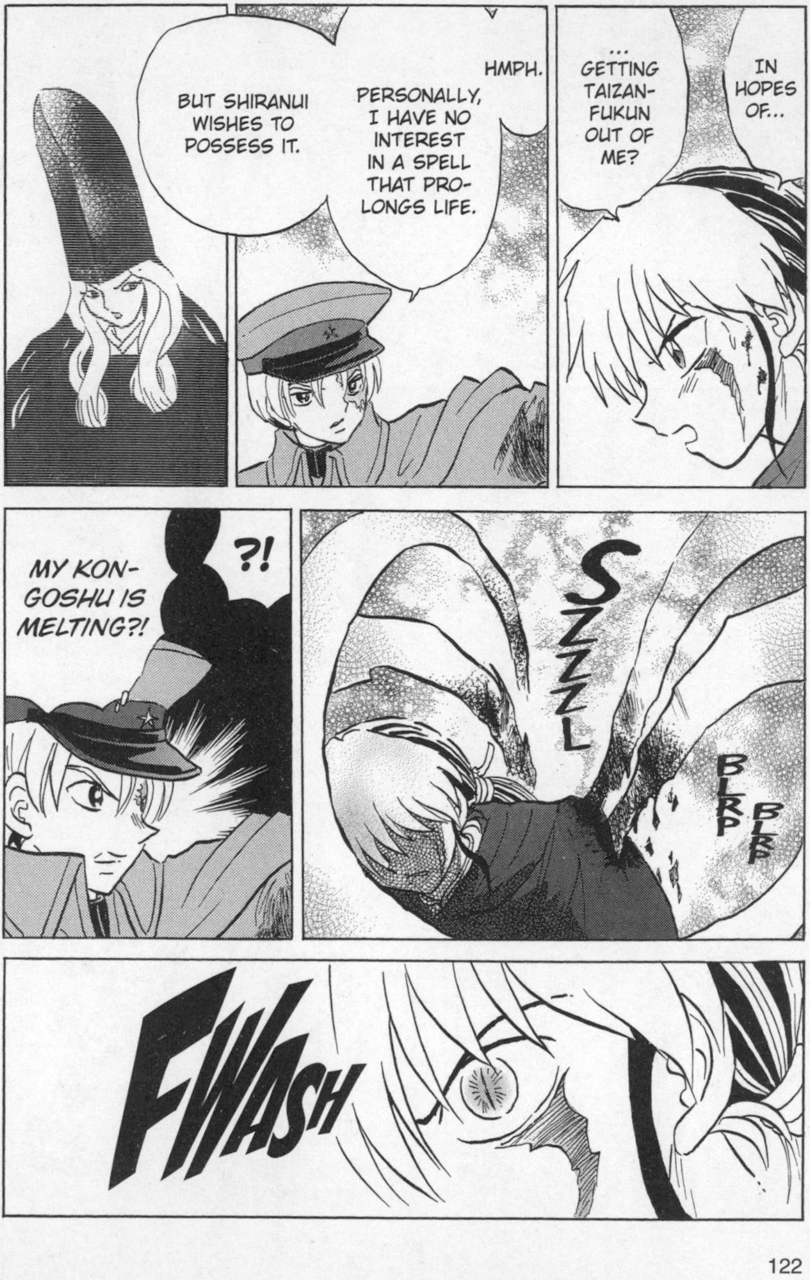
IN HOPES OF...
... GETTING TAIZAN-FUKUN OUT OF ME?
HMPH.
PERSONALLY, I HAVE NO INTEREST IN A SPELL THAT PRO-LONGS LIFE.
BUT SHIRANUI WISHES TO POSSESS IT.
SZZZZL
BLRP BLRP
?!
MY KON-GOSHU IS MELTING?!
FWASH

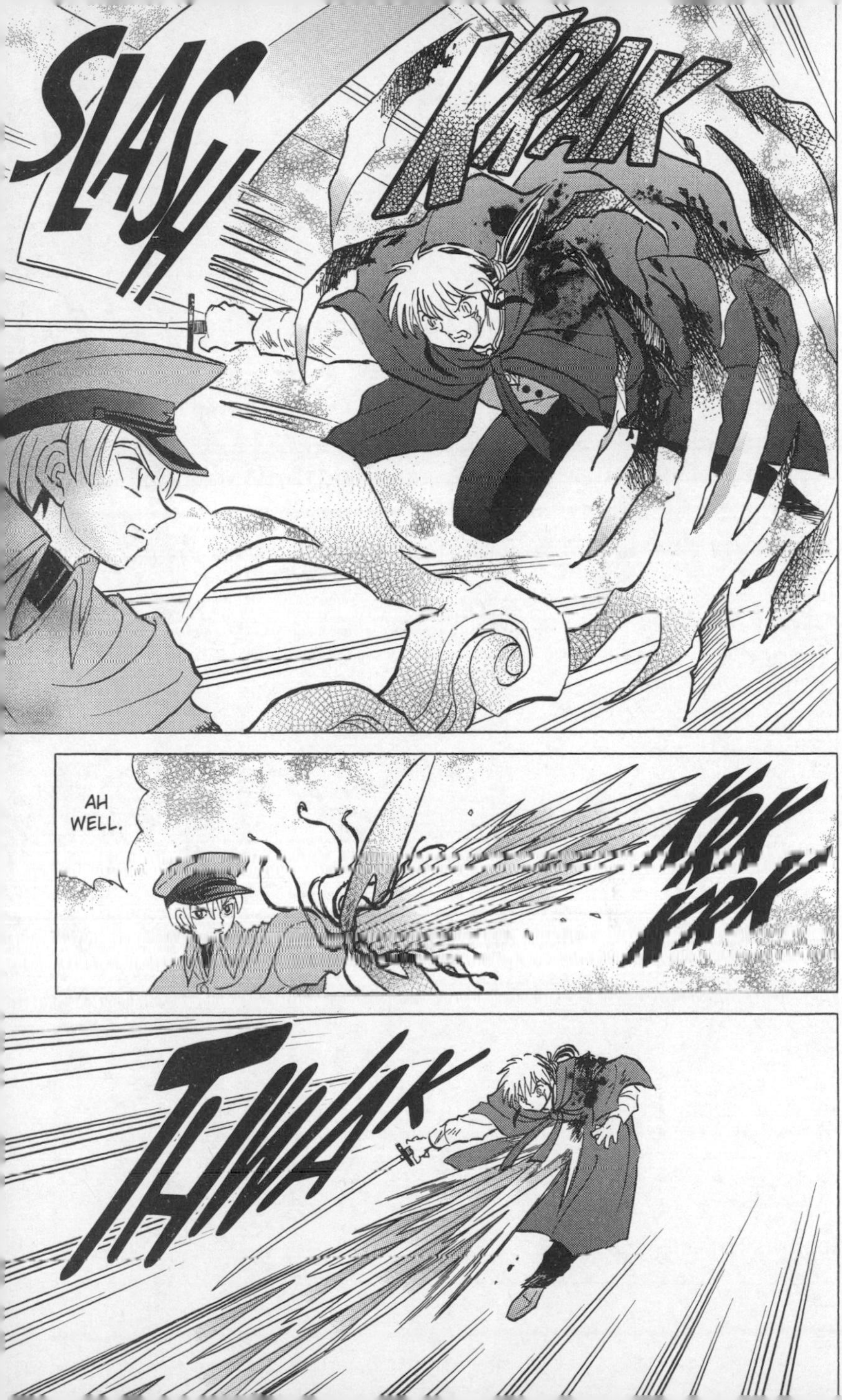
KRAK
SLASH
KRK
KRK
AH WELL.
THWAK

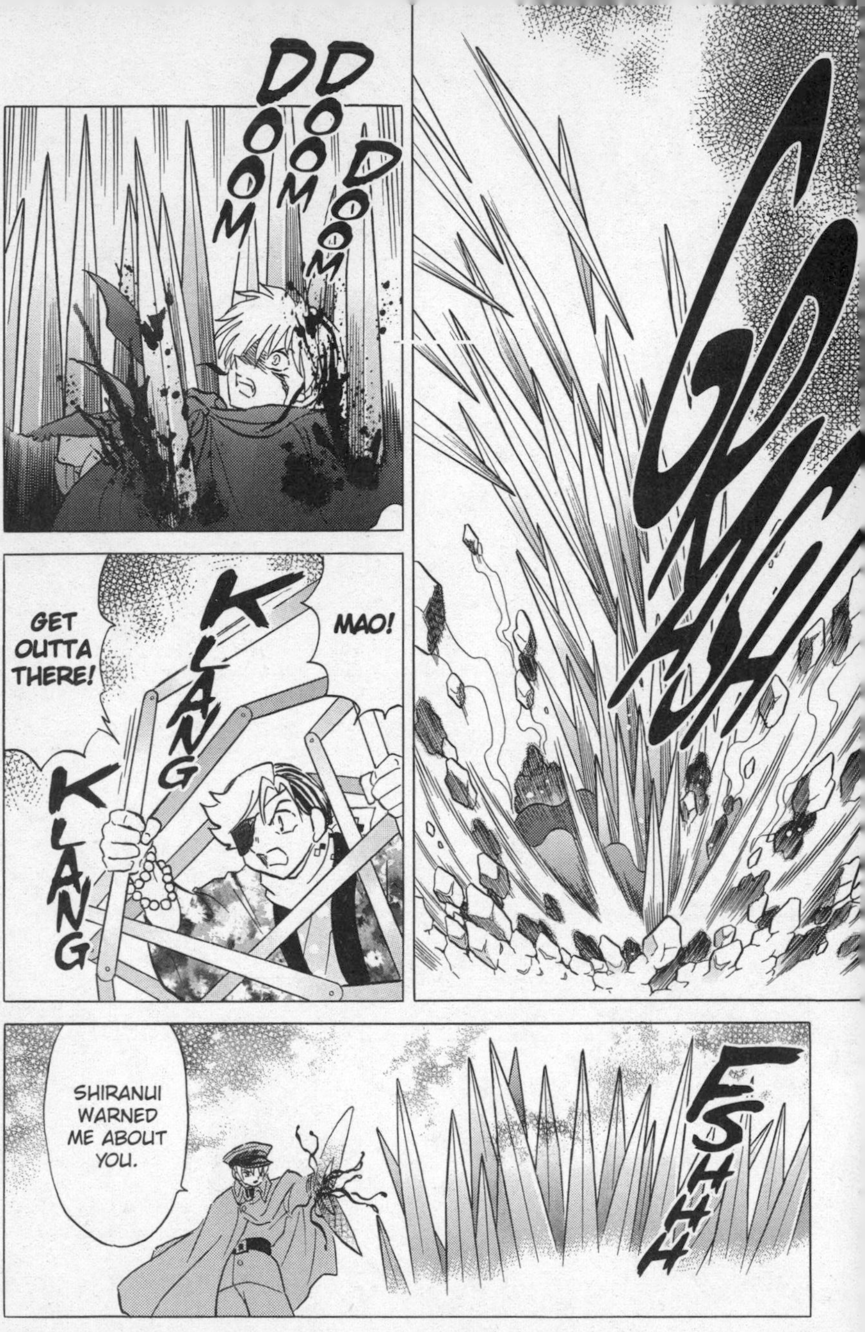
DDOOM DOOOM DOOOM
MAO!
GET OUTTA THERE!
KLANG
KLANG
FSHHHH
SHIRANUI WARNED ME ABOUT YOU.

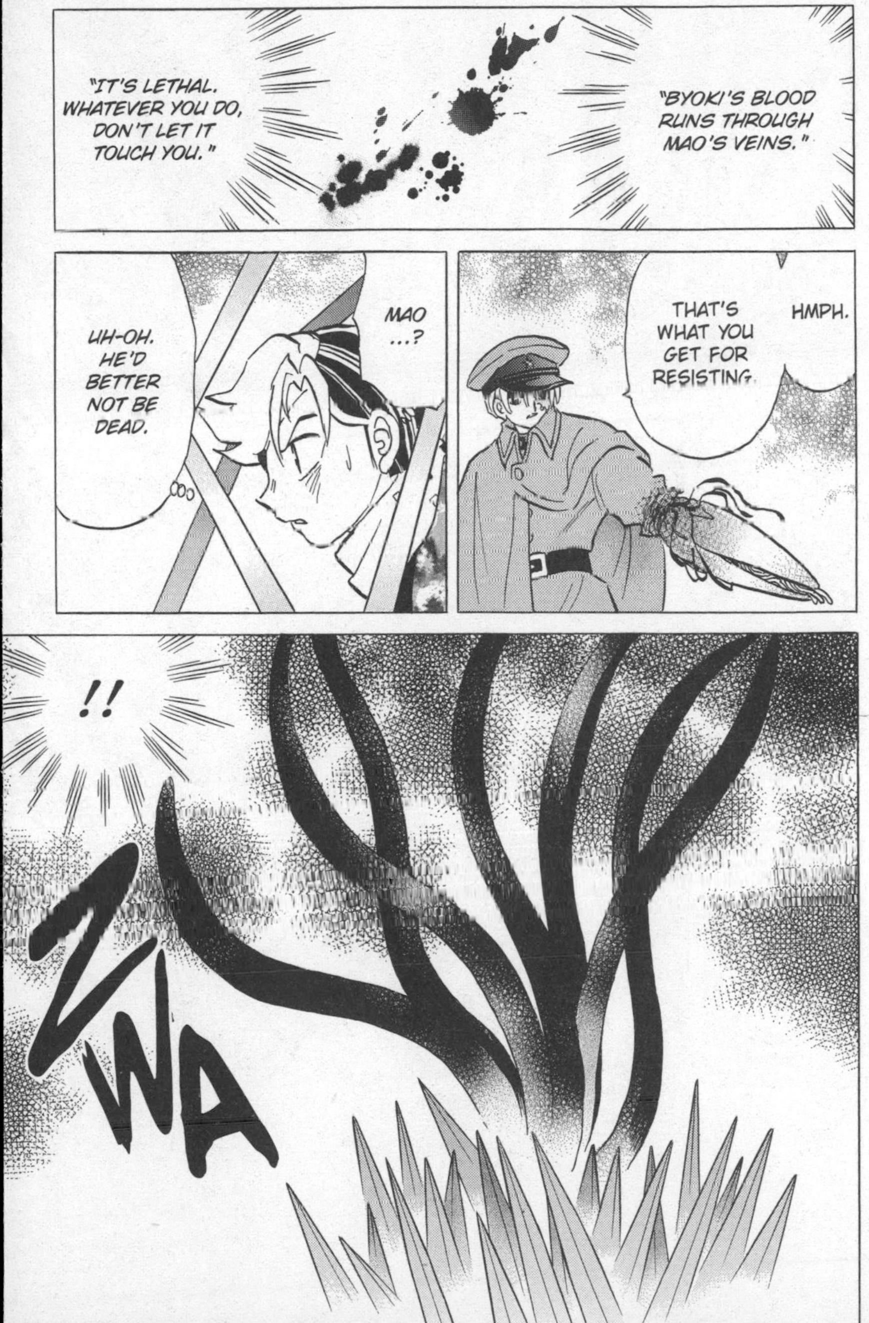
"BYOKI'S BLOOD RUNS THROUGH MAO'S VEINS."
"IT'S LETHAL. WHATEVER YOU DO, DON'T LET IT TOUCH YOU."
HMPH.
THAT'S WHAT YOU GET FOR RESISTING.
MAO ...?
UH-OH. HE'D BETTER NOT BE DEAD.
!!
ZWA

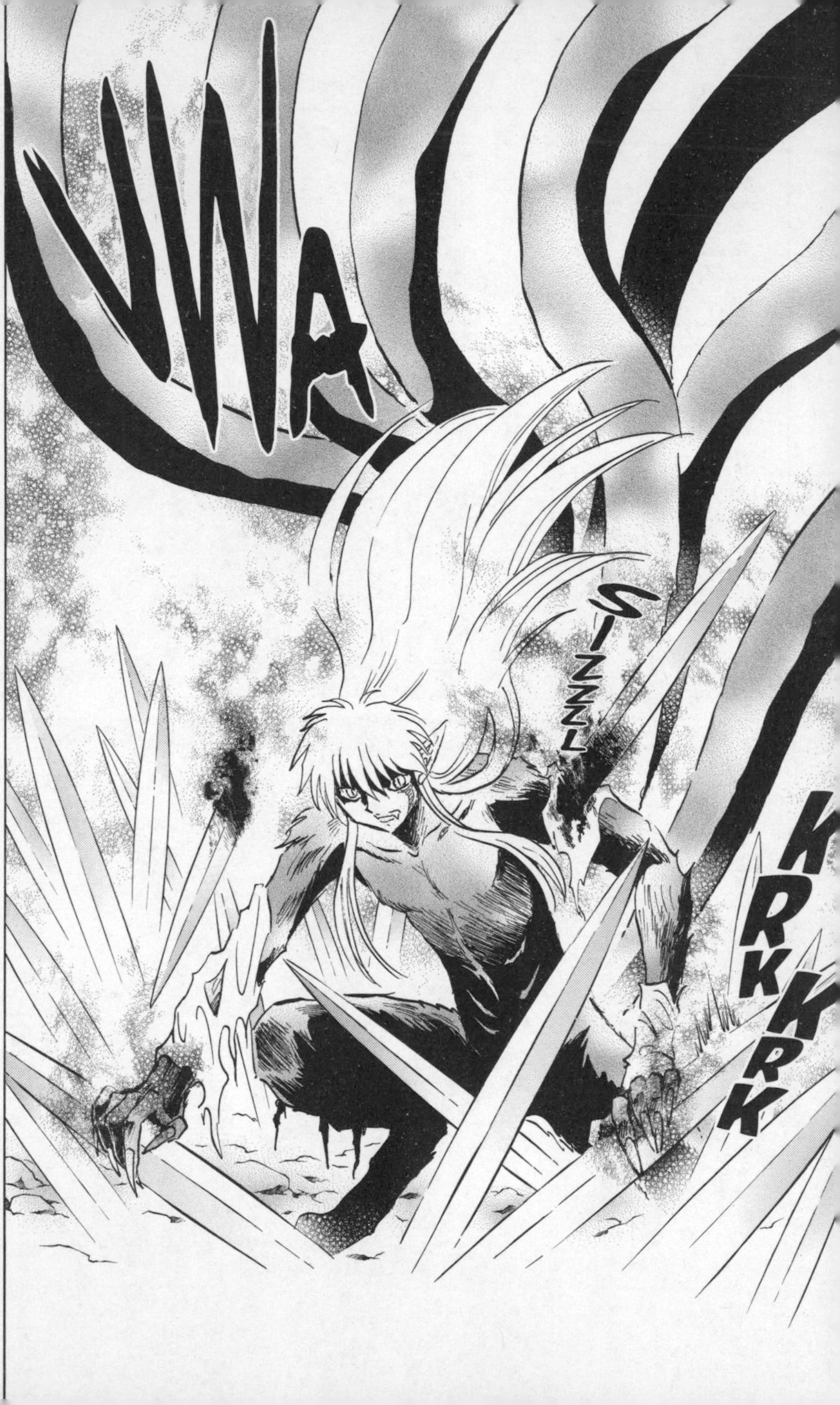
UWA
SIZZZL
KRKKRK

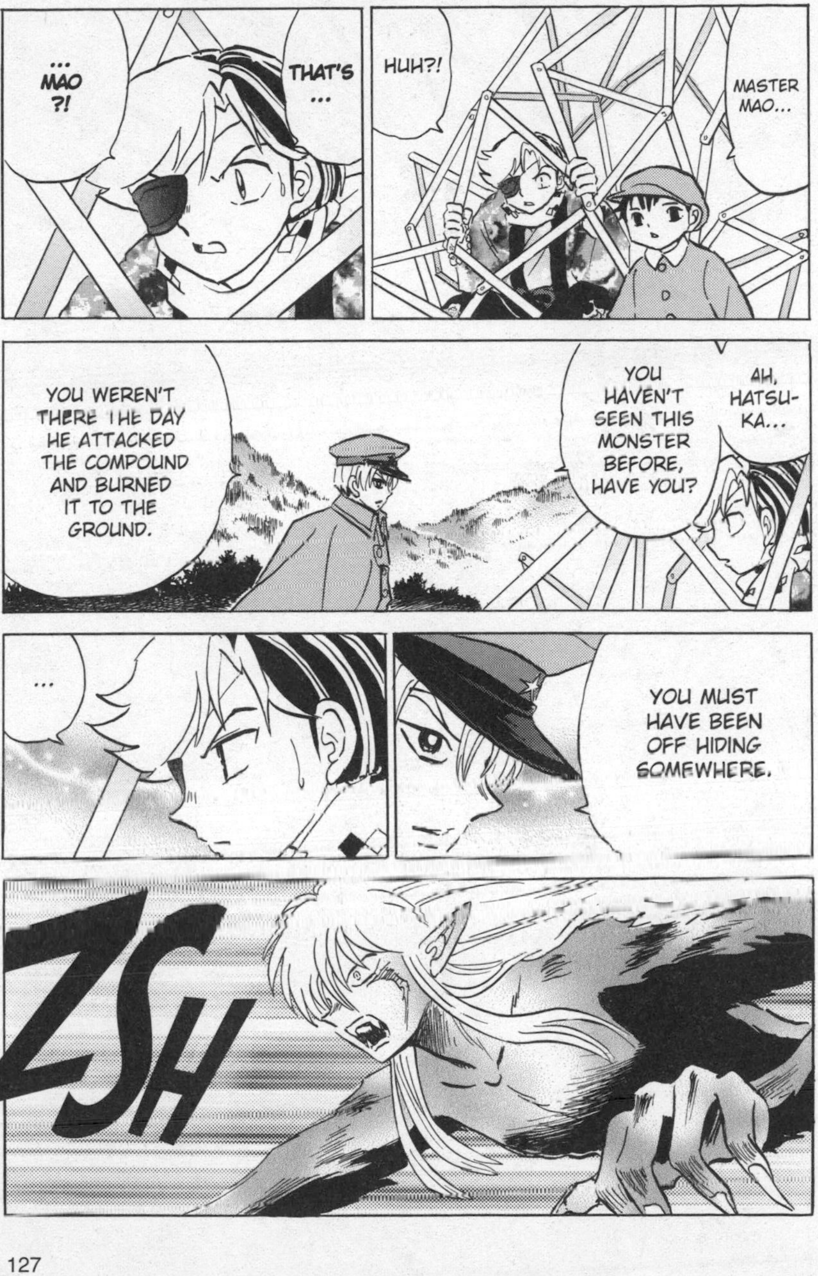
MASTER MAO...
HUH?!
THAT'S ...
... MAO ?!
AH, HATSU-KA...
YOU HAVEN'T SEEN THIS MONSTER BEFORE, HAVE YOU?
YOU WEREN'T THERE THE DAY HE ATTACKED THE COMPOUND AND BURNED IT TO THE GROUND.
YOU MUST HAVE BEEN OFF HIDING SOMEWHERE.
...
ZSH

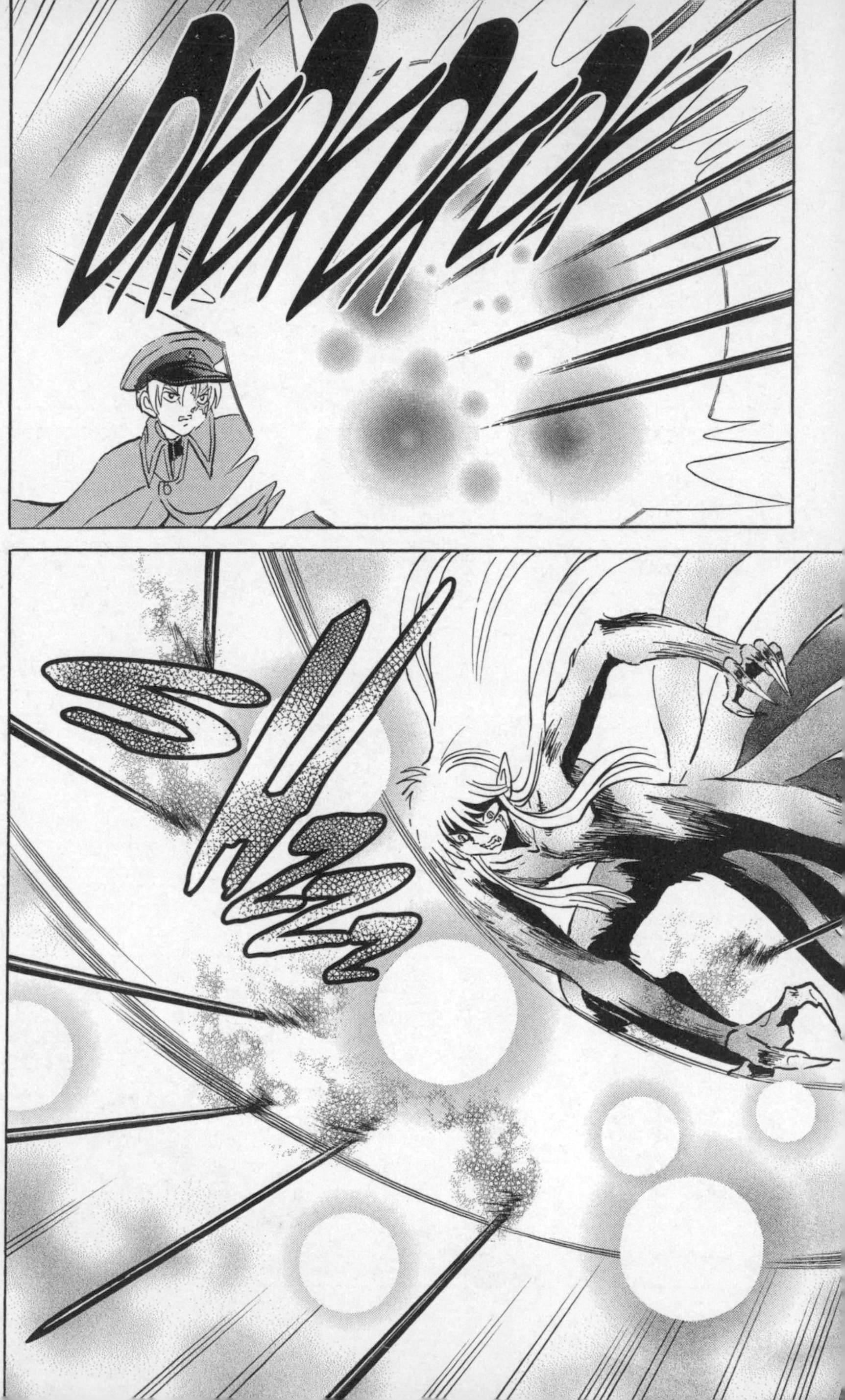

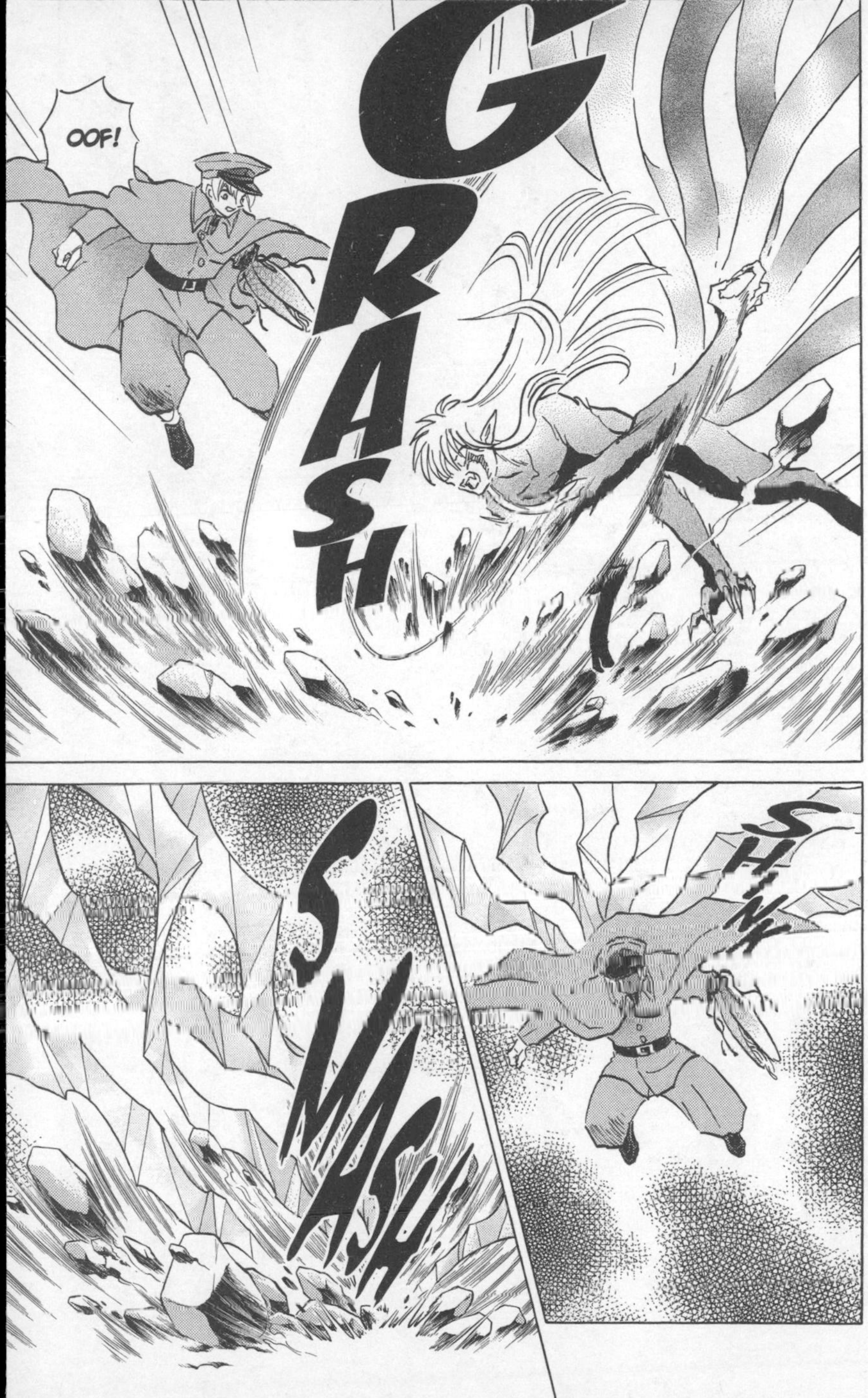
OOF!
CRASH
SHINK
SMASH

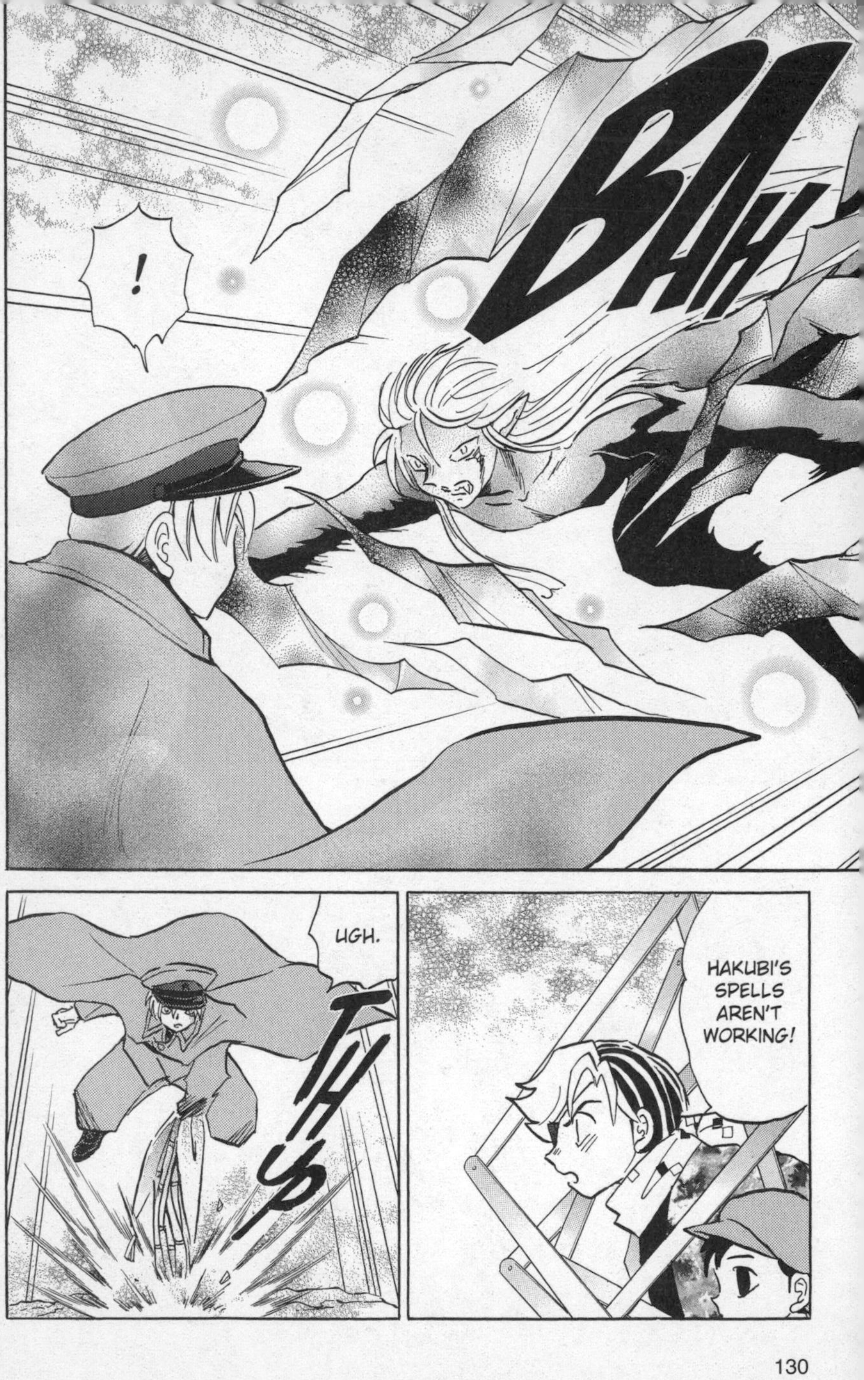
!
BAH
HAKUBI'S SPELLS AREN'T WORKING!
UGH.
THUP

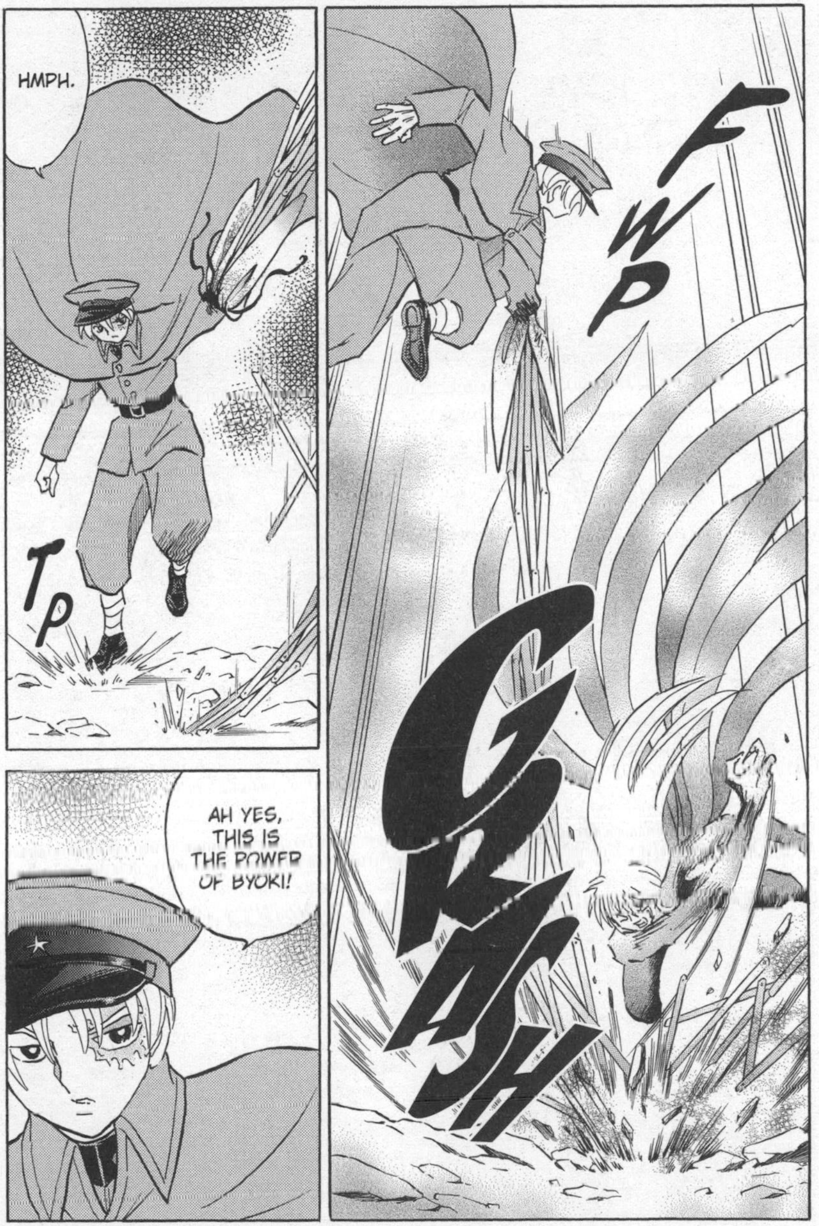
FWP
CRASH
HMPH.
TP
AH YES, THIS IS THE POWER OF BYOKI!

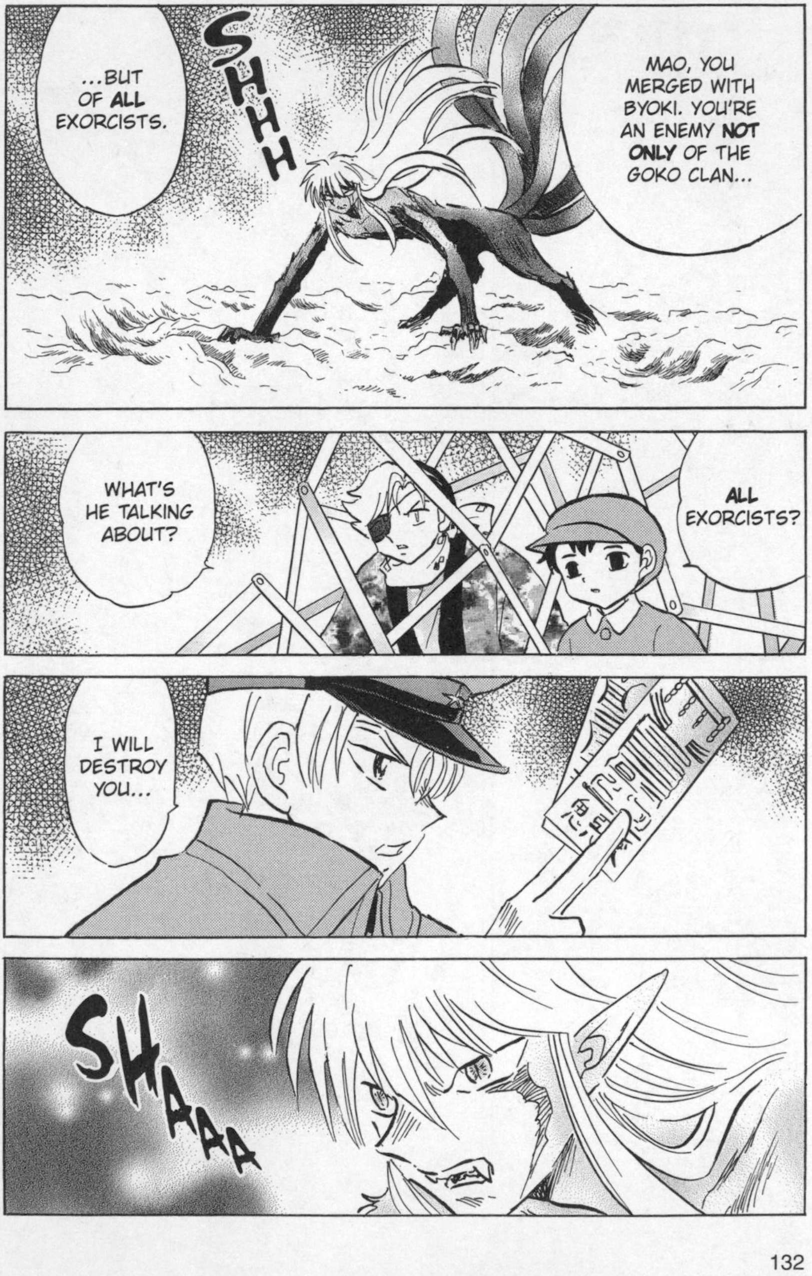
MAO, YOU MERGED WITH BYOKI. YOU'RE AN ENEMY NOT ONLY OF THE GOKO CLAN...
SHHH
...BUT OF ALL EXORCISTS.
ALL EXORCISTS?
WHAT'S HE TALKING ABOUT?
I WILL DESTROY YOU...
SHAAA

Chapter 8:
Beyond the Five Elements

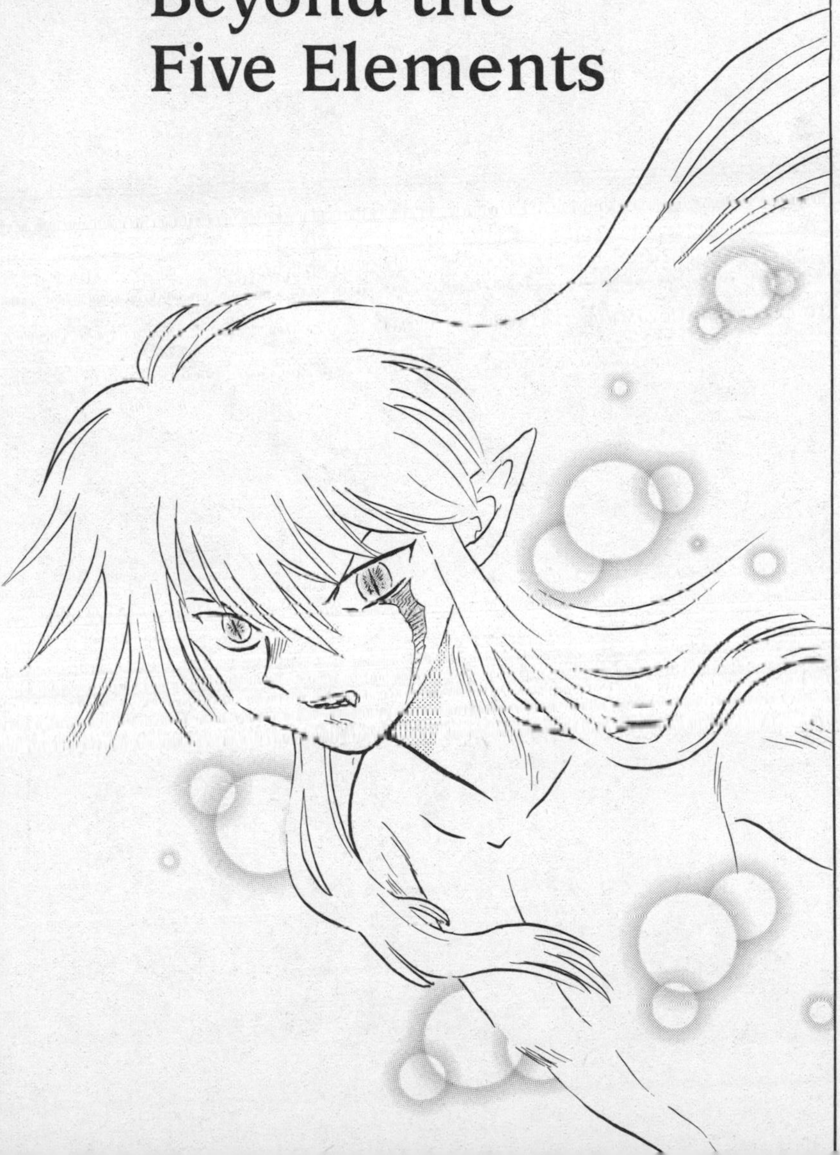

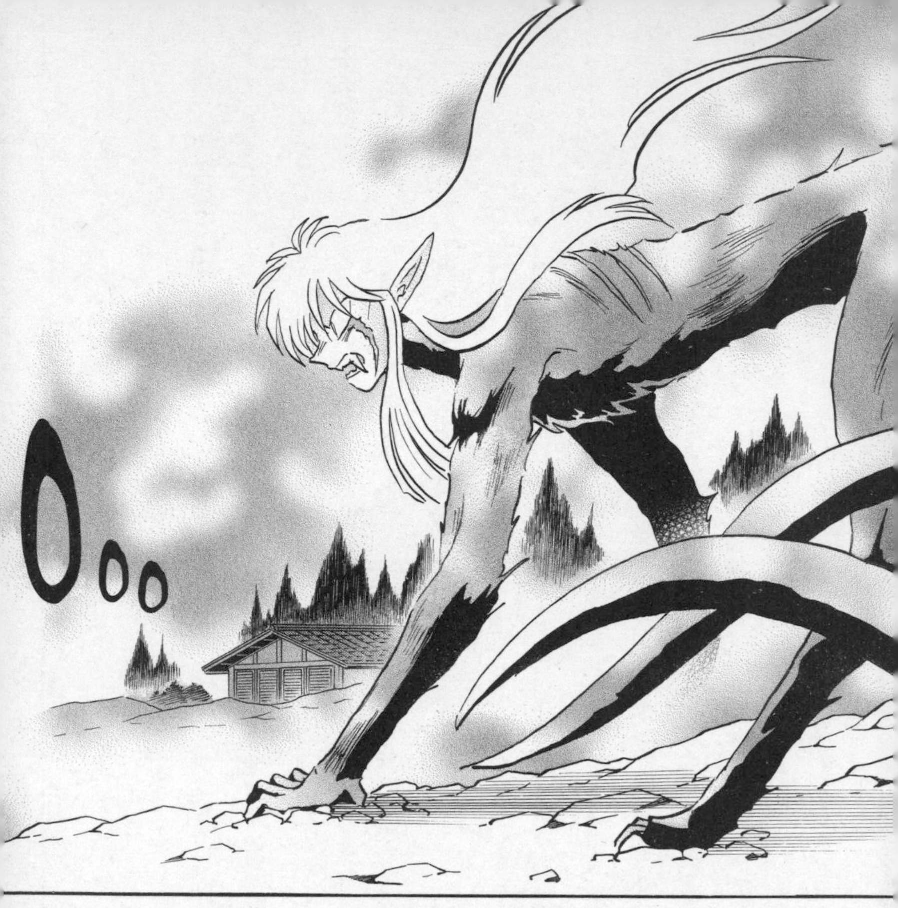
Ooo
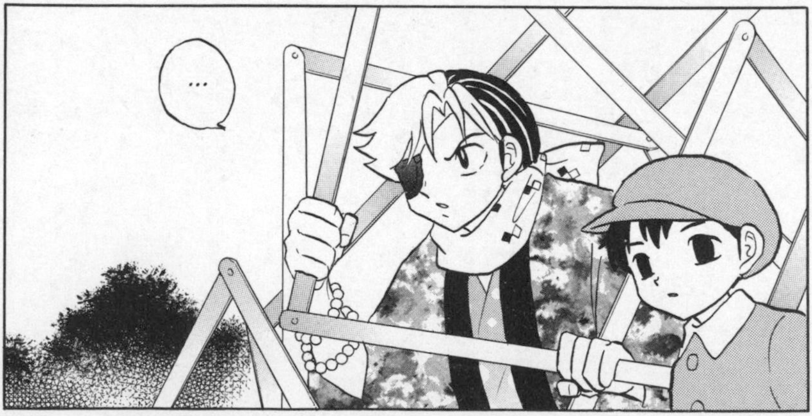
...

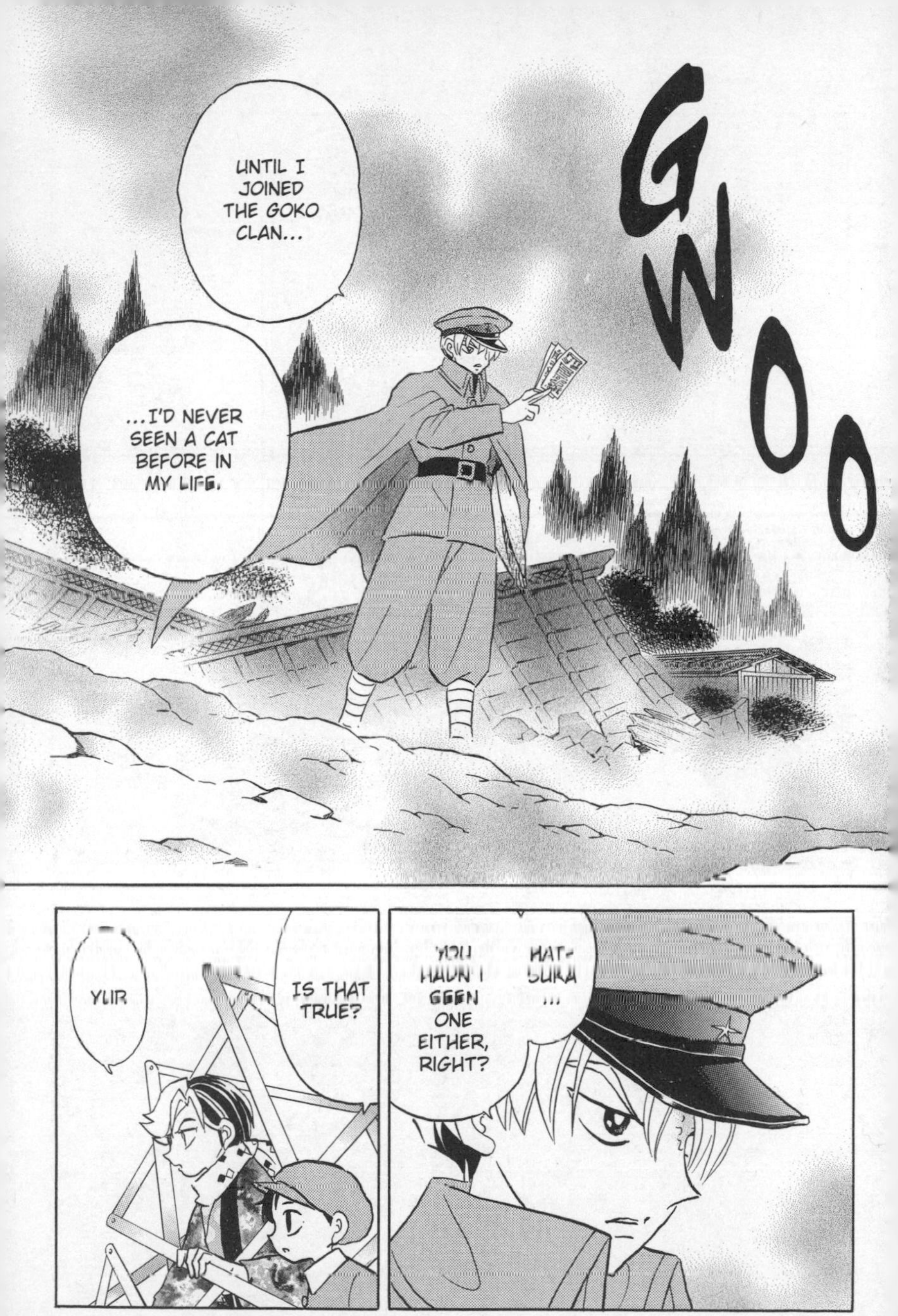
GWOO
UNTIL I JOINED THE GOKO CLAN...
...I'D NEVER SEEN A CAT BEFORE IN MY LIFE.
HAT-SUKA...
YOU HADN'T SEEN ONE EITHER, RIGHT?
IS THAT TRUE?
YUP

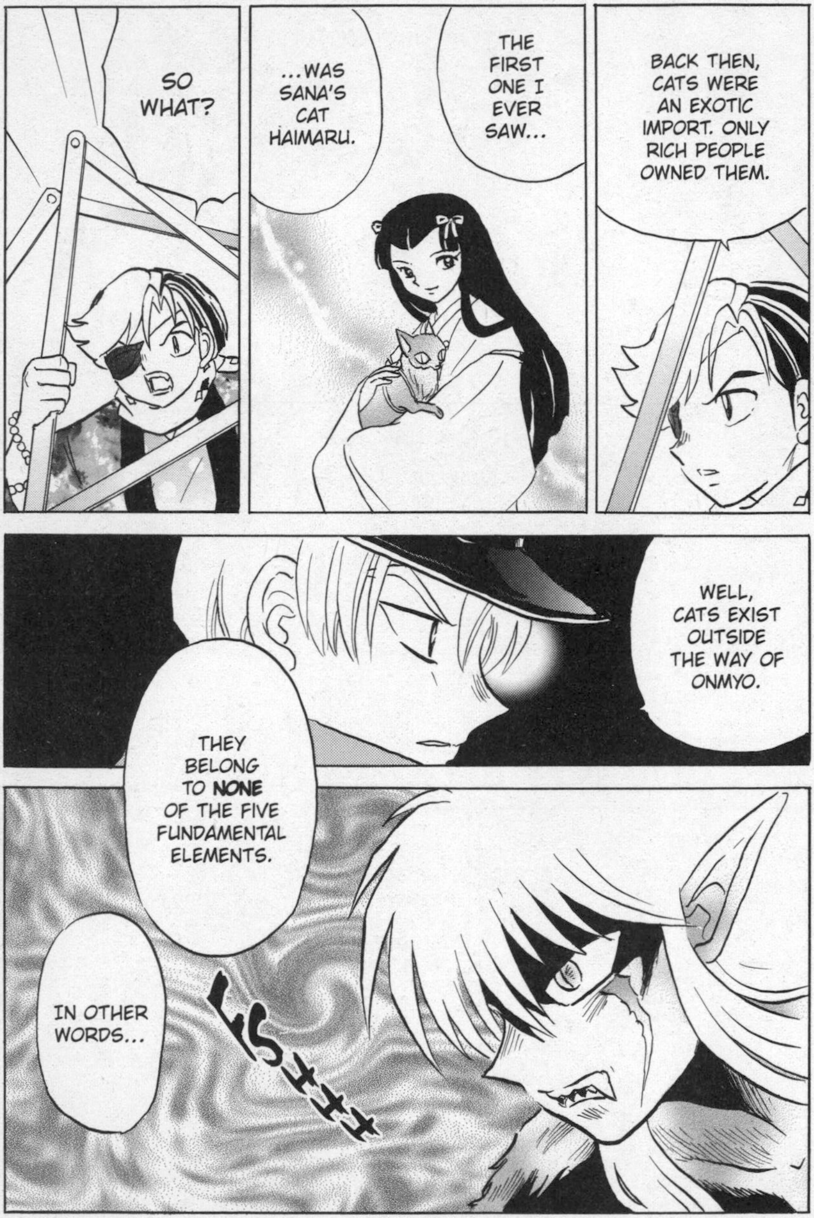
BACK THEN, CATS WERE AN EXOTIC IMPORT. ONLY RICH PEOPLE OWNED THEM.
THE FIRST ONE I EVER SAW...
...WAS SANA'S CAT HAIMARU.
SO WHAT?
WELL, CATS EXIST OUTSIDE THE WAY OF ONMYO.
THEY BELONG TO **NONE** OF THE FIVE FUNDAMENTAL ELEMENTS.
IN OTHER WORDS...

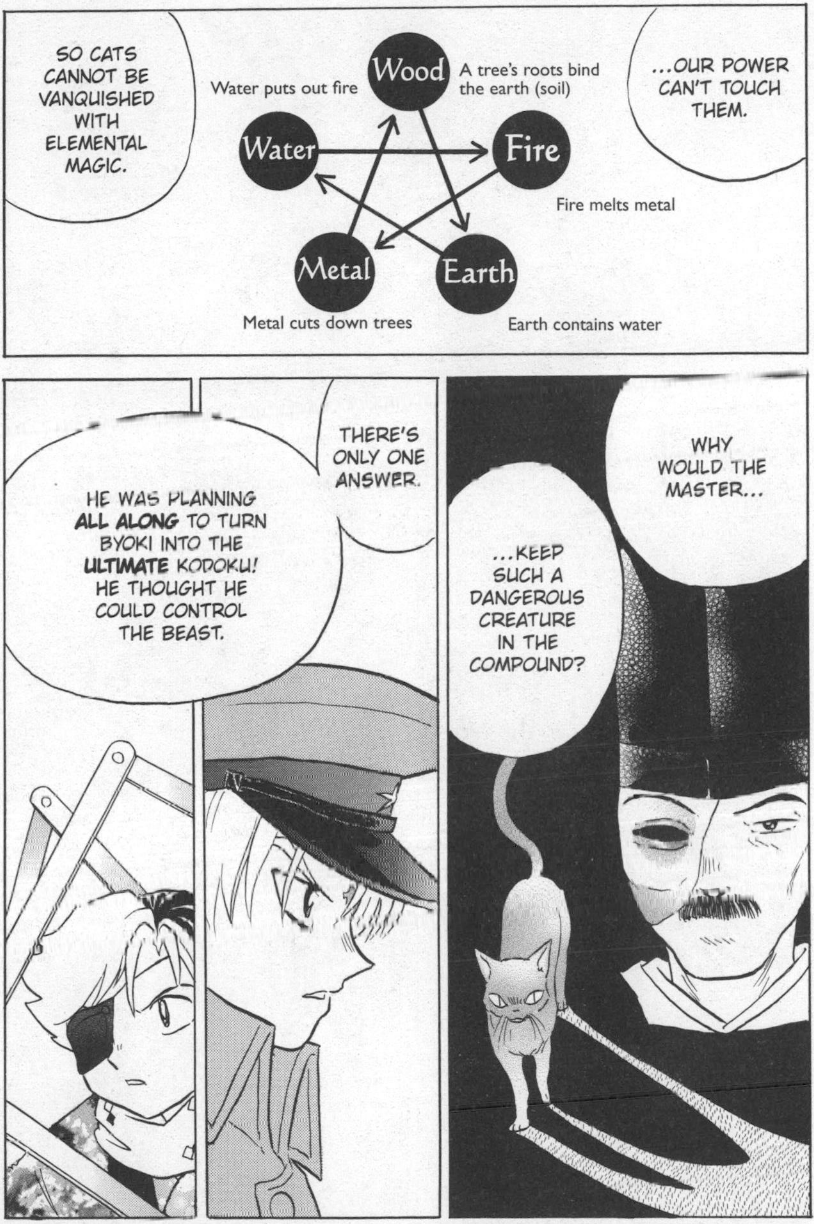
SO CATS CANNOT BE VANQUISHED WITH ELEMENTAL MAGIC.
Wood
A tree's roots bind the earth (soil)
Water puts out fire
Water
Fire
Fire melts metal
Metal
Earth
Metal cuts down trees
Earth contains water
...OUR POWER CAN'T TOUCH THEM.
WHY WOULD THE MASTER...
...KEEP SUCH A DANGEROUS CREATURE IN THE COMPOUND?
THERE'S ONLY ONE ANSWER.
HE WAS PLANNING ALL ALONG TO TURN BYOKI INTO THE ULTIMATE KODOKU! HE THOUGHT HE COULD CONTROL THE BEAST.

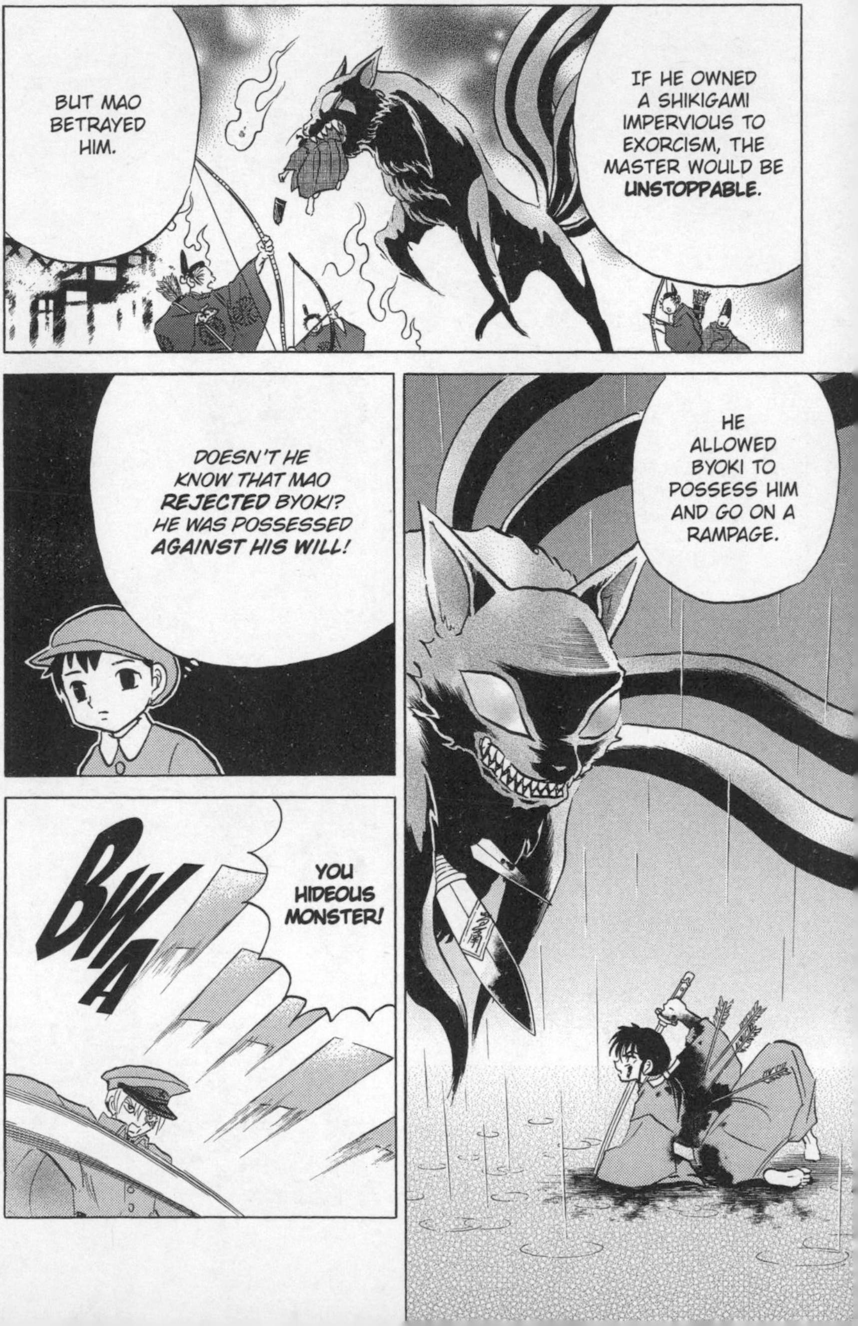
IF HE OWNED A SHIKIGAMI IMPERVIOUS TO EXORCISM, THE MASTER WOULD BE UNSTOPPABLE.
BUT MAO BETRAYED HIM.
HE ALLOWED BYOKI TO POSSESS HIM AND GO ON A RAMPAGE.
DOESN'T HE KNOW THAT MAO REJECTED BYOKI? HE WAS POSSESSED AGAINST HIS WILL!
YOU HIDEOUS MONSTER!
BWA

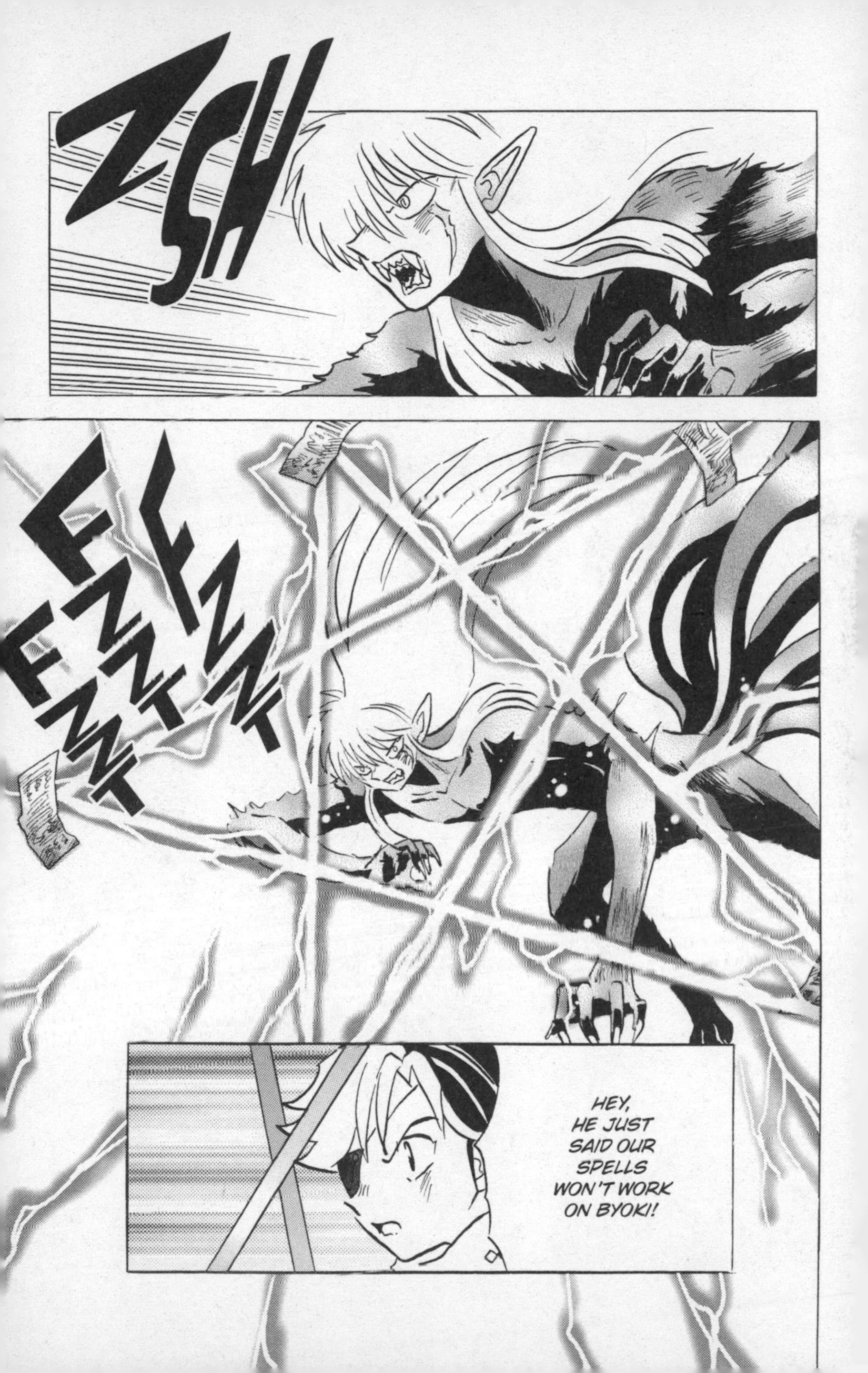
ZSH
FZZZT
FZZZZT
HEY, HE JUST SAID OUR SPELLS WON'T WORK ON BYOKI!

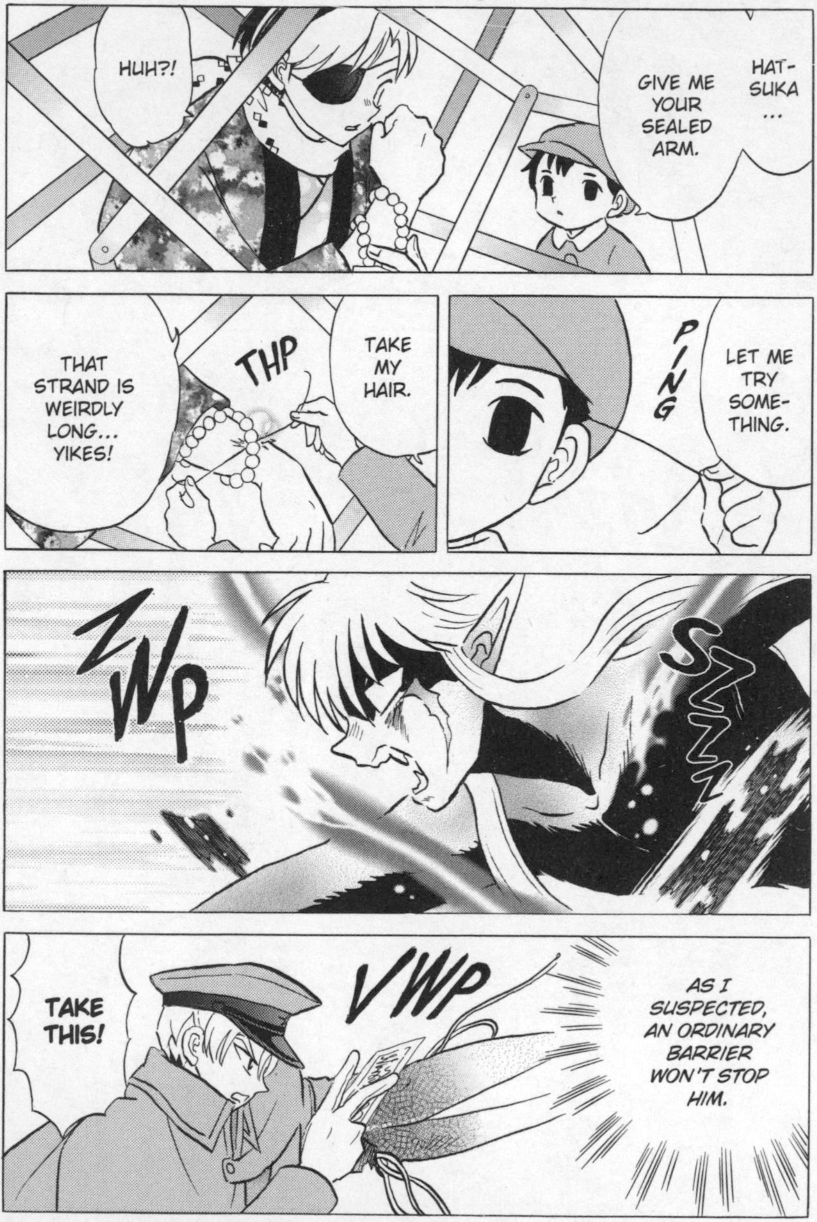
HAT-SUKA...
GIVE ME YOUR SEALED ARM.
HUH?!
LET ME TRY SOMETHING.
PING
TAKE MY HAIR.
THP
THAT STRAND IS WEIRDLY LONG... YIKES!
SZZZ
ZWP
AS I SUSPECTED, AN ORDINARY BARRIER WON'T STOP HIM.
VWP
TAKE THIS!

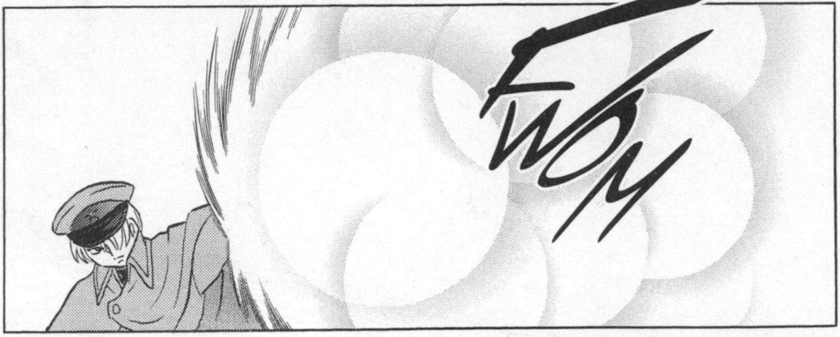
FWOM
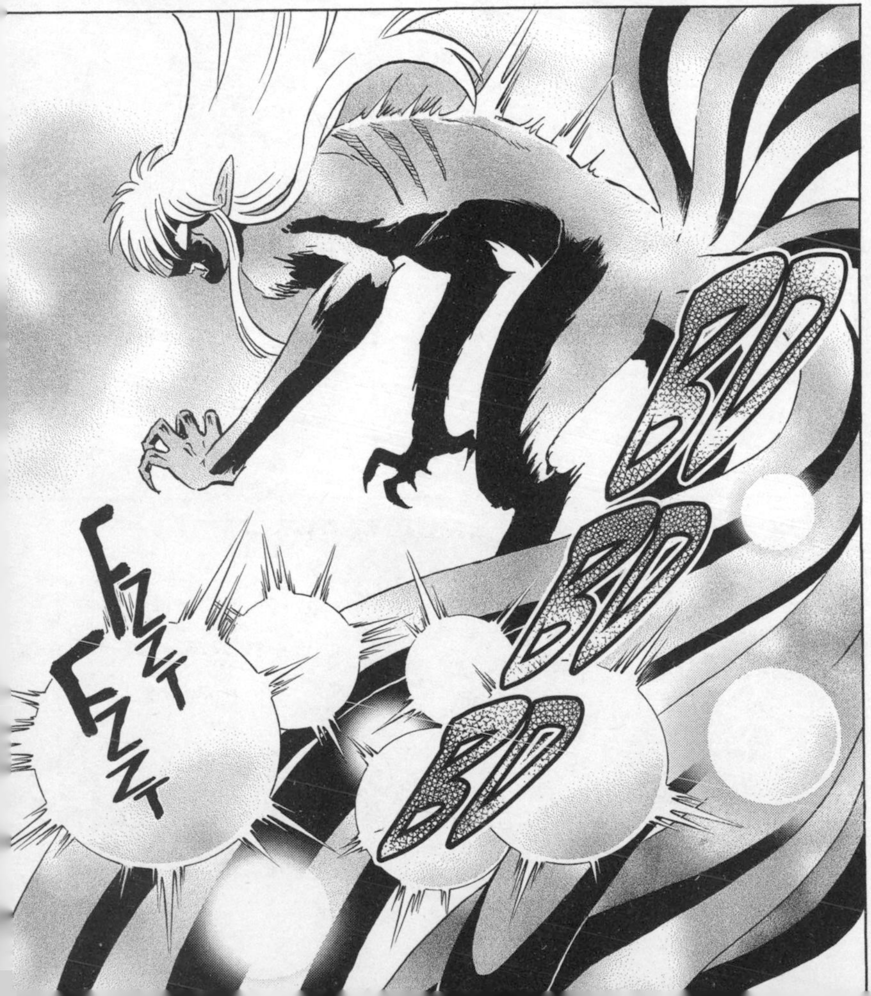
BZZ
BZZ
BZZ
FZZZT
FZZZT

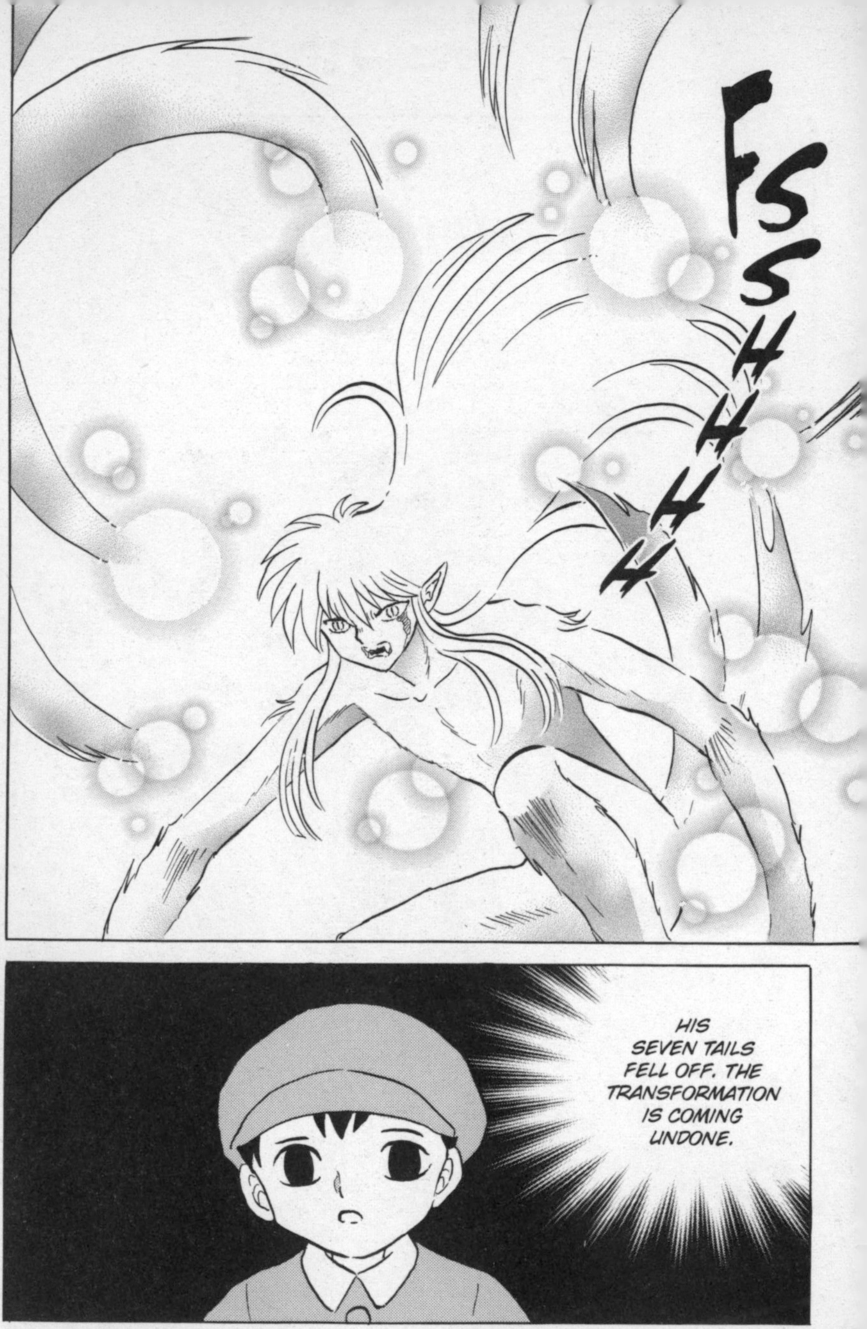
FSSHHHHH
HIS SEVEN TAILS FELL OFF. THE TRANSFORMATION IS COMING UNDONE.

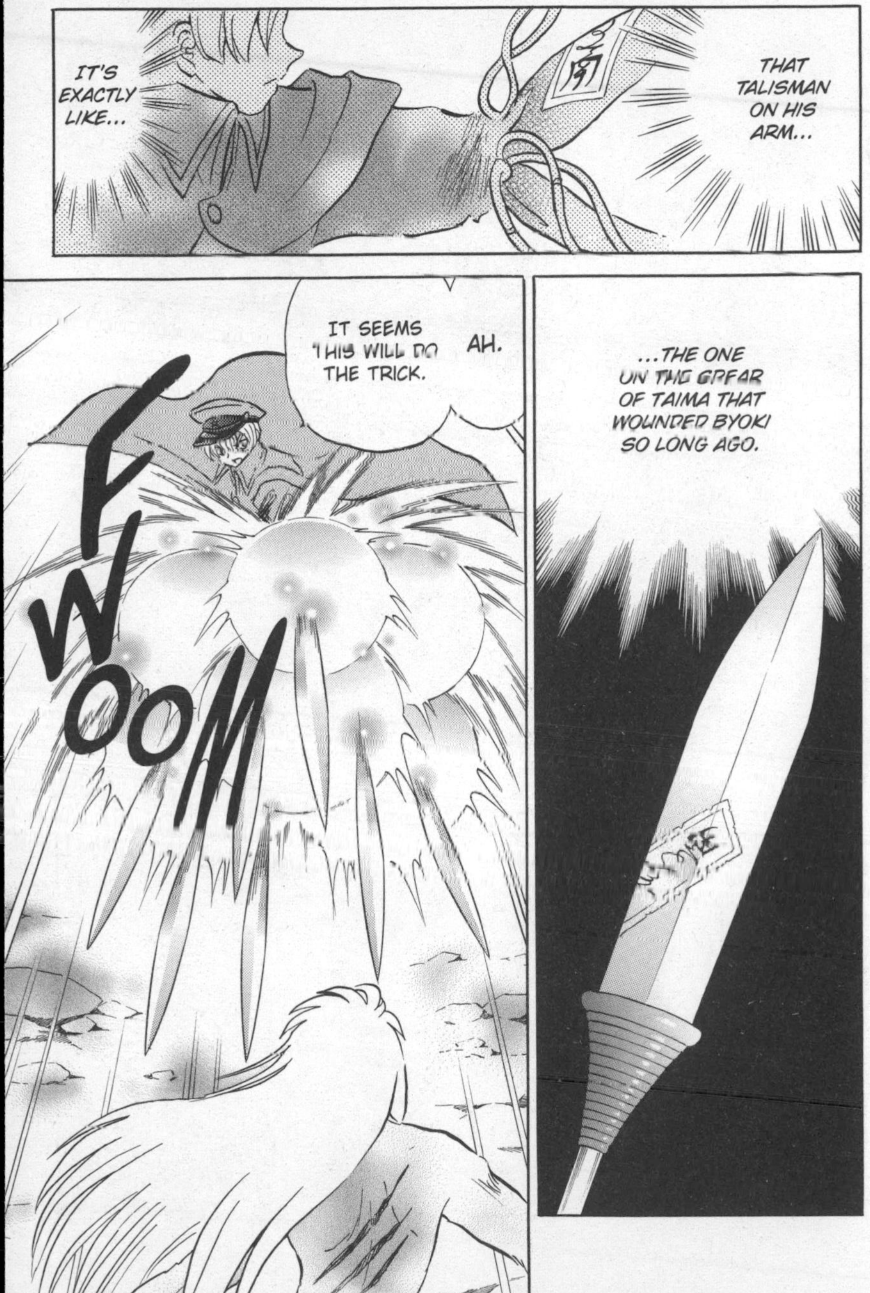
THAT TALISMAN ON HIS ARM...
IT'S EXACTLY LIKE...
...THE ONE ON THE SPEAR OF TAIMA THAT WOUNDED BYOKI SO LONG AGO.
AH.
IT SEEMS THIS WILL DO THE TRICK.
FWOOM

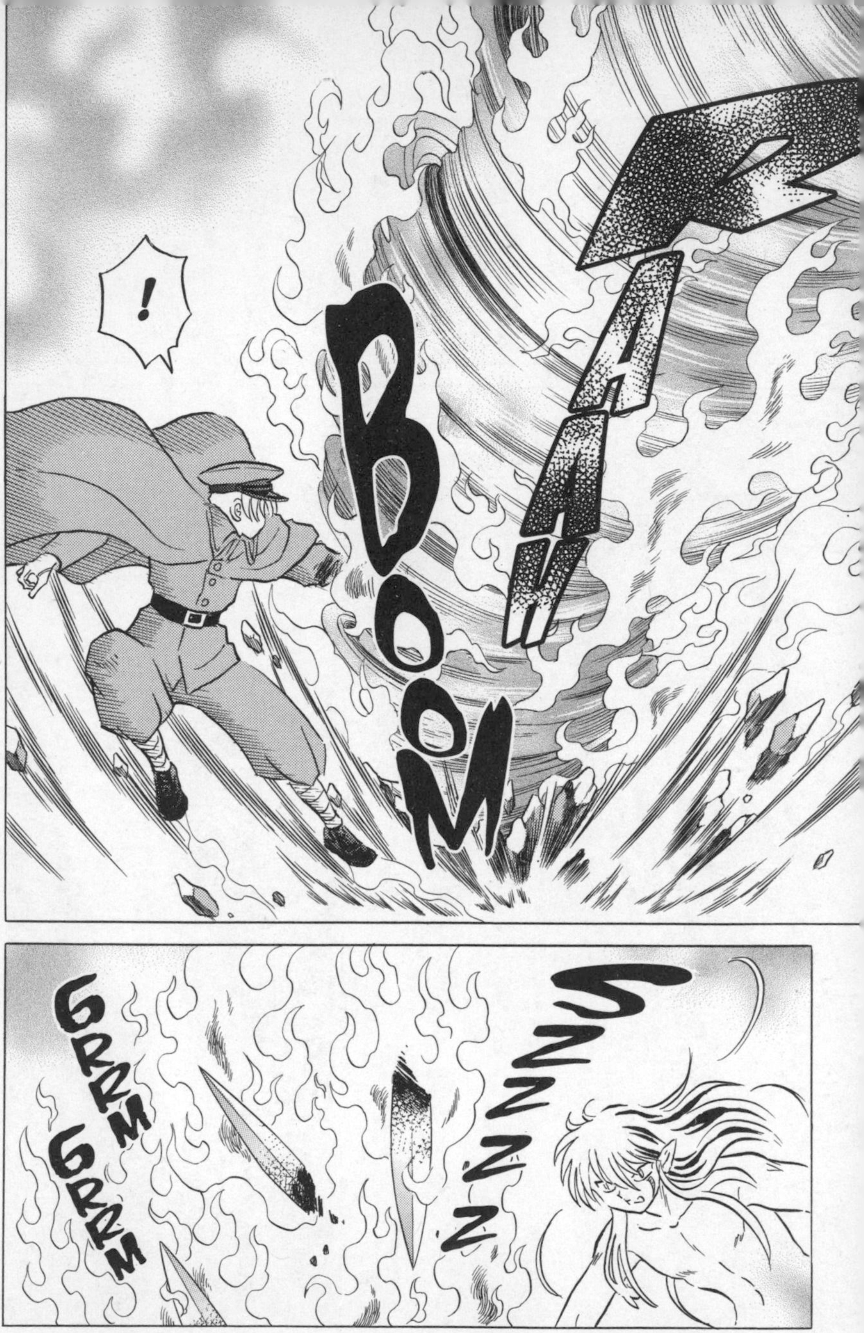
RAAH
BOOM
!
SZZZZZ
GRRRM
GRRRM

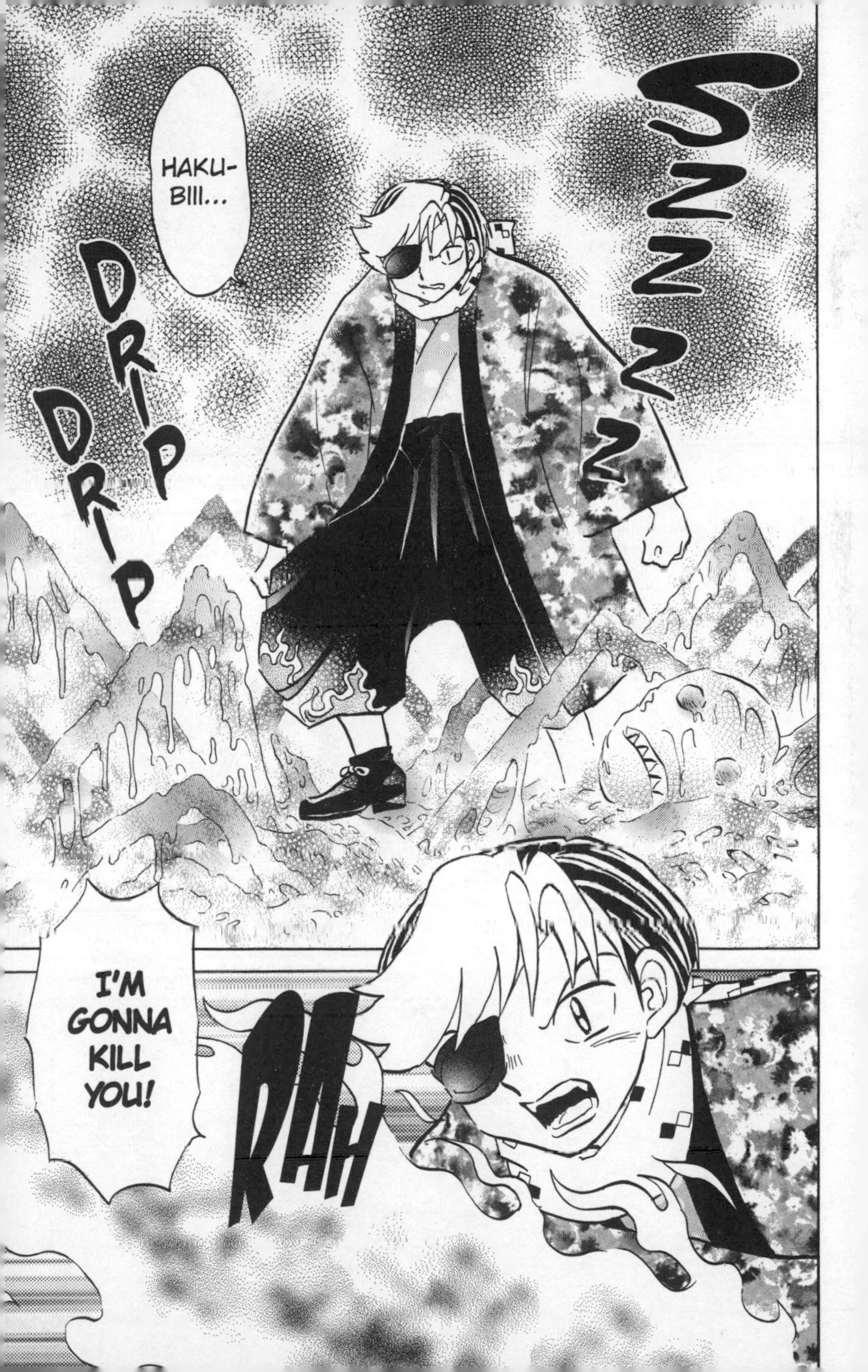
SZZZZ
HAKU-BIII...
DRIP DRIP
RAH
I'M GONNA KILL YOU!

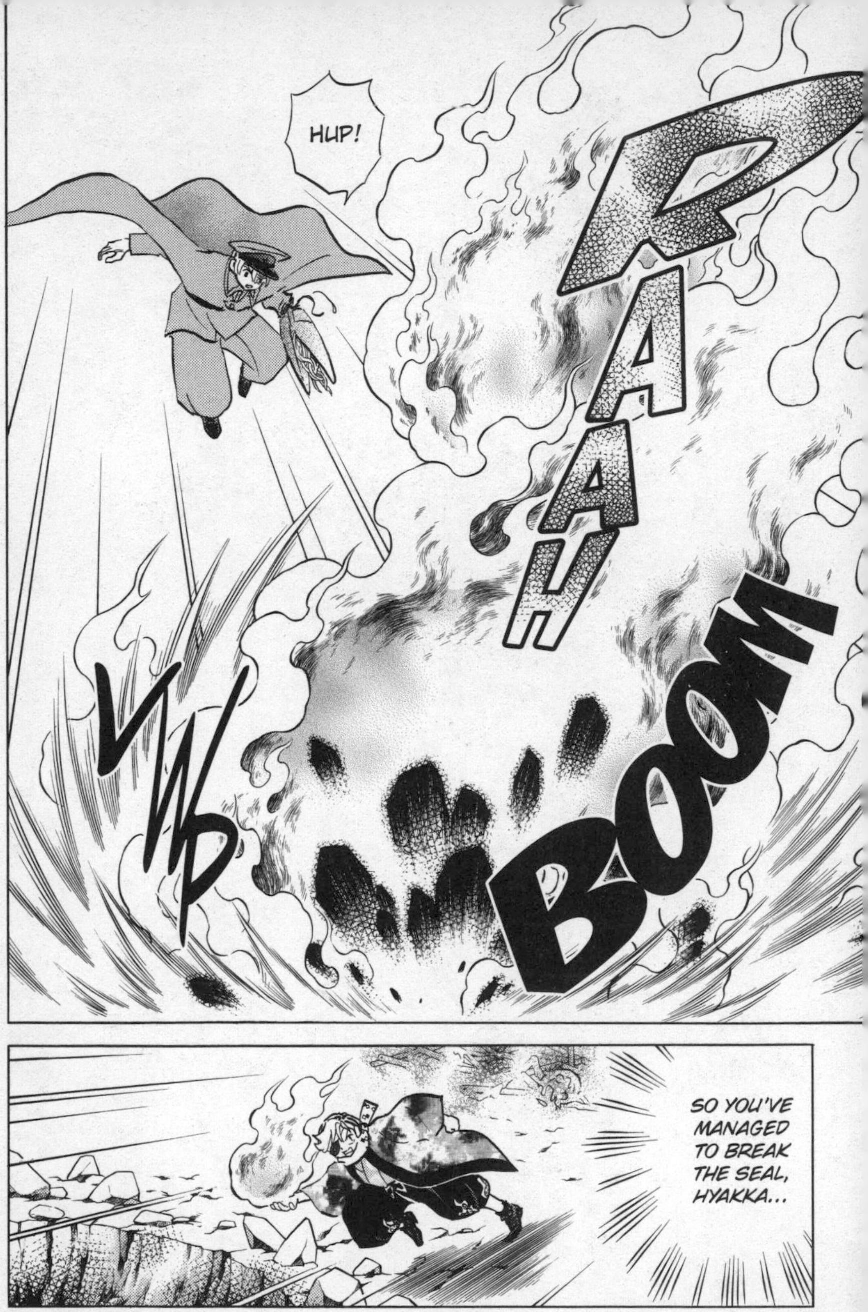
HUP!
RAAH
BOOM
SO YOU'VE MANAGED TO BREAK THE SEAL, HYAKKA...

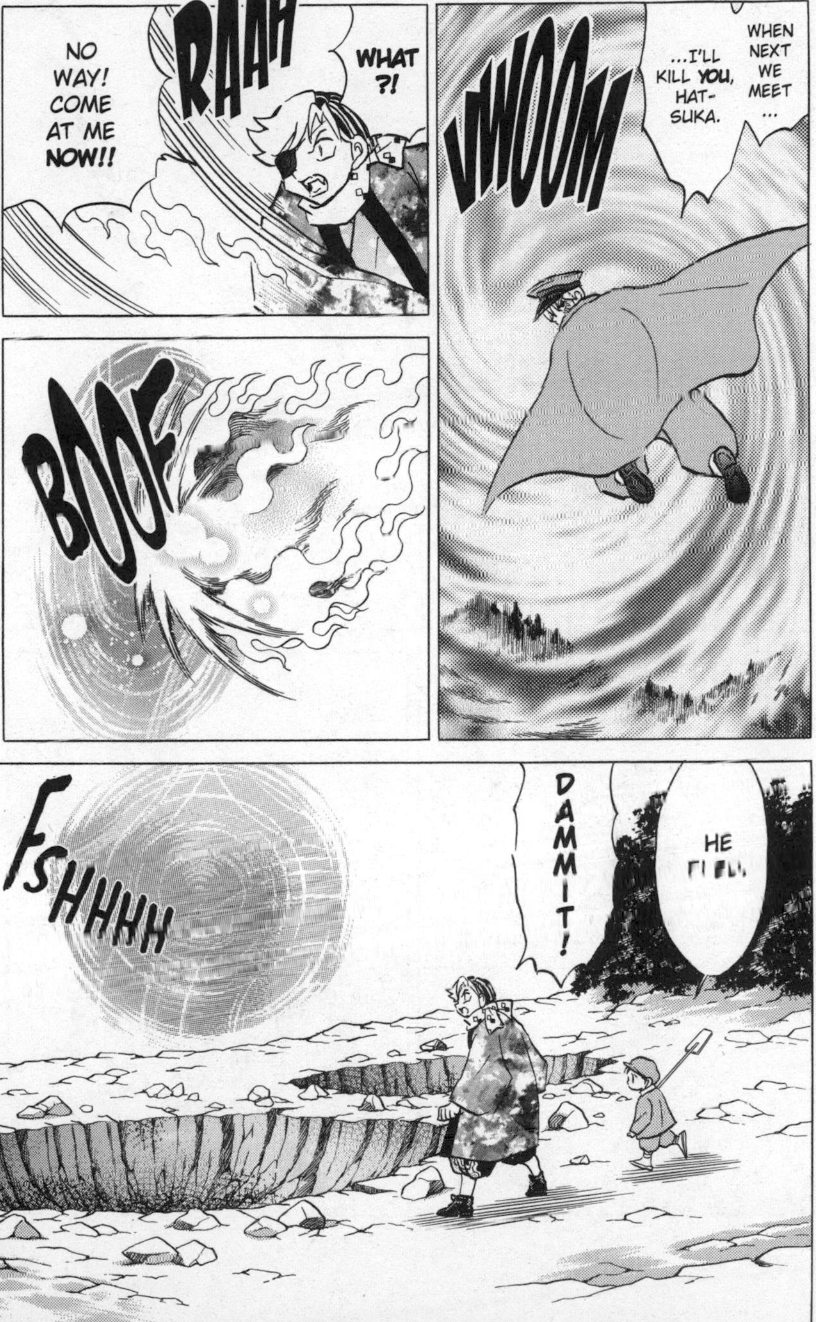
WHEN NEXT WE MEET...
...I'LL KILL YOU, HAT-SUKA.
VWOOM
WHAT?!
RAAH
NO WAY! COME AT ME NOW!!
BOOF
HE
DAMMIT!
FSHHHH

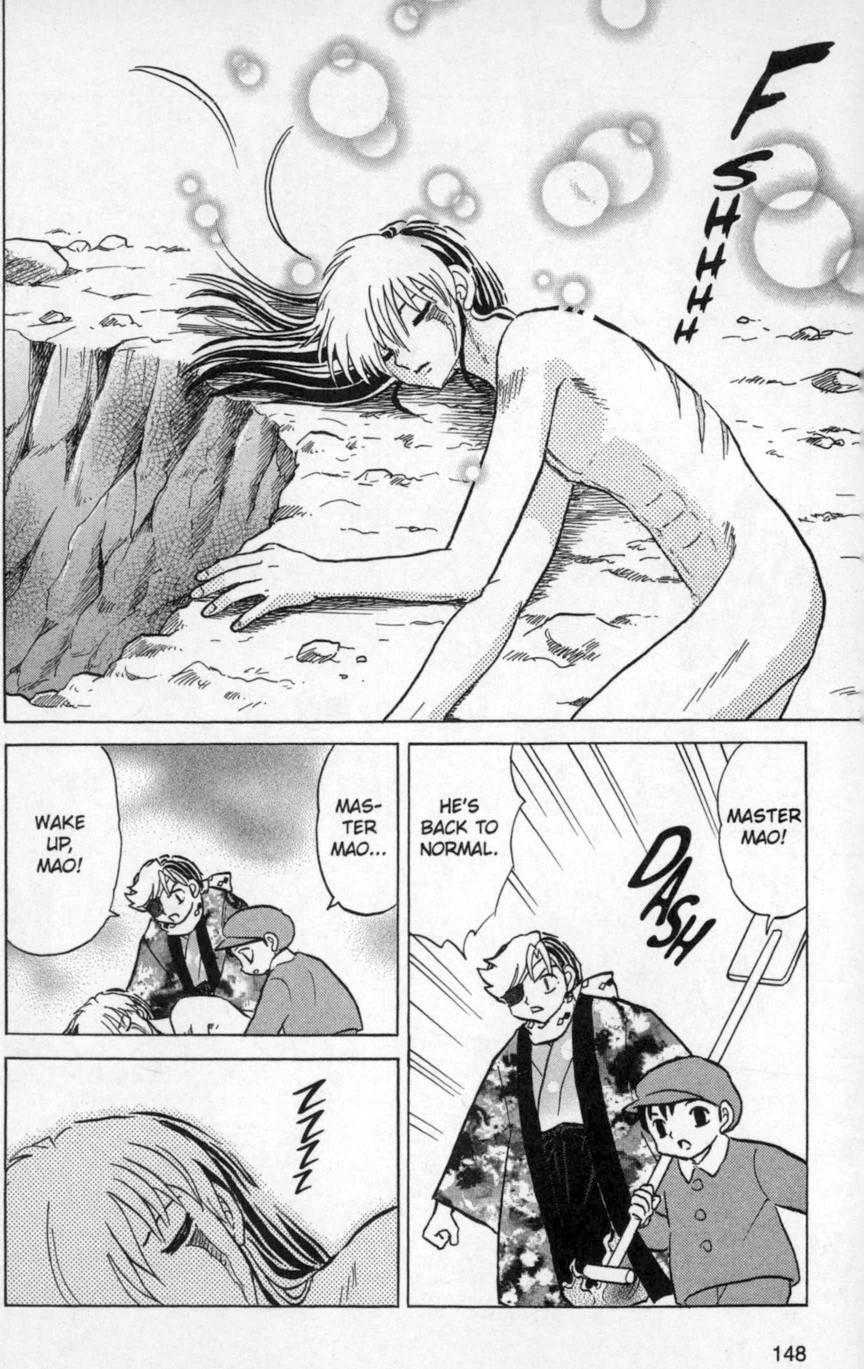
FSHHHH
MASTER MAO!
DASH
HE'S BACK TO NORMAL.
MAS-TER MAO...
WAKE UP, MAO!
ZZZZZ

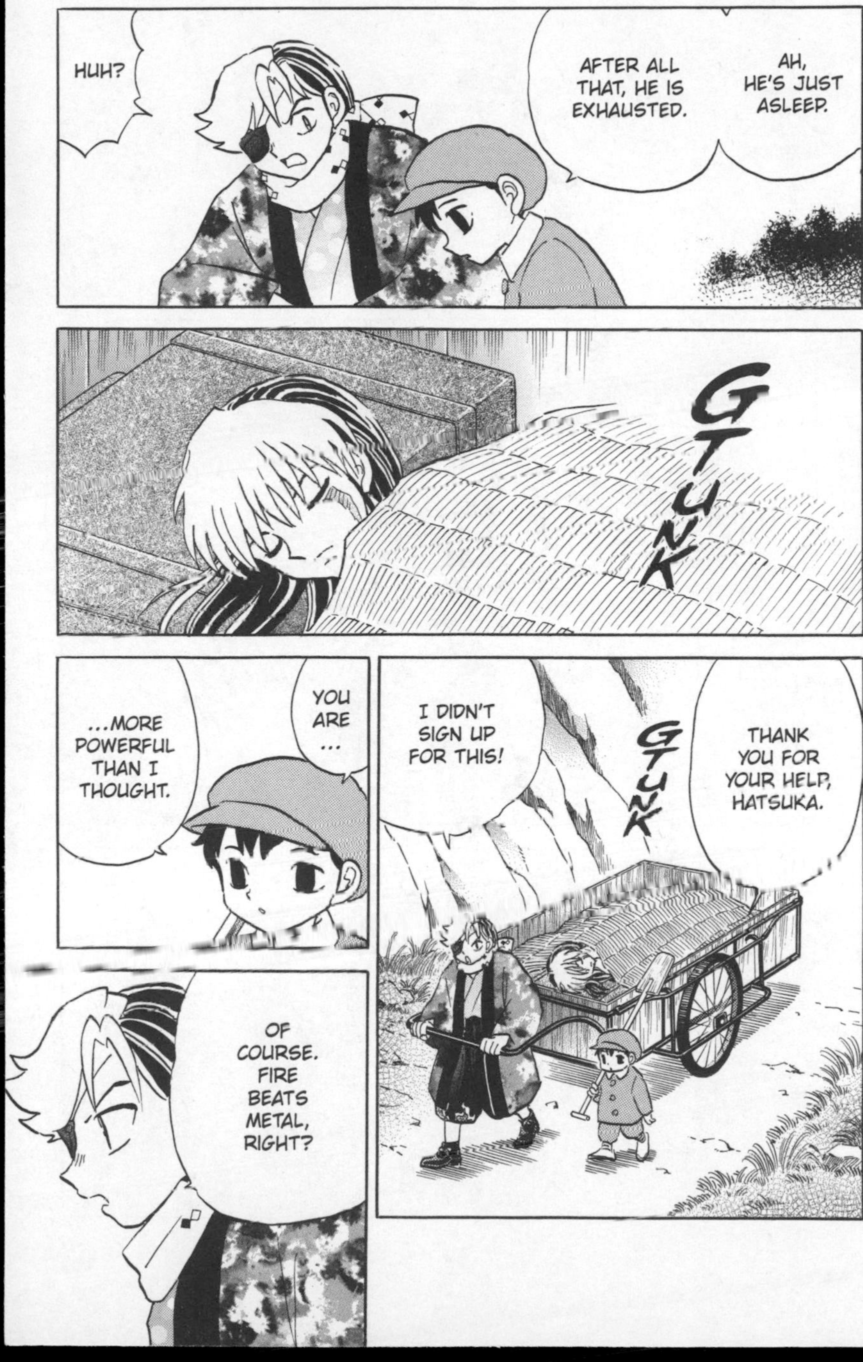
AH, HE'S JUST ASLEEP.
AFTER ALL THAT, HE IS EXHAUSTED.
HUH?
GTUNK
THANK YOU FOR YOUR HELP, HATSUKA.
GTUNK
I DIDN'T SIGN UP FOR THIS!
YOU ARE ...
...MORE POWERFUL THAN I THOUGHT.
OF COURSE. FIRE BEATS METAL, RIGHT?

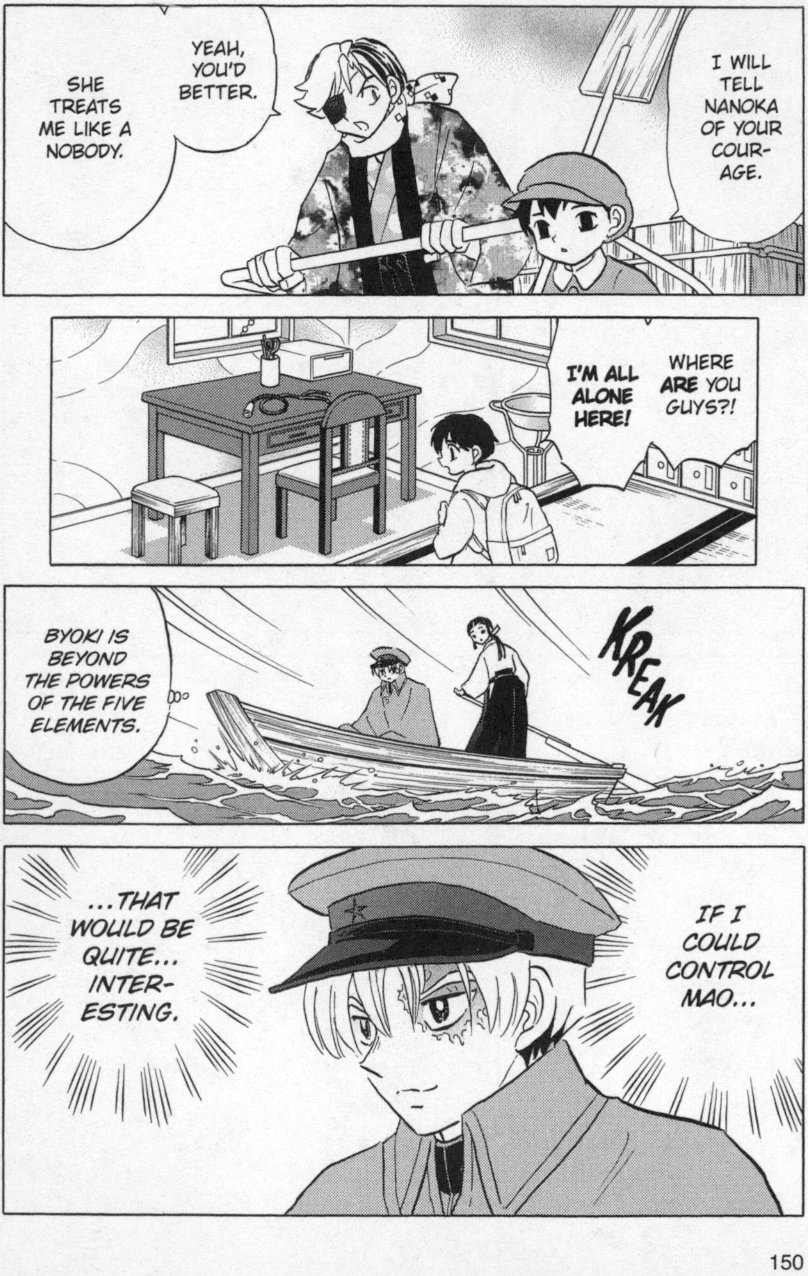
I WILL TELL NANOKA OF YOUR COURAGE.
YEAH, YOU'D BETTER.
SHE TREATS ME LIKE A NOBODY.
WHERE ARE YOU GUYS?!
I'M ALL ALONE HERE!
KREAK
BYOKI IS BEYOND THE POWERS OF THE FIVE ELEMENTS.
IF I COULD CONTROL MAO...
...THAT WOULD BE QUITE... INTERESTING.

Chapter 9:
He Won't Wake Up

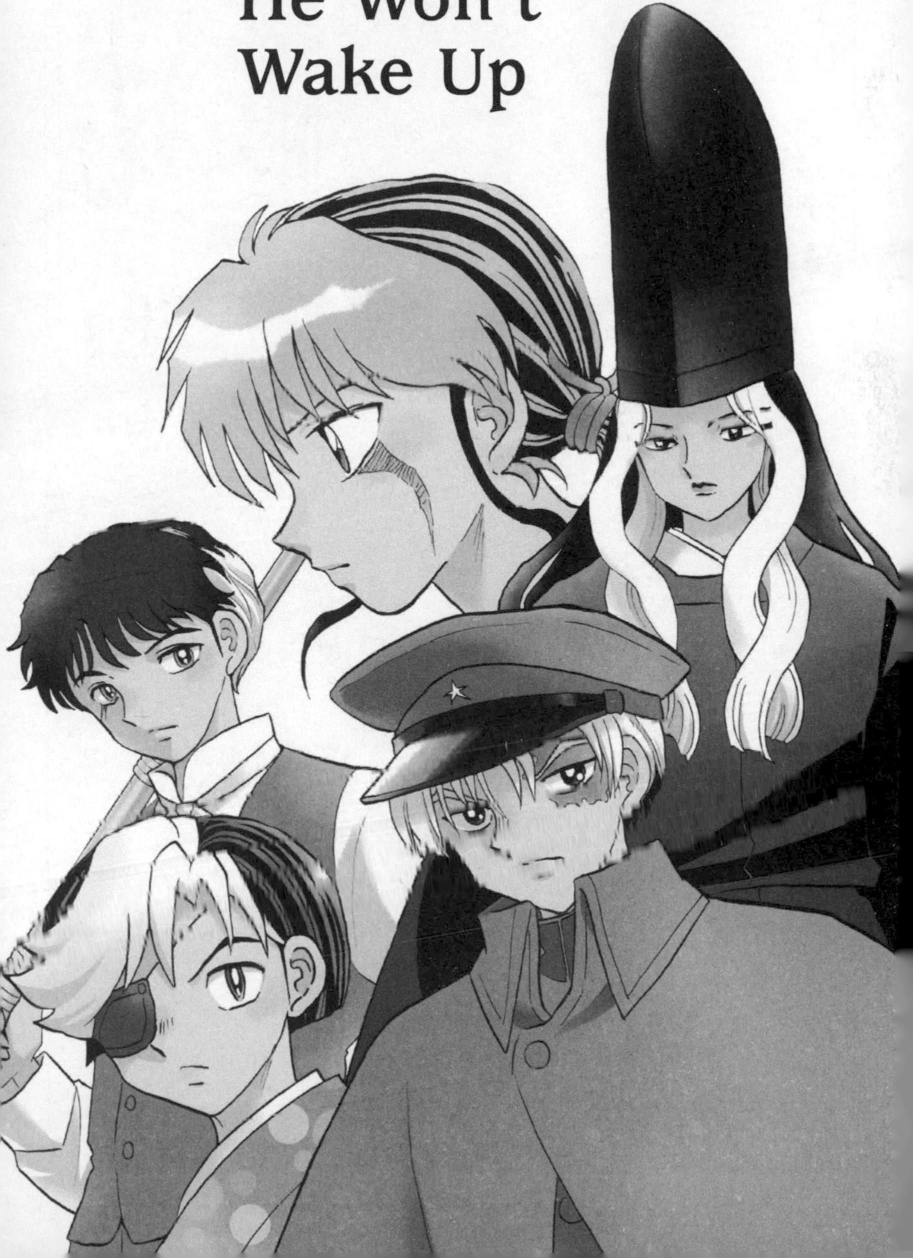

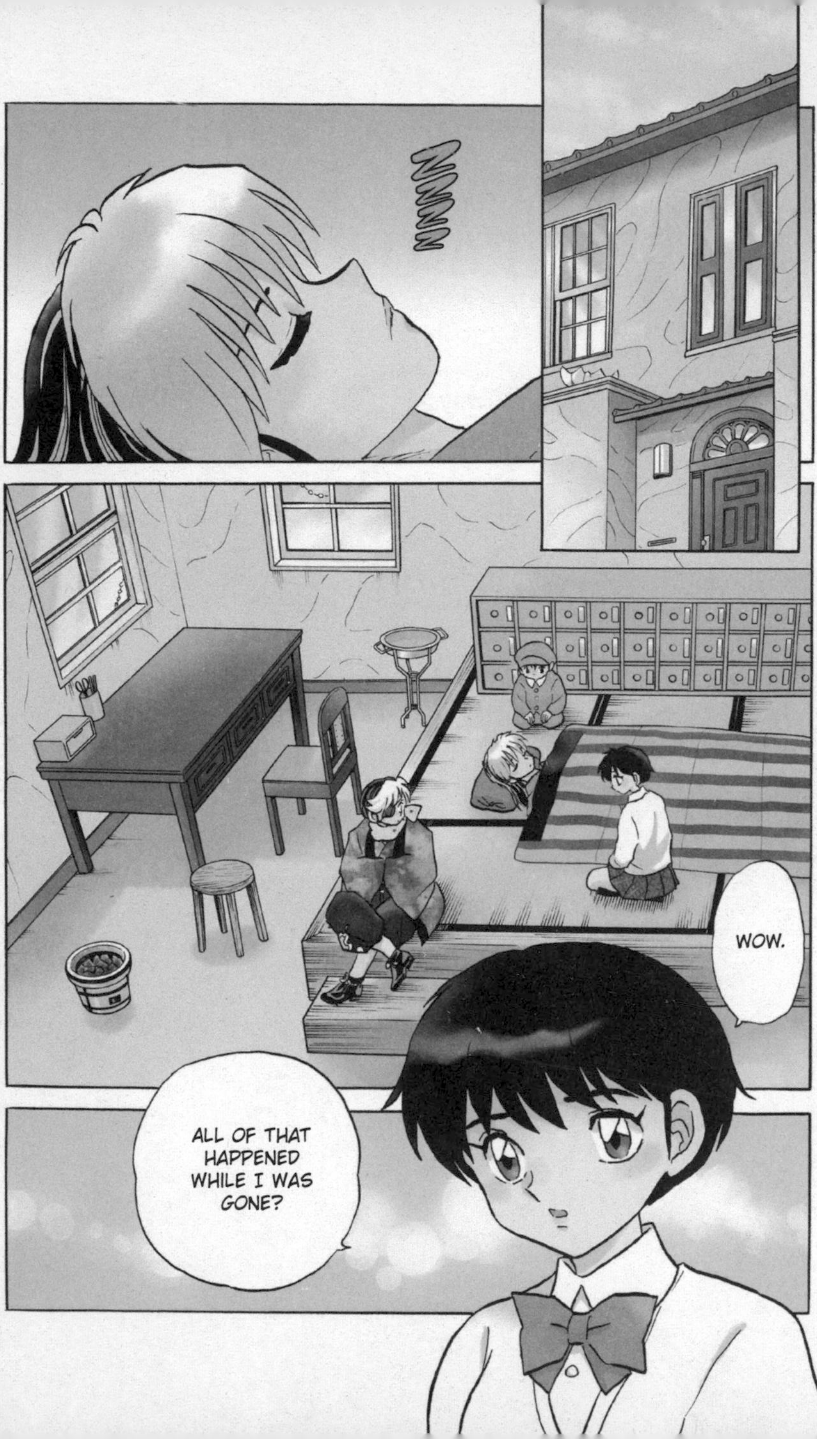
WOW.
ALL OF THAT HAPPENED WHILE I WAS GONE?

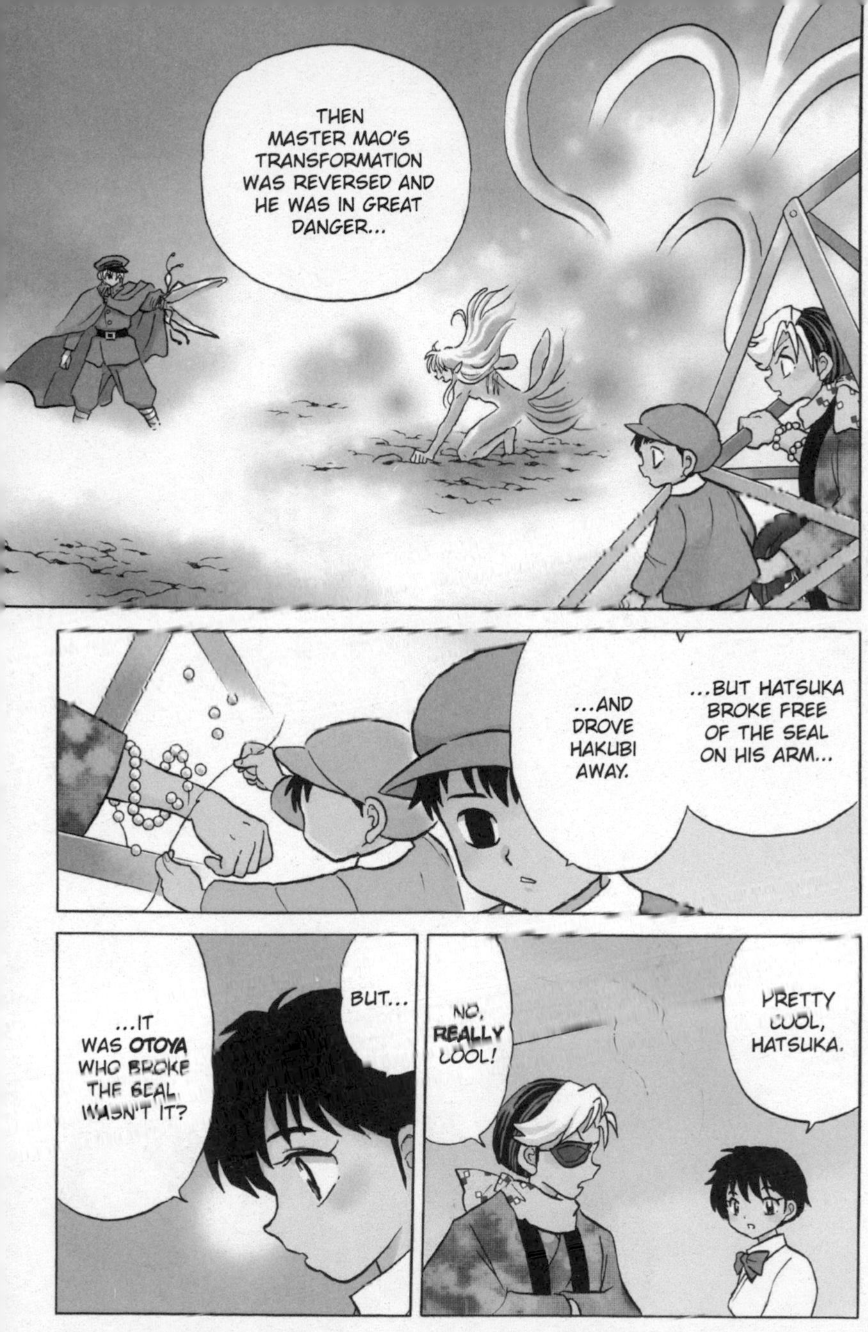
THEN MASTER MAO'S TRANSFORMATION WAS REVERSED AND HE WAS IN GREAT DANGER...
...BUT HATSUKA BROKE FREE OF THE SEAL ON HIS ARM...
...AND DROVE HAKUBI AWAY.
PRETTY COOL, HATSUKA.
NO, **REALLY** COOL!
BUT...
...IT WAS **OTOYA** WHO BROKE THE SEAL, WASN'T IT?

MAO

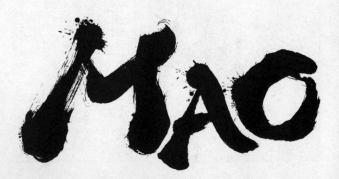

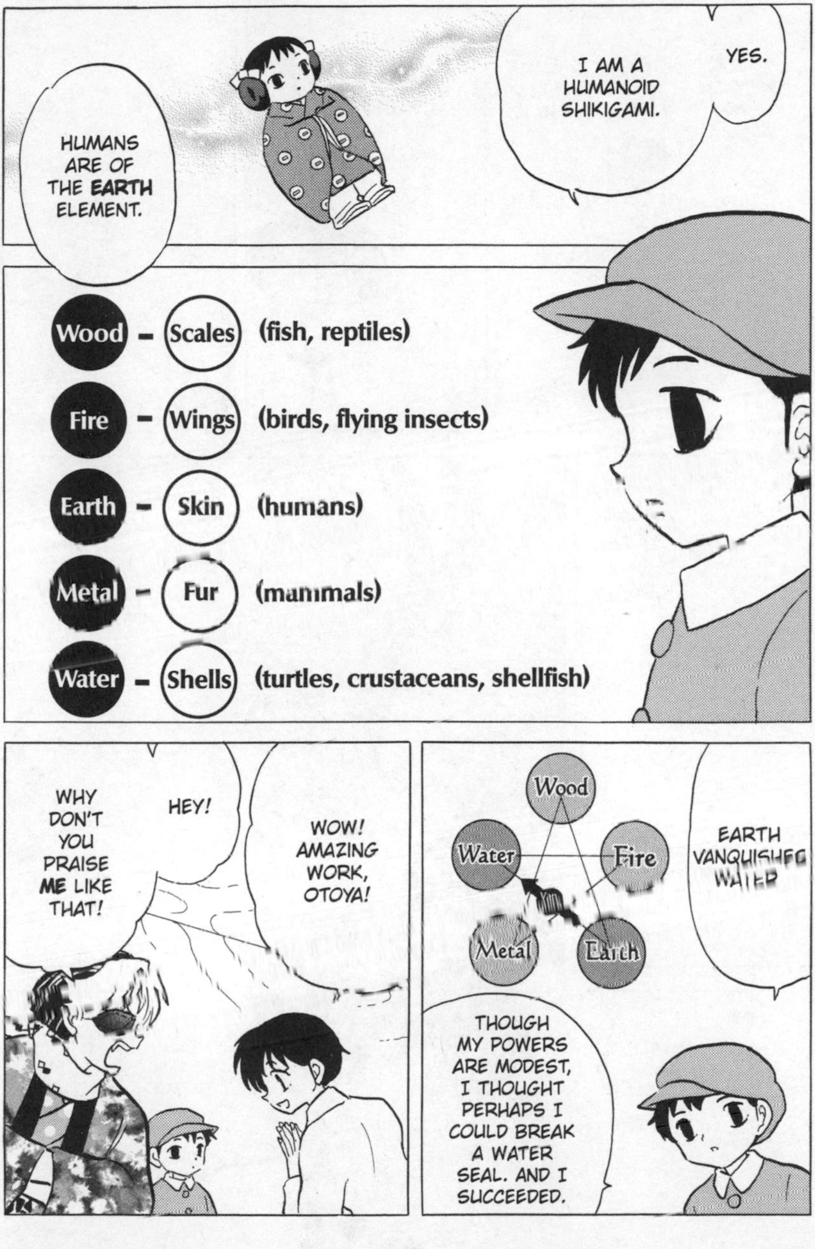
YES.
I AM A HUMANOID SHIKIGAMI.
HUMANS ARE OF THE **EARTH** ELEMENT.
Wood - Scales (fish, reptiles)
Fire - Wings (birds, flying insects)
Earth - Skin (humans)
Metal - Fur (mammals)
Water - Shells (turtles, crustaceans, shellfish)
EARTH VANQUISHES WATER
Wood
Water
Fire
Metal
Earth
THOUGH MY POWERS ARE MODEST, I THOUGHT PERHAPS I COULD BREAK A WATER SEAL. AND I SUCCEEDED.
WOW! AMAZING WORK, OTOYA!
HEY!
WHY DON'T YOU PRAISE **ME** LIKE THAT!

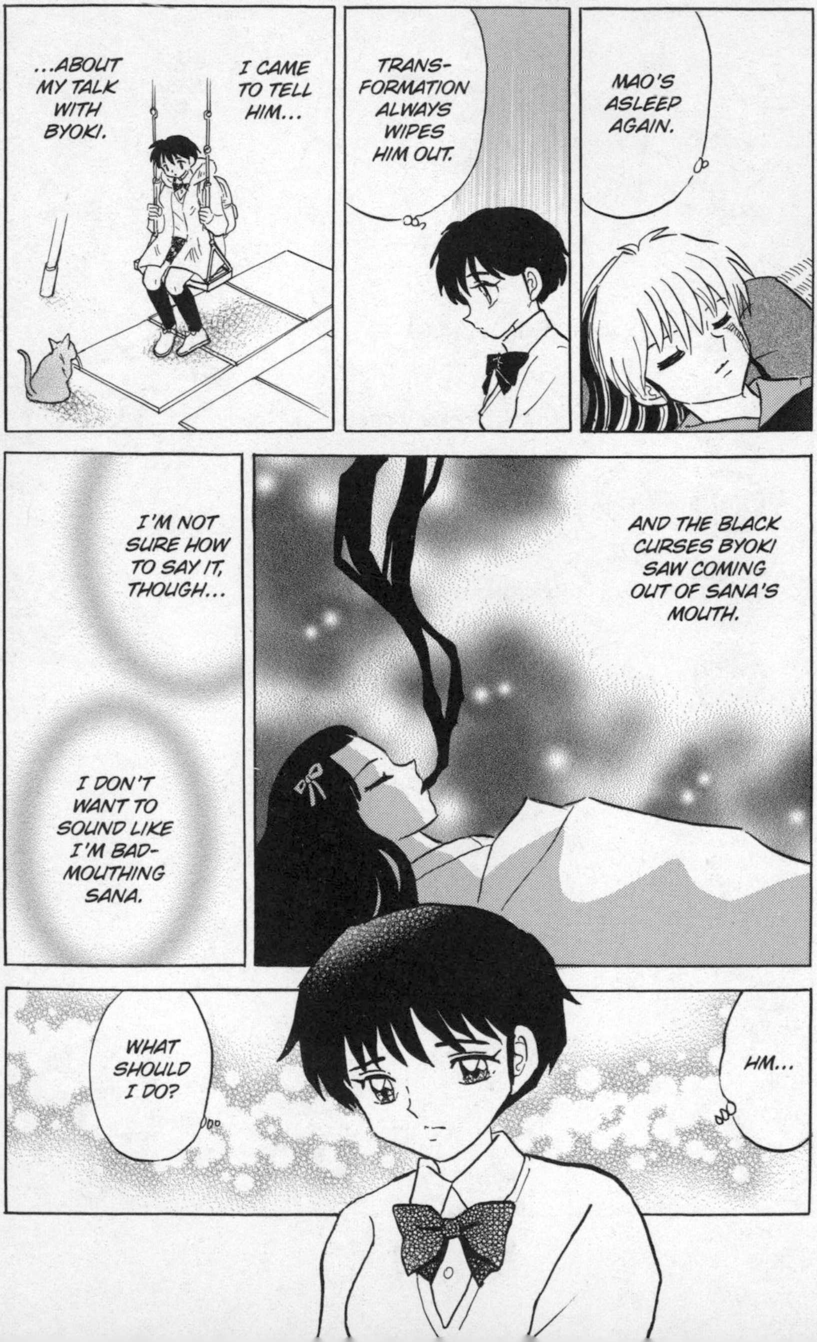
MAO'S ASLEEP AGAIN.
TRANS-FORMATION ALWAYS WIPES HIM OUT.
I CAME TO TELL HIM...
...ABOUT MY TALK WITH BYOKI.
AND THE BLACK CURSES BYOKI SAW COMING OUT OF SANA'S MOUTH.
I'M NOT SURE HOW TO SAY IT, THOUGH...
I DON'T WANT TO SOUND LIKE I'M BAD-MOUTHING SANA.
HM...
WHAT SHOULD I DO?

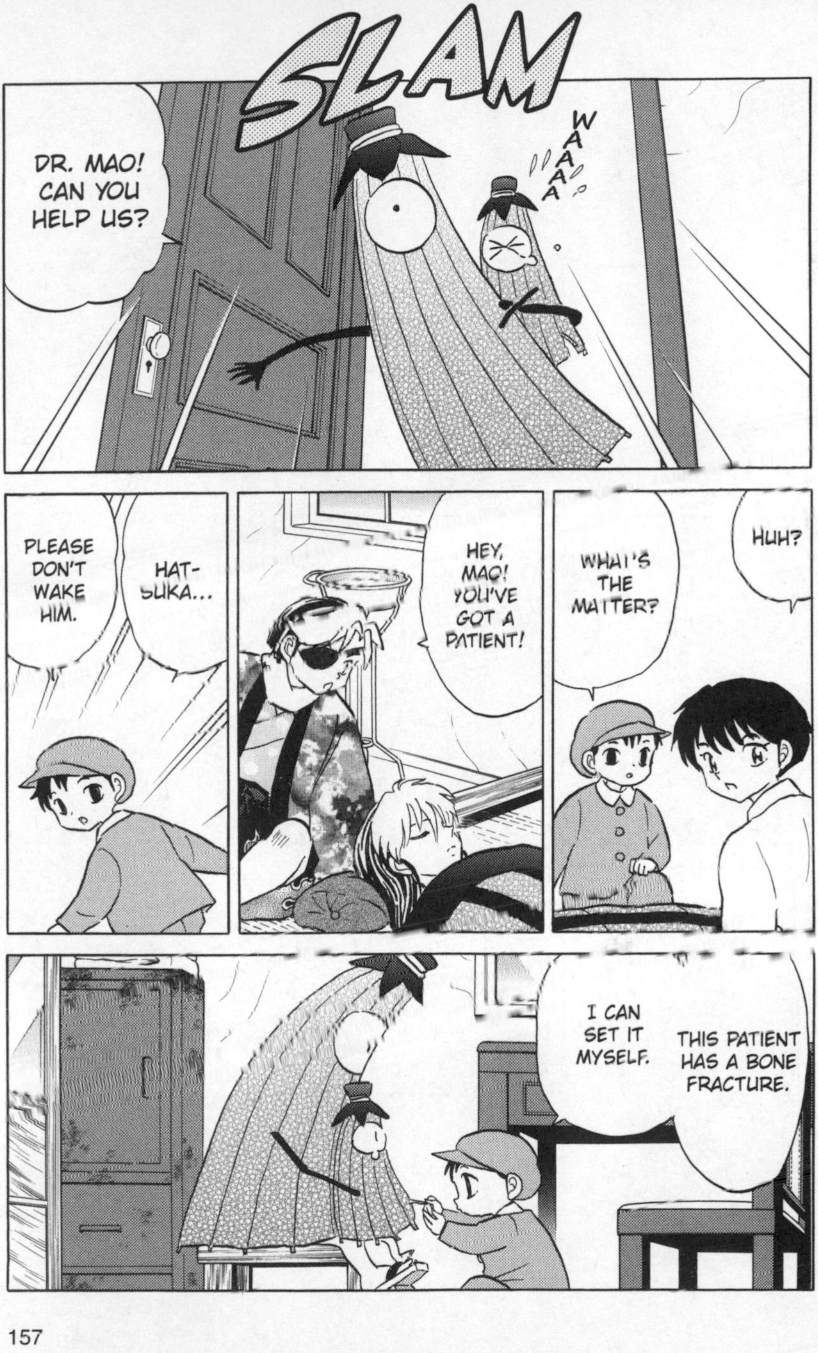
SLAM
WAAAAA
DR. MAO! CAN YOU HELP US?
HUH?
WHAT'S THE MATTER?
HEY, MAO! YOU'VE GOT A PATIENT!
HAT-SUKA...
PLEASE DON'T WAKE HIM.
THIS PATIENT HAS A BONE FRACTURE.
I CAN SET IT MYSELF.

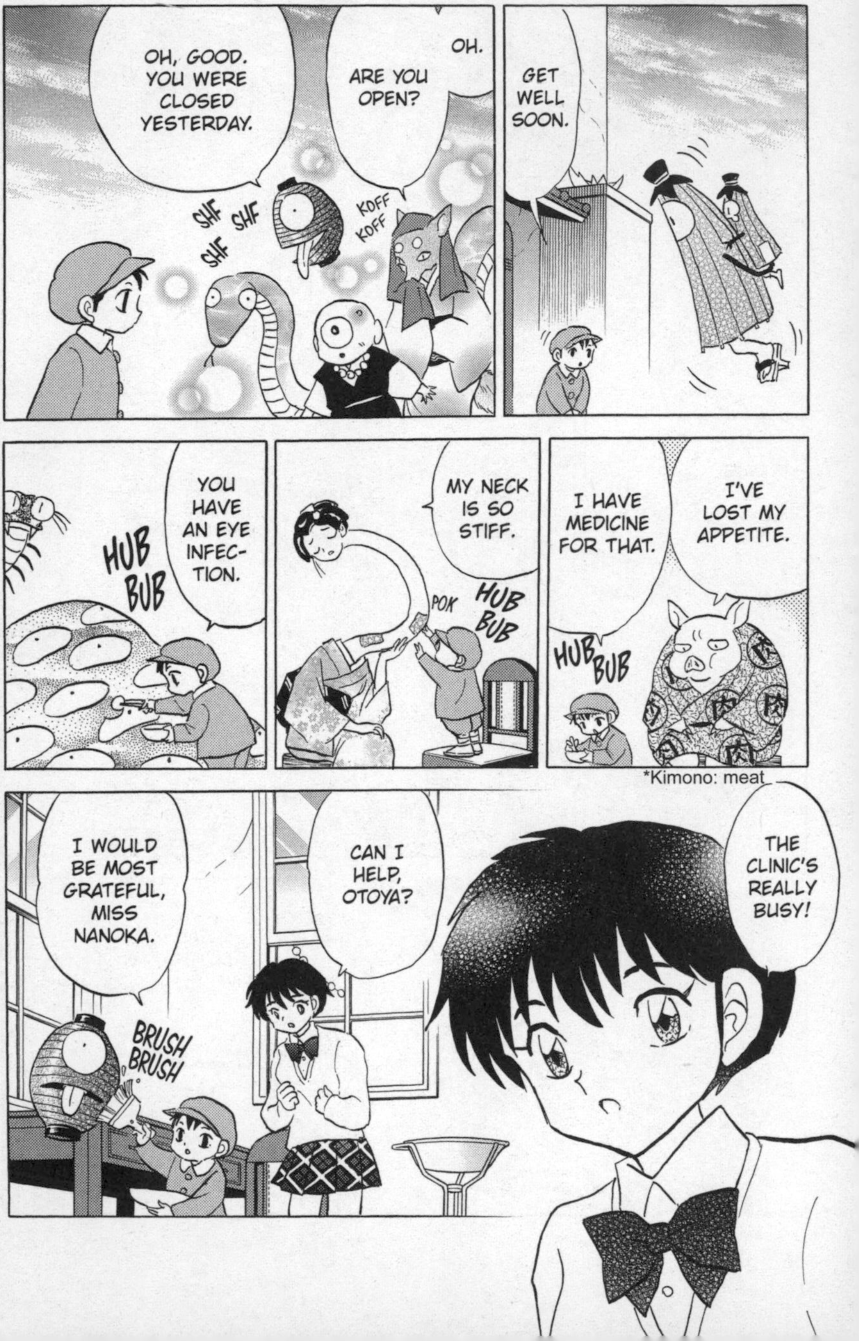
GET WELL SOON.
OH.
ARE YOU OPEN?
KOFF KOFF
OH, GOOD. YOU WERE CLOSED YESTERDAY.
SHF SHF SHF
I'VE LOST MY APPETITE.
I HAVE MEDICINE FOR THAT.
HUB BUB
MY NECK IS SO STIFF.
HUB BUB
POK
YOU HAVE AN EYE INFEC-TION.
HUB BUB
*Kimono: meat
THE CLINIC'S REALLY BUSY!
CAN I HELP, OTOYA?
I WOULD BE MOST GRATEFUL, MISS NANOKA.
BRUSH BRUSH

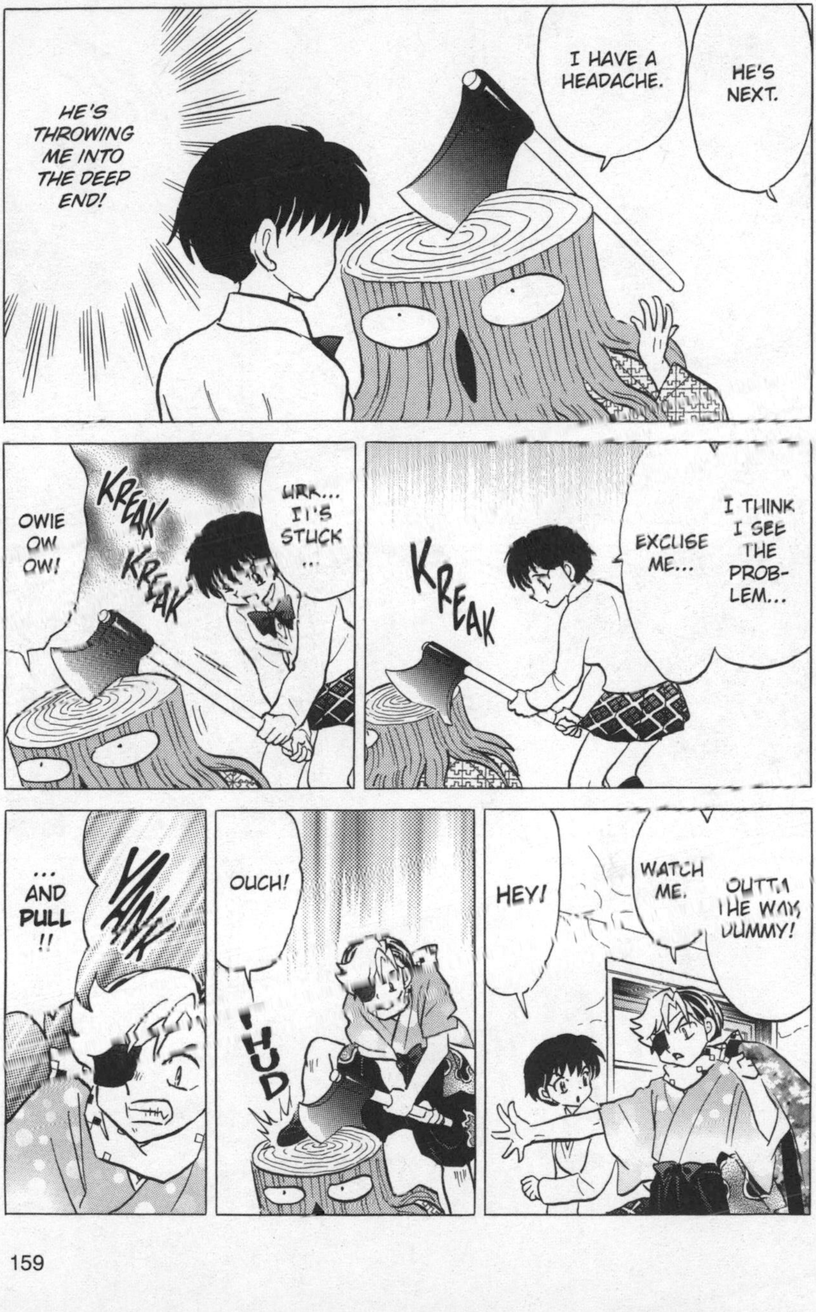
HE'S NEXT.
I HAVE A HEADACHE.
HE'S THROWING ME INTO THE DEEP END!
I THINK I SEE THE PROB-LEM...
EXCUSE ME...
KREAK
URK... IT'S STUCK ...
KREAK KREAK
OWIE OW OW!
OUTTA THE WAY DUMMY!
WATCH ME.
HEY!
OUCH!
THUD
YANK
... AND PULL !!

GOT IT OUT!
FWOMP
FWIP
WUPPA
ROLL
THUD
SHF SHF...

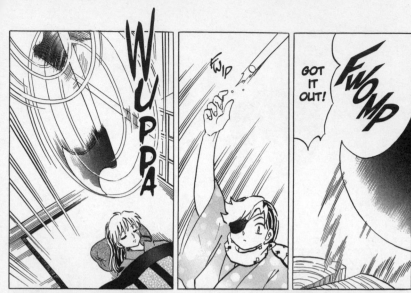

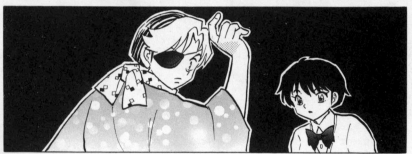

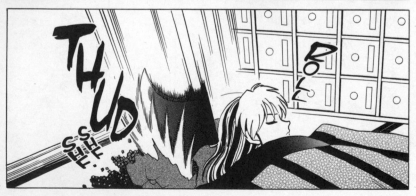

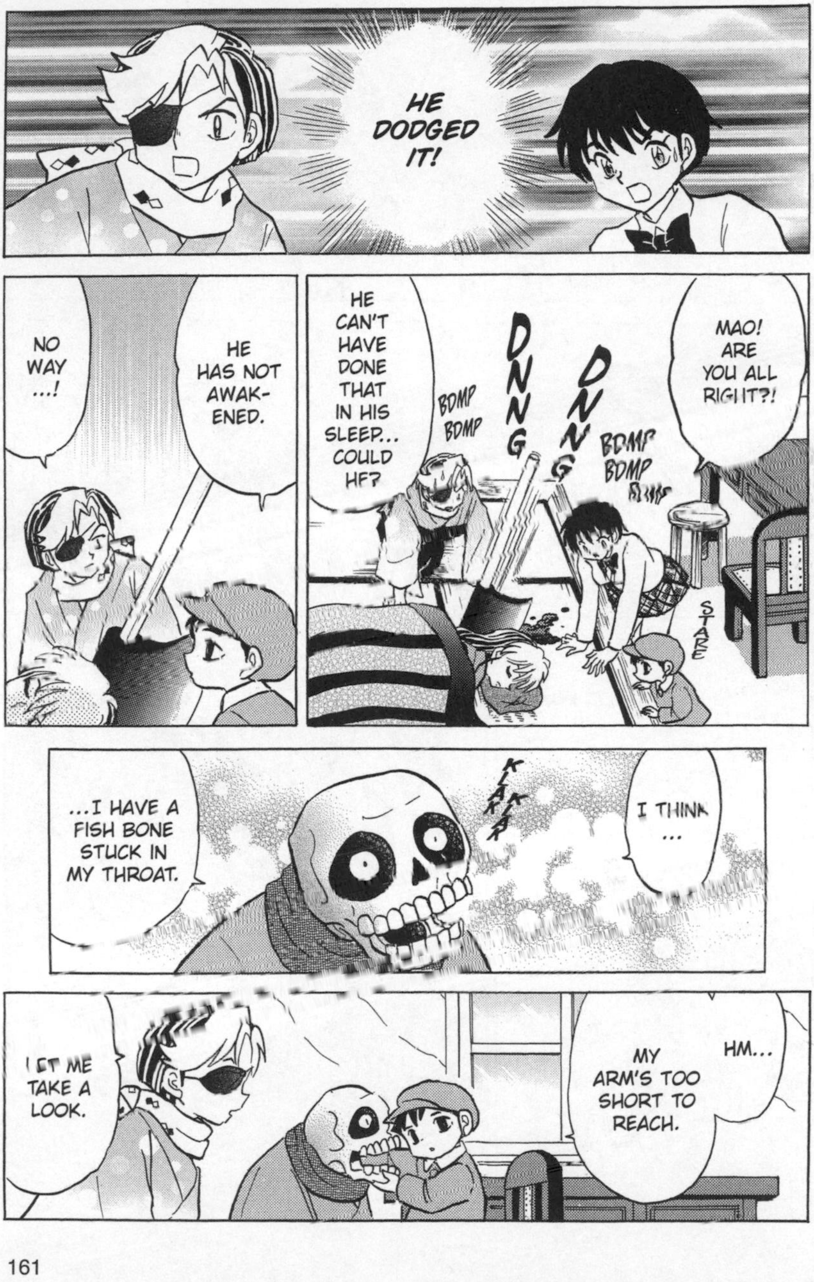
HE DODGED IT!
MAO! ARE YOU ALL RIGHT?!
DNNG
DNNG
BDMP BDMP
BDMP BDMP
HE CAN'T HAVE DONE THAT IN HIS SLEEP... COULD HE?
STARE
HE HAS NOT AWAK-ENED.
NO WAY ...!
I THINK ...
KLAK KLAK
...I HAVE A FISH BONE STUCK IN MY THROAT.
HM...
MY ARM'S TOO SHORT TO REACH.
LET ME TAKE A LOOK.

OTOYA, DOES THIS DECOCTION LOOK READY TO YOU?
BLUP BLUP BLUP
A LITTLE LONGER.
SHF SHF
I THINK I'VE GOT IT...
FWOMP
CRASH
TOK TOK TOK TOK
WHAT ?!
YOU PULLED OUT THE PATIENT'S VERTEBRA.
NOT A FISH BONE, EH?

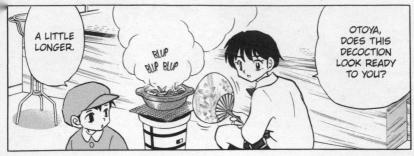

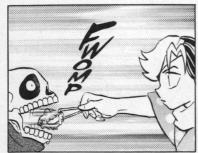

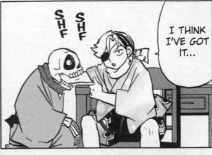

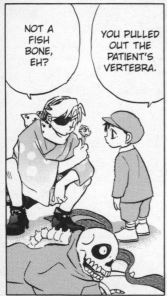

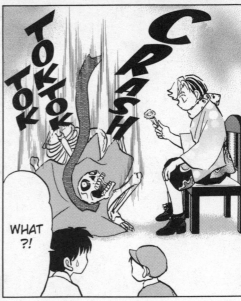

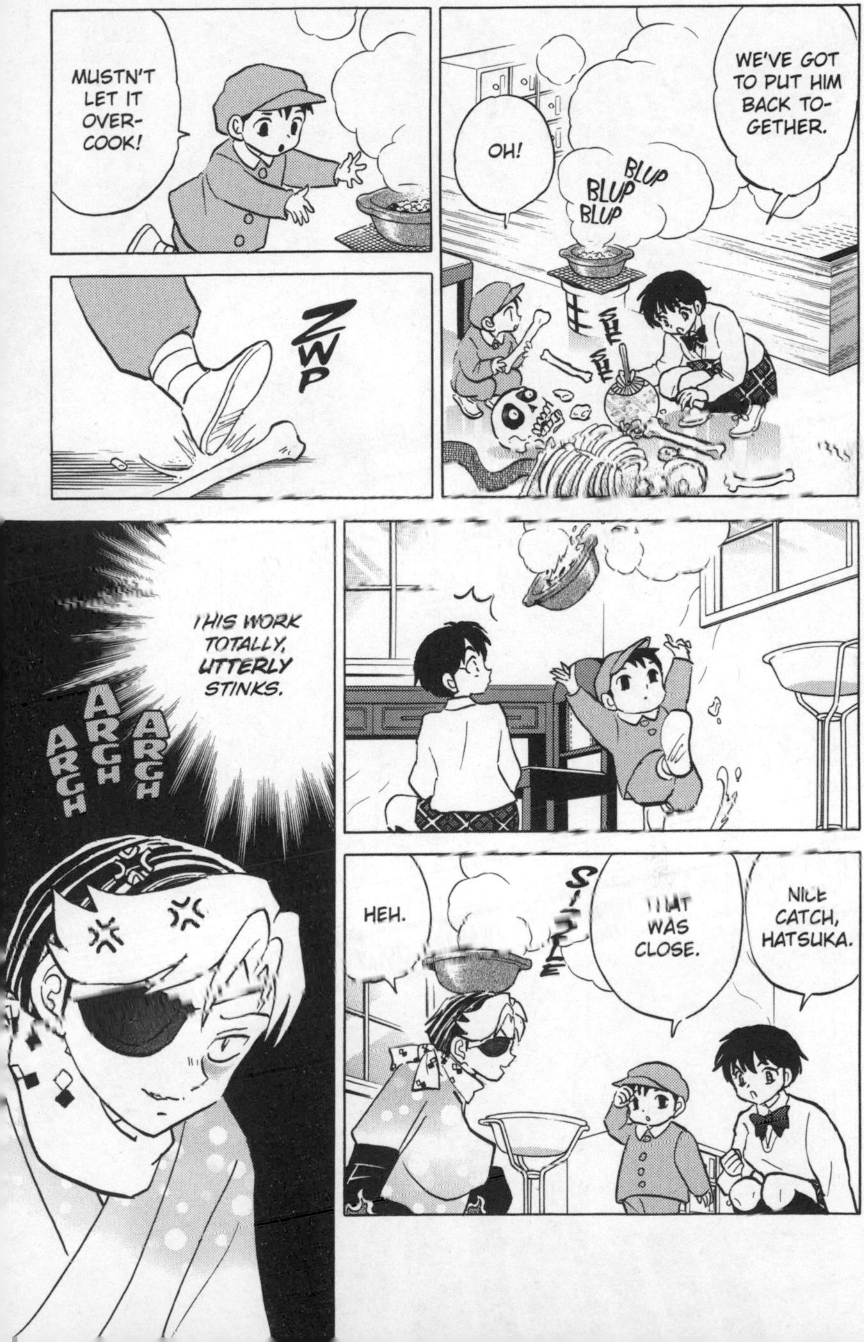
WE'VE GOT TO PUT HIM BACK TO-GETHER.
OH!
BLUP BLUP BLUP
MUSTN'T LET IT OVER-COOK!
ZWP
NICE CATCH, HATSUKA.
THAT WAS CLOSE.
HEH.
THIS WORK TOTALLY, UTTERLY STINKS.
ARGH ARGH ARGH

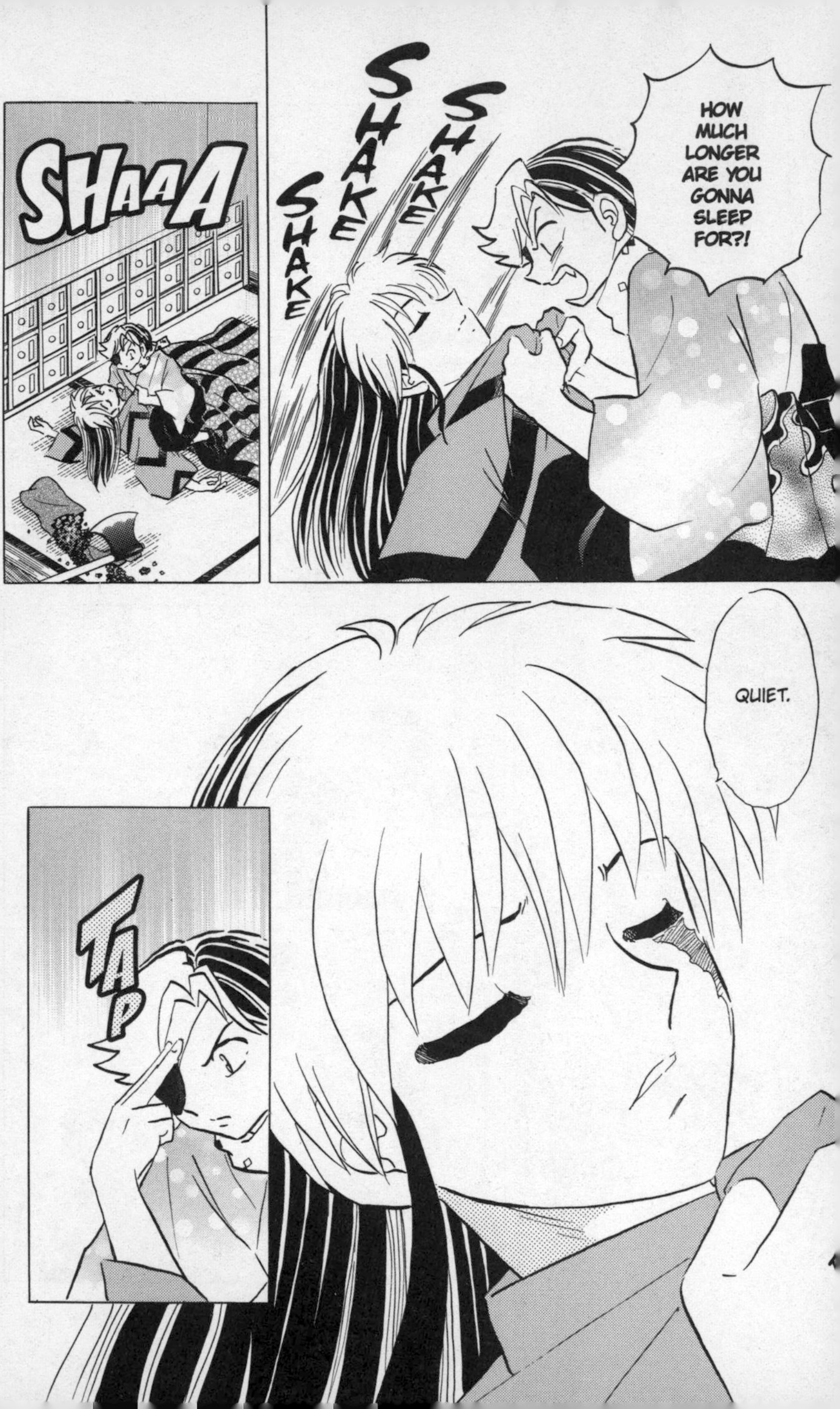
HOW MUCH LONGER ARE YOU GONNA SLEEP FOR?!
SHAKE
SHAKE
SHAKE
SHAAAA
QUIET.
TAP

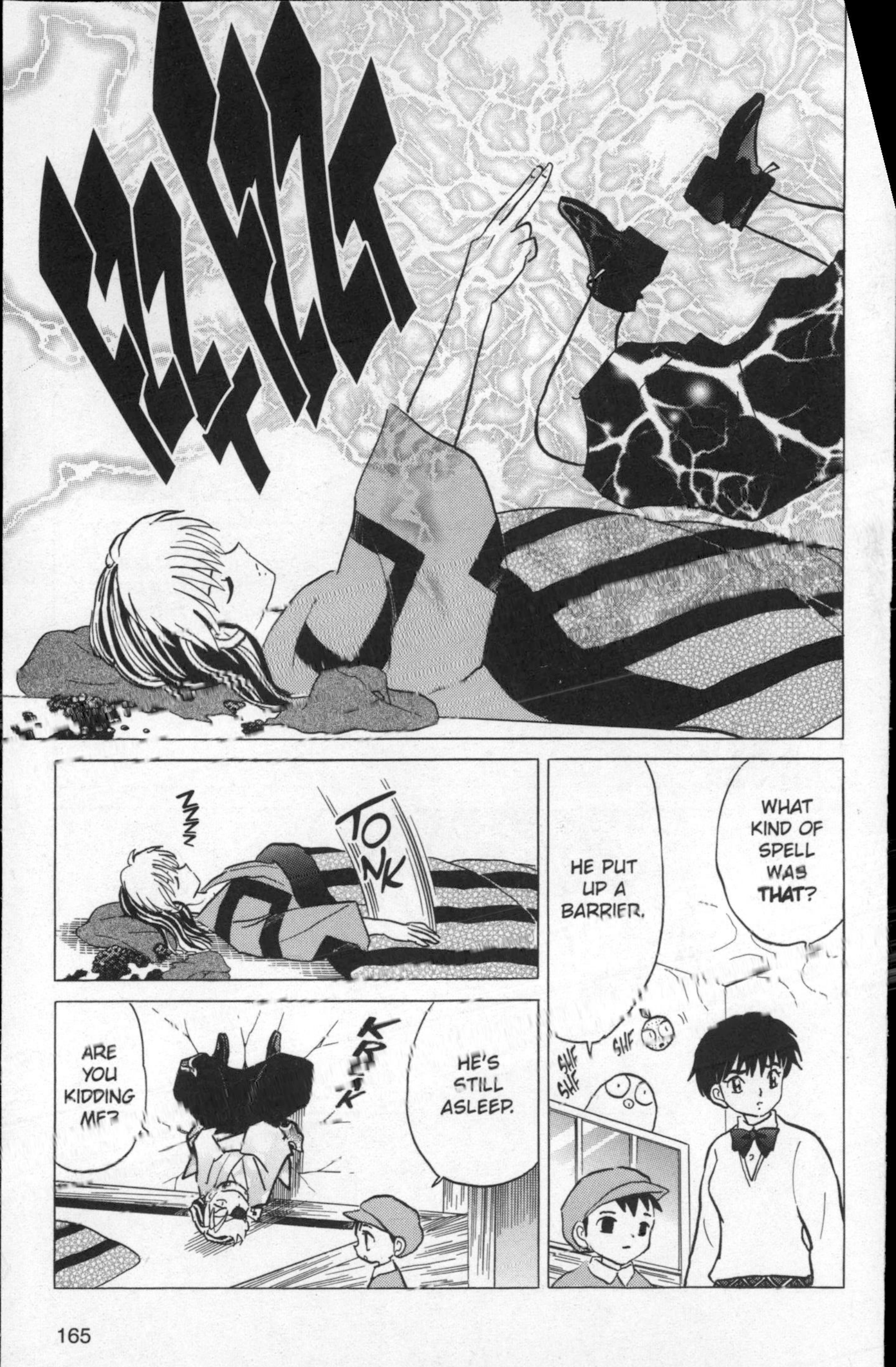
WHAT KIND OF SPELL WAS THAT?
HE PUT UP A BARRIER.
SHF SHF
SHF
ZZZ
TONK
HE'S STILL ASLEEP.
KRIK
ARE YOU KIDDING ME?

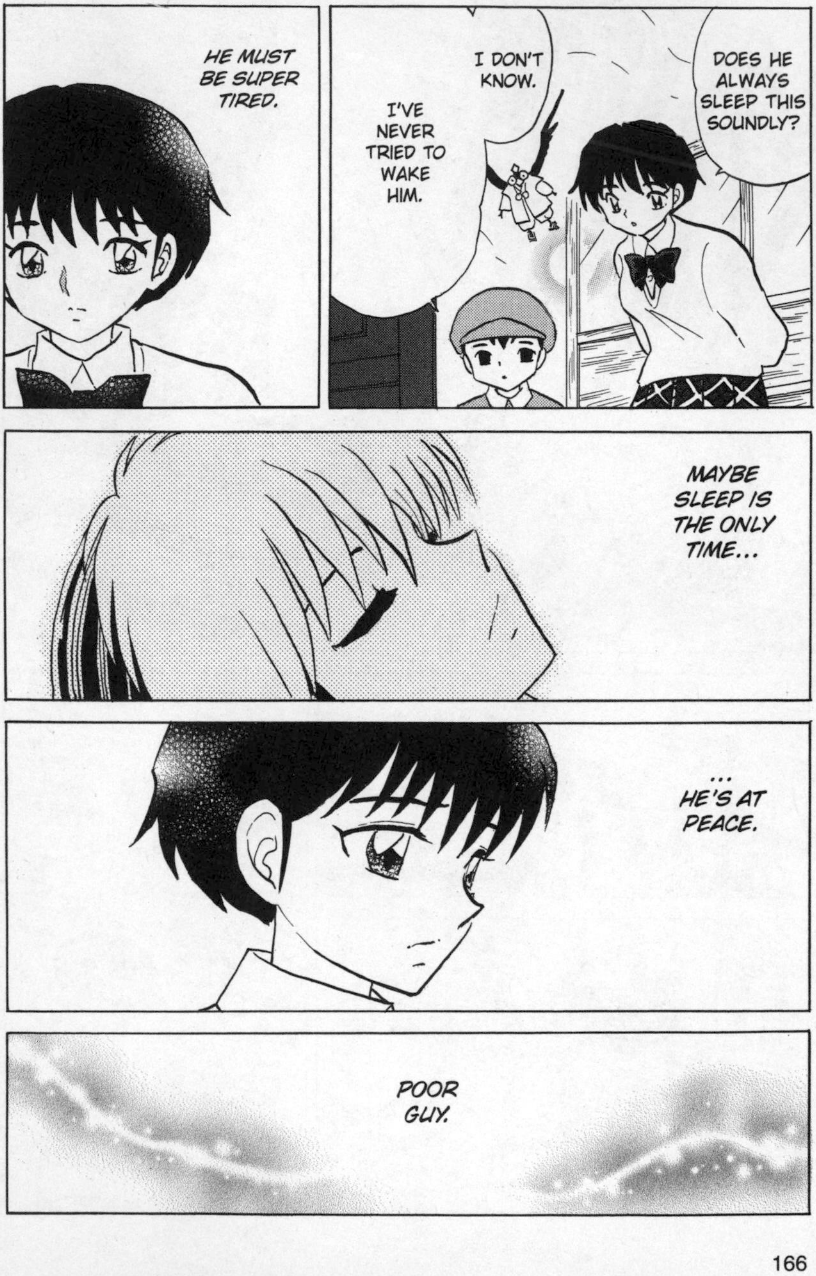
DOES HE ALWAYS SLEEP THIS SOUNDLY?
I DON'T KNOW.
I'VE NEVER TRIED TO WAKE HIM.
HE MUST BE SUPER TIRED.
MAYBE SLEEP IS THE ONLY TIME...
... HE'S AT PEACE.
POOR GUY.

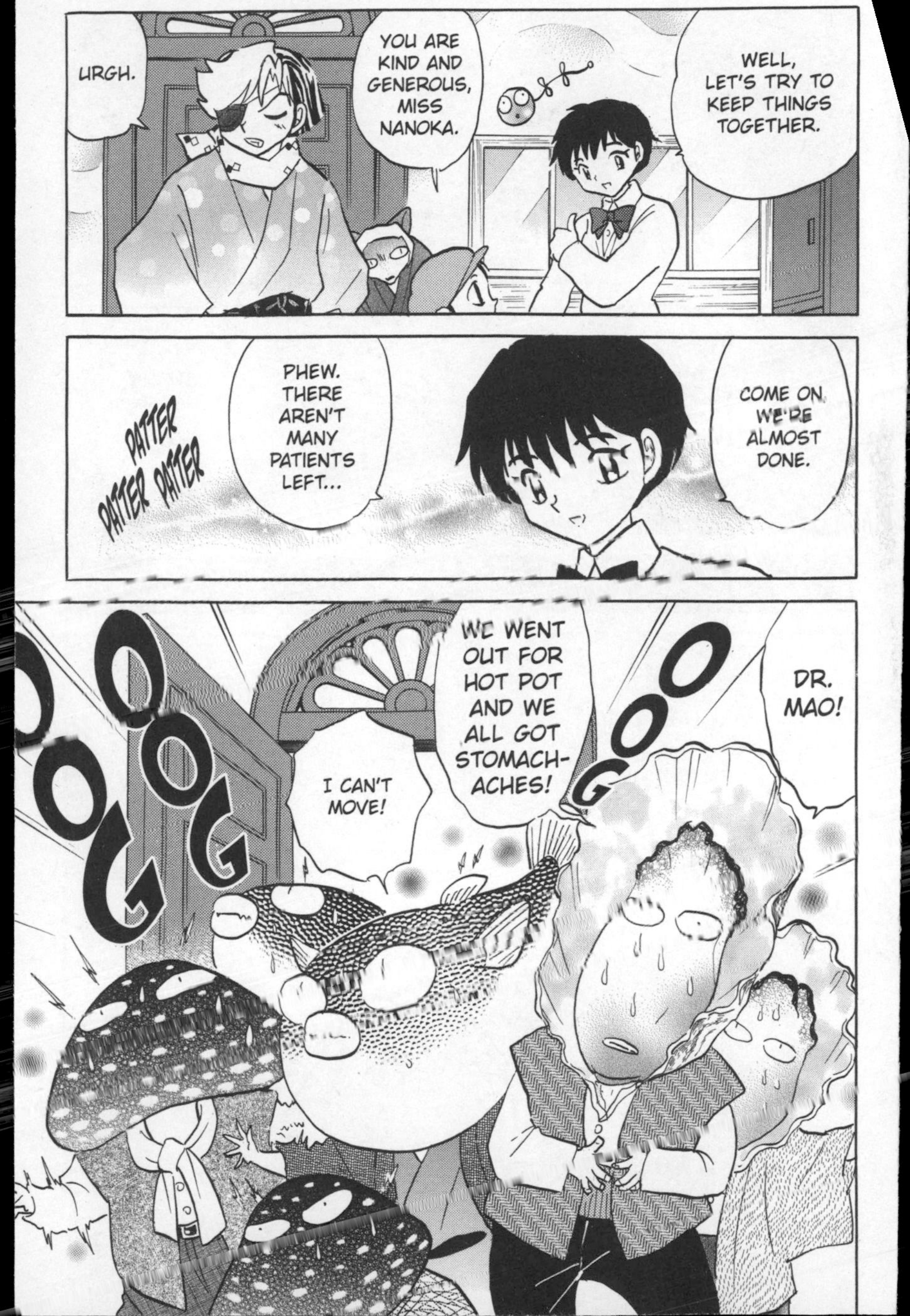
WELL, LET'S TRY TO KEEP THINGS TOGETHER.
YOU ARE KIND AND GENEROUS, MISS NANOKA.
URGH.
COME ON. WE'RE ALMOST DONE.
PHEW. THERE AREN'T MANY PATIENTS LEFT...
PATTER PATTER PATTER
DR. MAO!
WE WENT OUT FOR HOT POT AND WE ALL GOT STOMACH-ACHES!
I CAN'T MOVE!

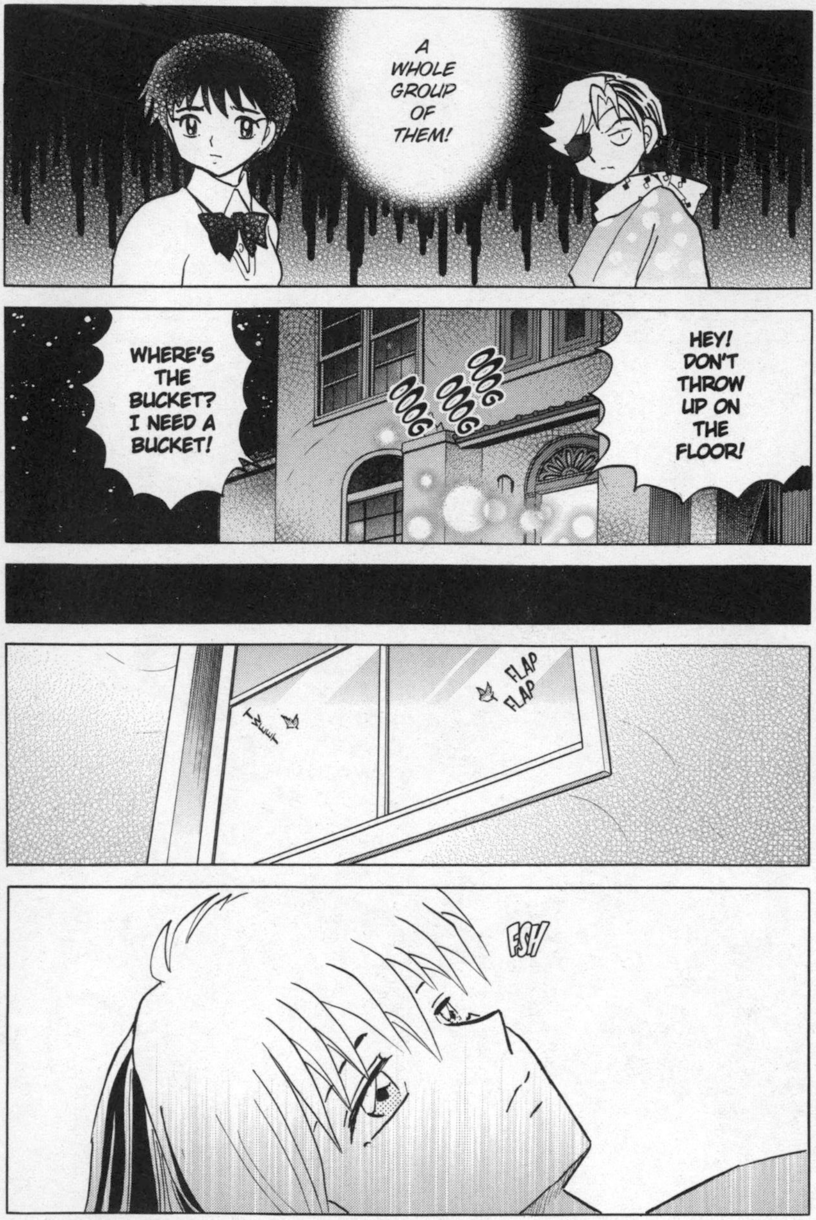
A WHOLE GROUP OF THEM!
HEY! DON'T THROW UP ON THE FLOOR!
OOOG OOOG OOOG
WHERE'S THE BUCKET? I NEED A BUCKET!
FLAP FLAP
FSH

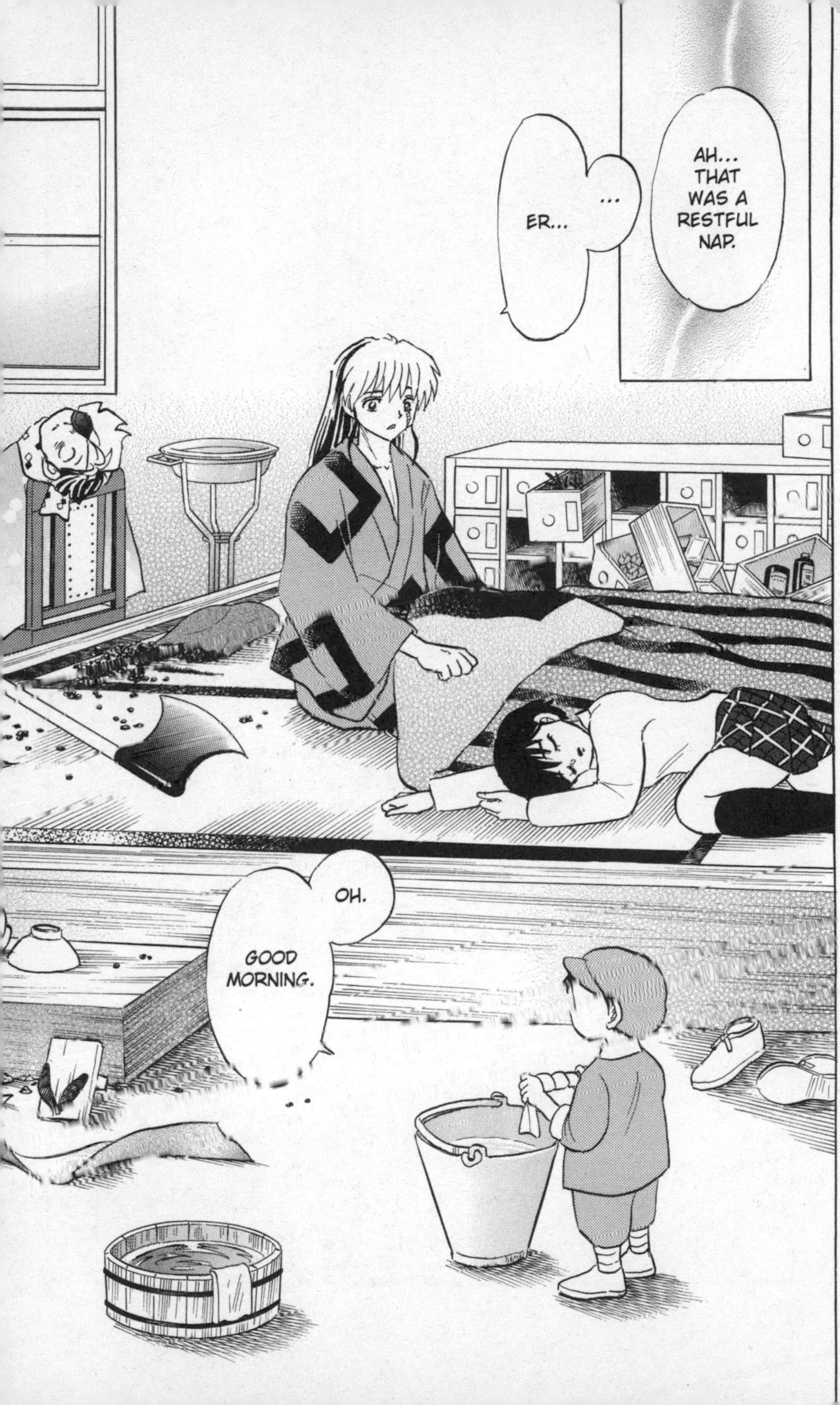
AH... THAT WAS A RESTFUL NAP.
...
ER...
OH.
GOOD MORNING.

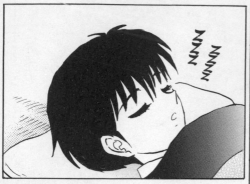

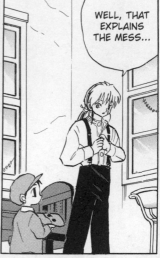

WELL, THAT EXPLAINS THE MESS...
ZZZZ
ZZZZ
SNERK
THEY STAFFED THE CLINIC FOR ME, EH?
HOW NICE OF THEM.
I'M GLAD TO SEE...
...YOU BACK AT YOUR STATION, DR. MAO.
SORRY TO KEEP YOU WAITING.
WE WERE STARTING TO WORRY.

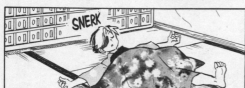

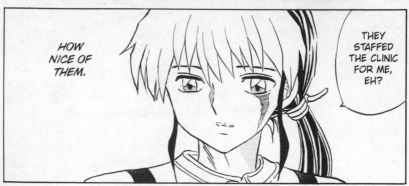

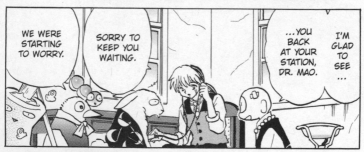

Chapter 10:
Maogui

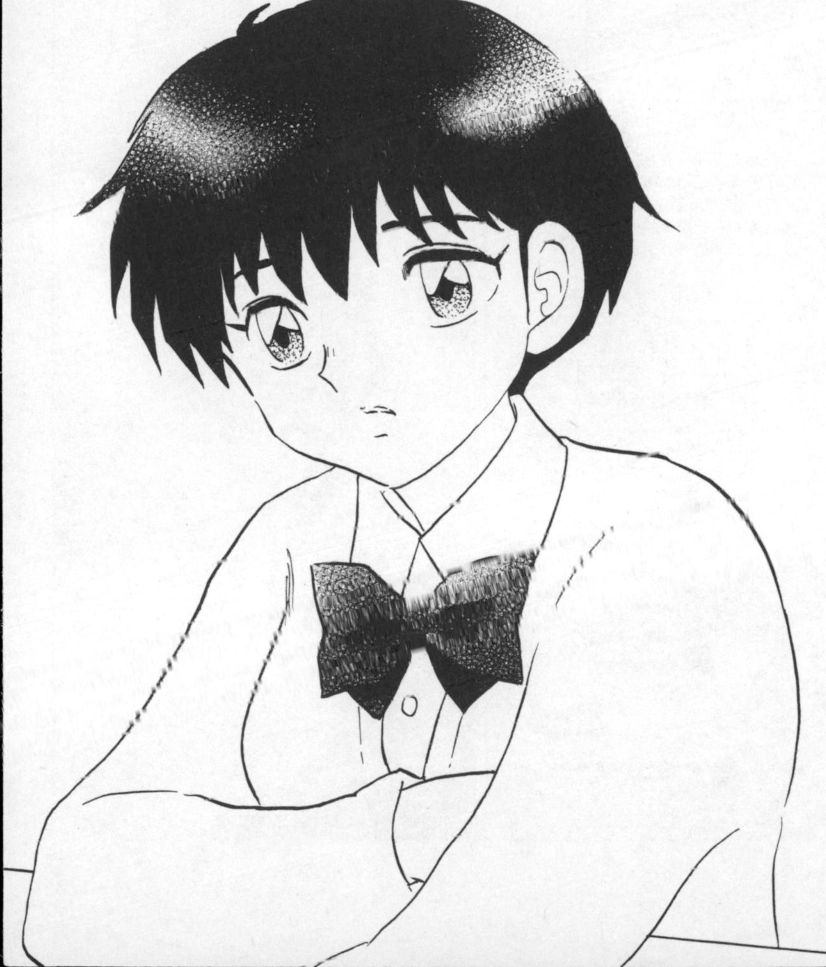

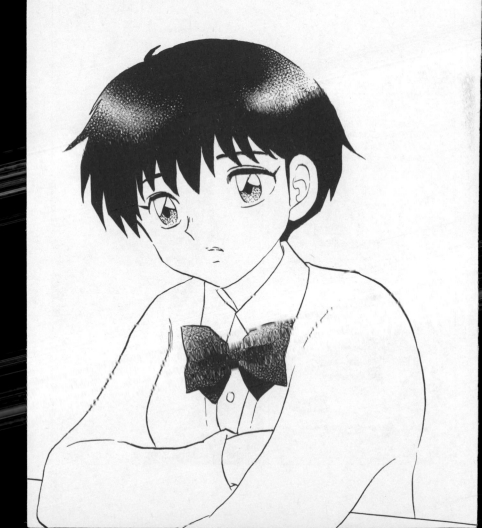

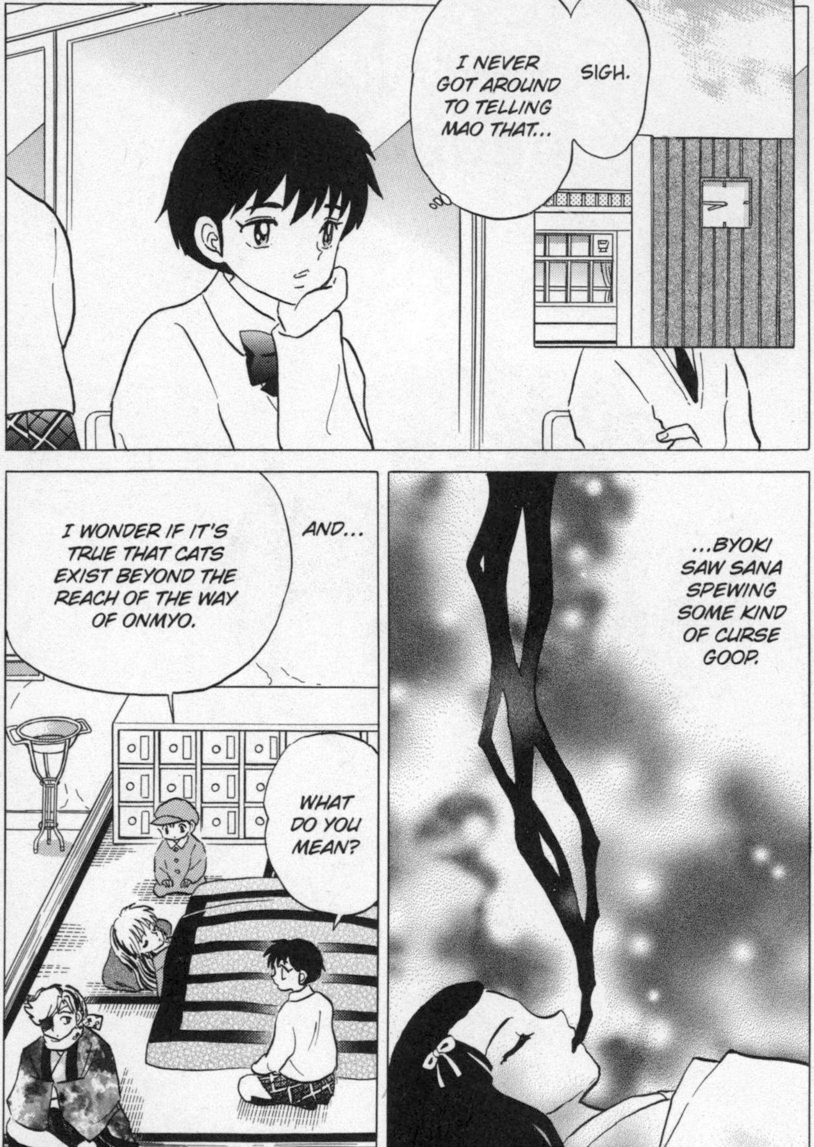
SIGH.
I NEVER GOT AROUND TO TELLING MAO THAT...
...BYOKI SAW SANA SPEWING SOME KIND OF CURSE GOOP.
AND...
I WONDER IF IT'S TRUE THAT CATS EXIST BEYOND THE REACH OF THE WAY OF ONMYO.
WHAT DO YOU MEAN?

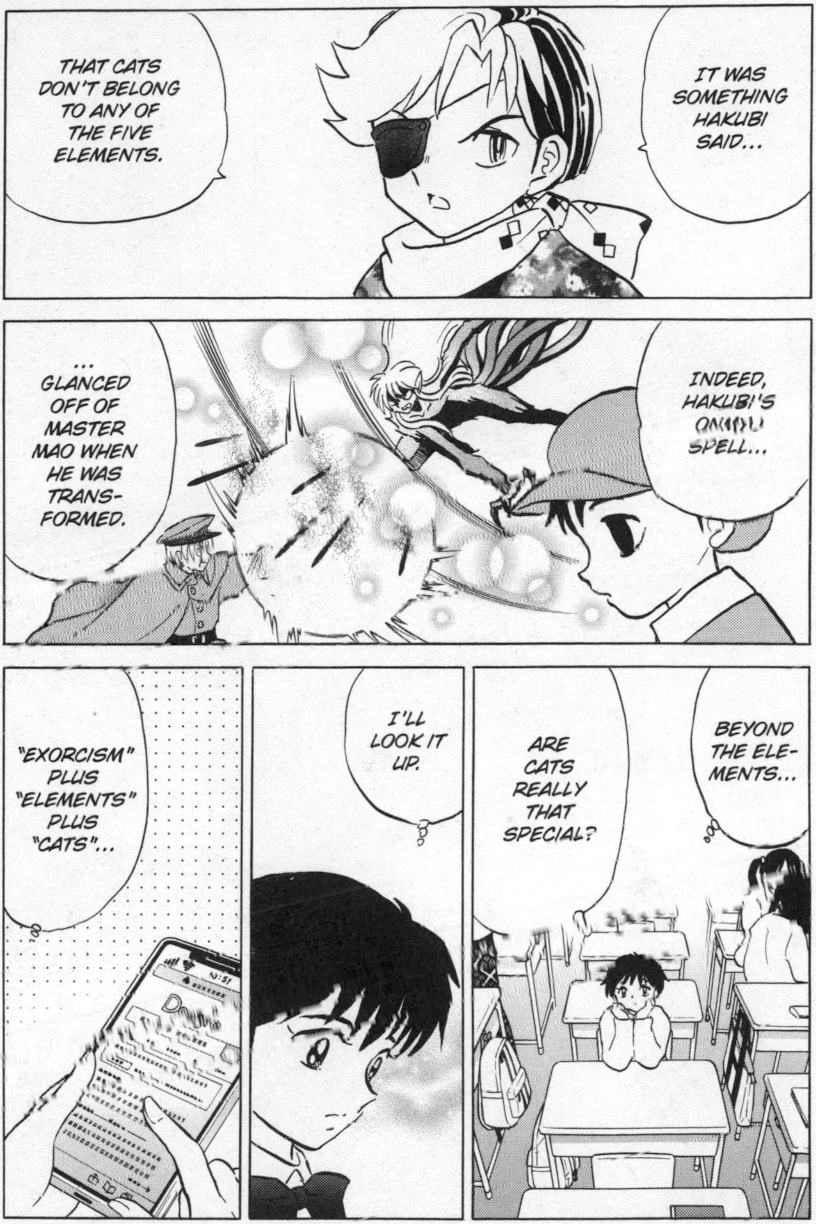
IT WAS SOMETHING HAKUBI SAID...
THAT CATS DON'T BELONG TO ANY OF THE FIVE ELEMENTS.
INDEED, HAKUBI'S SPELL...
...GLANCED OFF OF MASTER MAO WHEN HE WAS TRANS-FORMED.
BEYOND THE ELE-MENTS...
ARE CATS REALLY THAT SPECIAL?
I'LL LOOK IT UP.
"EXORCISM" PLUS "ELEMENTS" PLUS "CATS"...

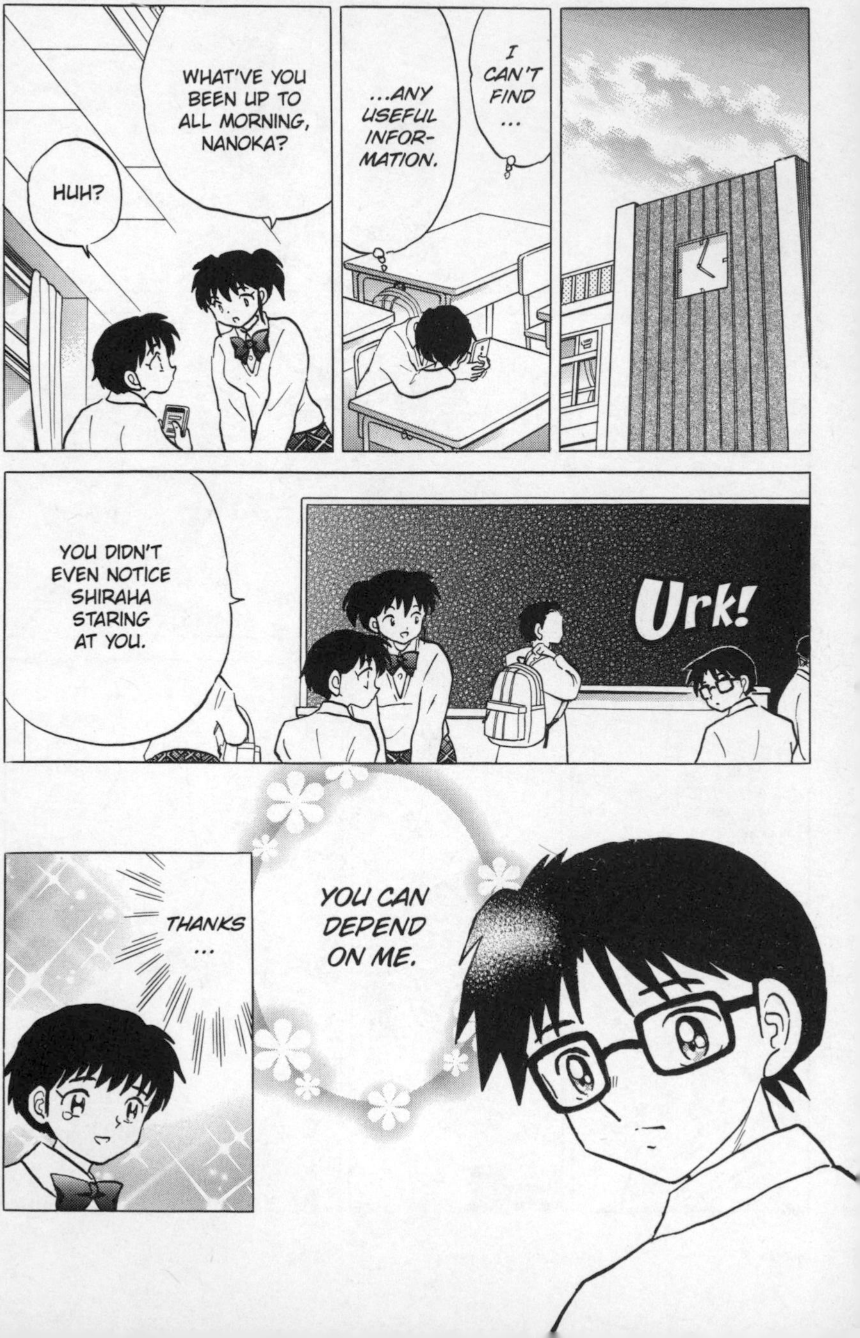
I CAN'T FIND ...
...ANY USEFUL INFORMATION.
WHAT'VE YOU BEEN UP TO ALL MORNING, NANOKA?
HUH?
Urk!
YOU DIDN'T EVEN NOTICE SHIRAHA STARING AT YOU.
YOU CAN DEPEND ON ME.
THANKS ...

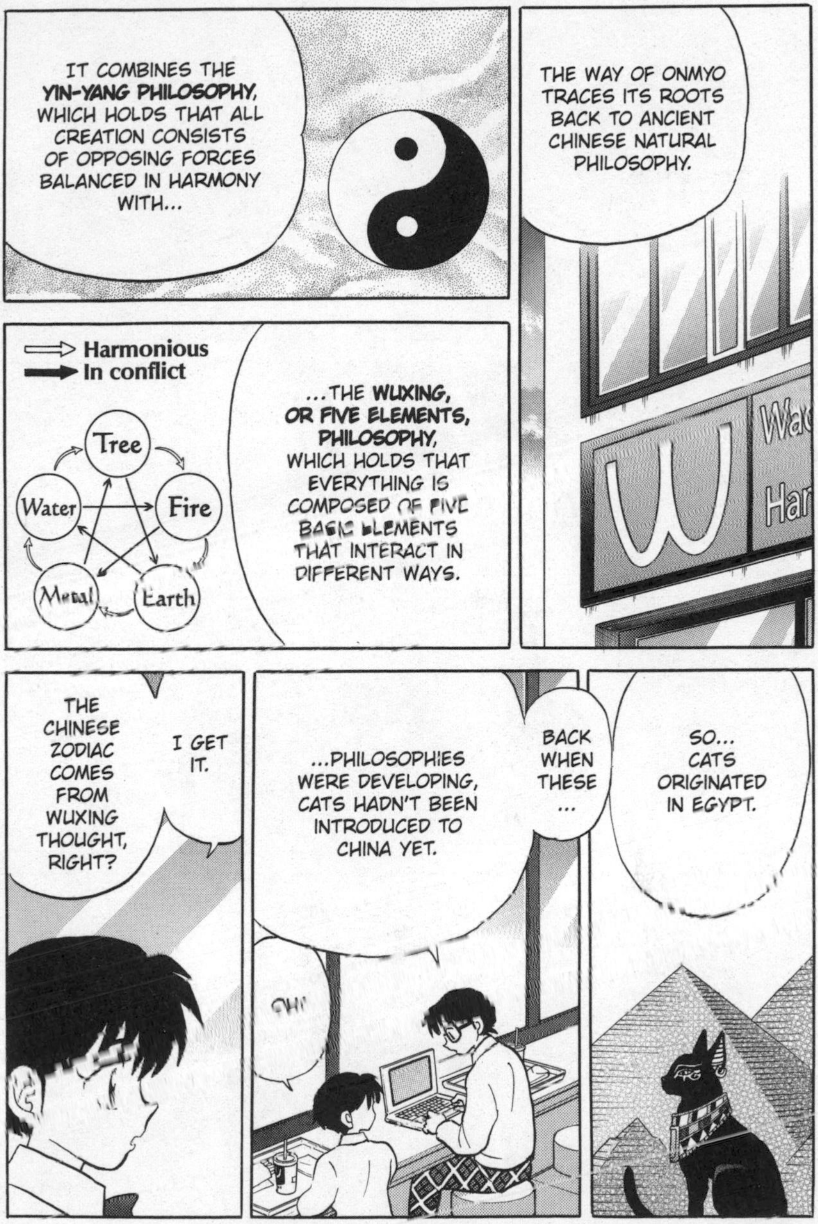
THE WAY OF ONMYO TRACES ITS ROOTS BACK TO ANCIENT CHINESE NATURAL PHILOSOPHY.
IT COMBINES THE **YIN-YANG PHILOSOPHY**, WHICH HOLDS THAT ALL CREATION CONSISTS OF OPPOSING FORCES BALANCED IN HARMONY WITH...
...THE **WUXING, OR FIVE ELEMENTS, PHILOSOPHY**, WHICH HOLDS THAT EVERYTHING IS COMPOSED OF FIVE BASIC ELEMENTS THAT INTERACT IN DIFFERENT WAYS.
Harmonious
In conflict
Tree
Fire
Earth
Metal
Water
SO... CATS ORIGINATED IN EGYPT.
BACK WHEN THESE ...
...PHILOSOPHIES WERE DEVELOPING, CATS HADN'T BEEN INTRODUCED TO CHINA YET.
OH!
I GET IT.
THE CHINESE ZODIAC COMES FROM WUXING THOUGHT, RIGHT?

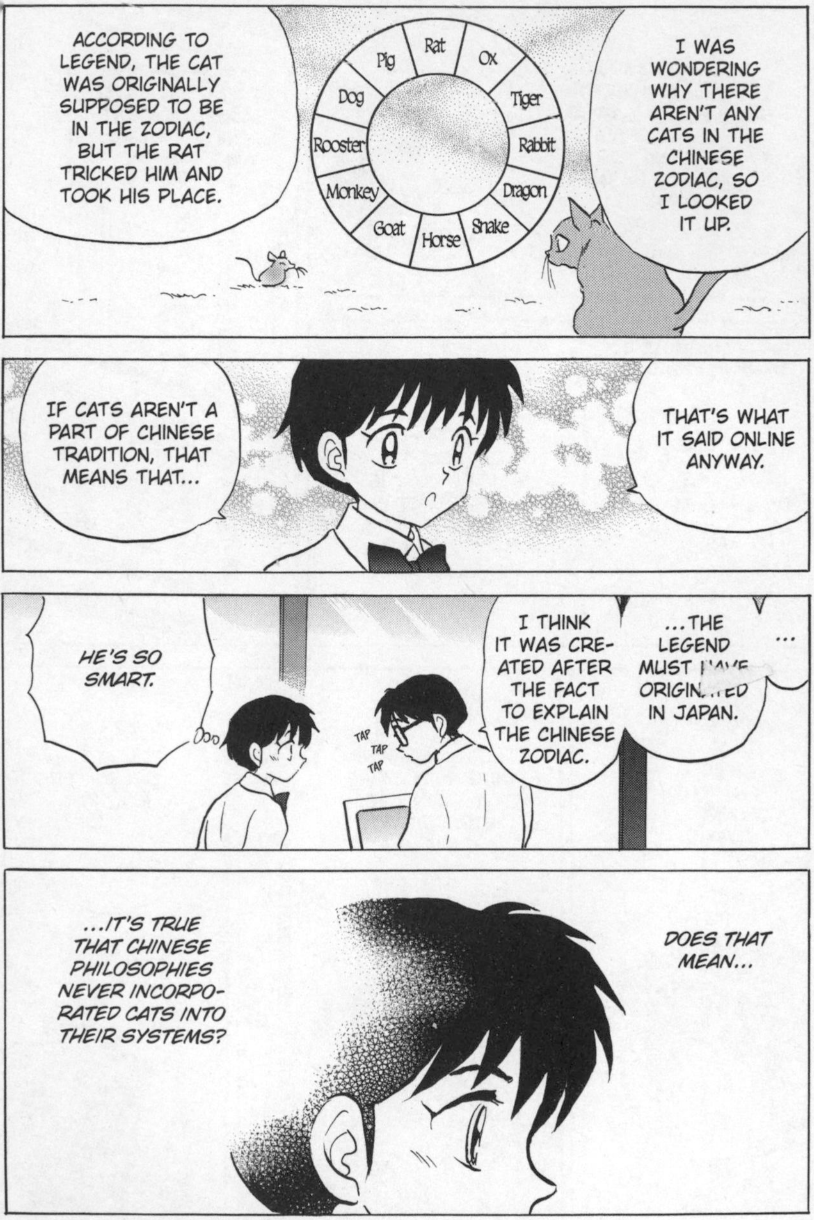
I WAS WONDERING WHY THERE AREN'T ANY CATS IN THE CHINESE ZODIAC, SO I LOOKED IT UP.
Rat
Ox
Tiger
Rabbit
Dragon
Snake
Horse
Goat
Monkey
Rooster
Dog
Pig
ACCORDING TO LEGEND, THE CAT WAS ORIGINALLY SUPPOSED TO BE IN THE ZODIAC, BUT THE RAT TRICKED HIM AND TOOK HIS PLACE.
THAT'S WHAT IT SAID ONLINE ANYWAY.
IF CATS AREN'T A PART OF CHINESE TRADITION, THAT MEANS THAT...
...
...THE LEGEND MUST HAVE ORIGINATED IN JAPAN.
I THINK IT WAS CREATED AFTER THE FACT TO EXPLAIN THE CHINESE ZODIAC.
TAP TAP TAP
HE'S SO SMART.
DOES THAT MEAN...
...IT'S TRUE THAT CHINESE PHILOSOPHIES NEVER INCORPORATED CATS INTO THEIR SYSTEMS?

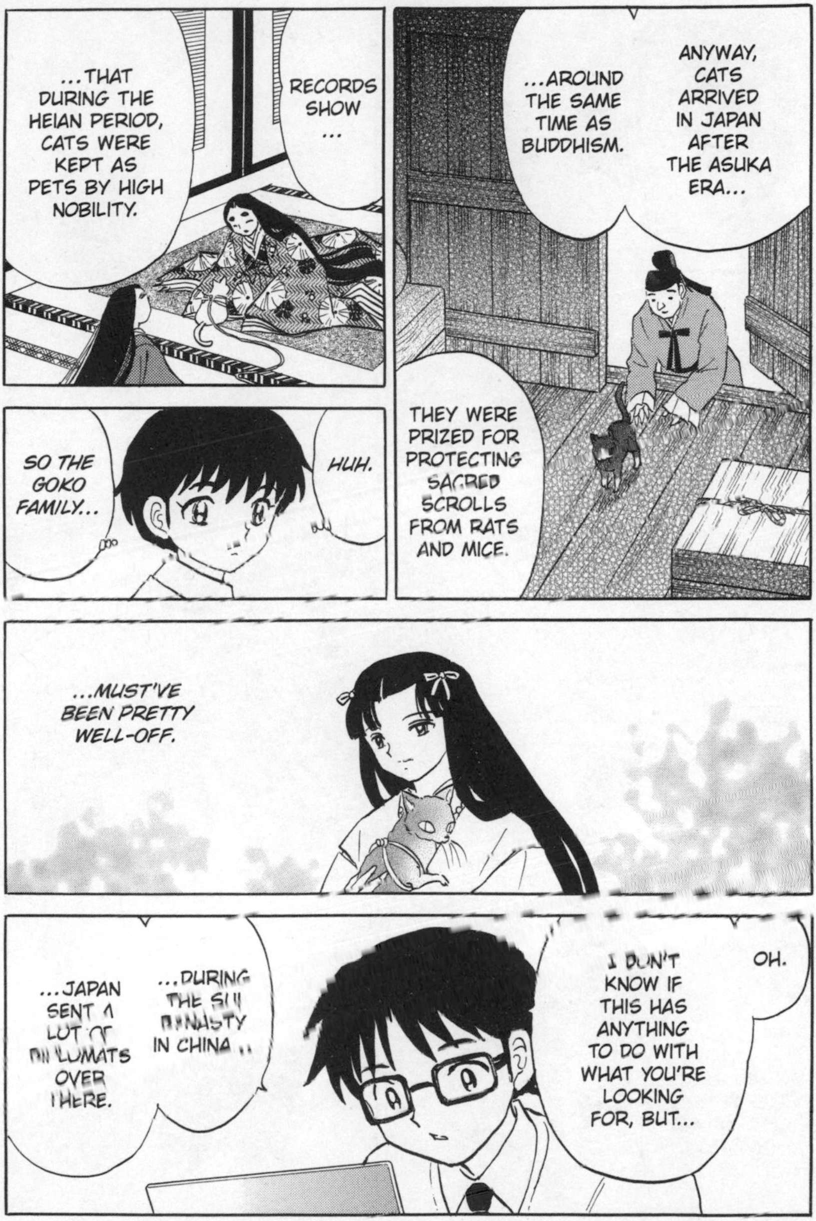
ANYWAY, CATS ARRIVED IN JAPAN AFTER THE ASUKA ERA...
...AROUND THE SAME TIME AS BUDDHISM.
THEY WERE PRIZED FOR PROTECTING SACRED SCROLLS FROM RATS AND MICE.
RECORDS SHOW ...
...THAT DURING THE HEIAN PERIOD, CATS WERE KEPT AS PETS BY HIGH NOBILITY.
HUH.
SO THE GOKO FAMILY...
...MUST'VE BEEN PRETTY WELL-OFF.
OH.
I DON'T KNOW IF THIS HAS ANYTHING TO DO WITH WHAT YOU'RE LOOKING FOR, BUT...
...DURING THE SUI DYNASTY IN CHINA...
...JAPAN SENT A LOT OF DIPLOMATS OVER THERE.

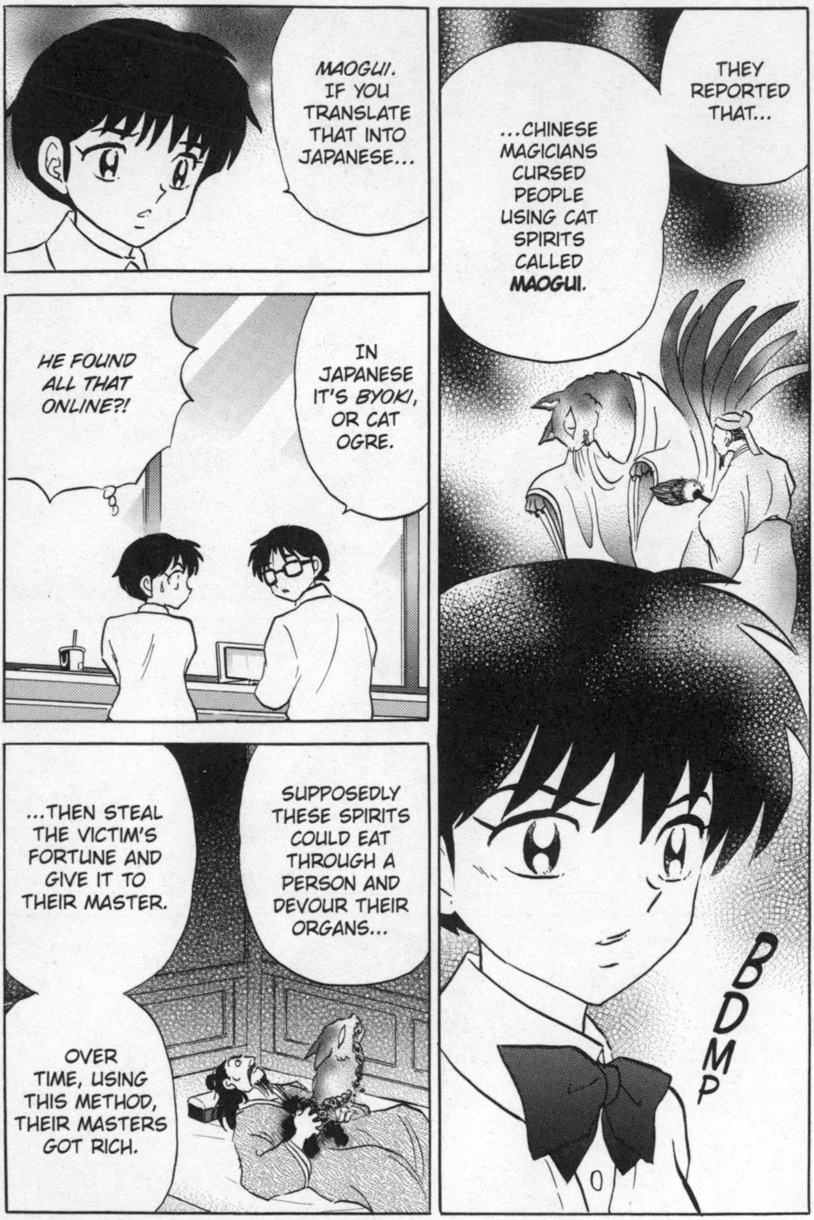
THEY REPORTED THAT...
...CHINESE MAGICIANS CURSED PEOPLE USING CAT SPIRITS CALLED **MAOGUI**.
BDMP
MAOGUI. IF YOU TRANSLATE THAT INTO JAPANESE...
IN JAPANESE IT'S *BYOKI*, OR CAT OGRE.
HE FOUND ALL THAT ONLINE?!
SUPPOSEDLY THESE SPIRITS COULD EAT THROUGH A PERSON AND DEVOUR THEIR ORGANS...
...THEN STEAL THE VICTIM'S FORTUNE AND GIVE IT TO THEIR MASTER.
OVER TIME, USING THIS METHOD, THEIR MASTERS GOT RICH.

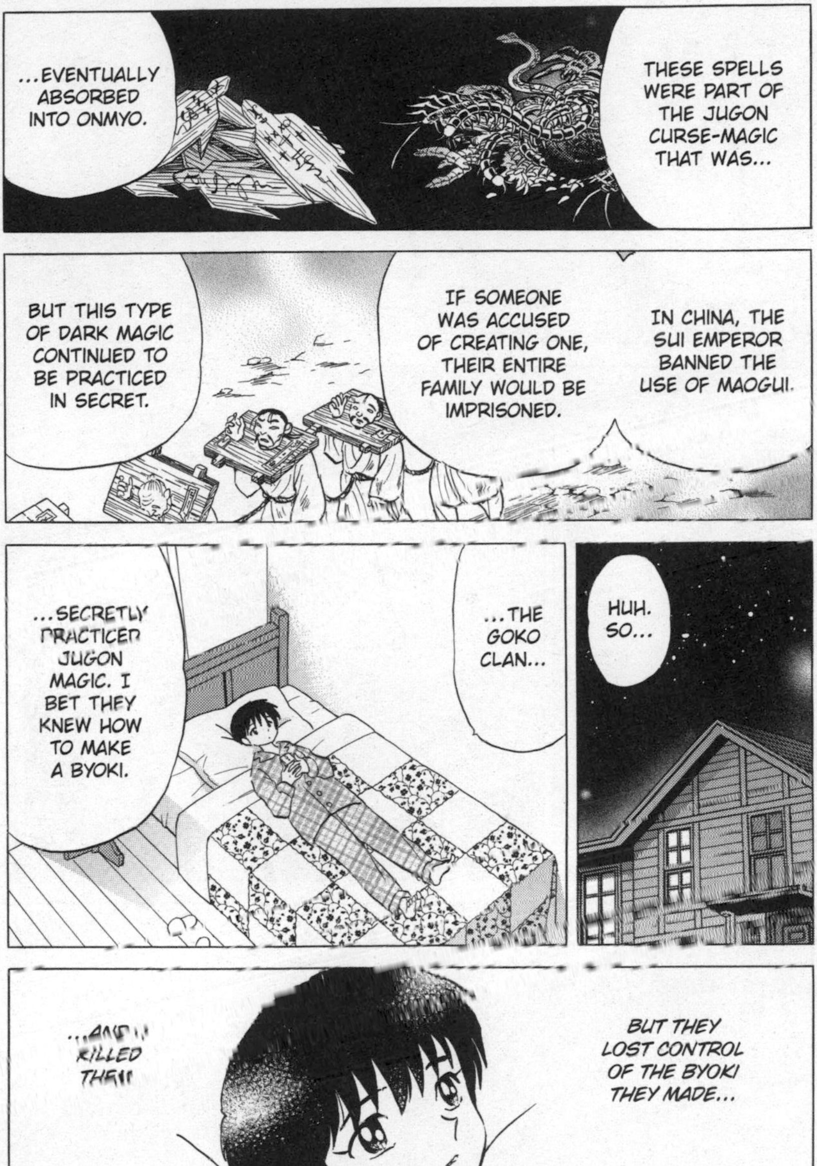
THESE SPELLS WERE PART OF THE JUGON CURSE-MAGIC THAT WAS...
...EVENTUALLY ABSORBED INTO ONMYO.
IN CHINA, THE SUI EMPEROR BANNED THE USE OF MAOGUI.
IF SOMEONE WAS ACCUSED OF CREATING ONE, THEIR ENTIRE FAMILY WOULD BE IMPRISONED.
BUT THIS TYPE OF DARK MAGIC CONTINUED TO BE PRACTICED IN SECRET.
HUH. SO...
...THE GOKO CLAN...
...SECRETLY PRACTICED JUGON MAGIC. I BET THEY KNEW HOW TO MAKE A BYOKI.
BUT THEY LOST CONTROL OF THE BYOKI THEY MADE...
...AND IT KILLED THEM

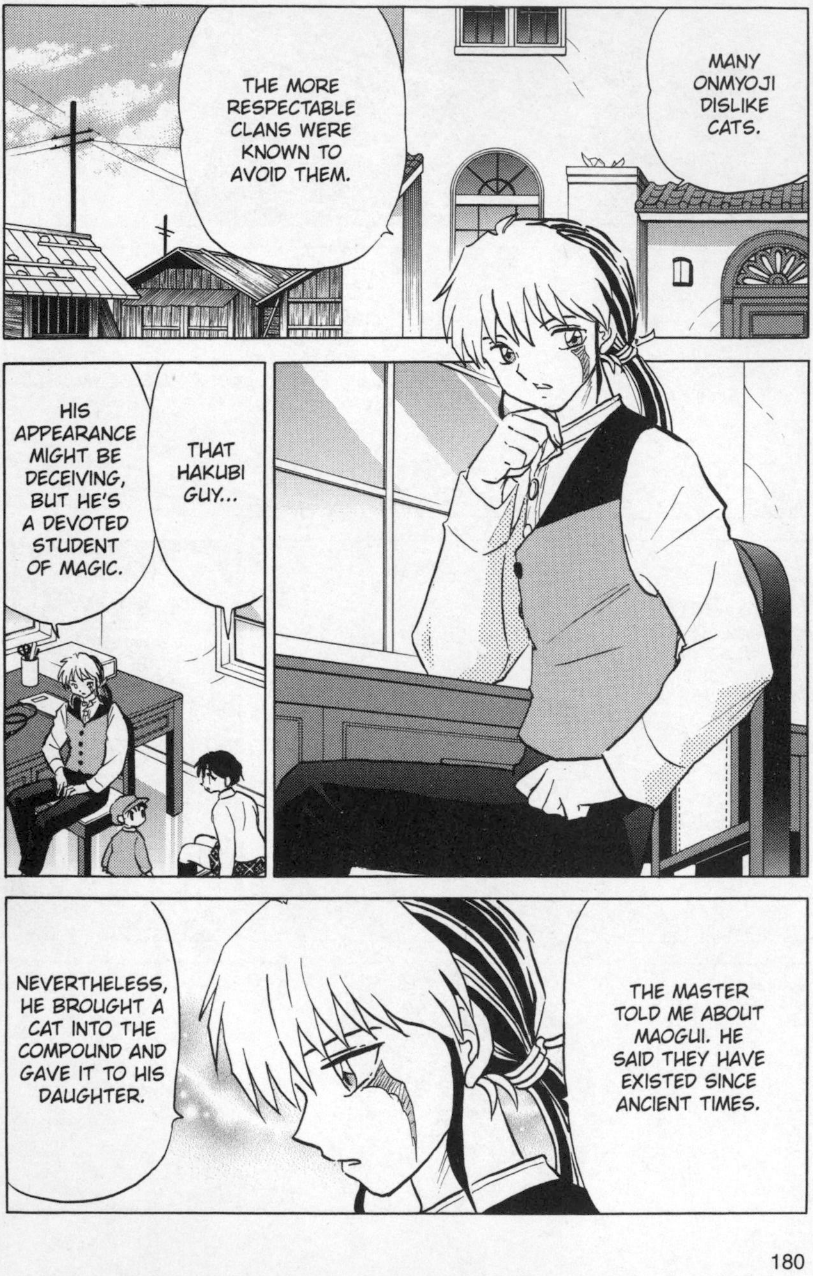
MANY ONMYOJI DISLIKE CATS.
THE MORE RESPECTABLE CLANS WERE KNOWN TO AVOID THEM.
THAT HAKUBI GUY...
HIS APPEARANCE MIGHT BE DECEIVING, BUT HE'S A DEVOTED STUDENT OF MAGIC.
THE MASTER TOLD ME ABOUT MAOGUI. HE SAID THEY HAVE EXISTED SINCE ANCIENT TIMES.
NEVERTHELESS, HE BROUGHT A CAT INTO THE COMPOUND AND GAVE IT TO HIS DAUGHTER.

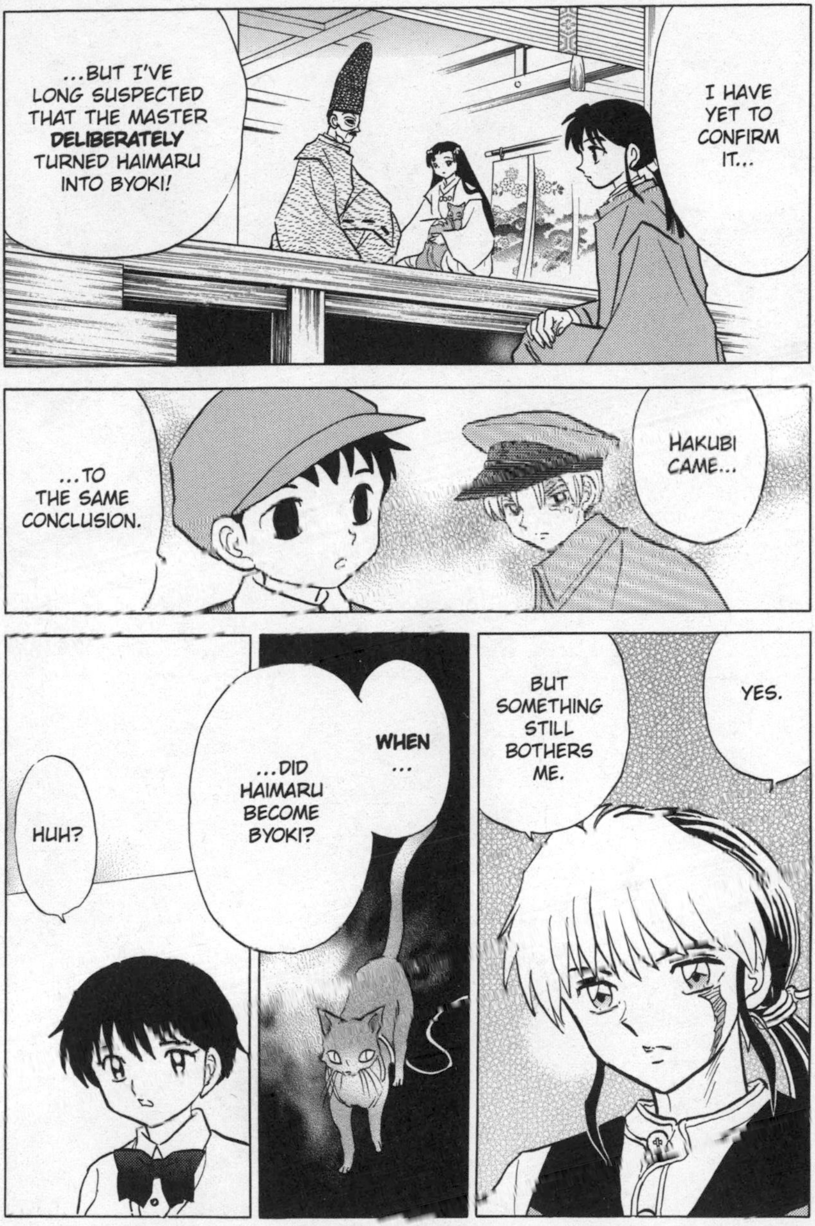
I HAVE YET TO CONFIRM IT...
...BUT I'VE LONG SUSPECTED THAT THE MASTER **DELIBERATELY** TURNED HAIMARU INTO BYOKI!
HAKUBI CAME...
...TO THE SAME CONCLUSION.
YES.
BUT SOMETHING STILL BOTHERS ME.
WHEN ...
...DID HAIMARU BECOME BYOKI?
HUH?

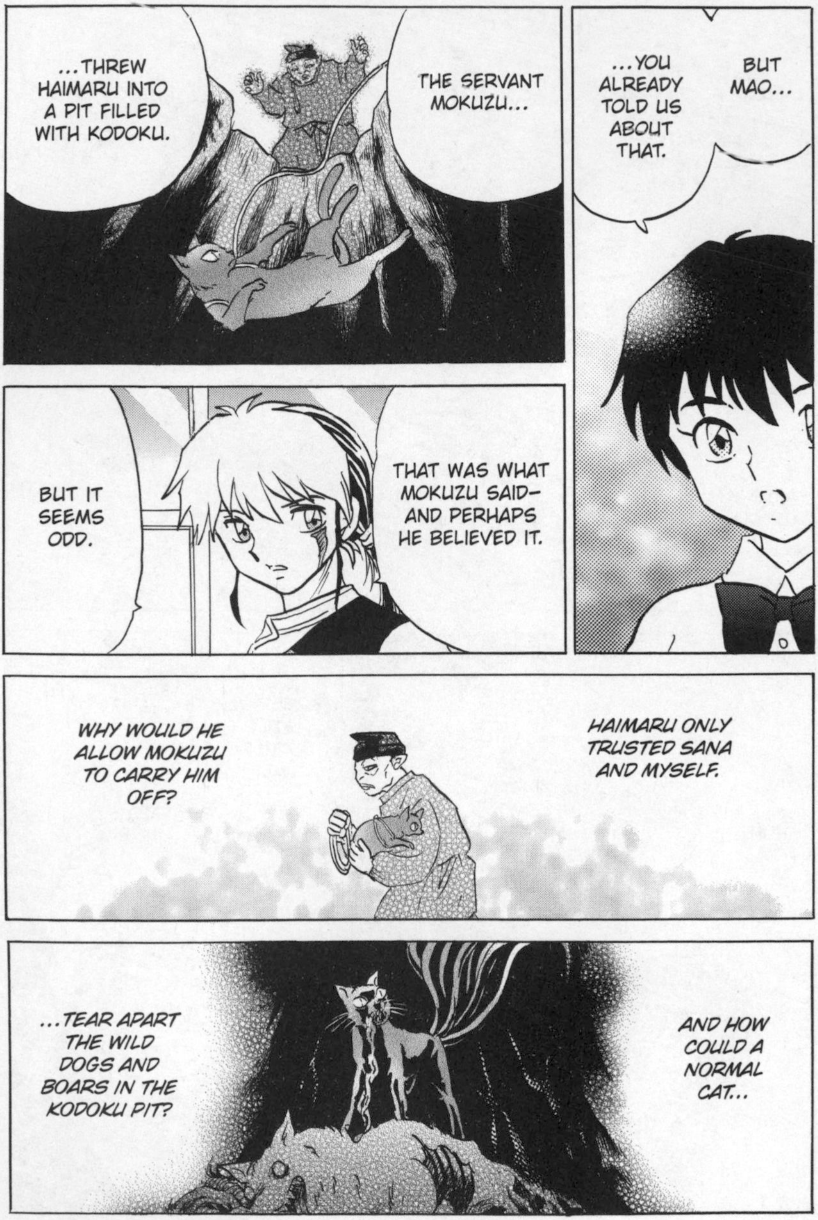
BUT MAO...
...YOU ALREADY TOLD US ABOUT THAT.
THE SERVANT MOKUZU...
...THREW HAIMARU INTO A PIT FILLED WITH KODOKU.
THAT WAS WHAT MOKUZU SAID—AND PERHAPS HE BELIEVED IT.
BUT IT SEEMS ODD.
HAIMARU ONLY TRUSTED SANA AND MYSELF.
WHY WOULD HE ALLOW MOKUZU TO CARRY HIM OFF?
AND HOW COULD A NORMAL CAT...
...TEAR APART THE WILD DOGS AND BOARS IN THE KODOKU PIT?

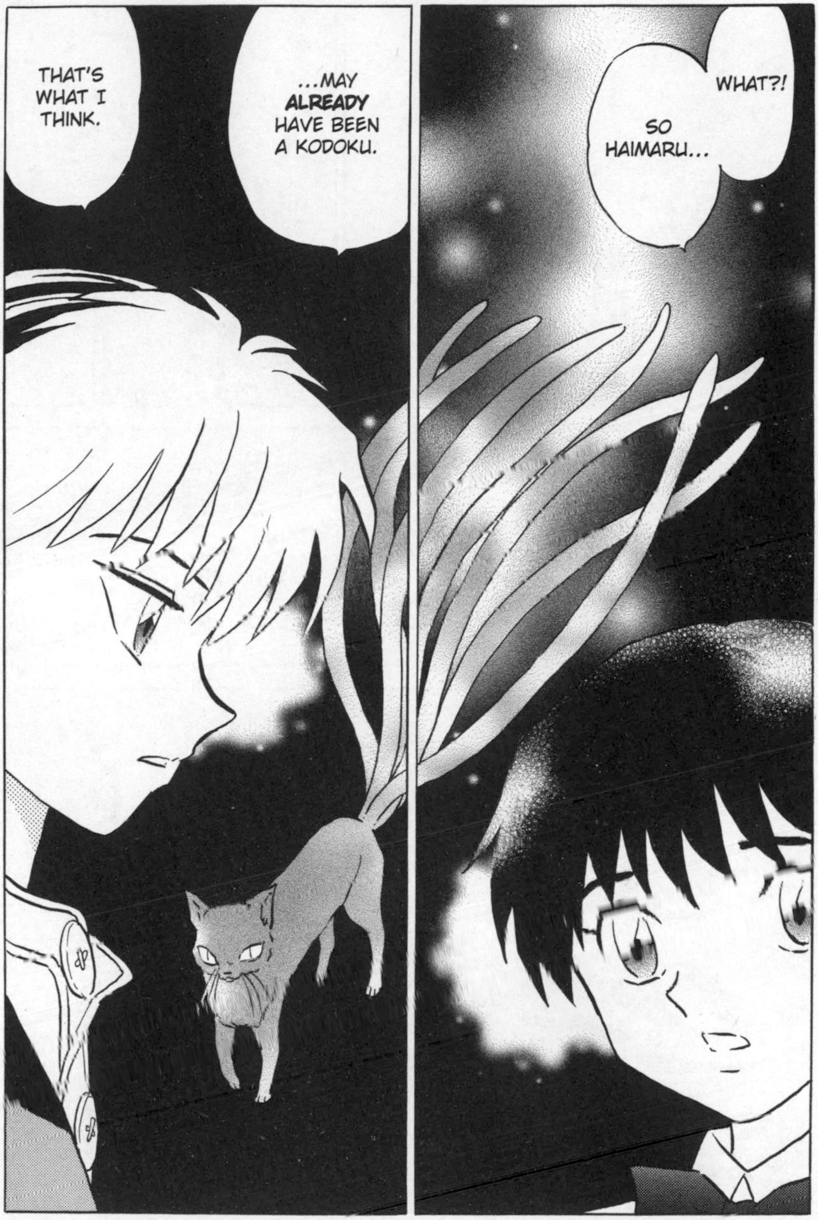
WHAT?!
SO HAIMARU...
...MAY **ALREADY** HAVE BEEN A KODOKU.
THAT'S WHAT I THINK.

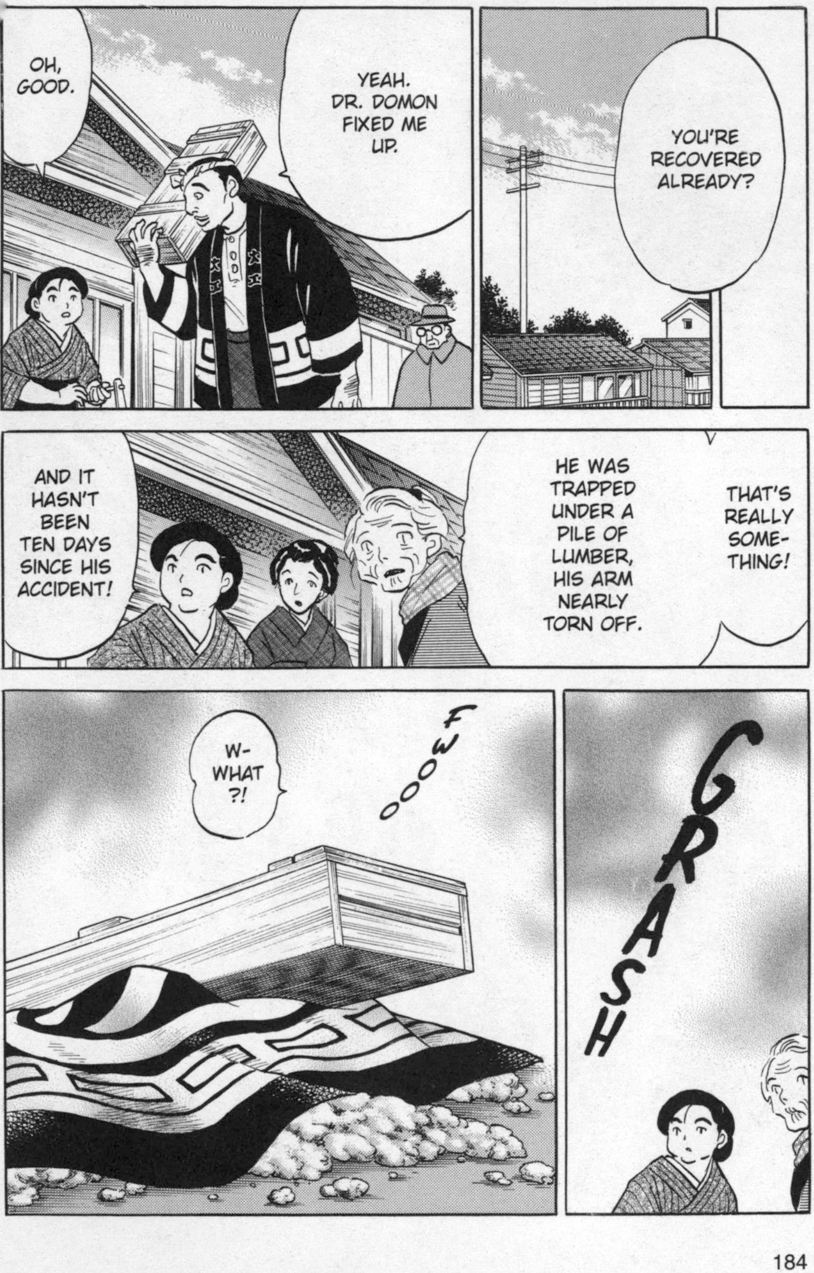
YOU'RE RECOVERED ALREADY?
YEAH. DR. DOMON FIXED ME UP.
OH, GOOD.
THAT'S REALLY SOME-THING!
HE WAS TRAPPED UNDER A PILE OF LUMBER, HIS ARM NEARLY TORN OFF.
AND IT HASN'T BEEN TEN DAYS SINCE HIS ACCIDENT!
CRASH
FWOOOO
W-WHAT?!

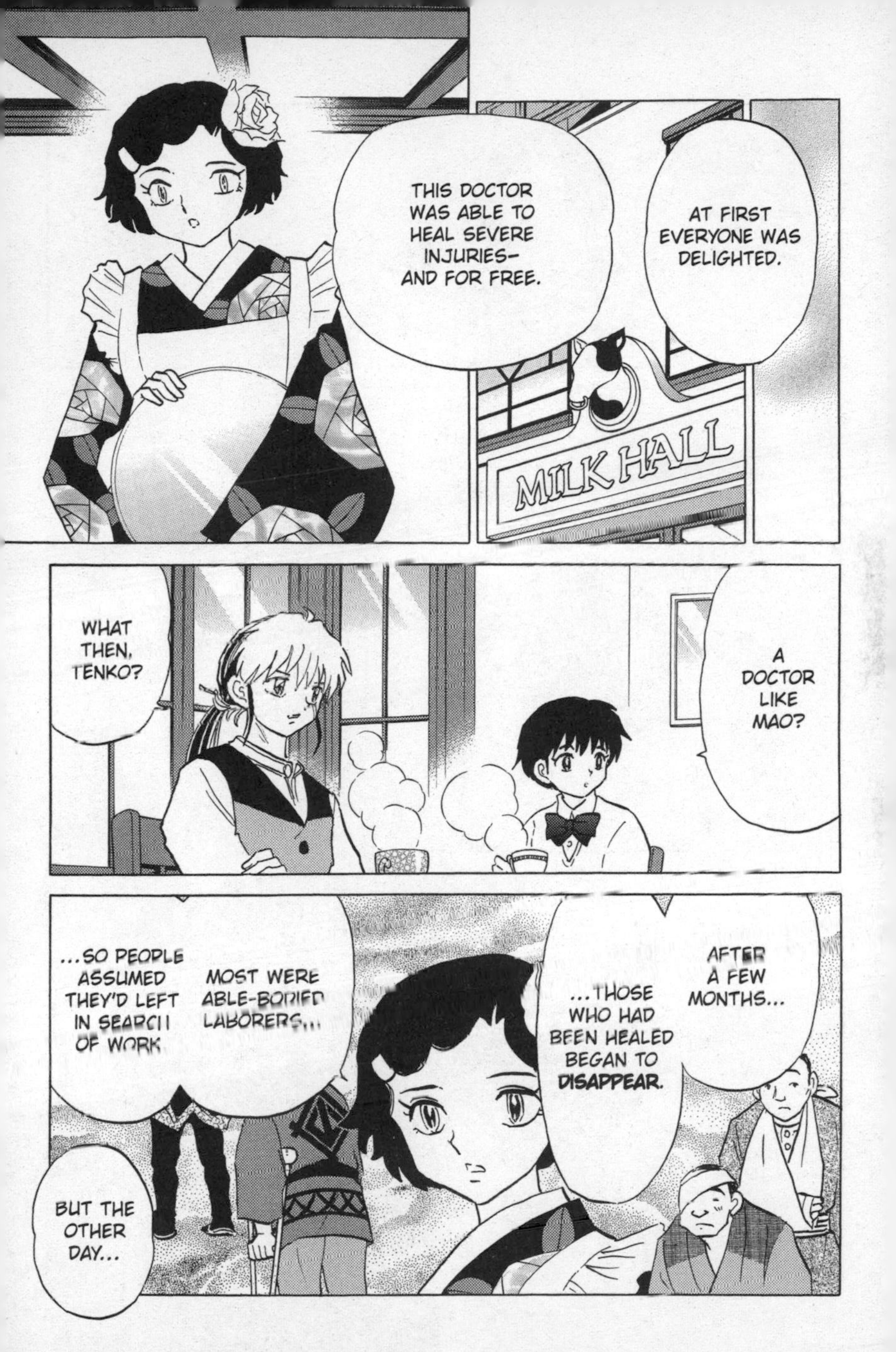
AT FIRST EVERYONE WAS DELIGHTED.
MILK HALL
THIS DOCTOR WAS ABLE TO HEAL SEVERE INJURIES— AND FOR FREE.
A DOCTOR LIKE MAO?
WHAT THEN, TENKO?
AFTER A FEW MONTHS...
...THOSE WHO HAD BEEN HEALED BEGAN TO **DISAPPEAR**.
MOST WERE ABLE-BODIED LABORERS...
...SO PEOPLE ASSUMED THEY'D LEFT IN SEARCH OF WORK
BUT THE OTHER DAY...

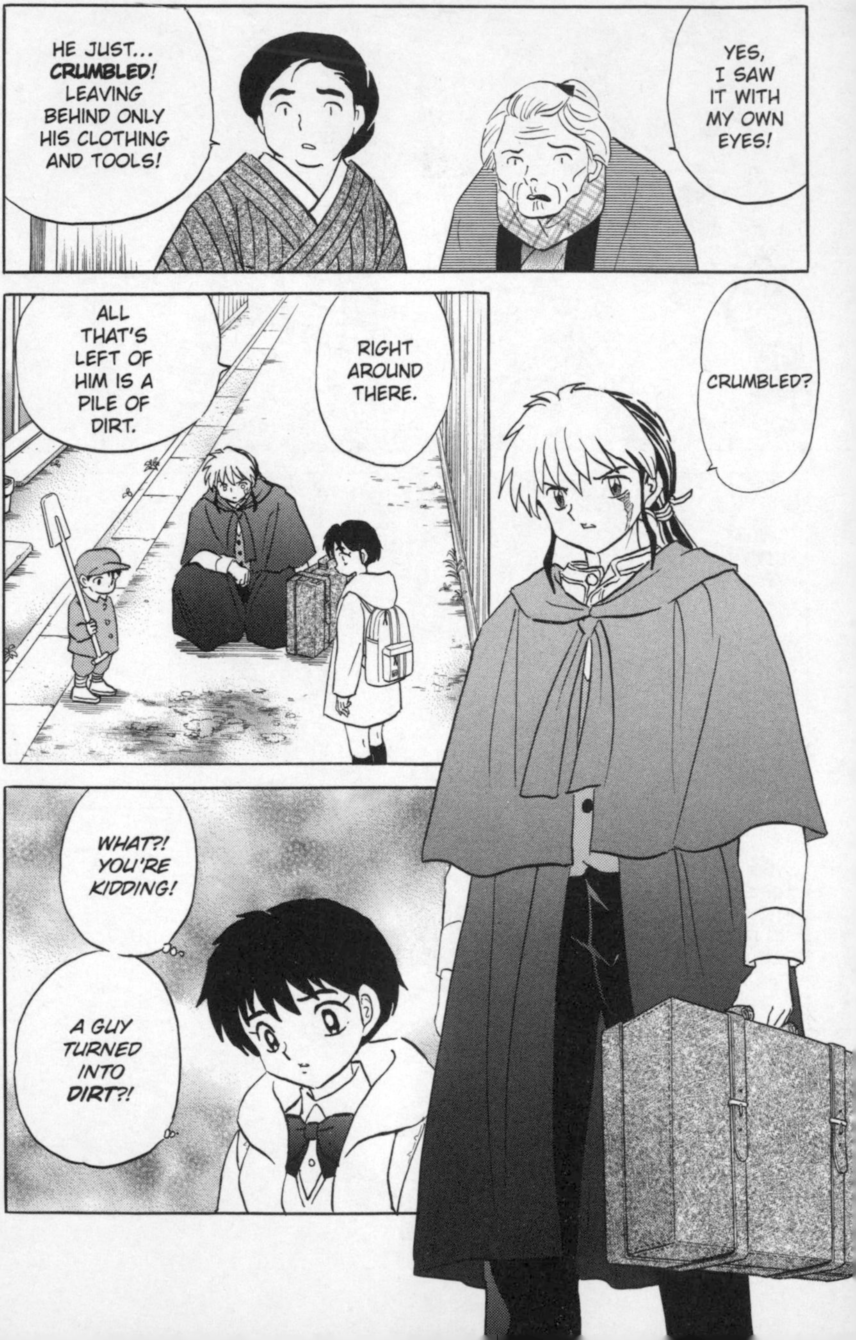
YES, I SAW IT WITH MY OWN EYES!
HE JUST... **CRUMBLED!** LEAVING BEHIND ONLY HIS CLOTHING AND TOOLS!
CRUMBLED?
RIGHT AROUND THERE.
ALL THAT'S LEFT OF HIM IS A PILE OF DIRT.
WHAT?! YOU'RE KIDDING!
*A GUY TURNED INTO **DIRT?!***

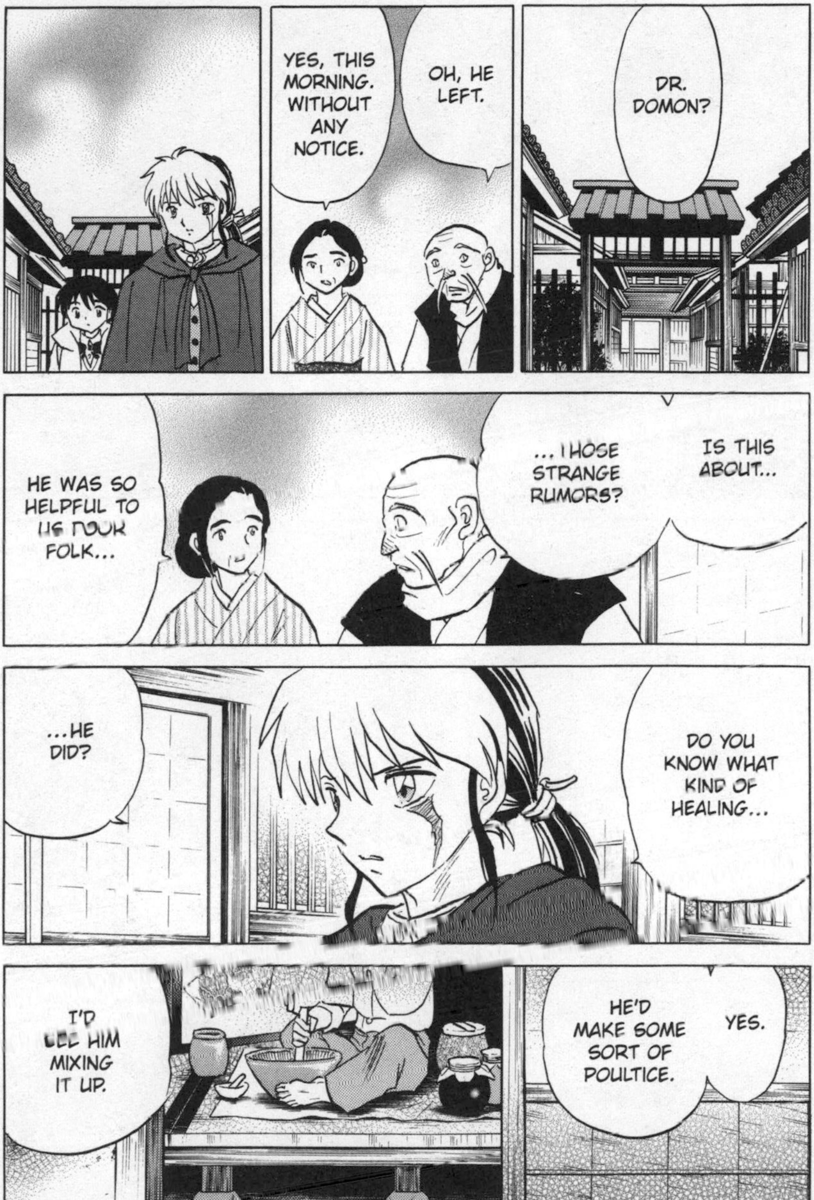
DR. DOMON?
OH, HE LEFT.
YES, THIS MORNING. WITHOUT ANY NOTICE.
IS THIS ABOUT...
...THOSE STRANGE RUMORS?
HE WAS SO HELPFUL TO US POOR FOLK...
DO YOU KNOW WHAT KIND OF HEALING...
...HE DID?
YES.
HE'D MAKE SOME SORT OF POULTICE.
I'D SEE HIM MIXING IT UP.

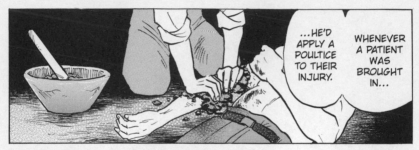

WHENEVER A PATIENT WAS BROUGHT IN...

...HE'D APPLY A POULTICE TO THEIR INJURY.

A FEW DAYS LATER, IT WOULD BE COMPLETELY HEALED.

JUST LIKE MAGIC!

WAS THAT MEDICINE...

...MADE OF SOIL PERHAPS?

BDMP

WHAT?!

TO BE CONTINUED...

MAO

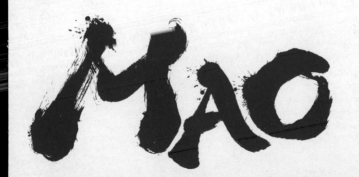

Rumiko Takahashi

The spotlight on Rumiko Takahashi's career began in 1978 when she won an honorable mention in Shogakukan's prestigious New Comic Artist Contest for *Those Selfish Aliens*. Later that same year, her boy-meets-alien comedy series, *Urusei Yatsura*, was serialized in *Weekly Shonen Sunday*. This phenomenally successful manga series was adapted into anime format and spawned a TV series and half a dozen theatrical-release movies, all incredibly popular in their own right. Takahashi followed up the success of her debut series with one blockbuster hit after another—*Maison Ikkoku* ran from 1980 to 1987, *Ranma ½* from 1987 to 1996, and *Inuyasha* from 1996 to 2008. Other notable works include *Mermaid Saga*, *Rumic Theater*, and *One-Pound Gospel*.

Takahashi was inducted into the Will Eisner Comic Awards Hall of Fame in 2018. She won the prestigious Shogakukan Manga Award twice in her career, once for *Urusei Yatsura* in 1981 and the second time for *Inuyasha* in 2002. A majority of the Takahashi canon has been adapted into other media such as anime, live-action TV series, and film. Takahashi's manga, as well as the other formats her work has been adapted into, have continued to delight generations of fans around the world. Distinguished by her wonderfully endearing characters, Takahashi's work adeptly incorporates a wide variety of elements such as comedy, romance, fantasy, and martial arts. While her series are difficult to pin down into one simple genre, the signature style she has created has come to be known as the "Rumic World." Rumiko Takahashi is an artist who truly represents the very best from the world of manga.

MAO
VOLUME 6
Shonen Sunday Edition

STORY AND ART BY
RUMIKO TAKAHASHI

MAO Vol. 6
by Rumiko TAKAHASHI
© 2019 Rumiko TAKAHASHI
All rights reserved.
Original Japanese edition published by SHOGAKUKAN.
English translation rights in the United States of America,
Canada, the United Kingdom, Ireland, Australia, and New
Zealand arranged with SHOGAKUKAN.

Original Cover Design: Chie SATO + Bay Bridge Studio

Translation/Junko Goda
English Adaptation/Shaenon K. Garrity
Touch-up Art & Lettering/James Gaubatz
Cover & Interior Design/Yukiko Whitley
Editor/Annette Roman

The stories, characters, and incidents mentioned in
this publication are entirely fictional.

Printed in the U.S.A.

Published by VIZ Media, LLC
P.O. Box 77010
San Francisco, CA 94107

10 9 8 7 6 5 4 3 2 1
First printing, July 2022

PARENTAL ADVISORY
MAO is rated T+ for Older Teen and is
recommended for ages 16 and up. This volume
contains fantasy violence.

viz.com

shonensunday.com

Coming in Volume 7...

While the ancient relationships and rivalries of the Goko clan continue to wreak havoc in the Taisho era, Mao and Nanoka pursue a mysterious doctor who violates the modern directive to "first do no harm." Next, mysterious human hairs reveal the secret location of Shiranui's lair and of a long-lost love. And then Kamon is captured. Who—and what—can save him?

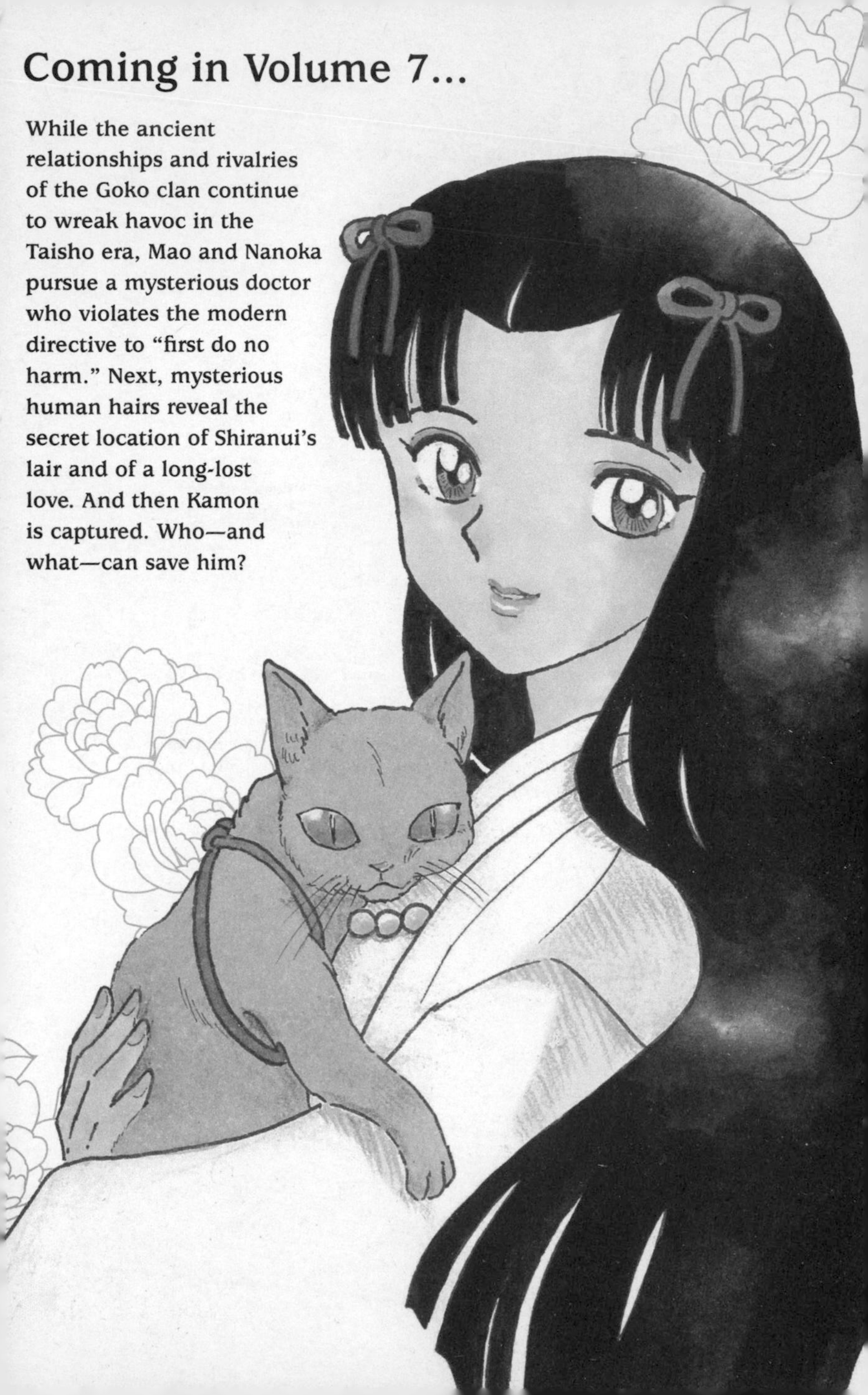